MAMA

ANTONIL

HASSLE FREE PRESS

Published in 1978 by Hassle Free Press
BCM Box 311 London WC1V 6XX

First published in Great Britain by
Antonil. 1978
in a limited edition of 350 copies
numbered and signed by the author.

ISBN 0 86166 000 5 PAPERBACK
ISBN 0 86166 001 3 HARDCOVER

Typeset by Red Lion Setters, Holborn, London
Printed by Dillcourt Ltd., London

for Verena

Credits

IN ENGLAND

Chien — who did the cover and line drawings...

Jonathan — who took some of the slides which inspired the drawings...

Margo — who did the maps...

Paul — who distributed the limited edition...

Steve — who leant me recent copies of "Unidad Indígena"...

Larry and Victor — who let me use the CALA...

IN COLOMBIA

Luis Horacio — who gave me a job...

Don Abel — who provided a roof, *Lena*, and an inexhaustible supply of tinto...

Carlos César — who travelled the same mule to Caquiona and Tierradentro...

Horacio, Ann and Eva — who voiced encouragement an an early stage...

Rubén — who let me watch his seedlings grow into bushes...

Mamita Santos — the ever dependable connection...

Monroy — who kept me up to date with the land struggle in Tierradentro...

Guillermo — who took me into the Western Cordillera...

David — who pointed out invaluable sources for an ethnohistory of the Cauca area...

Don Diego — who opened the *Archivo Central del Cauca* to me...

Bill — who provided the inside dope on dope...

And, above all, the Indians of the Cauca area and their respective *cabildos* — particularly those of San Andrés de Pisimbalá, Huila, Tóez, Togoima, Santa Rosa, Calderas, Guambía (El Cacique), Coconuco and Caquiona — who generously allowed me to remain in their territory, and willingly volunteered a wealth of information about coca. The anonymity of my principal informants is maintained through the use of pseudonyms in the text.

This book is dedicated to them and all those who made it possible for it to appear in its present form.

Contents

Appendices

THE CENTRAL AND NORTHERN ANDES showing adjacent areas of the Amazon basin.
NOTE: Hatched areas show mountains over 2000m.
CARIBBEAN SEA
PACIFIC OCEAN
VENEZUELA
COLOMBIA
ECUADOR
PERU
BRAZIL
BOLIVIA
Santa Marta
Cartagena
SIERRA NEVADA
Maracaibo
Coro
Caracas
Cumaná
Panamá
Sierra Nevada de Cocuy
Medellín
Tunja
Bogotá
Villavicencio
Buenaventura
Cali
CAUCA
MAGDALENA
Popayán
Pasto
Tumaco
Ipiales
Moçoa
Otavalo
Quito
Guayaquil
VAUPES
CAQUETA
PUTUMAYO
NEGRO
AMAZONAS
Manaus
Leticia
Iquitos
MARAÑON
UCAYALI
HUALLAGA
Pucallpa
Trujillo
Tingo María
Huánuco
LA MONTAÑA
URUBAMBA
Lima
Huancayo
Quillabamba
Cuzco
YUNGAS
La Paz
Cochabamba
Santa Cruz
Arica
N
Statute Miles
Kilometres

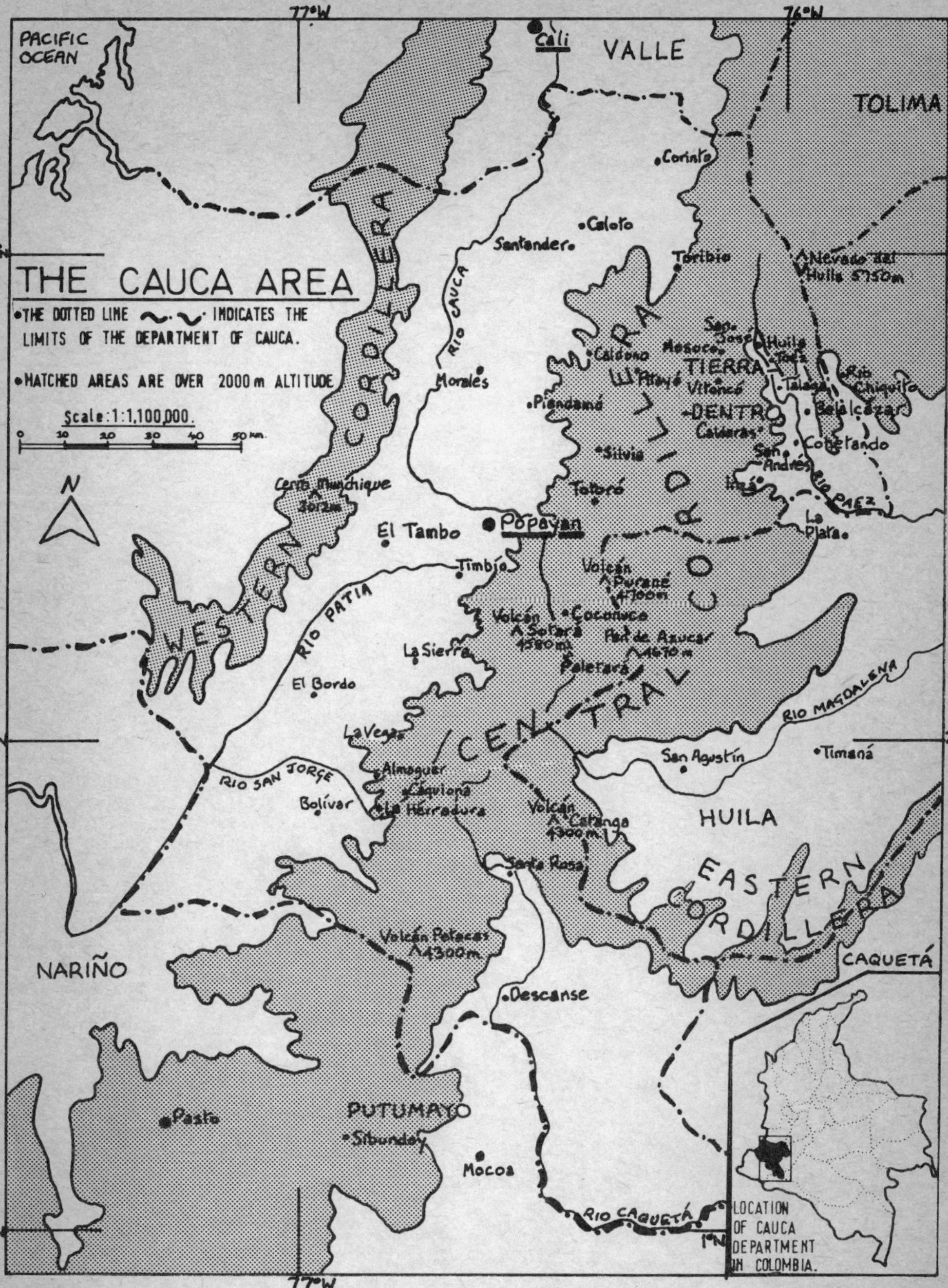

THE CAUCA AREA
•THE DOTTED LINE INDICATES THE LIMITS OF THE DEPARTMENT OF CAUCA.
•HATCHED AREAS ARE OVER 2000 m ALTITUDE
Scale: 1:1,100,000.
0 10 20 30 40 50 km.
N
77°W
76°W
3°N
2°N
1°N
PACIFIC OCEAN
Cali
VALLE
TOLIMA
Corinto
Caloto
Santander
Toribio
Nevado del Huila 5750m
RIO CAUCA
WESTERN CORDILLERA
CENTRAL CORDILLERA
EASTERN CORDILLERA
TIERRADENTRO
Caldono
Mosoco
Vitoncó
Calderas
Huila
Talaga
Rio Chiquito
Belalcázar
Cohetando
San Andrés
Inzá
RIO PAEZ
La Plata
Morales
Piendamó
Silvia
Totoró
Cerro Munchique 3012m
El Tambo
Popayán
Timbío
Volcán Puracé 4700m
Coconuco
Volcán Sotará 4580m
Pan de Azucar 4670m
Paletará
RIO PATIA
La Sierra
El Bordo
RIO MAGDALENA
La Vega
Almaguer
Caquiona
La Herradura
Bolívar
RIO SAN JORGE
San Agustín
Timaná
HUILA
Volcán Cutanga 4300m
Santa Rosa
Volcán Petacas 4300m
NARIÑO
CAQUETÁ
Descanse
PUTUMAYO
Pasto
Sibundoy
Mocoa
RIO CAQUETÁ
LOCATION OF CAUCA DEPARTMENT IN COLOMBIA.

Introduction

Story written out of old diaries and discarded bus tickets finds you back in Bogotá. It is the end of May, 1973, almost two years to the day since that first score, that opening gambit in a rapid sequence of missions as chronicler, as interpreter to a mis-marriage of cultures, to the nervous rubbing of frozen noses. Every time, it seems, the city hits you with the same nerve-tingling, sense-deadening coordinates: a seeping dampness underfoot, a chill freeze shot through the coke-thin air. Must be the old thirteenth floor Tequendama blues — anxious heart a-thumping, pumping minimal oxygen and vicarious thrills. Frame dissolves into a distant blurr of lush green fields and burnt-out volcanoes, the Sábana held within a timeless siege, its plateau encircled by the saw-toothed ridges of the Andes. You swallow the landscape whole, feeling that rarified atmosphere come on tight and uncomfortable in the lungs, a keen rush of fear erupting across the skin-deep surface of it all. Cold sweat as you walk past the dark-suited citizenry — their eyes empty ciphers, blank zeros held in catatonic suspense, hurriedly checking your face against the mugshot on the front page of their newspapers: *Detenido otro traficante gringo . . .*

Busts, Scams. Numbers, Deals. The rise and fall of the independent operator; flat pools of blood lying between the broken cobblestones of *atabobo*-Babylon. Bad old days no more. *La coca está en el culo de la madre del carajo* (a popular saying) . . . One day in '73, you wake up to feel a cold muzzle of grey automatic in the earhole. You got the message, kid? A puff of smoke deadened by the sound of downpour, a single no-watt, so-watt bulb strung from a leaning lamp-post. The light goes out on a back street behind the Hilton. Off-stage and shadow-bound, a pack of mangy street dogs are hoping for a corpse. First centurion: 'A hundred dollars or . . .' Second centurion: 'Extradition or life . . .' Easy deals no more. Take two on the automatic, aimed this time, and aimed at you.

So you got the message, kid. Riot police disgorge from cattle trucks and surround the intersection, beat sticks and gas cans at the ready. But what of your commitment to the service? to the subject? Your sense of responsibility to the coca theme? One morning you go uptown for an interview with the Director of the Instituto: 'Ah, a social history of the use of coca in Colombia . . . very interesting, very *polemical* . . . you have monies from some international foundation? no? . . . some link-up with the health authorities? no? . . . a doctoral research project at least? oh no? . . . I see . . .' Sound track stuck at the point of no return.

Bogotá the ugly — a heritage of doom and despair. All the while the radio news hangs heavy in the air: 'Official sources have described this morning's outbreak of violence as an act of premeditated provocation on the part of an extremist minority without any popular support . . . in a series of preventive measures, the military authorities have declared a state of siege and sealed off access to the Universidad Nacional . . . ' Far away, the hills echo back a distant soundtrack of steel ball-bearings on boxwood *carrito* carts, their reel and rasp muffled in the mist . . . ree ree, rra rra rra . . . a stench of corruption hangs in a pall over the dead-bled city, its shadow the carrion-feeding condor on the *peso* note . . . We huddle together and we wait, standing close to the door of the café and pretending to read the headlines of an El Espacio pinned to the rack on one side: *Descuartizó a su madre y luego se suicidó* . . .

Good fortune smiled in Popayán. Despite its petty chauvinism and small-town paranoia, it remains the most relaxed of Colombia's provincial capitals, the most easy-going. It has retained the placid colonial atmosphere of a town bypassed by industrial progress, the peace of its siesta hour disturbed only by the periodic sorties of the relatively inept young soldiers from the local NCO training college. On a fine, sunny day Popayán is a delightful place, with an excellent climate (av. temp. 18°C.), interesting street life and strong cultural traditions — not to mention what is probably some of the finest coca and marijuana in Colombia. It is not, however, the ideal place to simply score and hang out, for the town maintains a healthy disrespect for *gringo* tourists, and seldom greets the traveller with anything other than indifference, or even actual hostility. And personally to make matters worse, I arrived in the town in what were already pretty desperate straights. In a single month in Colombia I had been arrested, or narrowly escaped arrest, no less than half-a-dozen times, and my money was rapidly running out. True, I had the advantage of speaking good Spanish, but what I really needed was some kind of official *cover*, a cast-iron alibi for remaining in the area. As luck would have it, the local university was looking for someone to teach archaeology. 'That's my bag' I said, and in the absence of any other interested or accredited parties, they gave me the job. Just like that. I could hardly believe it . . .

Deep down, however, I could not help feeling that my return into the cloying embrace of academe was something of a sell-out, a relapse into pure careerism. Would not teaching obligations prevent me from spending more time in the field, in the neighbouring countryside itself? Fortunately, any such sentiments were very much misplaced, for — as the result of quite legitimate student unrest and unbelievably dim-witted government intransigence — the Faculty of Humanities was actually closed more than half the time that I was in the area, allowing ample time for travelling outside Popayán. I say 'fortunately' with good reason, for in view of an almost complete institutional collapse, it was not difficult to convince some of the students that nothing, literally nothing, could be expected from the classroom-and-examination system, or indeed from the professional structure of the social sciences as a whole. The very absence of any organized university curriculum allowed for a chink in the armour of the system's naive, uncritical scientism, a gap through which the actual day-to-day practice of liberation could penetrate the shell of so much empty rhetoric, so much ineffectual theory. This point of breakthrough, a veritable *punta de lanza*, was provided by the example of the Indians of Cauca, whom some of the students began to visit with increasing regularity at this time — first with a patronizing desire to 'educate', then with growing awe at the Indians' surprising degree of political effectiveness, and finally with real respect and a genuine desire to learn from their successes — taking advantage of the long 'holidays' which the administration of the University of Cauca periodically decreed.

All this was during a period in which thc Indian civil rights movement, CRIC (Consejo Regional Indígena del Cauca), was beginning to cause quite a stir in many rural areas, and both the students and myself found ourselves subject to considerable harassment by the police and the army — notably at Huila, Belalcázar, Corinto, Caldono, Jambaló and Coconuco. Travel in the cocaine-producing regions of southern Cauca was equally fraught with perils: the first night I slept in Bolívar, for example, I was rudely awoken at dawn by the town's police chief and the cold snout of his service .38. He had set up a bust worthy of front-page treatment by the press — both the mayor and the local magistrate had come along for their share of the glory — and the assembled company was more than a little disappointed to find that my research was seemingly legitimized by a very ambiguous Government script pinned to the inside of my passport. Other drug-busts verged on the absurd; in Cali, a city with a 'swinging' reputation, I was stopped with a group of friends at the entrance to a Santana concert and taken away to police headquarters for carrying white lime powder in a gourd. (It is remarkable that, despite an official prohibition on coca, the accompanying leaves aroused no interest whatsoever.) I attempted to explain that the lime was simply an alkaline reagent for chewing with the leaves, but my story was viewed with the utmost derision, and it was not until several hours later that we were finally released, once a high-ranking narc had deigned to classify the suspicious white powder as (officially) harmless.

Paez man.

These occasions, however, served to underline the very real necessity of working 'under cover'. The use of coca in Colombia is a very marginalized phenomenon, and deserved to be treated accordingly — by means of a marginalized, unofficial and unsponsored anthropology, a form of counter-intelligence whose justification could only be a heartfelt sympathy for coca and coca chewers themselves. Such a position necessarily required 'cover' of some sort, for — although in the company of actual coca chewers it was easy enough to come straight to the point — it remained extremely foolhardy to even discuss the subject of drugs with any of the more respectable citizens of the small provincial towns. After a few false starts, I found that the key word to use on such occasions was *historiador* — 'historian' — as *arqueólogo* was widely associated with tomb-robbing and trafficking in antiquities, and *antropólogo* or *etnólogo* were, at least in the eyes of the basically anti-Indian local authorities, terms with unmistakeably 'subversive' and 'communist' overtones. There was not, in any case, very much to be gained in the way of information about coca from those who never used the leaves themselves. The level of sheer ignorance with regard to coca — even among local white dope-smokers and student radicals — was literally staggering beyond belief, and I fear that very few Colombians would share the opinion that the plant is a vital and crucial element of their national heritage, one which deserves to be studied, defended, and even diffused among the population as a whole. In my experience, very few people — other than fellow coca chewers — were ever willing to contemplate the fact that a foreigner, an educated white man could possibly want to learn about coca leaves for their own sake. Among urban, middle-class Colombians, my motives were always construed to be very much more obscure. The fact is that in Colombia the word *coca* is universally associated with sensationalist newspaper headlines, and — whether the attitude is one of sniffing regard for refined cocaine, or one of high moral repudiation of the corruption produced as a result of the drug traffic — the common opinion of virtually the entire population is that the chewing of the leaf is foul, uncivilized, and more specifically, 'backward' and unhealthy.

The major reason for this is that — unlike the scene in Peru and Bolivia — the number of Colombian coca chewers is really very small, involving a total population of fifty or, at most, a hundred thousand individuals, which clearly cannot compare with the situation further south, where perhaps as many as six or eight million Quechua and Aymara Indians use the drug. Mainstream Colombian culture has little understanding or sympathy for its Indian minorities; they are considered anachronisms, remnants of another age, social dinosaurs who have survived only in the more inaccessible parts of the country — such as the Sierra Nevada de Santa Marta, the Amazonian rainforests, and a few isolated pockets within the major cordilleras of the Andes. One of these pockets, however — that

Paez woman

which is referred to throughout this book as 'the Cauca area', and roughly, though not exactly, conterminous with the *departamento* del Cauca, the administrative unit centred on Popayán — provides a very significant exception to the general rule. Here no less than 57 Indian reservations or *resguardos* still control a very substantial amount of land, and the indigenous population almost certainly reaches a figure of as much as 100,000 individuals altogether. (Other estimates vary from as low as 50,000 to as high as 235,000). Of these, over half speak the Paez language, a local dialect which forms part of the Macro-Chibcha linguistic family. At the present time they are distributed on both sides of the Central Cordillera — north of a line drawn between Totoró and Inzá, and south of the highest peak in the area, the Nevado del Huila — and in a few small communities in the Western Cordillera, notably in the *municipio* of Morales.

Another group, the Guambianos — of the *resguardo* of Guambía, near Silvia — speak a related, but mutually unintelligible language, and number close on 8,000. It is also likely that many of the other Indian groups living near Popayán — such as those in Coconuco and Puracé — at one time shared a language very similar to Guambianò. They have, however, suffered a great deal from the cultural and territorial inroads made into their communities, and today they only speak Spanish, though still maintaining a small area of land in *resguardos*, the shrunken vestiges of reserves assaulted for four centuries by the rapacious landowning aristocracy of Popayán. In southern Cauca, a handful of *resguardos* have likewise managed to survive in the more remote valleys of the Central Cordillera, but they too have lost their original languages and have assimilated a great deal of *mestizo* Colombian culture. In numerical terms, however, southern Cauca probably includes an Indian population of between 15,000 and 25,000, with well over half of it concentrated outside the reservations in areas such as the valley of the San Jorge river, where most of the old *resguardos* were extinguished over a hundred years ago.

The distribution of the coca habit in the Cauca area does not exactly fit the ethnic boundaries. The Guambianos, for example, abandoned the use of coca around the turn of the century, and — despite an otherwise strong respect for their cultural traditions — seem unlikely to ever seriously re-adopt the habit again. Even the situation in the rest of Cauca is not as homogeneous as might appear at first sight, and it is necessary to make a clear distinction between two main types of coca consumption in the area. One is that exemplified by the Paez Indians of Tierradentro, a traditional form of coca chewing which is often significantly at variance with the more acculturated pattern of the Spanish-speaking Indians and *campesinos* of southern Cauca. Such a dichotomy not only reflects obvious differences of external detail — such as a variety in the decoration of coca bags, or in the preparation of the lime reagent chewed together with the leaves — but also expresses cultural dissimilarities of a much more fundamental kind. For instance, coca amongst the Paez is considered not only an aid to hard physical work, but also a 'magical' plant — being widely employed in the context of shamanism, healing and divination. This is a dimension almost entirely lacking in southern Cauca, where the leaves are used pretty much exclusively as a stimulant, or as a medicinal herb for the treatment of certain clearly identified complaints.

This 'profanity' of coca in southern Cauca would explain why it is only here — and not in Tierradentro, where coca is rarely traded outside the immediate family circle — that the leaf has become a major cash crop, spawning first a flourishing trade in coca to the markets of the nearby towns and, in more recent years, a booming cocaine industry as well. The historical and economic implications of this difference of attitudes are discussed in some detail in chapters III and IV, but there is a sense in which the whole subject can also be related to underlying, present-day concepts of ethnic identity as well. Southern Cauca, along with the adjacent *municipos* of San Agustín and La Cruz — in the departments of Huila and Narino respectively — is an area characterized by an almost complete absence of any specifically 'Indian' culture. That is to say, native languages and many customs have been forgotten altogether, nearly all the original reservations have been split up into private holdings, and the racial composition of the rural population has received significant additions of European and African blood.

To a considerable extent, therefore, class conflict has substituted ethnic solidarity as the major determinant of social behaviour, and the cultural differences that exist in the area are those which separate the farm-dwelling *campesino* peasantry from the provincial petit bourgeoisie which dominates life in the municipal towns. Within such a context, coca chewing is found only among the more economically deprived *campesinos,* and it is clearly considered a trait which should be abandoned by any farmer who aspires to a respectable position in local affairs. It is interesting that the terms *chino* or *indio* are normally used to refer pejoratively to all the poorer members of the peasantry, irrespective of the colour of their skin. For this reason, no racist implications should necessarily be ascribed to their everyday usage, and the words only express a clear social denigration of any kind of behaviour — such as coca chewing — which is considered backward, ignorant, and symptomatic of poverty.

While it is not uncommon, therefore, to find *campesinos* — even those with clearly Caucasian racial features — chewing coca in the southern parts of the department, the same phenomenon becomes increasingly rare as one travels further north. In Tierradentro itself, social identity is more often defined in explicitly ethnic terms, and there exists considerable antagonism between the inhabitants of the proud, independent Paez reservations and the rapidly expanding white peasantry, anxious to convert the communal Indian lands into more profitable private farms. This situation leads to a notable degree of conflict between Indians and *blancos* — 'whites' in the cultural, and not necessarily the racial sense — as the split is quite evidently based on territorial and behavioural differences, rather than on simple economic inequalities.

For these reasons, any white settler who dares adopt the coca habit near an area of Paez predominance usually risks becoming something of an outcast among his own people, and is thought of as a man who has betrayed his race and his upbringing. It cannot, therefore, be at all surprising that very few converts to coca have emerged among the *blancos* of Tierradentro. And at the same time, it is quite easy to explain why a good number of the more 'progressive' Indians — those who have been led by the Church and the authorities into dissociating themselves from a 'savage' and 'primitive' past — have actually begun to abandon the coca habit, as if ashamed of its barbarity. The real irony remains that, in the name of progress, they have been encouraged to replace coca with the far more damaging combination of coffee and cigarettes. It is, therefore, particularly encouraging to note the attitude of CRIC, who in 1975 made the following statement regarding the use of coca:

> 'to conserve coca as part of Indian culture; for the purposes of shamanism and agricultural work, and as a medicine. It is necessary to stop trading coca with whites, because coca is a thing worthy of respect, and traders use it in a way which is not appropriate . . .' (from the General Conclusions of the 4th Congress of CRIC, Tóez, August 1975.)

This position has not been taken in isolation from the broader context of Paez resistance to ethnocide and incorporation by the enveloping Colombian society, CRIC's program includes the following seven points:

1. To recuperate reservation lands which have been lost.
2. To increase the size of the reservations and institute a self-reliant, communal economic system in the areas liberated from control by white landlords.
3. To strengthen the freely-elected Indian *cabildos* ('Councils') which govern each reservation.
4. To stop paying the illegal *terraje* ('land-tax') which makes the Indians, effectively, into share-croppers on land which is reality their own property.
5. To make people aware of the existing laws for Indians and to insist on their proper application.
6. To defend the history, language and customs of the Indians, and foster a new awareness of their own musical forms, their mythology,

and their traditional system of shamanism and herbal medicine.
7. To form Indian teachers to educate the children in their own language and culture.

Since its foundation in 1971, CRIC has scored a number of remarkable victories in attempting to carry through this program, and since early 1975 has succeeded in bringing out its own monthly newspaper, 'Unidad Indígena', which provides a wealth of detail about its current activities and those of like-minded Indian groups elsewhere in Colombia. A fuller account of the historical background and recent growth of CRIC can be found in Appendix C, and one should only add that its case has recently been taken up by that august body, the UN Working Group on Slavery of the Sub-Commission on the Prevention of Discrimination and Protection of Minorities: The UN Commission on Human Rights. The final recommendations made to the Committee were that the Government of Colombia should be asked to admit a UN sponsored investigatory mission to look into the following questions:

1. To ensure that titles to land were clearly defined and rightful claims supported at all times.
2. To ensure that central government laws are carried through locally without corruption.
3. To ensure that the Consejo Regional Indígena del Cauca (CRIC) is unequivocally established as a judicially accredited organization, with the power of the central government behind it.

(Survival International Review: Vol. 2 No. 3 — Summer 1977.)

Whether or not such initiatives are successful in exerting any effective pressure on the government in Bogotá remains, of course, very much in the realm of conjecture. Nevertheless, as Survival itself has pointed out: 'we do . . . feel it important to ensure that a voice on behalf of the indians is heard wherever and whenever possible . . . ' It is with a similar perspective in view that this book has attempted — by placing the use of coca not only in a subjective context, but also in that of a legitimate Indian struggle for self-determination and self-respect — to contribute both to a growing understanding of the much maligned coca leaves, and to a global commitment to protecting the economic, cultural and political rights of all ethnic and social minorities marginalized by the orthodoxy's crass conception of progress, misrepresented by the ethos of a paternalistic science, and repressed by the institutions of the authoritarian state. Rather than assuming to 'leadership', or membership of a revolutionary 'vanguard', the anthropologist must find his purpose in supporting and publicizing those movements where the people themselves are manifestly in control of their own destiny.

'The future organization of society should be carried out entirely from below upwards, by the abolition of the State and the free association of the workers and peasants . . . ' Michael Bakunin.

Note: Though the major Indian group in the Cauca area have been referred to throughout this study as 'the Paez', it has become common in this century to denote them in the plural in Spanish as *los Paeces* (with the stress on the first 'e') or, probably more correctly, as *los Páeces* (with the stress on the 'a'). In anycase, the Paez call themselves a quite different name — *nása* — which could be translated as 'we, the people' . . .

The pronounciation of Paez words, as written in this book, should follow Spanish usage, with the exception of those sounds — notably the 'sh' — which are absent from Spanish. While the results of such a transliteration are, admittedly, only very approximate, the obstacles to a more accurate rendering place it beyond the scope of the present study. As far as I am aware, no comprehensive linguistic analysis of the Paez language has ever been published, and remains a field which could fruitfully be explored in the future.

I. Mama Coca

'Suppose truth is a woman . . . '
Friedrich Nietzche: 'Beyond Good and Evil.'

There can be little point in denying that I first came to be interested in the coca leaf through a prior concern for its main alkaloid, cocaine. My introduction to the subject had been casual, almost accidental: I happened to be travelling through Colombia, and could hardly avoid running into some of the large number of dealers and smugglers who were then hanging out in the country, principally in the capital city of Bogotá. This was in the summer of 1971, the last year before the big-time mafias moved in on the old independent suppliers and squashed the open market. Cocaine, at that time, seemed to move around more commonly in kilos than in grams; and — with almost unlimited access to the product in a reasonably pure, uncut state — it would have been foolish, even irresponsible, not to have taken the opportunity for some thorough experimentation.

Now, let it be clearly stated, I have no criticism of cocaine insofar as its use as an occasional euphoriant is concerned. But — and this is the more crucial point — for every rush there is a corresponding jag, or drag, and in the end cocaine appeared to be unable, in strictly physiological terms, to balance the body's own metabolic equation. It is as if the drug were governed by some esoteric principle of diminishing returns; for at the higher levels of consumption — say, two or three grams a day — it became clearly counter-productive, even self-defeating. In such circumstances the use of cocaine failed to produce any real exhilaration, and only served to overcome the down accumulating from previous doses — leading to a repeated, but short-lived, return to feelings of normal fitness. In a sense, this was due not to any quality inherent in the alkaloid of cocaine itself, but principally to the very potency and speed of action of the drug in its refined, concentrated state. I became convinced that, in order to discover a dependable and truly balanced stimulant — something more exact than tea, coffee, or *yerba maté*, and less improvident than the amphetamines — it would be necessary to moderate the initial cocaine effect, to sustain it and prolong it at a steady level for several hours. Obviously, there could be no better place to begin this search than with the very plant — coca — from which cocaine had originally been derived.

On returning to Colombia in May 1973, therefore I was no longer greatly interested in using the dread cocaine itself, and instead my major preoccupation became that of learning how to chew coca leaves properly. Though this ran against the grain of orthodox, purely academic anthropology — and, as a result, produced a less than enthusiastic response from the authorities in Bogotá — it seemed clear that only in this way would I be able to reach any understanding of the Indian peoples who used the drug, and accorded it such a vital role in their daily lives. I had to admit, however, that this simple statement of intent — this espousal of a quite literally *amateur* approach — could never provide an entirely satisfactory framework for all the manifold aspects of the task at hand. Most importantly, it lacked any definition of the nature of coca itself, implying that mere personal events could somehow be isolated from their cultural and historical setting, to the point where they became no more than a rather gratuitous exercise in introspection. The problem remained that of discovering a foil, a counterweight to my own experience, something which could direct the development of research without subjecting it to the alienating constrictions of a formal methodology, without limiting it to the mere testing of preconceived hypotheses and mechanical models of human behaviour.

It was for this very reason that I began to find myself attracted — almost seduced, in a manner of speaking — by the enigmatic figure of Mama Coca, who somehow summarized in her shadowy, mythical personality the very nature of the drug itself. Coca and its alkaloids have almost always been associated with some sort of womanly or female principle: this had been made explicit — in my mind at least — by the slang of New York City, where cocaine is often known as 'girl' or 'lady', and in that of Spanish America, where the terms used esoterically — such as *la nieve* (Bolivia), *la perica* (Colombia), and *la tia blanca* (Peru) — are all feminine in gender.

Furthermore, I had enough prior experience of cocaine itself to know what this feminine principle entailed, at least in terms of the refined form of the drug. At first sniff, one would perhaps imagine that such a potent stimulant should be classified as pertaining to the aggressive, masculine realm. But this would be to ignore the very changeable quality of the cocaine experience, the very fickle nature of its associated euphoria, and in particular, the intense bitchiness it could produce on being abused. All of these traits were 'feminine' — at least in the traditional sense of the word — and they all tended towards a definition of the coca experience couched in terms of malleability, of sudden change and transformation.

Truth to tell, the original outline of the Peruvian Mama Coca had first made a conscious impression on me a few years previously, while leafing through Mortimer's classic 'Peru: a History of Coca.' Not being at that time sufficiently interested to begin a critical reading of the whole weighty tome, my attention had initially been captured by the many fine illustrations which graced its pages. Most notable of these was the frontispiece, which bore the title 'Mama Coca Presenting the Divine Plant to the Old World.'[1] It showed an Art Nouveau priestess in a long, flowing white robe, bedecked in extravagent jewels, and wearing an amazing feather head-dress. With the sickle in her right hand she had cut a few short branches of coca from the bush, holding them aloft in her left. She was placed on top of a boulder, her feet chest-high to a Spanish conquistador who stood with his right hand raised to receive the wondrous gift. Clad in a full suit of armour and carrying a double-handed sword, he presided over a background which included a group of Spanish soldiers leaning on their pikes and, in the distance, three small caravels at anchor in a placid bay.

Though this image was itself extremely evocative, I couldn't help being disappointed by the fact that the body of Mortimer's text contained precious little further reference to the coca goddess, other than to state that she was associated specifically with the star Spica, in Virgo, a fact that is certainly in keeping with her character.[2] The expression 'Mamacoca' seems to have been first used in English by Plukenet, in a botanical description of the plant contained in his 'Phytographia', a work published in London in 1692. Here Mama Coca was considered a deified name, roughly translatable as 'Mother of coca.'[3] A similar idea of maternity was also asserted by the proliferous Frazer, author of 'The Golden Bough.' He wrote that the Peruvians believed all crops to be protected by tutelary spirits which stimulated their growth, and which were always known as the 'mother' of the plant in question.[4] This was all very well as far as it went, but the transparent simplicity of Frazer's view seemed somehow to cry out for further elaboration, for a closer and more thorough appraisal of the Mama Coca idea in its indigenous setting.

In the first place, it appeared that Mama Coca should really be seen as a specific manifestation of a more general deity, the Mama or universal mother figure who is also represented in a great number of other guises as well. One of these was Mama Huaco, who is referred to as both the mother and the consort of Manco Capac, the legendary founder of the Inca nation. For politically expedient reasons Mama Huaco was often equated with the goddess Pachamama, or Mother Earth, whose central position in Andean religion significantly predated the Inca empire, and whose importance survived unaltered, even despite the imposition of an official Inca cult based on the worship of the Sun.

The Mama figure often had her identity complemented by that of a specific crop, and the Peruvian concept of magical power, or *huaca*, was a quality shared not only by the principal Andean deities and their shrines, but also by such drug plants as the coca bush. The mythical personage Mama Coca, therefore, not only represented that aspect of the universal Mama goddess concerned with enhancing the growth of coca, but also conveniently summarized the very magical potency, or *huaca*, of the coca leaf itself. In other words, even the very term 'Mama Coca' could be considered something of an ambiguous metaphor, referring at once to both the character of the supreme mother goddess, and to the specific *huaca* attributes of the coca plant.[5]

The Incas — naturally enough — could not fail to include this almost universal Andean figure of the coca goddess into their account of the genesis of their own people. In traditional mythology the original, nomadic Inca — Sinchi Roca — had united his mountain people with the inhabitants of the valley of Cuzco by means of his marriage with a woman named Mama Coca, the daughter of the chief of the village of Sanu. It was this alliance which eventually led to Sinchi Roca's conquest of the nearby site of Cuzco itself, and to the definitive foundation of the ethnic and social aristocracy which was later to be known by the name 'Inca'.

With this precedent foremost in their minds, it is understandable that a number of subsequent members of the royal family should also have been honoured with the name Mama Coca. One of these was the sister of the last great Inca, Huyana Capac, who ruled from 1491 to 1526. She was abbess of the *acllahuasi*, or temple of the virgins, in Cuzco, and is said to have fallen victim to the 1528 plague epidemic carried to the Pacific coast by the first white explorers, and already felt throughout the central Andes at least seven years before the Spanish Conquest took place.[6]

The legendary chastity of this particular woman has often been attributed to other manifestations of Mama Coca, but this association is rather doubtful, to say the least. On the contrary, most mythical accounts of the origins of coca tend to be associated with some act of sexual indulgence, or even of actual defilement, a feature that would certainly seem to be in keeping with coca's — and indeed, cocaine's — widespread reputation as an aphrodisiac. In the case of a myth recorded near Cuzco in 1571, the original Mama Coca figure is described in the following terms:

> '...she was a very beautiful woman and because she had an unclean body they killed her and cut her in half and buried her, and from her a bush was born which they called *ma macoca* and *cocamama*, and since then they began to eat her, and it was said that they carried her in a pouch, and this could not be opened to eat her except after having copulated with a woman, in memory of her...'[7]

It is clear, from its female gender, that the pronoun (her) refers to the woman in the myth and not to the bush (*el arbol*; masculine in Spanish). She is explicitly associated with 'unclean' attributes, and the complex of eating her, of opening the bag which contains her, is necessarily conditioned by some preliminary sexual indulgence. It is less clear whether this refers to the need to copulate before every chew of leaves, or only prior to the very first attempt. Given the regularity of the chewing habit, the former possibility seems highly unlikely, and thus it would appear that initiation into coca may have been considered — at least at one time — as an indication of arrival at the age of puberty.

Perhaps this association of the origins of coca with a woman's body, and with a profane genital sexuality, would be less notable were it apparent only in the specific cultural context of the central Andes. But this is not the case, and the almost universal nature of a female coca spirit is made manifest by the existence of similar accounts in a good number of areas which are entirely divorced — both geographically and culturally — from the cilivizations of Peru. Two thousand miles away in the Sierra Nevada de Santa Marta, the oral traditions of the Kogi Indians seem to show the very same association of coca with female origins. In Kogi mythology, coca — like all of plant life — is ultimately a gift of Gualchóvang, the earth mother figure who brought about the primal genesis from out of the still waters. More specifically, it is true, the male civilizing hero Sintana seems to have been the main figure responsible for creating the first bush of coca, but this he did by transforming the body of a woman who had been living in attendance on Gualchóvang.[8]

In addition there are two other Kogi myths which deal with alternative versions of the origins of coca, rendering more apparent the exact role of women in the affair. In one of these, Sintana's daughter Bunkeiji used a characteristic female subterfuge to abscond some coca leaves from the mythical ancestor *mama* Ili, who was the only one to possess any at that time. (Note: The Kogi use the term *mama* as a title for male shamas and ritual specialists, and are not in the Peruvian sense of mother or tutelary goddess.) On returning to her father, Bunkeiji found him lying on the floor, as if dead. She put the coca leaves into his mouth, and her brother Mirvuixa added the necessary lime. Sintana sneezed and came back to life, with a stream of blue butterflies issuing from his mouth.

The other myth regarding coca is not associated with any major cultural heroes, but only with one particular mythical ancestor, known as *mama* Teyuna. In this account, a certain man had a daughter who could produce large quantities of leaves just by shaking them out of her long hair, thereby providing her father with all the coca he needed. Wishing to acquire a supply of these leaves, *mama* Teyuna disguised himself as a bird, and began to frequent the river where the girl went usually to bathe. Their relationship flourished, despite her father's opposition, to the point where the bird began drinking the girl's saliva straight from her mouth. Asking if the girl loved him, and receiving an encouraging reply, the bird asked her to pull a string that was hidden among the feathers on his head. At this point, his disguise fell away, and a naked *mama* Teyuna came forward to embrace the girl passionately . . . Later on, returning home, he shook his head and two coca seeds fell out of his hair. These he planted, and from there he spread the plant to all his neighbours.[9]

Turning to the Amazonian cultural area, the myths seem to repeat the already familiar pattern, associating the origins of coca with the sexual functions of a pervasive female spirit. One account in particular, taken from the Desana — a Tukanoan group in the Colombian Vaupés region — describes the birth not only of coca, but also of the hallucinogen *yajé* (**Banisteriopsis** spp.) In this, the daughter of a mythical figure called Wai-Maxse — the Lord of Beasts — was in extreme menstruation pains, and had gone down to a beach on the river bank where she lay rolling over in the sand. An old Desana woman was passing by, and tried to help her to her feet, but the daughter twisted over in such a violent spasm that one of her fingers came away in the old woman's hand. The story is repeated for another of Wai-Maxse's daughters, and on being planted in the ground, the two lost fingers produced respectively the *yajé* and coca plants.[10]

A similar story — interesting for its inversion and re-location of many minor details — has recently been reported among the Maku, forest Indians whose territory neighbours on that of the Desana. Here it concerned a daughter of Old Snake Man, the Master of Fishes, who lived under a waterfall. Several of his offspring had surfaced through the water in the form of snakes, then peeled off their skins and become human. One was captured by a mythological male ancestor of the Maku and became his wife. She noticed that he made his coca from the scrapings of a reed and, considering this rather inferior stuff, suggested that they visit her father's sub-aquatic abode to acquire a supply of the real thing. Her father was asleep at the time, but at the moment they pulled the first leaves from his coca bush he awoke with a start, feeling an intense pain as if his finger had been pulled off. The woman tried to hide the coca leaves — first in her mouth, then under her armpit, and then finally up her vagina — but this caused her body to erupt in the characteristic tumours of ganglionic tuberculosis. Though they finally made it back to the surface with the coca, this precedent would seem to stress the unsuitability of coca for female consumption, a feature which is widely reported all over Amazonia.[11]

Admittedly, these myths are often characterized by many specific differences of detail, but clearly there is also one major theme underlying them all. This concerns not only the intervention of a female agent in the origins of coca, but also specifies that this intervention occurs in a distinct realm, that of the sexual reproductive processes. Indeed, the identity of Mama Coca as a 'mother' and tutelary deity might easily be considered a subsidiary elaboration of this original mythical genesis — rather than the other way round — for Mama Coca obviously possessed no absolute or independent existence before the domestication of the first coca bush. This point is not merely an academic quibble, as it implies a fundamental distinction between the Indian concept and the more rarefied Western view, which often seems to presuppose the existence of an idealized Mama Coca, a goddess who somehow exists independent from — and prior to — any material manifestation of the bush.

In this context, it is worth pointing out that the 1571 report from Cuzco had only used the expressions *ma macoca* and *cocomama* in a very restricted sense, to describe the coca bush itself. It appears, however, that at least the second of these two terms — *cocomama* — was also employed in the early seventeenth century to denote certain small idols which presided over the coca harvest in particular plantations. According to an original source, dating from 1620, these idols could be made from any material, such as wood, cloth and various different metals.[12] Frazer, however, would have it that the representations of the 'divine mother' must be made from elements of the plant itself, in this case, leaves of the coca bush.[13] In either eventuality, it could be argued that the individual magical images, or *cocomamas*, were not really symbolic figures at all, nor did they represent any all-embracing coca godhead. Instead, they could be seen quite simply as magical objects in the worship of certain *huaca* powers contained in the coca plant itself, as examples of a pantheism more strictly substantial than metaphysical. Rather than confirming the existence of some pervasive, universal coca goddess, the case of the *cocamama* idols could well imply that the Indians considered an abstract Mama Coca figure as superfluous, that is to say, both possible and unnecessary, since a completely sufficient relationship was already manifest to all in the mutual interaction of specific coca bushes and their own complementary idols.

Any attentive reader may have noticed that the original argument regarding the nature of Mama Coca now seems to have come round in a complete circle, and stands almost directly opposed to its own point of departure, which suggested the existence of an irreducible female nature or essence in coca, and the idea of Mama Coca as a tutelary deity or 'mother of coca'. This idea of an essential divinity — of Mama Coca as an identifiable member of the divine pantheon, desporting herself on the slopes of an Andean Mount Olympus — would seem to result from a characteristically Western misinterpretation of Indian cosmology, a typically Platonic reduction of the diffuse Indian spirit to a piece of statuary, a clear-cut and universal form. In this idealized scheme, the flow of magical power (*huaca*) is from goddess to plant; the abstract Mama Coca godhead is an obvious necessity, since she constitutes the course around which an entire structure of significance is organized. On the other hand, the native idea of Mama Coca must be seen as entirely situational, as an inversion of the Western logical structure, for the *huaca* of a specific manifestation of Mama Coca springs from a close proximity to the coca leaves themselves. Nothing could be clearer, in this respect, than the seventeenth century report of individual cocomama idols guarding over their respective coca plantations. Likewise, in the mythological context, it should be recognized that the intervention of an ancestral female figure does not serve primarily as a precedent for a divine Mama Coca, but instead acts principally to explain the origins of the coca bush itself, the material manifestation, not the abstracted goddess.

It is precisely this contextual 'meaning' of the various Mama Coca myths, that allows for the occasional inversion of the female attributes, producing the apparent anomaly of a masculine Mama Coca. Among the Barasana Indians — another Tukanoan group in the Vaupés drainage — coca seems to fit into a complex set of behavioural or conceptual opposites, being considered a 'male' quality not in the abstract sense, but rather simply in its capacity to complement the 'female' manioc. This observation underlines the necessity of viewing the different versions of the Mama Coca myth always in culture-specific terms, and in this context, it is worth pointing out that the Barasana can certainly produce a mythological precedent for their own, rather idiosyncratic, view of coca as a masculine element. Interestingly enough, the myth concerns the almost universal theme of sexual intercourse — hardly surprising, since it is the human model for all procreation — but in this case, it was the man involved, rather than the woman, who was then transformed into the first domesticated coca bush. As a result of this, all Barasana coca groves are laid out in the shape of a T or a cross, in recognition of the posture of the copulating male, prostrate on the ground.[14]

Returning to the Central Andean area, there is even a sense in which the very expresson 'Mama Coca' could simply have resulted from an elaborate play on words. In the first place, the word coca was not original to Quechua, the language of the Inca state, but rather stemmed from the Aymara *kkoka*, a generic term which meant tree or bush, irrespective of species. The early Quechua dictionaries — such as that of González Holguín — all use the word coca in compounds, indicating that the imported Aymara term had been tacked on to more ancient usages. One of these compounds was *ttupa coca*, which indicated the small-leaved species of coca from the Peruvian coast, **Erythroxylum novogranatense** var. **truxillense**. Another was that employed to denote the larger leaved species from the eastern slopes of the Andes, **Erythroxylum coca**; it was reported by different sources as *mamosh coca, mumush coca,* or even *mamas coca.*

While not wishing to labour the point, it might be feasible to consider whether this latter usage provides an alternative or supplementary explanation of the very etymology of the words Mama Coca. The expression would thus have come to mean the original and ancient coca of the eastern slopes of the Andes, as opposed to the more common and indiscriminate coca, a term imposed all over the New World by the Spanish in their quest for administrative and linguistic uniformity. Furthermore, the term could eventually have blended with local denominations for wild species of coca, again reinforcing the idea of Mama Coca as a prehistoric prototype to present-day cultivated coca. For example, the name 'mamacoca' is still used by the local Indians to describe a species of wild coca (**E. mamacoca** Mart.) growing in the Huallaga basin near Huánuco, Peru.[16] 'Mama Coca' could therefore be seen — at least in the cultural context of the Central Andes — as a form of shorthand notation, its baroque proliferation of meanings serving to refer at once to the wild coca plant, its mythical female progenitor, its tutelary or protecting spirit, the graven image of this god, and finally, even a specific type of coca leaf grown on the eastern slopes of the Andes. None of these meanings would necessarily exclude any other, all would imply the possibility of alternative 'readings', additional interpretations of an intentionally ambiguous message.

Clearly, then, it would be useful to consider Mama Coca as the paradigm for a particularly adaptable and open-ended conceptual system. Even in restricting interpretation to the very simplest of schemes, Mama Coca represents a blurred and indefinable point in the interpenetration of two poles — on the one hand the principle of feminine fecundity and growth, and on the other the magical *huaca* of the coca bush itself. Clearly the temptation is to try and fix a point at which this nebulous interpenetration of coca and femininity may be reduced to a simple intersection, that is to say, a point which establishes clear boundaries between the 'mama' and the 'coca' components which together make up the chimeral entity known as Mama Coca. In discovering and defining such a point, Mama Coca would herself be objectified, boiled down to a simple mathematical formula. It is precisely this kind of approach which lies at the root of so much of Western conceptual fetishism, including, incidentally, the image of Mama Coca which figures as frontispiece to Mortimer's history of coca. Her Anglo-Saxon features betray the fact that she is an entirely ethnocentric construct, a romantic phantasy produced in complete isolation from the Andean context of coca chewing, a mirror of our own civilization's enormous capacity for mystification.

For all these reasons, any outsider's idea of Mama Coca is likely to be quite out of touch with the sometimes contradictory concepts which are invoked by the South American coca chewers themselves. In the case of the Cauca area, where I did my own field work, the very idea of a female coca spirit was so extremely diffuse, so inexplicit, as to be almost wholly unidentifiable. For a long time I even considered abandoning the very question of Mama Coca entirely, as her association with a certain kind of facile hip mysticism was likely to constitute something of a bind, an unnecessary drawback. If, in the end, I did preserve the quest for her identity as the major theme of this study, I did so prompted less by the concrete mythological precedent of the Central Andes, than by the need to define some model for my investigation, some model that could actually transcend the usual kind of maladapted and *a priori* methodological tools used by so many anthropologists in the field. The attraction of Mama Coca lay precisely in her lack of clear definition. It was this diffuseness of outline, this inherent instability which could itself serve as investigative framework, as a complement to my own direct — and essentially formless — experience in the field.

The notion remained rather hazy, however, and I was fortunate to chance on a short paragraph which clarified the outlines of the sort of abstracted femininity which I had ascribed to Mama Coca. It had been written by the Elizabethan poet John Donne, and come from his early prose writings — 'Paradoxes and Problems' — in a section entitled 'A defence of women's inconstancy';

> 'That Women are Inconstant, I with any man confess, but that Inconstancy is a bad quality, I against any man will maintain: For every thing as it is one better than another, so is it fuller of change; the Heavens themselves continually turn . . . so in Men, they that have the most reason are the most alterable in their designs, and the darkest or most ignorant, do seldomest change; therefore Women changing more than men, have also more reason . . .'[17]

I could not help thinking that a formal recognition of the type of feminine inconstancy described by Donne could, in fact, serve as a very appropriate vehicle for expressing the many changes likely to be encountered in any approximation to the experience of using coca. The quest for Mama Coca was therefore not really a quest at all, but rather, simply a continuous process of definition. The pursuit of her inconstant image would lead inevitably to the repeated attainment of partial goals. Goals which, on being reached, would merely become thresholds onto a further stage of the investigation. It did not, therefore, appear at all surprising that my research should oscillate between the differing approaches found in sociological, pharmacological, ethnographic or historical frameworks of social inquiry. Rather, it seemed that the direct coupling of a subjective experience of coca with the various theoretical and cultural approaches to the subject — both those discernible in the written sources, and those indicated to me by *companeros* in the Cauca area — would, in fact, constitute the only possible approach to a personal definition of the elusive Mama Coca.

It was perhaps inevitable that this approach would finally lead to an encounter with a real, substantial Mama Coca — an elderly Paez widow who, besides being an excellent informant, also had the capacity to arouse me sexually in a manner I had never before experienced. Throughout the latter half of 1973, I often found myself visiting her house in the valley of San Andrés de Pisimbalá, and though we never established any actual physical contact, the bonds between us grew to the point where I was repeatedly recognizing her features in my dreams, more often than not in some clear association with coca leaves. Her adult sons clearly found our relationship a source of some considerable amusement, and all the more since I usually brought her gifts of coca and received in return her own home-baked lime powder. This was a fine white substance which, being kept in a pear-shaped gourd of distinctly phallic outline, obviously lent itself to a good deal of explicit sexual joking, along the lines of 'young man comes to old woman to fill his *tuka* (gourd) with white powder . . . '

Not until I had known her for more than six months did I decide to try to overcome her natural coyness, explaining as respectfully as I could my identification of Mama Coca with her own person. As if to call into question such overbearing seriousness, she began to giggle uncontrollably, lifting her skirt above the knee and adopting all the coquettish poses of a girl thirty years her junior. Then she proceeded to ply me with her own domestic *núsa* — fermented cane juice — and before very long we were both quite pissed. All the preceding sexual tension seemed somehow to evaporate on being made explicit, and thereafter we always remained the very best of platonic friends. I was just getting up to leave, glad of this release from such pent-up emotions, when she suddenly remarked: 'That woman, the one with the coca, you must be careful, understand? She has got you *encantado* (bewitched), and is capable of killing you just like that . . . ' She broke a twig expressively in her hand, and threw it away into the bushes. I later learned that her husband had died from a similar affliction, or infatuation, staying up all night, chewing coca and wandering about the countryside until he collapsed through sheer exhaustion. She was worried, therefore, that this malign Mama Coca spirit was somehow working through her, operating without any conscious control on her part. She suggested that I get in touch with her brother — a very highly respected shaman in those parts — and attempt to thrash out the obsession with him directly. It is to this point, therefore, that I shall return in the last chapter of the book, for in terms of my own subjective, existential preoccupations, it was precisely this whole question of the way to deal with the 'objectification' of Mama Coca that became the single most important aspect of my field work in the Cauca area.

II. Coca and the West

'They were very ugly in manner and appearance; all had their cheeks bulging with a certain green herb which they chewed constantly, like cattle. They could hardly speak, and each carried two gourds hanging from his neck, one filled with the herb he had in his mouth, and the other with a white flour that looked like powdered plaster. From time to time they would wet a stick, dip it in the flour, and then put it in their mouths . . . mixing the flour with the herb . . . and, amazed at such a thing, we could not understand its secret . . .'

A letter by Americo Vespucio, dated September 4th, 1504, describing his journey to the north coast of South America in 1499.[1]

It seems likely that Vespucio's letter was the very first written report on the use of coca, a habit which — as we have seen — was a good deal more widespread in the early sixteenth century than it is today. Most of the early accounts were concerned with describing the custom along the Caribbean coastline, an area where it has long since disappeared, along with most of the indigenous inhabitants. Furthermore, nearly all descriptions were marked by the same blank incomprehension apparent in Vespucio's letter, and it was not until many years later — after the Conquest (1533) and stabilization of the new colony of Peru — that any attempt was made to provide a serious explanation of the coca habit.[2] Even such a perceptive chronicler as Pedro Cieza de León, writing about the Cauca area in the early 1540s, found it difficult to suppress his feeling of distaste:

'In the other villages subject to the cities of Cali and Popayán they go about with small coca leaves in their mouths, and they extract from little gourds a certain mixture that they make, and put it also in their mouths, keeping it there a while and doing the same with some earth which is like lime . . . On asking the Indians why they always have their mouths full of that herb — which they do not eat, but merely hold between their teeth — they said that they feel little hunger and find themselves full of strength and energy. I think that it must have some such effect, though it appears to me a bad habit and a vice, and suitable for such people as these Indians . . .'[3]

With time, however, news of the extraordinary qualities of coca began to filter back to Spain, often to be confused — at least initially — with information pertaining to other drug plants, such as tobacco. A summary of the ideas current at the time is to be found in Nicolas Monardes' celebrated New World herbal, the 'Historia Medicinal', first published in Seville in 1574. The 1577 English translation by John Frampton can be found as the heading to Chapter V of this book. Monardes' work was also rendered into Latin by the director of the Emperor's garden in Vienna, Charles L'Ecluse (or Clusius), and published under the title 'Exoticorum' (Antwerp, 1582); as well as forming the basis for Claude Duret's discussion of coca in the 'Histoire admirable des plantes . . . ' (Paris, 1605).

Despite all this written recognition of the drug's marvellous qualities, it seems clear that the actual consumption of coca never really caught on in Europe. In this respect, the case of coca differed notably from that of two other New World drug plants — chocolate and tobacco — whose popularity began to increase beyond all measure in the seventeenth century. To a very great extent, the reason for this must lie in the initial difficulty of learning how to chew coca properly, especially when compared with the relatively simple chocolate-drinking and tobacco-smoking habits. The painful cauterization of the soft mucous membrane of the mouth — an inevitable consequence of any careless application of the lime powder used with coca leaves — as well as the almost universal aesthetic discrimination against what was considered an 'ugly' habit, would both have prevented any widespread adoption of coca by the Spaniards in the New World, and its subsequent diffusion back to the European metropolis. Indeed, this situation has hardly changed even today, and despite the easy assimilation of a great number of drugs by modern society, it is unlikely that coca chewing — as opposed to cocaine sniffing — will ever become a fashionable trend.

EARLY SPANISH CAMPAIGNS AGAINST COCA

It is but a short step, however, from simple distaste to outright condemnation, and wishing to discover something in the coca habit which was more censurable than mere ugliness, the Spanish authorities soon had recourse to the superior wisdom of the Church. Accustomed to tales of witches and their 'flying ointments' — a common obsession in late medieval Europe — the very ingestion of any psychoactive plant substances was widely believed to involve some sort of diabolic perversion. The efficacious use of scapegoating against the European witches provided the model for cultural repression in the Americas, and it became customary to refer to the Indian use of drugs by means of the colourful expression *hablar con el demonio* (to speak to the devil).[4] As a result of the jealous vigilance of the holy fathers, the taking of potent hallucinogens and psychedelics soon became a very hidden, surreptitious practice, and for this reason there exist very few contemporary reports on the subject.

Such was not the case with coca, however, which was widely employed not only as a magical herb, but also as a daily stimulant in the normal course of agricultural work. Its use, therefore, could not easily be hidden from the authorities; and perhaps for this very reason coca came to be selected as a prime target in the missionary campaign then beginning to bear down on the native Americans. The first ecclesiastical council of Lima (1551) chose simply to condemn coca outright, considering it a major obstacle to the spread of Christianity. Diego de Robles stated bluntly: 'Coca is a plant which the devil invented for the total destruction of the natives.'[5] By 1569 clerical interests had prevailed upon the King to send out the following recommendations to Peru:

> '... that certain inconveniences follow from the uses and customs of the Indians of this land regarding the cultivation of coca, since it is an important element in their idolatries, ceremonies, and witchcraft, and they pretend that carrying it in their mouths they do receive strength, which is an illusion of the devil, according to what some experienced people have said ... '[6]

Friar Antonio de Zúniga, in a letter to the King dated July 15th,1579, claimed that the use of coca had been the cause of his failure to convert the heathens, and suggested that all the plantations be destroyed and the Indians working them be sold off as slaves.[7] The good friar was enough of a realist, however, to recognize that his proposals were unlikely to be accepted. In the first place, the habit was so widespread that any effective suppression would have required the policing of almost the entire population of the Andes, as impossible a task then as it is today. More significantly, the coca trade had soon become the single most important source of agricultural revenue in all Peru, providing the livelihood not only of the Indian and Spanish growers, but also yielding a significant income — through the extraction of tithes and tributes — to both the Crown and the very Church itself.

Concern with the coca 'problem', therefore, tended to recede gradually as time wore on, and came to concentrate instead on the glaring abuses which had emerged as the result of unscrupulous commercial practices on the part of greedy Spanish and *mestizo* speculators. In the 1560s, Juan de Matienzo completed the first detailed and careful study of the production of coca in Peru, backing up his case with a virtually irrefutable theological argument in favour of the plant:

'. . . since God created coca in this land rather than in any other, it must have been necesary for the local inhabitants, because God did nothing in excess, nor to no effect . . .'[8]

More significantly, he dedicated considerable attention to the health risks involved in picking the harvests, since this required sending large numbers of high-altitude Indians into the humid, insalubrious *montana* regions, from where they returned plagued with terrible diseases — that is, if they ever returned at all. As a result of such reports, and their impact on the administrative zeal at Philip II's court, a number of edicts or *Ordenanzas* were decreed concerning the treatment of the Indian labour force. On the 17th December 1563 '. . . the Spanish are forbidden to force the Indians to work in the exploitation of the coca crop . . .'; and in 1573 more specific recommendations were made, detailing a number of restrictions on the Indian workload, and stating the maximum period (one month) that highland labourers could be forced to remain in the *montana*. It is unlikely that these laws were ever very vigorously applied — the standard response of the colonists to such instructions was the ironic little phrase *se obedece, pero no se cumple* (the order is obeyed, but not carried into effect) — and by the end of the sixteenth century the chewing of coca, together with all the abuses associated with its exploitation, had become a widely accepted fact of life in the Andes.

THE FIRST NON-INDIAN COCA CHEWERS

At the same time, there evidently occurred some relaxation of the earlier intolerant attitudes towards the habit, with the use of coca — principally, perhaps, in the form of teas — spreading among black slaves and white settlers alike.[10] An official of the Spanish Inquisition, on a mission to Quito between 1623 and 1628, described the Dominican and Augustinian monks of that city in the following terms:

'Sire, they do take coca in these two orders with the greatest abandon, a herb in which the devil has invested the most essential of his diabolic tricks, and which makes them drunk and out of their senses, so that being beside their normal selves they say and do things unworthy of

Christians, and even less of ecclesiastics. I think that if the Inquisition does not use a very strong hand with such an infernal superstition, all this will be lost . . .'[11]

Despite such evidence of coca's infiltration into the cloisters, the most thoroughly documented case of a white man's use of coca still remains that of Francisco Martín, one of the members of Micer Ambrosio's first expedition into the jungle areas of north-eastern Venezuela (1529-1531). Having distinguished himself throughout by his courage and resistance, Martín was chosen to form part of a small subsidiary force whose mission was to take a large booty in captured gold back to the original Spanish settlement at Coro, on the Caribbean coast. Wandering aimlessly through the deep rainforests which surround Lake Maracaibo, the small band were eventually reduced to eating their horses, and in the last resort, even the human flesh of their Indian porters, a fact which was recorded with horror and disbelief by the chroniclers of the time. With their strength failing, they were finally forced to bury the treasure and Martín — with an injured leg — was left to die by his three remaining companions.

According to the blood-curdling description written by Pedro de Aguado, our hero's hunger was so great at this point that he was forced to eat the uncooked penis of an Indian who had fallen victim to the three other Spaniards. In total desperation, he finally threw himself into a river, and seizing hold of a log floated downstream to an Indian village which lay a few leagues distant. He had the good fortune to be reasonably well received, and despite the opposition of the young men of the tribe, he eventually married the chief's daughter, becoming a celebrated warrior and an almost legendary healer and diviner throughout the land. When he was finally discovered again by the Spanish, many years later, he was found to have adopted all the local customs — including Indian dress and body paint, and, naturally enough, the coca habit as well.

Scandalized at such a brazen repudiation of Christian values, and more important still, recognizing him as the sole survivor of an expedition which had lost an incalculable treasure in buried gold, they forced Martín back to Coro. Appropriately enough, he never succeeded in locating the treasure again, and twice he escaped from his Spanish captors and returned to his wife and children in the Indian village. With regard to his fondness for coca, Pedro de Aguado is most explicit:

'. . . and even after he had left the company of these Indians he used it many times, because the Indian customs had suited him so well that he considered them a natural thing . . .'[12]

Considering that large numbers of the early colonists lived at very close quarters with their new Indian subjects, it is perhaps surprising that more of them did not follow Martín's example. In any case, a number of the more perceptive witnesses of the time did actually make the effort to point out a few useful therapeutic applications for the plant. An early account of coca chewing near Cumana, on the Venezuelan coast, describes a black stain forming on the teeth of the Indian *coqueros:* '. . . the dark colour remaining thereafter for a whole lifetime, and neither do the teeth rot, nor do they ever ache . . .'[13] The Jesuit Priest, Bernabé Cobo, confirmed this observation through his own experience in Peru:

> 'It happened to me once that, on calling a barber to pull out one of my teeth which was becoming loose and hurting a good deal, the barber told me that it was a pity to pull the tooth, as it was still good and healthy. A fellow priest who was present at the time advised me to chew coca for a few days, and this I did, with the result that the pain was banished and the tooth became as firm as the rest.'[14]

Cobo also mentioned various other qualities of the leaves: their local use in applications to broken bones and infected flesh wounds, their suitability for stomach disorders and compulsive vomiting, and the ability of the smoke of smouldering coca seeds to halt bleeding in the nose. As a result of these and other observations, it soon became acceptable for white people to use coca — at least medicinally — and the disgust and blank incomprehension of the earlier period began to give way to an almost grudging respect for the plant. By the beginning of the seventeenth century this had produced a reasonably stable and balanced pattern of consumption — one which was to remain virtually unchanged until the discovery and commercialization of cocaine. With the profits of the trade firmly in the hands of powerful colonial interests, the vast mass of the population were allowed or even encouraged to continue chewing coca. Various other groups — black slaves, in particular, and the occasional white *campesino* as well — probably also adopted the coca chewing habit as an aid to hard physical work. Even the more respectable colonists were forced to recognize the occasional usefulness of the miraculous leaf, preparing it in teas and using it as an almost universal panacea for a wide range of digestive and nervous complaints.

THE ISOLATION OF COCAINE

There is a great lack of published literature on coca in the seventeenth, eighteenth and early nineteenth centuries, and this would seem to reflect the stability of usage which was characteristic of this period. True, a new kind of scientific interest in the plant was beginning to emerge: botanists such as Joseph de Jussieu and Aimé Bonpland made original field collections of the different varieties of coca plant, and in 1786 Lamarck published the classic description of the typical economic species, **Erythroxylum coca.**[15] In Colombia — or rather, in the colony of New Granada — this interest was reciprocated by the celebrated *expedición Botánica*. In March, 1784, under the direction of Celestino Mutis, this group collected and illustrated the coca of Mariquita, in the Middle Magdalena valley near Bogotá, thus recording the first botanical sample of what was later to be identified as the species **Erythroxylum novogranatense.**[16]

A number of British officers also published short accounts of the coca habit in their books about the war of independence against Spain, but these were mainly limited to pointing out its parallels with the use of betel in India and the Far East.[17] Some adventurous authors even suggested that coca be introduced in England as a temporary expedient in times of famine, but — alas! — they were not taken very seriously.[18] The trouble was that very few literate people had ever chewed coca leaves themselves, and thus they did not really know what to say in its defence. It is this which makes the case of General Miller — commander of the British volunteer force during the Peruvian campaign of 1824 — such a very remarkable exception:

> 'Nothing obtains the good will of an Indian sooner than his being requested to spare a little coca. He pulls out his pouch with an air of utmost satisfaction, and seems anxious to have it supposed that he feels the honour most sensibly. General Miller often chewed it . . . '[19]

Miller was not alone in his enthusiasm for coca, however, and a few years later its use was also praised in the writing of the notable Andeanist, Clements Markham, who visited Peru in 1859:

> 'I chewed coca, not constantly, but frequently, from the day of my departure from Sandia, and besides the agreeable soothing feeling it produced, I found that I could endure long abstinence from food with less inconvenience than I would otherwise have felt, and it enabled me to ascend precipitous mountain sides with a feeling of lightness and elasticity and without losing my breath. This latter quality ought to recommend its use to members of the Alpine Club, and to walking tourists in general.'[20]

Appropriately enough, it was this same year of 1859 which also ushered in the single most important development in the history of coca — the isolation of cocaine and its recognition as the principal active alkaloid in the coca leaf. Though the example had passed unperceived by the international scientific community, the basic principle of cocaine extraction had, in fact, already been pioneered by the Indians of the Guajira peninsula, on the border between Colombia and Venezuela. The Guajiro system involved boiling ground coca leaves in a solution of water and lime powder, the latter produced by grinding burned sea-shells.[21] In this way, there emerged a thick, viscous syrup of coca which clearly contained a very potent charge of alkaloids, and whose nature was not greatly removed from the unrefined 'base' or *pasta* of cocaine that is a common feature of today's illicit trade.

A great deal has been written about the original 'discovery' of cocaine, and it is not the object of this study to mediate between the conflicting claims of Gaedeke — who isolated what he called Erythroxyline, in 1855 — and of Albert Niemann — who is usually credited with the formal recognition of cocaine, sometime in 1858 or 1859. After morphine was discovered in 1803, great strides forward had been made in alkaloid chemistry, and it was almost a foregone conclusion that coca would finally yield up its elusive 'essence' to the impassive scrutiny of the test tube.

What is more surprising, perhaps, is that the isolation of cocaine did not lead to any great interest in devising new applications for the drug. Probably the single most important reason for this failure lay in the very sceptical treatment commonly given to accounts of coca chewing in its native context. The powers attributed to the leaf were widely considered to be delusions or superstitions quite in keeping with the 'savage' status of the Indians who used it; and the travellers who claimed — along with Miller and Markham — that they had experienced noticeable effects from the leaves, were usually dismissed simply as eccentrics whose naive enthusiasm had been allowed to cloud their better judgement. As we shall see, Western medicine was to pay dearly for this self-inflicted shortsightedness.

THE WONDER DRUG

Cocaine had to wait all of twenty-five years before a practical application for it came to be recognized in medical circles. Originally inspired by reports describing its use by the Prussian army on field exercises, the young Sigmund Freud decided to begin experimenting with cocaine on himself, employing the drug as an all-purpose stimulant and mood-raising tonic. His intriguing findings, however, were neither well received nor very widely publicized, and it remained for his fellow student in Vienna — Carl Koller — to apply cocaine in a hitherto unrecognized capacity, that of a local anaesthetic. Overnight his discoveries revolutionized the art of surgery, and by the winter of 1884-1885 cocaine had become one of the most hotly debated issues in the medical establishment of the time.[22]

Initially, at least, cocaine was clearly considered something of a wonder drug, and its surgical applications were universally hailed as a breakthrough in modern science. Its applications as a stimulant, however, or as a substitute for morphine — precisely those aspects which most interested Sigmund Freud — were on the whole rather less enthusiastically received. The stereotypes of opiate addiction soon came to be associated with cocaine as well; being subsequently publicized through such vehicles of mass communication as the serialized adventures of Sherlock Holmes. By the late 1880s, denunciation of a new vice, cocainism, had become the order of the day, and Freud felt the need to point out:

> 'All reports of addiction of cocaine and deterioration resulting from it refer to morphine addicts . . . Cocaine has claimed no other, no victims of its own.'[23]

Freud was largely right, of course, but being only an insignificant houseman at the time, his professional superiors had little patience with the academic niceties of his argument. In any case, it can hardly be doubted that the underlying reason for cocaine's identification with morphine — and for its subsequent misclassification as an especially dangerous drug, as enshrined in the Harrison Act of 1914 — must have originated in the widespread unwillingness to consider seriously the cultural precedent of coca as it is used in the Andes. To judge from Freud's major paper on the subject — 'Uber Coca' published in July 1884 — most accounts limited themselves to occasional remarks about Indian 'endurance' while chewing coca leaves, or merely repeated the misconceptions culled from that untrustworthy chronicler, Inca Garcilaso de la Vega, best known for his dubious assertion that coca had originally been the strict prerogative of the Inca aristocracy.[24]

Indeed, one of the most noticeable aspects of the whole affair was precisely the revolution which the discovery of cocaine produced in 'civilized' perceptions of the coca habit. Rather than being a mere curiosity, a colourful detail used to enliven travellers; accounts of voyages through the Andes, coca very quickly came to be considered — at least by interests favourable to cocaine — as a 'sublime leaf', the 'divine plant of the Incas'. Given the lack of detailed information on the coca habit, it is perhaps understandable that so many authors should have simply assumed that whatever was true for cocaine also held for coca, and vice-versa. Freud himself was uncompromising in this respect:

> 'The experiments carried out recently with the cocaine prepared by Merck in Darmstadt alone justify the claim that cocaine is the true agent of the coca effect . . . '[25]

It was in order to remedy this misconception that William Golden Mortimer undertook what is probably the single most important and comprehensive work yet to have been written on the subject, his 'Peru: A

History of Coca', first published in New York in 1901. This book was based on a truly encyclopaedic attempt to blend the medical research of the time with opinions then current in the field of Andean studies, and — given the fact that considerable new information has been made available in the intervening seventy-five years — it is surprising to note just how much of Mortimer's material has simply never been bettered elsewhere. Above all, it is to Mortimer, and to his main informant, Henry Rusby, that credit must be given for opposing the official view that cocaine necessarily incorporates all the myriad qualities of the coca leaf. As Rusby himself put it:

> 'With certain restrictions it may be said that the properties of cocaine, remarkable as they are, lie in an altogether different direction from those of coca as it has been reported to us from South America.'[26]

At the same time while not wishing to belittle Mortimer's numerous and valuable contributions to the subject, it would still be excusable to point out that there remains one major flaw in his argument. The issue is an important one, for it seems a little unfortunate that he should have gone so far in distinguishing between coca and cocaine, only to succumb finally to the commercial interests so apparent in his publicity on behalf of M. Angelo Mariani, the manufacturer of a range of coca-derived wines and elixirs that were enjoying a considerable vogue at the time.[27] First placed on the market in 1863, the original Vin Mariani had soon conquered the palates of large numbers of notable citizens, including more than one Pope and head of state. As a result of this success, it had spawned countless imitators, including the cocaine-bearing prototype of Coca Cola, first manufactured in 1886, by John Smyth Pemberton of Atlanta, Georgia.

PHARMACOLOGY: A MODERN INQUISTION

Mortimer, however, can surely be forgiven this trifling pecadillo, especially if one stops to consider the gross dishonesty which became common in so many of the subsequent medical surveys of the coca habit. It is, perhaps, quite significant that his work was very seldom referred to by any of the later school of bullshit pharmacologists, that particularly twentieth-century breed of 'drug abuse' specialists and international narcotics bureaucrats. This is hardly surprising, however, since Mortimer emphatically did not support the morphine-derived 'addiction' theory which many other authors have wished to employ in explaining the coca habit of the Andean Indians. The first champion of this line of thought had been Eduard von Poeppig, a German who travelled extensively in Peru in the years 1827 to 1832, and whom Mortimer described euphemistically as

'... not an enthusiastic admirer of Indian customs ...'[28] Bearer of a puritanical sense of propriety, coca was only one of the many aspects of Indian life which he found shocking and depraved, and he described at length the terrible symptoms — including insomnia, headaches, and finally even death — of what he took to be terminal cases of coca addiction.[29]

Poeppig's dismal account of the Indian coca chewer, together with a few laboratory experiments on cases of chronic intoxication produced by means of large intravenous injections of cocaine, provided most pharmacologists with all the evidence they needed to condemn the use of the coca leaf. Indeed, in many cases, professional reputations did not rest on any original research at all, but on the use of unrestrained dogmatism and wild, inflammatory rhetoric. A case in point is provided by Louis Lewin, the distinguished toxicologist, who published in 1924 a book called 'Phantastica', for a long time considered almost a bible on the effects of psychoactive drugs. With regard to coca, his argument began — characteristically enough — by restating the by now common misconception that '... the use of the leaves and that of cocaine produce very similar results as regards the actual symptoms and final form of the cocaine evil.'[30] Were this not enough, he proceeded to reaffirm the even more characteristic confusion between coca and the opiates, rubbing it in with a vehemence that harked back to the darkest days of the Spanish Inquisition:

> 'The prolonged toxicomaniac abuse brings about by gradual development graver symptoms, the manifestations whereof are apparent among those eager coca-eaters (*sic*) of South America, the *coqueros*. Physically and morally they behave like opium-smokers. A cachectic state appears, with extreme emaciation accompanied by a gradual change in demeanour. They are old men before they are adult. They are apathetic, useless for all the more serious purposes of life, subject to hallucinations, and solely governed by the one passionate desire for the drug, besides which everything else in life is of inferior value.'[31]

Given Lewin's fiery appeal to everything that is most ethnocentric and culturally intolerant in modern medicine, it should come as no surprise that his ideas were widely appreciated by the social elite which forms the bulk of the medical profession in South America. In 1936, the Department of Pharmacology at the Faculty of Medicine in Lima initiated a series of investigations into the coca habit, and soon a good number of local researchers had established solid reputations in the field of condemning what they chose to call — so clinically — *el cocaísmo* or *la cocamanía*. Foremost among these was Dr. Carlos Gutiérrez-Noriega, whose findings tended to emphasize the social issues involved in coca chewing, including such gems as the relationship between this habit and 'the existence of acute and chronic mental alterations.'[32]

The fact that his observations were somewhat at variance with the definition of sanity current among the Indians themselves did not, of course, detract from his argument nor prevent Gutiérrez-Noriega from becoming established as the major official specialist on the coca issue. After all, the accolade he and his collaborators received for their work seems to have been almost entirely dependant on the confirmation they gave to the cultural prejudices of white, city-bred Peruvians, most of whom must have nodded with grave satisfaction on hearing the illustrious physician state that: '. . . the use of coca, illiteracy, and a negative attitude towards the superior culture, are all closely related . . .'[33] Other authors were soon feverishly elaborating on the themes first pioneered by Gutiérrez-Noriega; stressing that coca chewers were usually 'alienated' and 'anti-social', as well as 'inferior' in intelligence, initiative and adaptability, and that they suffered 'behavioural abnormalities' such as an absence of ambition, and an indifference to economic problems.[34]

In any case, having established the main ideological thrust to their campaign, these same 'experts' then proceeded to invite the United Nations to conduct a full international inquiry into the coca 'problem', hoping in this way to rip off research money and finally bring enough political pressure to bear on their unfortunate countrymen to achieve their ultimate aim, which was '. . . to free a people from the slavery of an addictive drug.'[35] From the outset, the bias of the U.N. Commission of Inquiry on the Coca Leaf was underscored by the background of the man chosen to be its titular head, one Howard B. Fonda, at that time vice-president of Burroughs Wellcome and Co. and a director of the American Pharmaceutical Manufacturer's Association. Arriving in Lima airport on the 12th September 1949, he was quoted by the press as stating that the use of coca was undoubtably harmful, that it was possibly the cause of 'racial degeneration' among the Indians, and that the findings of the Commission would definitely confirm the correctness of his assumptions.[36]

What is perhaps more surprising, is that this kind of badly informed scaremongering should actually have been so widely accepted, even respected, by the public opinion of the time. After all, the arrival of the U.N. Commission did happen to coincide with a period characterized by an almost complete absence of cocaine on the world market of illicit drugs, and the anti-coca offensive could not, therefore, unlike more recent drives against the growing of opium poppies, really be justified in terms of any major public health hazard afflicting the industrialized capitals of the West. Why, then, did the 1940s and early 50s witness such a major campaign against the chewing of coca?

The answer, surely, must lie in that period's abiding obsession with material progress and development, and with the elimination of any traits — such as coca chewing — which might remain subversively alien to the bland stereotypes of the new consumer society. The initiative for such a pervasive attack on traditional ways of life must clearly have stemmed from those social groups who had most to gain from the process of modernization, including both the local *criollo* oligarchy and petit bourgeoisie, and — more specifically — the multinational interests of industrial capitalism. It may even be possible to narrow the focus still further, and suggest that the particular period under consideration — the Second World War and its sequel — constituted a veritable high-water mark in the ascendancy of the United States in Latin America, a grand flowering of *yanqui* expansionism in its classic phase.

The dollar inevitably brought in its wake such figures as *míster* Fonda, along with a thriving new pharmaceutical industry and many ill-considered Public Health schemes as well. More often than not, these exploited the issue of hygiene as a means to disguise straightforward neo-colonialism, and many supposedly altruistic medical campaigns found their real objectives in undermining the cultural independence, political autonomy, and economic self-sufficiency of large numbers of the rural peasantry. In the case of coca, the real issue may not even have been the supposed evils of the chewing habit at all, and one suspects that the vociferous campaign against the drug may have found its major function as a cover for official double-dealing behind the scenes. It should, therefore, come as no surprise that the military junta then in power in Peru should have seized the opportunity to establish, by means of *Decreto-Ley* no. 11046 (June 13th, 1949), a government monopoly on the whole domestic and export coca trade. Particularly significant was the fact that — under the terms of Article 6 of this law — all profits from the business were to be the exclusive preserve of the Armed Forces.

This sort of action, naturally enough, was always held to be in the best interests of the peasantry itself, despite the fact that nobody ever deigned to ask them their opinion. The banner of improving health standards conveniently substituted the older religious mission as an excuse for any kind of high-handed paternalism. In point of fact, effective medical assistance remained at a bare minimum, and through the Andes surged instead a flood of mass-produced cigarettes and confectionery, fertilizers, insecticides, antibiotics, and — perhaps most sickening of all — the *gringo* sugar-based derivative of their own drug, Coca Cola. In place of the real thing, the white man could only offer a bottle full of artificial colouring and corrosive gases.

In the face of such obvious colonialism, it is hardly surprising that any self-respecting Andean peasant should keep a healthy distance between himself and any marauding medical experts who might have strayed out into the countryside. Fortunately, most of the anti-coca lobby were perfectly content to sit in their laboratories, doing battle with their intellectual rivals, the heretics in the Peruvian medical profession who actually dared to defend the use of coca, considering it a means of accommodating the body to the strains of living at high altitudes. Foremost among this group was Dr. Carlos Monge, a well-respected figure with twenty years' experience as the founder and director of the Institute of Andean Biology. The Institute's record included a good deal of pioneering research on the adaptation of the human organism to survival at extreme altitudes, and clearly, its direct observation of the use of coca in its native context had produced conclusions quite at variance with the rarified theories emanating from the Department of Pharmacology. A series of articles in the 1952 and 1953 issues of the anthropological journals, 'Peru Indígena' and 'América Indígena', provides written evidence of the increasingly acrimonious exchanges which took place at this time between the conflicting parties in the coca debate.[37]

Dr. Monge opened his repudiation of theU.N. Commission by pointing out that its three month period of investigation had hardly been sufficient to back up its very sweeping and widely publicized conclusions. He indicated that the Commission's insistence on the impaired work performance of habitual coca chewers radically contradicted his own findings, which showed that coca was an important element of man's cultural adaptation to the harsh climate and oxygen-deficient atmosphere of the Andean highlands. He also questioned the Commission's assumption that coca chewing was in some sense a 'cause' of malnutrition, observing that none of the diseases normally attendant on malnutrition — such as pellagra, beriberi, scurvy or rickets — had ever been present in the Peruvian *sierra*.

This point regarding malnutrition was of fundamental importance, for the very basis of Gutiérrez-Noriega's 'explanation' of the coca habit lay in the reciprocal relationship which he had established between food scarcity and the Indian use of leaves: 'The habitual chewer prefers the drug to food . . . From this, a vicious circle is established; one begins to chew coca in order to suppress hunger, but later the subject loses his appetite and eats little because he chews coca . . . '[38] In other words, Gutiérrez-Noriega saw coca chewing as both cause and effect of chronically inadequate food supplies, a circular argument which — at least in political terms — was obviously endowed with some considerable appeal. In particular, many of the older school of socialist theoreticians felt a need for just such a neat, mechanical interpretation of the coca habit, and what better than to explain it away as a minor cultural aberration 'forced' on the native population by conditions of extreme economic exploitation.[39]

One must credit Dr. Monge, therefore, with considerable courage for resisting this kind of facile simplification of the coca phenomenon — coming, as it did, from both sides of the political spectrum — and for arguing his case convincingly to the Peruvian government, who chose to ignore the tactless recommendations of the U.N. Commission. In Colombia, on the other hand, no reputable authority saw fit to defend the coca habit, despite the fact that throughout the Cauca area it was still common in the 1940s for white employers — even missionary priests[40] — to include a daily ration of coca in their payments to agricultural labourers. On his appointment as Minister of Hygiene, a local medical worthy from Popayan, Dr. Jorge Bejarano, decided to make political capital out of the issue, introducing Decree no. 896 of March 11th, 1947, which outlawed the cultivation, distribution, sale and possession of coca leaves throughout the country. Though this legislation provided local police forces with another favourite excuse to harass the Indians and *campesinos* of the Cauca area, its effective implementation — by means of a crop substitution program — was unfortunately undermined by the same sort of bureaucratic inertia which is a constant feature of all Colombian public life. The Ministry of Hygiene — having originally proposed the law — then transferred responsibility for its effective execution to the Ministry of Labour, who passed the buck to the Ministry of Agriculture, who in turn decided that the campaign must be financed by the agrarian banks and credit agencies. Within two years the project had come to a complete standstill, soon to be forgotten in the heat of the *Violencia*, a civil war of catastrophic proportions which particularly affected many of the Paez Indians' coca-producing areas.[41]

For the next fifteen years, the coca issue lay relatively dormant, only to be revived in Peru in the mid-60s by a research team from the school of Hygiene and Public Health at John Hopkins University, Baltimore. Supported by a grant from the Research and Developmet Command of the United States Army, Drs. Buck, Sasaki, Hewitt and Macrae undertook what they chose to call an 'epidemiologic' study of the 'noxious' effects of coca leaf chewing among the residents of the village of Cachicoto.[42] Though guided by a crushingly 'objective' methodology — including such glories of the age as 'random selections' by means of IBM cards, and phases of study conducted 'independently' by the various 'specialists' — they appear to have been quite unable to form a dispassionate evaluation of the very hypotheses which they had set out to test, and which, to nobody's surprise, had been drawn entirely from the conclusions of the already discredited U.N. Commission. Predictably enough, the results of the study fully confirmed all their own original expectations, namely:

> '...that coca chewing is associated with an inferior nutritional state; that chewers have a higher prevalence of conditions resulting from poor personal hygiene; and that the work performance of coca chewers is inferior to that of a comparable control group.'[43]

In order to produce such a very gratifying result, a number of graphs and statistics were shown to demonstrate the coca-chewers' inferior skin-fold thickness and lower serum albumin and serum cholesterol counts, but at the same time, the fact that these figures only just verged on the border of statistical significance was very carefully and deliberately glossed over. In truth, as an example of the manipulation of statistics, the study of Buck *et al.* must be almost without peer in the recent annals of science. Their prejudice is rendered further apparent by the repeated use of the word 'paradoxical' to describe findings which do not fit their original thesis. One example of this concerned '. . . the paradoxical reduction of the percentage of coca chewers infested with amoebae . . . '[44], while another attempted to explain away another puzzling factor, the lower tuberculin sensitivity of the coca chewing group.[45]

On balance, however, perhaps the most significant feature of this study was its complete failure to discuss what the investigators saw fit to dismiss in terms of '. . . the culture — associated glorification of its (coca's) use . . . [46] It is hard to imagine a more distant and uninvolved form of scientific inquiry, or a more transparent lack of sympathy for the people subjected to the investigation. Anthropologists have, in general, been rather slow to repudiate the basic assumptions of this kind of approach, perhaps through fear of the Research and Development Command of the U.S. Army, or more likely, out of a rather out-moded and inappropriate respect for the methodology of such hard-core, high-status sciences as epidemiology. The time is clearly ripe for a frontal assault on all forms of alienating orthodoxy, and particularly on the solemn mystifications which pass as 'science' where coca is concerned.

POST-1968 DRUG STUDIES NEW WINE IN OLD BOTTLES?

The arrival and diffusion of novel drug habits among previously unaffected social groups — especially Western, middle-class youth — has served to underline the insufficiencies of any explanation of such events couched purely in straight pharmacological terms. Two main failures can be identified in the old approach: firstly, its facile reduction of major historical events and cultural processes to the status of mere 'problems' of Public Health; and secondly, its inept assumption that a drug must necessarily perform in social contexts the same action as that observed in the laboratory. Recent research — particularly that concentrating on the sociological and economic features of individual drug habits — has served to uncover a number of quite glaring disparities between the perceived effects of a single drug taken in differing social contexts, and as a result, the importance of the cultural component in shaping a given drug experience has become increasingly well recognized.

On account of its widespread popularity and demonstrated inoffensiveness, marijuana (**Cannabis spp.**) has been a recipient of a good deal of the new research initiatives promoted by the advent of more enlightened attitudes[47] Perhaps most significant of all, the widespread use of many common and legal drugs — such as coffee, tobacco and alcohol — has been subjected to much closer scrutiny than before, unmasking their carefully groomed public image as harmless 'non-drugs', and thus calling into question the rather arbitrary twentieth century distinction between what is licit and what is illicit in terms of drug consumption.[48]

Coca has been less fortunate in this respect, a fact which would seem to result both from cocaine's more 'dangerous' profile — in law enforcement terms — and from the marked dissimilarity between the Indian habit of chewing leaves, and the urban user's custom of sniffing or shooting cocaine. All the more significant, therefore, is the work of those few authors who have attempted to redress the unfavourable balance of scientific opinion with regard to coca, and place its usage within the proper context of its historical, social and ethnomedical background.[49]

The contribution of Joel Hanna, in particular, deserves full credit for dispelling a number of worn-out misconceptions about the use of coca in Peru. He suggests, for instance, that hunger — caloric deficiency — should not be considered a driving force in the use of coca; thus putting the whole obsessive question of malnutrition back into a more realistic perspective, where it can be seen as a function of poverty and insufficient land, rather than as either cause or effect of the habit of chewing coca. He also states that his physiological tests — despite the unlimited availability of free coca leaves to his Indian subjects — were not able to confirm any of the favourite medical bogies about coca 'addiction': there was no evidence of psychological disturbances or withdrawal symptoms, nor did he notice any significant modification of working efficiency and energy requirements while under the influence of coca leaves. The only clear-cut effects of coca chewing — an accelerated heart-rate during submaximal effort, increased endurance under stress, and a mild constriction of the blood vessels — all appear to be features which are of considerable biological assistance in the Andes, increasing resistance to cold weather and high altitudes, and providing an added capacity for hard physical work. Above all, he stresses the economic importance which coca possesses in the rural society of Peru, and its role in establishing reciprocal patterns of exchange and social solidarity between otherwise independent and self-sufficient Andean communities.

Burchard and Bolton's studies, on the other hand, are perhaps less concerned with the broader cultural issues than with devising a new focus for the pharmacology of coca chewing. Neither appears very keen to endorse all of Hanna's observations on the physiological effects of coca, preferring to suggest instead that metabolic changes in the coca chewer's body may, in the long run, be more important than cold resistance and increased work capacity in explaining its use. In keeping with this opinion, both feel that the really crucial biological function of coca lies in its action on the glucose level in the blood: '... chewing coca leaf does in fact raise blood glucose levels and may in reality be a cultural mechanism for the management of blood glucose homeostasis problems.'[50] They see the use of coca as a cultural adaptation to conditions of hypoxia — caused by the shortage of oxygen at high altitudes — as well as a nutritional balance to a diet rich in carbohydrates, but relatively weak in animal protein: '... coca may prevent the rapid decline in blood glucose which typically follows the initial rise in glucose concentrations after meals rich in carbohydrates.'[51]

It would clearly be churlish to underestimate the importance of these findings, for they have contributed a significant new emphasis to the understanding of the coca habit. But it can only be fair to point out, however, that this recognition of the glucose effect had already been noted by the indefatigable Gutierrez-Noriega as early as 1947.[52] I also have the feeling that Bolton and Burchard are most at home when concentrating on what seem — at least from the anthropological point of view — rather tangential issues, being less interested in the Indians' own view of their coca habit than in the vision afforded from the comfortable distance of a laboratory, albeit a laboratory-in-the-field. Burchard, for example, writes:

> 'My major aim in this paper is to move away from a traditional cocain-model of coca chewing and towards an ecgonine-model, since ecgonine rather than cocaine is probably the central alkaloid involved in coca chewing.'[53]

In other words, though the name of the alkaloid is changed, the traditional chemical model of behaviour remains intact, and the different forms of cultural control over a given drug experience are still not entered into the equation, or not, at least, until *after* the basic physiological measurements have been made.

A number of unnecessarily extreme positions seem to result from this kind of gratuitous reductionism. Feeling an understandable repugnance towards equating the coca habit and the urban use of refined cocaine, neither author seems willing to admit that coca chewing may actually be any fun, that is, that coca might be used as much for its euphoriant properties as for its ability to raise the glucose level in the blood. If, for example, we are to believe Burchard's statement that ecgonine has '... little or no central stimulating effect on the sympathetic nervous system; no anaesthetic or euphoric properties...', and that '... the addicting (*sic*), euphoric, and anaesthetic action of cocaine can only occur when the molecule is intact...[54], then it would also follow that his version of the pharmacology of coca chewing — in which all cocaine is degraded to ecgonine before being absorbed into the human body — would not produce any sensation of local anaesthesia in the mouth, nor indeed, any feeling of euphoria either. At least with respect to the question of anaesthesia, I think almost any coca chewer would flatly deny this opinion, for the freeze produced on the gums is one of the clearest and most characteristic features of the drug.

> Bolton is even less compromising in his attitude: 'In the amounts ordinarily consumed by the Indians, coca produces no euphoric effects to my knowledge. And most definitely, Indians do not chew coca to become stoned (*sic*). Oddly enough, some American students who joined me in the field in 1974 insist that they did experience euphoria while chewing coca. Initially I attributed their reactions to the powers of suggestion rather than the powers of chemical substances. However, it is worth pointing out that these students ingested enormous amounts of coca leaves, amounts considered excessive by the Indians . . . Since Indians do not chew coca in quantities sufficient to produce these physiological effects, we can safely put aside this issue: the answer is *irrelevant* to the question of why Andean Indians chew coca.'[55] (stress added)

Certainly, my own perception of the coca effect would tend to confirm the euphoria reported by Bolton's students, and I do not think that this feeling can really be attributed to any excessive indulgence in the use of coca leaves. Personally speaking, I hardly ever chewed more than an ounce of leaves a day, considerably less than many of my Indian informants, and well within the range described by Burchard and Bolton for the Indians of the Central Andes. And though it is true that most coca chewers do, in fact, usually talk to strangers about their coca habit in terms of its effectiveness in combating cold, tiredness and hunger, this does not necessarily exclude the perception of euphoric effects as well. Indeed, what is 'euphoria' if it is not the ability to overcome — both physically and mentally — the slough of such depressing circumstances as cold, tiredness and hunger?

The problem, therefore, appears to be one of definition, of the tailoring of conceptual categories to fit specific cultural contexts. 'Euphoria' is defined in the Oxford English Dictionary simply as 'a feeling of well-being', but to Burchard and Bolton it seems to have undertones of the Rolling Stones on a coast-to-coast tour, and they are anxious to avoid the associations of coke-sniffing in the dressing-rooms. To an Indian, however, 'euphoria' may be an idea covered by other terms, or even a wholly indefinable mood — like the vague feeling of optimism which accompanies physical fitness, or the perception of an indescribable crispness in the air. If questioned by an ethnographer, the 'euphoric' Indian is likely to simply flash a knowing smile, or indicate with a twinkle in his eye what is basically a very personal, inscrutable and intimate state of well-being. The very word 'euphoria' is difficult to translate, even into another English synonym. The Spanish term used to describe the sensation attendant on coca chewing is *armado*, which has the sense of 'cocked' or 'wired' or 'coiled-up-and-ready-to-spring.' Any of these metaphors could be interpreted in terms of a highly attuned and stimulated brain and nervous system, and significantly, it is in these organs that the 'euphoric' properties of cocaine have been shown to act.

In the case of the Cauca area, reference was always made to the 'heat' of the wad of coca as it sat in the mouth, and a wad was only removed once it had gone so 'cold' that it could no longer be revived with additional doses of lime powder. Absorbed through the mucous membranes of the mouth — and producing local anaesthesia, an effect again associated with cocaine rather than ecgonine — this 'heat' was seen to reside for a while in the body before being dissipated as the anaesthesia wore off. It does not seem unreasonable to suggest that — at least in Paez terminology — the 'heat' or *báhia* produced by coca chewing was itself the local category comparable to our own more intellectualized 'euphoria'. The evident relish with which the word *báhia* was associated would seem to confirm that impression, as would the attendant facial expressions of contentment, satisfaction, pleasure and exhilaration.

Though Burchard and Bolton do both make the occasional polite nod in the direction of cultural interpretations of the coca habit, their underlying scheme does seem to imply that it can only be 'explained' by recourse to its physiological effects, and not by reference to its ultimate impact on social behaviour and personal sensibilities. The main danger of this approach is that it usurps all responsibility for distinguishing fact from fiction — for stating what is pharmacologically 'real' — thereby making it more than easy to dismiss any subjective reports of euphoria, such as those reported by Bolton's students. In this way, the question can simply be deemed 'irrelevant' to the pharmacological perception of the effects of coca chewing, 'irrelevant' that is, because it cannot be measured physiologically in any clearly quantifiable terms.

There is, of course, a very good historical reason for this tendency to de-emphasize — at least in 'straight' ethnomedical circles — the euphoria or cerebral stimulation produced by coca leaves. Pharmacologists are at present undertaking a very substantial and fundamental change in their attitude to illicit drugs, and not only with respect to coca. The days of orchestrated hysteria and rabid antipathy to any kind of illegal drug consumption — of the erroneous, but widespread, assimilation of all such habits to the opiate-inspired model of 'addiction' — are fortunately drawing to a close. Theories regarding the physiological effects of various drugs are in the process of revision and redefinition, and there is evidently a desire to tread very carefully in restoring the balance of opinion. For this reason, any professional position which is marginally more tolerant than that of its immediate precursors must necessarily be defended and justified repeatedly, and in terms which show the most impeccable regard for the orthodox methodology of drug research. Pharmacologists, after all, have to depend on a barrage of sustaining technology to ply their trade; and their grants must be answerable to official bodies which are often not at all sympathetic to the new approach. As John Kaplan, the Professor of Law at Stanford University, has recently pointed out:

> 'Often an elite will have a vested interest — not just a material interest, but perhaps more important, a prestige interest — in maintaining positions that they have taken earlier. In some sense, admitting that they were wrong about something, even if reasonably wrong, calls into question their entire capacity to govern.'[56]

Such a situation — one in which many new and original findings are deliberately ignored or suppressed through political interest[57] — must, in the end, force official investigators to operate with a quite undue amount of caution, a caution which is often translated into methodological paralysis and sheer lack of imagination. In particular, there seems to be a widespread unwillingness to consider the positive and, indeed, moral aspect of a given drug habit, the fact that it might be seen as a creative and socially cohesive force, capable on the one hand of reaffirming traditional values, and on the other, of promoting rapid cultural and political change. Even on those rare occasions when such a moral dimension does come to be recognized, the impact is reduced by the fact that it is almost exclusively ascribed to 'primitive' rural peoples, and not to the supposedly 'alienated' members of the urban drug scene.

Tidy dichotomies of this kind may not always, however, necessarily reflect the experience of individuals who share a direct, personal experience of both types of drug culture. Neither party exists in complete isolation, and there can be little doubt that both are already exerting a considerable amount of mutual influence. The urban pattern of drug consumption is rapidly spreading into rural areas — in Colombia, the cases of marijuana and **Stropharia** mushrooms (see Appendix A) are particularly explicit in this respect — affecting the structure of traditional economies, and even the very cultural context in which the drug is used.

Furthermore, it is clear that any form of behaviour depends for meaning on its social and economic setting, and therefore, there can exist no true or absolute state of 'alienation'. Such behaviour is relative, 'alienated' only with reference to the norms of the society which surrounds it. As it is commonly used in drug abuse surveys, the term alienation usually implies one out of two fundamentally different and contradictory positions: the first characterized by the common media image of escapism and self-indulgence, and the other by a more radical stance, based on the possibility of effective political challenge to the oppressive norms of mainstream Western society. In the former case, a new drug habit can readily become absorbed into the prevailing orthodoxy, assimilated into patterns of consumption already predetermined by some well-established psychostimulant, such as alcohol or tobacco.[58] To judge from the classified ads in such a magazine as 'High Times', this has already been the case of many middle-class marijuana smokers, a fact which must be of great consolation to the dominant commercial interests.

In a different and more revolutionary context, however, the use of a drug may serve to ritualize the experience of social solidarity, to give conscious expression and explicit focus to an otherwise diffuse gut-reaction of cultural malaise. An excellent example of this may be provided by the use of *ganja* or the 'holy weed' by members of the Ras Tafari movement in Jamaica, itself a positive response which has emerged not from the antecedent of any particular 'traditional' culture, but from a deliberate and considered rejection of the sterile neo-colonial realities of the twentieth century. More often than not, however, such movements are callously excluded from the official register of drug phenomena, rendered somehow less modern, less relevant, by their classification in that ambiguous no-man's-land marked 'millenarian'. By this means, the possibility of creating new and dynamic forms of ritual behaviour — novel social applications for a recently adopted drug habit — can conveniently be avoided in any further discussion of the future political implications of the different drug cultures presently emerging in the advanced industrialized societies of the West.

In a paranoid moment — perhaps induced by an understandable indulgence in too much urban drug-taking — one might legitimately suppose that there exists a conscious, CIA-directed conspiracy to deny that any such innovative, drug-based ritual behaviour could seriously challenge the cultural predominance of the orthodox escape valves of consumer society — the pathetic round of booze, coffee, and cigarettes — or undermine the profits of the industries they maintain. To suggest this in academic circles, for instance, would be likely to provoke raised eyebrows and embarrassed reminders of the fiasco of the counter-culture in the late 1960s. To the masters of supposedly progressive opinion, any idea that new drug habits might serve to undermine the status quo is simply laughable, a case of naive libertarian idealism, quite out of keeping with the harsh historical realities of the present day.

Yet, at the same time, the function of drug-induced ritual behaviour in protecting the cultural continuity of 'primitive' or 'traditional' peoples is widely recognized, even respected, by the very same authorities. Part of the answer to this puzzling inconsistency may lie in the fact that, among such peoples, drug consumption is usually seen as a conservative trait, whereas in the West it is normally considered innovative, at least in the case of the youthful use of illicit substances. What may be less well recognized is the fact that primitive conservatism and youthful radicalism are often both directed at the same ultimate objective, the taming and humiliation of the monster machine of state bureaucracy and industrial capitalism.

It is not, therefore, at all surprising that many urban drug users should seek orientation from the more honest, traditional and well-balanced drug cultures, a truth which is self-evident throughout the entire length of the *gringo* trail in South America. There seems to be an increasing, albeit unconscious recognition of the fact that merely indulgent drug consumption — the 'alienation' the narcotics bureaucrats talk about — must give way increasingly to drug consumption of the ritualized, socially activating kind, and to a solidarity with other, non-bourgeois drug consumers and producers the world over.

The rigid separation of the globe into 'primitive' and 'alienated' drug cultures exists, therefore, precisely in order to prevent any collective revolt by the groups under study, any pincer movement by the victims on both sides of the fence, any mass repudiation of the official scientism which maintains the established authorities on drug use in their posts. Burchard's contrast between the ecgonine-model involved in coca chewing, and the cocaine-model of urban coke sniffing, implies much more than a simple recognition of the admittedly rather different pharmacology of these two forms of the drug. Above all, it arises from an ideological need to separate the fundamental moral issues into two convenient stereotypes: the indulgent doper and the somehow better balanced Andean Indian.

Youthful anthropologists and travellers in general — probably some of the few individuals with a direct experience of both forms of drug culture — are therefore faced with a major responsibility, that of challenging these stereotypes, both in their own experience in the field, and in the explicit denial of the separation between 'them', the Indians, and 'us', the dopers. Above all, they should take the step common in earlier times — but thoroughly taboo in our own century — of proselytizing in favour of the drug under consideration, and actually recommending its use to those who have no prior experience of the drug themselves. This positive responsibility must necessarily supersede the old type of purely negative responsibility, the position marked by a weak-kneed fear of the unknown, by a hesitant ignorance which invariably recommends only caution, delay and immobility.

Such an aggressive, pugnacious attitude can only, it is true, be legitimately recommended with regard to drugs known not to possess any seriously toxic or addictive properties. But even subject to such a limitation, there are many substances which could find useful applications in weaning drug abusers away from more dangerous synthetic compounds, and back to natural, organic substances. An emphasis on coca and marijuana, for example, would serve to de-mystify the supposedly 'dangerous' image of these drugs, and could be used to replace the far more damaging dependence on cocaine itself, or on the amphetamines, or even on the worn-out trio of alcohol, tobacco and coffee.

The use of a drug as a ritual catalyst — or as an agent of political and cultural consciousness-raising — must, therefore also be accompanied by an initiative designed to keep its profile radically antithetical to the 'straight' orthodoxy of Western civilization. Tendencies towards the manipulation of illicit drugs as a new mechanism of social repression, as yet another growth area of the consumer society, must also be subject to a rigourous and thorough-going criticism. Above all, any new initiative must be based on considerable knowledge of the capacities and limitations of the drug itself; knowledge, let us say, of the order of that which makes coca a central and positive element in Andean society, and which springs not from an abstracted pharmacology, but from a clear understanding of the subjective effects of the drug on oneself. It would seem clear, therefore, that to unilaterally limit research to any single, specific aspect of the drug — its internal chemistry, for instance — is really tantamount to intellectual suicide, since it eliminates the possibility of ones experience of the thing influencing one's concept-of-the-thing, and indeed, seems to imply that one's concept-of-the-thing will invade and finally pre-empt one's experience of the thing.

All coca is a single body, no aspect of it can really be usefully isolated from any other. It is for this reason that I originally suggested the *figura* of Mama Coca, herself a shapeless, almost indefinable entity, an empty receptacle implying the possibility of an almost infinite number of changes in one's opinion of the coca leaf. To counter any accusation that this approach involved no more than a wallowing subjectivism and self-indulgence, it must be pointed out that the very process of acquiring and using a drug necessarily involved the assistance of other people, itself provoking the questions which had to be asked, indicating the directions which had to be taken. Perhaps most important of all, this approach — the methodology of the conscious and self-critical drug user —would be able to overcome the redundant causal scheme employed by so many authors on the subject, the obsessive concern with the question of why people chew coca, so evident in the studies of Burchard and Bolton, for example. Precisely because it says nothing about the expectations of drug users themselves — about the conceptual framework which gives their drug habit its meaning — the causal analysis can only remain of relatively minor significance, and it is unlikely to generate much enthusiasm among present or potential coca chewers. In the end, dedicated drug users are not concerned with why at all — they are concerned with how.

III. Botany, Archaeology, Colonial History. The Development of the Coca Trade

'Nor Coca only useful art at Home,
A famous Merchandize thou art become;
A thousand Paci and Vicugni groan
Yearly beneath thy Loads, and for thy sake alone
The spacious World's to us by Commerce known.'

Dr. Abraham Cowley. 'History of Plants.' (1662).

THE BOTANY OF COCA

An Aymara myth, one of the only such accounts not to centre on a female Mama Coca figure, describes with great candour and realism what is likely to have been involved in the first discovery of coca's qualities by man. A group of highland Indians had attempted to establish a colony in the *yungas*, the warm, humid slopes of the Bolivian Andes which lead down to the Amazon basin. Having angered the gods by burning down the native forest cover, their houses and crops were swept away by torrential rainfall, and the Indians were forced to take refuge in some nearby caves. When they finally emerged again, after many days of stormy weather, they found nothing but desolation all around them. Weak with hunger and despair, they came across an unknown shrub with leaves of brilliant green, which they gathered and put into their mouths to stay their hunger. The remedy thus discovered seemed so effective that the cultivation of this bush was later to provide the main motive for all Aymara occupation of the *yungas*.[1]

The coca referred to in this myth must be **Erythroxylum coca** Lam., the major economic species of the plant, cultivated on the eastern slopes of the Andes from Bolivia to Ecuador, and in adjacent areas of the Amazon basin. For a long time it was believed that all cultivated coca belonged to this species, but recent work by Dr. Timothy Plowman has confirmed the existence of at least one other cultivated species, **E. novogranatense** (Morris) Hieron.[2] This he has tentatively subdivided into two main types: the first being the 'typical' **E. novogranatense**, the coca grown in the northern Andes of Colombia and Venezuela; and the other the variety **truxillense** (Rusby) Machado, once widely distributed all along the coastal strip and eastern valleys of Peru, but today restricted to the vicinity of Trujillo and the Upper Maranón drainage. Both cultivated species form part of the pantropical genus **Erythroxylum** — of the family **Erythroxylaceae** — a very large genus which may contain as many as 250 species altogether. Many other species of **Erythroxylum** are sometimes used for medicinal purposes — **E. anguifugum** and **E. campestre** in Brazil;[3] **E. tabascense (syn. E. macrophyllum) in Mexico;[4] E. orinocense** and **E. acutum** (the *coca de mono*, or 'monkey's coca') in Colombia[5] — but they are not subject to formal cultivation, nor are they ever chewed. Furthermore, a number of other wild plants — such as **E. hondense, E. cataractarum, E. gracilipes**, and **E. carthagenense** — are often confused with the cultivated species, but none contains cocaine.[6]

All members of the genus usually grow as shrubs or small trees in open thickets or in the understory of primary and secondary forests. Though no extensive and truly wild populations of **E. coca** have survived down to the present, the facility shown by this species of escaping from cultivation, and reproducing itself by means of purely spontaneous propagation, would tend to suggest that the original wild coca plants were not greatly different to the cultivated forms. The removal of wild coca bushes from their original shaded or semi-shaded environment, and their subsequent cultivation in open fields, would seem to be designed to increase the availability of sunlight, thus producing a more abundant yield of leaves and possibly also potentiating the production of desirable alkaloids. Exploitation of the leaf, rather than of the reproductive organs of the plant, appears to have reduced the effect of artificial selection in modifying the botanical characters of the coca plant. For this reason, none of the drastic genetic and morphological changes normally associated with food crops — and none of the extreme dependence on propagation by man — seems to have occurred in the history of the coca plant.[7]

Given the very widespread present distribution of **E. coca** — all along the eastern slopes of the Central Andes — it seems virtually impossible to pinpoint the exact geographical origin of the species, though the central location of the Peruvian *montana* region — and particularly the Huallaga valley — may well imply that it was this area which first witnessed its domestication. Most authors have suggested a process by which an original discovery of the properties of coca was followed by a progressive increase in consumption, to the point where it became necessary to supplement the wild sources with plants transferred into horticultural contexts, and located nearer to the centres of human habitation. It is probably in this way that **E. coca** was introduced to the Amazon basin, spreading as far as the lower Putumayo and Vaupés regions of Colombia. Tolerance of the intense heat and poorly drained soils of this area has not been achieved without some sacrifice, however, and **E. coca** continues to reproduce relatively poorly in the lowlands, being propagated mainly by means of stem cuttings, rather than by seed. At the same time, the increasing frequency of contacts with other climatic regions of Peru — such as the relatively arid Maranón valley, or the desert coastline — would have led to a gradual, progressive isolation of a 'dry-adapted' coca — **E. novogranatense** var. **truxillense** — with the final emergence of effective sterility barriers between the two species. In turn, the diffusion of this species northwards into Colombia would have led to the establishment of the 'typical' variety of **E. novogranatense**, the species of coca still cultivated today in the Cauca area and in the Sierra Nevada de Santa Marta.

It was this species — 'Colombian coca', or *hayo*, as it was known in northeastern Colombia — which was taken at the turn of the century to Jamaica and to the Royal Botanic Gardens at Kew, being thereafter distributed to many areas of the Old World tropics, such as India (Darjeeling and Assam), Ceylon, Indonesia (Java and Sumatra), Hong Kong and the British colonies in Africa. Since it is clearly **Erythroxylum novogranatense** which concerns us most directly in the Cauca area, it would be worth considering the character of this species in greater detail.

The leaves of **E. novogranatense** are generally speaking smaller and thinner than those of **E. coca**, and their colour tends towards a much brighter and more yellow hue — a feature noticeable even in the dried leaves, though more remarkable while still growing on the branch. The bush of **E. novogranatense** also has a far greater ecological tolerance than that or its sister species, being able to thrive both in the seasonally dry climate of the Cauca and Magdalena valleys, and in the constant humidity and poorly drained soils of the tropical lowlands. In comparison, **E. coca** is most intolerant of drought, and its failure to set seed in those areas of the Amazon basin where it has been introduced would also tend to indicate that it is unhappy with the poor drainage and high temperatures of that area.

The tolerance shown by the Colombian variety is less pronounced, however, in the **E. novogranatense** var. **truxillense** of the Peruvian coast. The adaptation of this strain to irrigation techniques and the extremely arid climate of the Pacific seaboard has meant that it is no longer capable of being transferred into more humid environments. Nevertheless, both forms of **E. novogranatense** are significantly different to **E. coca** in their chemical structure. They sometimes contain a lower yield of cocaine, but this is balanced out by a higher yield of other associated alkaloids, and particularly by the presence of large quantities of methyl salicylate (wintergreen oil), which would account for their excellent flavour and their reputation as a 'sweeter' chew than the leaves of **E. coca**[8].

COCA IN ANDEAN PREHISTORY PART I: THE CENTRAL ANDES

This overview of the botanical genus **Erythroxylum** may allow some of the more strictly archaeological details to be put into a rather better perspective. There is little secure dating on the emergence of coca as a cultivated crop, but the available evidence would tend to suggest that this plant — like a great number of other cultigens — was being exploited long before the emergence of any objective markers of its presence, such as pottery representations of individual coca chewers, or finds of their associated paraphernalia such as coca bags and lime gourds, both of which are very common in the context of the later civilizations of Peru. Indeed, it seems likely that coca was being used for many years prior to the advent of formal agriculture in the Andes. Ethnographic parallels would indicate that hunter-gatherer bands have a remarkably detailed knowledge of the flora that surrounds them, particularly where medicinal or drug plants are concerned, and there can be little doubt that coca must have been discovered originally in exactly this type of social context, among the small groups of nomadic Indians who occupied the Andes in the immediate post-glacial period.

Centuries of experimentation with the leaves, both as a masticatory and in the form of teas, would ultimately have led to a recognition of the usefulness of an alkaline reagent in potentiating the alkaloids released from the chewed quid of coca. At the outset, this could have occurred quite accidentally; as for instance, with the chance addition of ash to leaves as they were dried over the family hearth. In any case, the subsequent importance of coca — notably, in the incipient agriculture of many preceramic groups — can certainly be demonstrated by the archaeological record on the Peruvian coast, an area where very dry conditions have allowed a good deal of vegetable matter to remain intact in the local burial middens. The earliest identifiable coca leaves and lime containers have been reported from the north coastal site of Huaca Prieta, being ascribed to the preceramic VI period, which falls between 2500 and 1800 B.C. A slow diffusion southwards of coca — and the related agricultural complex — would seem to be supported by a rather later carbon date of c.1300 B.C. from

View of the statue known as *el coquero*, at the site of El Tablon, near San Andrés de Pisimbalá, Tierradentro.

Asia, the southernmost of the early village sites on the Peruvian coast.[9]

It is quite likely that this gradual spread had its origins well beyond the confines of what is today Peru. One should point out that — although the Preceramic VI level at Huaca Prieta yielded no pottery — the incised designs on certain gourds bear strong similarities with the pottery decoration of the Valdivia phase on the coast of Ecuador. For a long time it was thought that Valdivia, despite its pottery, was exclusively a fishing culture, and all the original sites were beachside middens with maritime refuse. In recent years, however, inland sites with definite evidence of agriculture have been discovered, and one figurine has been excavated which shows the head of a man with the characteristic protuberance in his cheek caused by the chewing of coca leaves.[10]

This discovery probably pushes back the date of the original human use of coca to at least 3000 B.C. and would suggest that it may have been introduced to the Peruvian coast from Ecuador, along with other tropical products such as manioc and peanuts. Admittedly, such a possibility would seem to run counter to the botanical evidence, which supports the idea of an original diffusion of **E. coca** out of the Peruvian *montana*, with its progressive adaptation to the arid conditions of the upper Maranón basin and the valleys of the Pacific coast, and the ultimate definition of a distinct 'dry-adapted' species of coca, **E. novogranatense** var. **truxillense**.[11] This is not the only example of a situation where the botanical and archaeological data appear to be in conflict, however, and a similar discrepancy has also been noted with respect to other tropical crops on the Peruvian coast. It should also be stressed that the consensus of archaeological opinion has recently tended to de-emphasise the possibility of cultural contacts across the main cordillera of the Andes — both in the preceramic period and in the early formative cultures which span the period between 1800 and 900 B.C. — and this would seem to place in question any excessive reliance on a trans-Andean diffusionist theory to explain the early history of coca.[12]

Of course it is certainly feasible that Valdivia could itself have received coca from the eastern slopes of the Andes, and were this shown to be the case, the essential features of the botanical argument would clearly remain unchanged.[13] However, it may be worth pursuing our anti-diffusionist hypothesis one stage further, and suggest that Valdivia could actually have domesticated its own species of coca, one which already grew in a wild state on the Pacific side of the Ecuadorean Andes. This wild progenitor — a proto-typical **E. novogranatense** — could have then followed the archaeologically well-defined routes of influence radiating from Valdivia; southwards along the Peruvian coast — producing the variety **truxillense** — and northwards into the Colombian Andes where it would have given rise to the 'typical' form of **E. novogranatense**. In this context it should be noted that precious little work has been done on the botany of

Erythroxylum in Ecuador, a country in which the use of coca has today almost entirely disappeared.

Another difficulty in ascribing the emergence of **E. novogranatense** to an original diffusion of **E. coca**, lies in the fact that there do not appear to have been any agricultural groups in the *montana* early enough to have actually served as 'donors' of the coca bush to the coast. Neither the *montana* nor the adjacent areas of lowland *selva* can show any signs of sedentary agriculture before about 1800 B.C., and this is substantially later than the evidence for coca on the Pacific side of the Andes. All the same, it would still be worth considering the record as it stands, for the humid conditions of the *montana* make it extremely unlikely that direct evidence for the coca habit — such as lime gourds or coca leaves themselves — will ever be forthcoming from this area.

The early Tutishcainyo pottery phase in the Ucayali basin, close to the present-day town of Pucallpa, could easily represent one of the first groups to introduce coca into the Amazonian lowlands. This possibility is certainly enhanced by the similarities of the pottery with the earliest ceramic phase at Kotosh, a site located at 1950 metres in the Huallaga valley, and thus bordering on the upper altitude limit of the species **E. coca**. Given the strategic location of Kotosh — near the modern town of Huánuco, and in the vicinity of a *montana* region justly famous for the quality of its coca — it would certainly not be surprising if its inhabitants had learned of the properties of this plant and brought it under cultivation. And, granted the extremely laborious nature of coca picking, could not this tiring agricultural activity provide a possible explanation for the enigmatic pair of crossed hands which were modelled in plaster and embedded in the wall of the first temple ever constructed at Kotosh?

COCA IN ANDEAN PREHISTORY PART II: THE NORTHERN ANDES

Though the archaeology of the Central Andes provides considerable insight into the prehistory of the coca habit in that area, the situation in the northern Andes — and particularly in the Cauca area — is much less clear-cut. The proliferation of marginally different varieties of coca bush throughout the area has led to considerable confusion in the literature, including the misclassification of a good deal of the cultivated coca in Colombia as either **E. coca** or **E. hondense**. It seems clear that — excepting the Amazonian areas of the lower Putumayo and Vaupés drainages — all coca cultivated in Colombia must belong to the species **E. novogranatense**. This point had already been recognized in the 1540s by that perceptive chronicler, Don Pedro Cieza de León, who made a very

View of the same statue from the other side. Compare the geometrical designs on the semi-obliterated coca bag with the style of the *kuétan yáha* worn by the present-day Paez.

specific and unambiguous reference to the 'small coca' used near Cali and Popayán at this time.[14]

All the same, the question of the exact origins of Colombian coca must necessarily remain almost entirely conjectural, as direct evidence for the use of this plant only appears relatively late in the archaeological record. Following an anti-diffusionist line, one would certainly like to be able to suggest an independent domestication of the coca bush in Colombia, but no truly wild populations of **E. novogranatense** are yet known to exist, despite the occasional occurrence of 'escaped' coca plants in localities close to the traditional centres of cultivation.

It seems difficult, therefore, to avoid the truism that coca spread to Colombia out of the more advanced agricultural societies of Peru and Ecuador. The problem, in this case, is one of time-lag and direction; for if coca was being cultivated in Valdivia as early as 3000 B.C. it seems strange that it should have taken as much as two-and-a-half millenia to appear in the Cauca area, no more than four hundred miles away. The answer to this problem must surely lie in the fact that the highlands of southern Colombia appear to have been very sparsely inhabited then, and what few inhabitants there were at that time plainly did not include pottery-making or sedentary agriculture among their skills. These people left no traces save the occasional heavy point, a weapon which suggests the persistence of a nomadic, hunting way of life. Though it may be comforting to think of them chewing some sylvan species of **Erythroxylum** as they moved around the mountains, the evidence is hardly convincing, and we must wait for the first truly sedentary agricultural communities in order to demonstrate even the likelihood of widespread coca chewing.

Surprisingly enough, it is not along the main ridge of the Andes that the first neolithic or Formative peoples appear to have entered the Cauca area, but rather, from the lowland areas to the east and west. Even in these few well-established cases, however, the fragile nature of the links between the early ceramic cultures of Cauca and the supposed parent groups outside the area would tend to confirm the impression that the occupation must have occurred as a slow valley-by-valley process, not as an identifiable sequence of major migrations. On the Pacific coastline of Colombia, the culture of Tumaco points to maritime links with Ecuador, and even with Panamá and the west coast of Mexico. This settlement appears to have encouraged a gradual expansion inland through such cultures as Calima I, in the Western Cordillera near Cali. During approximately the same period — 700 to 200 B.C. — a group noted for its large painted tombs also established itself in Tierradentro, on the eastern slopes of the Central Cordillera. The vivid geometrical decoration within these tombs bears many close parallels with the type of design commonly executed in the Amazon by Indians under the influence of the hallucinogen *yajé*

(**Banisteriopsis** spp.), and although the archaeology of the adjacent lowland areas — the drainage of the Caquetá and Putumayo rivers — is virtually unknown, it is still feasible that something like the Peruvian relationship between *montana* and *selva* was also a feature of the early agricultural peoples of the upper Magdalena basin, and that it may have included the introduction of coca via the Amazon.[15]

Neither Tierradentro nor Calima I, however, can show any direct evidence for the use of coca, and their early prominence would not necessarily exclude the possibility of other, almost simultaneous, contacts existing between the Cauca area and the northern highlands of Ecuador. Not far from Tierradentro lies the group of sites centred around San Agustín — that of the Horqueta period, with its characteristic 'incised rectilinear' decoration — would point to important links running southwards along the main ridge of the Andes.[16] Since, in turn, pottery quite like that of the earlier coastal Valdivia culture has also been found in the northern highlands of Ecuador, it is possible that this influence could have resulted in the introduction of the hypothetical **E. novogranatense** of the Ecuadorean coast.

Certainly the two-and-a-half millenia which elapsed between Valdivia and the first manifestations at San Agustín would have allowed such a slow process of diffusion to have run its course. Furthermore, the geographical continuity of the coca habit along this route stands in marked contrast to its virtual absence on the Pacific coast of Colombia, and to its relatively patchy distribution in the neighbouring areas of the Amazon basin. Coca long continued to be a major crop in all the areas to the immediate south of Cauca, as may be demonstrated by the finds of seated polychrome figurines in the tombs of Narino — the southernmost department of Colombia — which often show a pronounced swelling of the cheek. In Ecuador itself there is extensive evidence of the continued importance of coca right up to the Inca and Spanish conquests, most notably in the figurines of the Bahia phase (500 B.C. — 500 A.D.) on the Manabí coast.[17]

In any event, it is indisputable that coca soon constituted a major and characteristic element of Indian adaptation to life in the Cauca area. Direct evidence for this appears in a number of contexts, none of which are dateable to much earlier than 50 A.D. This is the threshold normally accepted for the beginning of the megalithic cultural climax at San Agustín, whose hallmark is its impressive stone statues, many of which show protuberant cheeks, while others represent figures carrying small pouches slung across their chests.[18] Though such details do not, in themselves, constitute undeniable evidence of the use of coca, the likelihood of this interpretation being correct is certainly enhanced by the existence of another semi-destroyed statue at the site of El Tablón, pertaining to an epigonal manifestation of the San Agustín style, and located in the valley of San Andrés de Pisimbalá, very close to the painted tombs of the

Tierradentro culture. Though the head and limbs of the monolith have been completely destroyed, it is still possible to discern without any difficulty the representations of both coca pouch and lime gourd hanging on either side of the figure — at about the height of the hips, as they are worn today.

The carving of the coca pouch is so similar in size and shape to the contemporary versions worn by the Paez Indians, that one is clearly led to suspect more than a mere coincidence. The geometric design on the coca bag of today is a faithful copy of the statue original, and — perhaps less surprisingly — even the representation of the lime gourd possesses the very same dimensions as the one used now. In addition to the statue evidence, various undated burials in the Tierradentro region, and closer to Popayán itself, occasionally include pottery jars containing lime, and the *monsenor* in Belalcázar has the remains of a carved lime gourd in his collection of local antiquities.

Also undated is the archaeological culture of Quimbaya, found in the middle Cauca drainage near the present city of Pereira, and very famous for the fine quality of its gold work. Quimbaya finds have included large gold lime containers and their attendant spatulae, as well as numerous gold figurines represented with these very same implements in their hands. A number of these pieces can be seen in the Gold Museum in Bogotá, most notably one gourd-shaped lime container — all of 23.4 cm. high and weighing over one kilo in high-carat gold — which was discovered with its original lime still intact. The British Museum also possesses at least one very fine gold figurine in the Quimbaya style; the piece is hollow and has a narrow opening on top of the head, a certain indication of its use as a lime container.

Moving north and east of the Cauca valley, the chroniclers Castellanos, Piedrahita and Simon all speak of the widespread use of coca among the Muiscas of the plateaux surrounding Bogotá and Tunja. They mention its special application on the all-night fasting and meditation of the Muisca priests, as well as the fact of its being buried with the grave goods of the dead, and burned as an offering to the gods. Piedrahita states that in the early seventeenth century the use of coca remained very prevalent in the region around Bogotá, being mainly produced in the vicinities of Soata and Duitama. It would appear that the habit of chewing coca survived in this area at least until the late eighteenth century, and in all probability small pockets of isolated usage can still be found today.[19]

COCA IN ANDEAN PREHISTORY
PART III: COCA AND TOBACCO IN NORTHERN COLOMBIA

Though naive generalizations about the culture of large and widely dispersed linguistic groupings are often quite misleading, there does appear to be a reasonable case for ascribing the use of coca to almost all the known representatives of the macro-Chibcha stock of languages. From the Colorados and Cayapas of north-western Ecuador, to the Kogi of the Caribbean slopes of the Sierra Nevada de Santa Marta, there exists a clear relationship between the coca habit and the distribution of the various Chibcha dialects. Indeed, if coca was the preferred drug of the highland areas, it was hardly an unknown quantity in the northern lowlands of Colombia either, being particularly popular in the Tairona civilization of Santa Marta and in the rich gold-working kingdom of Sinu, located in the jungles inland from Cartagena.[20] At the same time, however, the inhabitants of the lowlands also shared a very high regard for another drug plant — one which appears to have been domesticated originally further east, in the Amazon and Orinoco basins.

This drug was tobacco (**Nicotiana** spp.), and its association with a tropical forest culture has led certain authors to ascribe its diffusion to a hypothetical westward spread of Arawak and Karib speaking peoples into the territory of what is today Colombia.[21] The overlapping of these coca and tobacco habits in northern Colombia is of singular importance, for personal experience would tend to confirm that a combination of the two allows the individual user both an 'up' (the stimulant, coca) and a complementary 'down' (the neural retardant, tobacco). Furthermore, the adoption of each other's drugs may well indicate a certain interaction between the inhabitants of lowland and highland areas, and a possible mixture of originally Chibcha, Arawak and Karib linguistic groupings.

There is considerable evidence that such a mixing of drug cultures did occur quite extensively, and though most of the Indians of the northern Colombian lowlands have long since disappeared, a very similar process is still taking place among the many tribes of the Amazon basin.[22] Though in the vicinity of Popayán — as, indeed, throughout most of the Andean highlands — tobacco only appears to have been used in the context of shamanic rituals and curing ceremonies, it was also employed for more secular purposes by the neighbouring peoples to the north, such as the historical Quimbaya Indians of the middle Cauca valley. That coca and tobacco were often enjoyed together — at least in the region around Cali — is also suggested by Cieza's sixteenth-century account mentioning two quite separate additives to coca. One was the common 'earth which is like lime . . .', but the other was 'a certain mixture which they make . . .', that was 'kept in small gourds . . .', their custom being to 'put it also in their mouths . . .'[23]

It is likely that this mixture involved a preparation of tobacco, an interpretation which is strongly supported by a parallel case that survives to this day among the Kogi of the Sierra Nevada de Santa Marta, who use a

Statue from Moscopán with swollen cheek. At present in the Casa Mosquera museum in Popayán.

tobacco extract known as *ambira* as an additive to coca leaves.[24] This syrup is prepared by the decoction of green tobacco leaves in water, to which various flours (*Manihot* or *Maranta* spp.) are added to give the mixture consistency. The extract is kept in a small gourd known as *noai*, a name also given to an alternative preparation of tobacco resin, one which is made in the form of a solidified cake.

This name *noai* is particularly significant in the light of an early seventeenth century mention of a substance called *anua*, which was widely used as a supposedly intoxicating booster to coca in the Eastern Cordillera north of Bogotá.[25] The comparison with present-day Kogi usage would imply that this was almost certainly a tobacco extract. One might consider, therefore, not only the middle Cauca drainage, but also much of north-eastern Colombia as well, as areas particularly rich in the mixture of tobacco and coca drug cultures. Further cases to support this view would include that of the Chibcha-speaking Tunebo of the Sierra Nevada de Cocuy, who at the present time cultivate and chew tobacco as well as coca, and that of the Karib-speaking Motilones of the Sierra de Perijá, on the Colombo-Venezuelan border. Although the main psycho-stimulant of the latter group is now tobacco, they are known to have used coca in the past, and this appears to have been due to commercial contact with the Chibcha-speaking tribes of the neighbouring Sierra Nevada de Santa Marta.[26]

It might be appropriate to conclude this section with a consideration of what seem to be the major features in the adoption of the coca habit by the Indians of South America. At the time of the Spanish Conquest, the use of coca had spread as far east as Caracas, Cumaná, and maybe even Trinidad, and had penetrated as far north as Panamá and Nicaragua. Southwards the Incas had carried it to Tucumán in Argentina, and in the space of recent memory Bolivian labourers have introduced it across the Chaco into Paraguay. In the nineteenth century its use was established well into the central Amazon near Manaos, and presumably the habit might eventually have spread further, up into Mexico on the one hand, and across into the uplands of eastern Brazil on the other.

Only the effective decimation of the native population, and the incorporation of the remnant groups into a predominantly white and European culture, can convincingly explain the decadence of the coca habit in many areas where it was once extant. Such would be the case of the Pacific coast in Peru and Ecuador, the Caribbean shores of Colombia and Venezuela, most of the highland regions of the latter two countries, and indeed, in more recent years, the Amazonian lowlands themselves. In addition, it may be possible to point to the emergence of certain political and economic factors in this century — such as the occasional misguided prohibitions of coca on 'health' grounds, and the competition for coca leaves produced by the cocaine industry — forces which together have resulted in a further decline of the number and prominence of *coqueros*, even in such predominantly Indian areas as the south of Colombia, and the highlands of Ecuador and northern Peru. It is necessary, however, to underline the fact that none of these pressures have been engendered as the result of any repudiation of the drug on the part of the indigenous population. Quite on the contrary, it would be fair to assume that the custom of chewing coca would have survived, and even flourished and spread, were it not for the lamentable fact of European colonization.

COCA: AN INCA MONOPOLY?

Traditional accounts of the history of coca have usually sought to emphasize that the production, distribution, and consumption of coca in pre-Hispanic Peru was always a monopoly held firmly in the hands of a jealous Inca elite, and to assume that the lesser citizens of the empire were necessarily excluded from the enjoyment of this rare and aristocratic privilege.[27] Notwithstanding its obvious appeal to critics of the coca habit, the actual credibility of this idea would appear to be more than a little undermined by the abundant evidence of coca chewing in pre-Inca archaeological contexts, and more significantly, by the widespread survival of many less monopolistic tendencies in the organization of the coca trade itself, both during the Inca period, and right through into the Spanish colony. And while the Inca state would certainly have been capable of controlling the flow of coca leaves in and out of the marketplace of Cuzco — supplied basically from the nearby coca-producing districts in the lower Urubamba valley — it hardly seems likely that such restrictive practices could have affected to an equal extent all the diverse and sometimes unruly peoples who formed part of its vast and far-flung empire.

In support of this argument, it should be noted that many of the rather diffuse, non-centralized patterns of pre-Inca trade have recently been highlighted by detailed studies undertaken of the cases of two ethnic groups in particular, peoples who actually managed to maintain some degree of economic independence throughout the period of Cuzco's ascendancy in the Central Andes. These were the Chupaychu Indians of the Huánuco area — traditionally an important centre of coca production — and the Lupaqa, an Aymara-speaking group centred on the valley of Lake Titicaca. Both were the objects of extensive administrative reports or *Visitas* written in the 1560s at the instigation of the Spanish crown.[28] Careful examination of these texts has revealed many significant features of the native economic system; and while it is true that both groups had progressed beyond the stage of straightforward face-to-face reciprocity which characterizes small, essentially egalitarian communities, it is also quite apparent that neither had acquired the sort of centralized economic structures which usually accompany the emergence of city-states or large territorial empires.

Furthermore, in view of their success in resisting the harsh economic realities of the Inca and Spanish conquests, it is perhaps not surprising that both the Chupaychu — a relatively small group of 10,000 — and the Lupaqa — with a much larger population of 150,000 — should actually have shared many comparable features in their exploitation of an essentially similar range of environments. Lacking both the centralized economy and the true class society of the Incas, most of the highland Indians of the Central Andes seem to have been characterized by relatively simple, semi-hierarchical chiefdom structures, organized around the collective worship of particular tribal divinities (*huacas*), and subdivided by means of an interlocking web of clan allegiances. Central authority would itself have been a function of well-defined needs, such as military defence or the ritual propitiation of the gods, and would have served less to enhance the wealth and status of any particularly powerful hereditary elite, than to act as an economic funnel, redistributing the produce of areas marked by a considerable degree of ecological diversity. The basic grains and foodstuffs grown in the middle-altitude basins — the main centres of population — would thus have come to be supplemented by a wide range of exotic resources drawn from relatively small outlying colonies, located either at very high altitudes — for access to llama wool and salt — or in the sub-tropical valleys lower down. It would be difficult to overestimate the importance of coca leaves as a motive for the occupation of the lower altitudes, for although the *montana* or *yungas* also produced other desirable items — cotton, gold, spices, and the colourful plumage of jungle birds — it must have been, above all, the need to assure a steady and independent supply of coca that drove most ethnic groups to settle at least a few of their members in that humid and unhealthy zone.

With the emergence and consolidation of these peripheral colonies, all trade could have been organized within single chiefdoms, and there would have been little need for formal marketplaces or commercial relations with other Indian peoples. Furthermore, such colonies would have rendered unnecessary the control of any continuous extension of territory outside the main nucleus, and the tribal unit would not have felt compelled to defend any distant or unmanageable frontiers. Instead, they could have concentrated their efforts on the sources of those particular products most in need, establishing discontinuous settlements or 'islands' of competing ethnic groups. At the same time, the settlers in these peripheral 'islands' would only have been semi-permanent in their functions, and since they retained the right to a house and land in the major nucleus of population, they could also be depended on to maintain close links of solidarity with the parent group. In this way, each tribal unit in the Central Andes would have been able to control an independent access to all the diverse items produced throughout the area, and maintain a vertical hegemony over a wide range of differing eco-niches.

The situation on the Pacific coast of Peru may — initially, at least — have been quite similar to that of the highlands, but in the long run the denser coastal populations must have produced much greater pressure on the available resources than is evident in the mountains. A court case of 1559, dealing with the ownership of the coca plantations in Quivi, in the upper Chillón valley, describes a contest between at least four different ethnic groups with claims to the bushes in question. Competition in these areas was a serious matter, for the upper stretches of the coastal valleys were not only important for their coca, but also for their control of the water which fed the agricultural irrigation system further downstream.[29] Indeed, the extreme importance of the water supply to many emergent civilizations led in certain cases — most obviously, on the north coast of Peru — to the abandonment of an earlier discontinuous pattern of ethnic settlement, and produced in its place the institution of a territorial state, with clearly defined borders and a centralized, bureaucratic control of irrigation.

In the first instance, this development may not have radically altered the classic Andean patterns of economic redistribution, and did not necessarily imply the advent of commerce and commercial relations as such. But ultimately the substitution of a multi-ethnic state system for the previous forms of exchange within single tribal entities was to have very noticeable effects on the structure of the Andean economy. The surplus generated by the state would tend to accumulate, losing its previous redistributive function, and being employed instead to enhance the special status of the urban aristocracy and priesthood. Various attendant developments can be ascribed to this centralizing tendency, among them craft specialization, the emphasis given to the construction of impressive ceremonial buildings, and the pursuit of a long-range trade in certain rare luxury items, a factor which would in turn have involved the emergence of a mercantile class within the governing elite.

It is worth pointing out, however, that although such systems have a great continuity on the coast of Peru, in the mountain regions there are very few traces of any real persistence of 'state' structures, as such, before the emergence of the Inca empire. In this case, the relative novelty of the continuous form of territorial organization in the highlands could serve to explain why there was still so much evidence of the survival of less complex economic systems in the area at the time of the Spanish Conquest. For reasons of political expediency, the Inca administration simply could not have afforded to alienate its newly subject peoples with a wholesale disruption of their own native economies. It could, and did, exact tribute directly from the central redistributive agencies of each conquered nation;

a feat normally achieved through the imposition of Inca divinities — particularly the *huaca* of Inti, the Sun — in a dominant position within the shrines of the local gods. All in all, therefore, the initial policy seems to have been merely to cream off a percentage of the goods produced by each newly conquered territory, while leaving the indigenous production system itself almost intact. Within this scheme, any idea of the Inca 'monopolizing' the whole Andean coca harvest is patently absurd, for the Inca retained little control over the leaves that remained for local consumption after the tribute had been paid.

At the same time, of course, it is also quite clear that the city of Cuzco and its vicinity — the Inca homeland — could never have depended entirely for its coca on the tribute of dubiously loyal subjects, and a need must have been felt to assure an independent supply of leaves, employing a completely state-controlled network which itself may have given rise to the idea of an Inca 'monopoly'. By settling groups of labourers in the *montana* — initially in the Urubamba valley below Macchu Picchu — the Inca could have been assured of all the coca needed for state functions, such as that used for diplomatic gifts, and that consumed by the army, the nobility, the religious temples, and the *chasquis* (messengers). The only group to have suffered under such an arrangement would have been the humbler citizens of Cuzco itself, since they would have lost any direct access to the Urubamba, their own traditional source of coca, and would have become dependant for supplies on an overstretched state bureaucratic system. In times of shortage this system could only be relied on to supply the most pressing needs of the state and the Inca elite, and thus the common man might have been unable to secure any leaves at all — a deprivation which would have been felt in terms of class discrimination, of an Inca 'prohibition' on coca chewing by the toiling masses.

In any case, the most significant aspect of the Inca system must have been its appropriation of the very productive process itself, for it would not have been enough to simply intercept an already established pattern of trade, in the manner demonstrated for such recently conquered peoples as the Lupaqa and the Chupaychu. There exists an extensive report describing one of these state-controlled Inca coca plantations written in the 1560s, and dealing with the *yungas* of Songo, Chacapa and Challana, in an area of what is today Bolivia. The Aymara-speaking Indians who formed the main bulk of the population in these valleys appear to have lost any original allegiance to their parent groups in the highlands, living permanently in the *yungas* and being accustomed to producing their coca exclusively for the Inca.[30] At first sight, it could be argued that this kind of peripheral colony constitutes no more than a simple extension of the traditional, ethnically-based redistributive system of the Andes, but this would be to ignore tribal loyalties to the more impersonal bureaucratic structure of the Inca state. The colonists of Songo no longer maintained the right to a house and land in the highland areas where they had originated, and furthermore, they were working on state-owned land in the capacity of a state-organized labour force. With the means of production — in this case, coca bushes — held firmly in the hands of an absentee landowning class, it would not be unfair to say that the Inca system replaced a simple redistributive mechanism with a particularly original form of state capitalism, thereby giving birth to the first true rural proletariat in South America.

This process becomes even more apparent if one stops to consider the evidence for Inca imperialism on the central coast of Peru. This was an area always treated as conquered territory by the highland invaders, and a number of coca plantations on the upper course of the Chillón river were actually annexed outright, and their produce dedicated to Inti, the Inca god of the sun. Not being able to trust the local population with the collection of their harvest, the Inca administrators introduced a group of their own specially organized mass labour force, the *mitimaes*.[31] This type of action — forcible dispossession, followed by recolonization — was perhaps the most drastic form of disruption suffered by the coca producers in the Inca period; and taken with the two other systems employed by the Inca — the exaction of tribute, and the establishment of entirely new state-controlled plantations, as at Songo — it could be said to form part of a three-pronged assault on the reciprocity and self-sufficiency which characterized the original economy of the coca leaf.

It was probably this remarkable contrast between the centralized Inca organization, and the earlier patterns of reciprocity and redistribution, which itself produced the idea that the Inca had somehow 'monopolized' the coca trade in pre-Hispanic Peru. Given that a large share of the Peruvian coca crop seems to have remained outside of effective Inca control, it could be argued that the coca monopoly was an ideal towards which the policy-makers in Cuzco were tending, but which they had not yet managed to implement efectively throughout the full extent of the empire. It might even be tempting to remove the ideal of a coca monopoly from its specific Inca context, as it is a very pervasive theme in Peruvian history, and may first have been attempted by the state structures which preceded the Inca empire, and about which we are lacking any detailed information. The persistence of the coca monopoly as an ideal is evident, furthermore, throughout the colonial and republican periods in Peru, and right down to the institution of the present-day Government agency ENACO (Empresa Nacional de la Coca).

COCA BECOMES BIG BUSINESS

To some considerable extent, therefore, the early Spanish emphasis on the prior existence of an Inca coca monopoly must have obeyed the need to find a credible precedent for the wholesale disruption of the traditional Andean economy which began to take place in the latter half of the sixteenth century. It is no accident that the major spokesman for the official view was Inca Garcilaso de la Vega, the son of a mixed marriage between a Spanish *conquistador* and a minor Inca princess, and thus the perfect mouthpiece for the new *criollo* elite then beginning to emerge in Peru. After a basically anarchic period of civil wars following the Conquest by Pizarro, the accession of Philip II to the throne of Spain in 1556 soon found itself reflected in an almost obsessive amount of legislation, a veritable administrative offensive designed to cement the control of the crown over the undisciplined colonies in the New World. This legislation tended to concern itself primarily with the issues which affected Spain's earnings, that is to say, it was mainly directed at controlling the production of gold and silver, and its ultimate remittance to the Treasury in Seville.

Since mining activities in Peru were inconceivable without plentiful supplies of coca, it was realized early on that the coca trade would soon become a source of income second only to the precious minerals themselves. Accordingly, the plantations owned by the Inca were first taken over by the crown, and then distributed in *encomienda* to the leading citizens of the new Spanish colony. Again citing Inca precedent, reforms were introduced in the tribute laws in 1558, so that dues could be paid directly to the king's representatives in coca leaves.[32] By this means, the crown was simply recognizing one of the most traditional functions of coca in the Andes, that of serving as a medium of exchange.

In addition, many powerful individuals began planting new bushes to supply the ever-increasing demand from the mining areas. The 1568 report from the *yungas* of Songo showed that in the 33 years that had elapsed since the Conquest, the area dedicated to the cultivation of coca had increased substantially. The heirs of the *conquistador* Alonso de Alvarado received in 1568 an annual production of 18,000 pounds of coca from their estate in Songo, but they considered this quantity insufficient, and were demanding the repayment of old debts from their tenants to the tune of 128,000 pounds in all.[33]

Their greed was perhaps understandable, for this quantity was worth a tidy fortune. Already in the 1540s coca had been considered the single most important agricultural product in the Andes, and a number of Spanish colonists had begun to dedicate themselves wholeheartedly to the trade which sprung up around it.[34] In particular, the fabulous silver mines of Potosí provided an almost insatiable market for coca, and an annual turnover of one million *pesos* worth of leaves (the contemporary equivalent of 4,550 kilos of gold) was not at all uncommon, comparing favourably with the relatively modest 400,000 *pesos* expended on food and clothing.[35]

Furthermore, as a result of the fact that coca fetched fully twice as high a price in Potosí as it did in Cuzco, it also became popular to engage in a good deal of long-range coca trading as well. Using llamas and mules as beasts of burden, it was not unusual for single dealers to set out on this route with as much as 60,000 pounds of leaves in a single shipment. The profit involved in such a transaction would be of the order of 7500 *pesos*, or just over 34 kilos of gold. Even in the 1560s, such a sum would have been enough to retire comfortably for life.[36]

It is clear, therefore, that the present get-rich-quick attitude in the cocaine business is by no means a novel phenomenon, but on the contrary, has always been an intimate part of the extractive temperament of the white man in America. Much of the cultural splendour of the Golden Age in Spain was, therefore, built not only on the backs of countless forced labourers in the mines of the Andes, but also on the profits of the trade which supplied them with the only stimulant which made the infra-human conditions of their work bearable. In a moment of sublime irony, one might consider the possibility that the 'Catholic Kings' were, in fact, the first godfathers of the drug traffic. Indeed, the coca trade was plainly considered altogether too lucrative for the leaf ever to be banned for its supposed Satanic properties — as some priests would have wished, notably, those who condemned it at the ecclesiastical council in Lima in 1551. When a Franciscan monk wrote to the king in 1579, he stated that the reason why the Bishop of Cuzco was failing to suppress the 'pernicious' coca habit was precisely because he derived a major portion of his income from the Church tithes levied on the value of the coca crop.[37]

So great is the impact of the glowing reports describing the fortunes to be made with coca in the sixteenth century, that historians have often used this material to demonstrate that indigenous consumption was subject to a huge and deliberate increase at the hands of ruthless Spanish entrepreneurs. Interested solely in the enslavement of their work force, the colonists are attributed with the encouragement of a morally debilitating drug habit, or in the words of one recent author, a vice which figures among the 'sterile retaliations of the condemned.'[38] The dubious nature of this assumption becomes increasingly apparent if one stops to consider the real details of the trade's organization, and not only in the mining situation, but in the traditional agricultural communities which formed the backbone of the native subsistence economy.

It has already been stated that a considerable amount of inter-altitude reciprocal exchange was still being practiced by the peoples of highland Peru as late as the 1560s. The survival of such an ethnically-based system, despite the disruptive effects of the Inca empire and the subsequent Spanish Conquest, indicates that at least part of the coca trade remained in the hands of small-scale, cooperative undertakings. Clearly such structures could only supply close kinsmen and other ethnic allies, and no doubt they also came under considerable pressure whenever subject to the new economic forces at large in the Andes. A case in point would be that of the coca-producing areas of the Huallaga basin, which were rapidly transformed in the wake of the discovery of mercury mines near Huancavelica.[39]

Nevertheless, one should not confuse changes in the commercialization of coca with assumptions as to the absolute increase in the consumption of coca by the — at that time — diminishing Indian population in Peru. In all probability consumption per capita remained at a reasonable constant, and what changed was simply the manner in which coca was supplied to the broad mass of the population. The mining situation provided the initial impetus to concentrate coca production in certain areas, and channel the bulk of the trade through the hands of a Spanish merchant class. By the 1570s there is considerable evidence of the disruption of other forms of labour organization as well, changes which inevitably came to be reflected in the patterns of the coca trade.

During this decade, the viceroy Toledo undertook a campaign of 'reductions' aimed at defining the colonial work levies, or *encomiendas*, in terms of clearly delimited geographical localities, and not in those of the traditional ethnic loyalites. While this may have been promoted by a great deal of ignorance regarding the native social stuctures, it is difficult to avoid the conclusion that it could also have formed part of a quite deliberate policy. The reduction of the number and diversity of the ecological zones occupied by any particular ethnic group might be seen as a conscious act aimed at better controlling the Andean population, all the more effective since it deprived each group of the peripheral resources which allowed it some degree of economic self-sufficiency and political autonomy.[40]

Clearly enough, the interruption of the traditional pattern of coca exchanges would be one of the more lucrative aspects of this reorganization. In future not only the mine workers, but also the broad mass of high altitude farmers as well, would all be forced to buy their coca in the white-controlled marketplace. Concurrent with this reorganization of the distribution end of the coca trade, there was obviously considerable interest in producing a maximum yield from the coca plantations themselves. Again, it is questionable whether this involved an absolute increase in the production of coca in Peru, or whether it simply implied the concentration of coca plantations in what were economically the most viable localities. Reports of the increased harvests of coca in certain areas must be balanced against a recognition of the fact that in other parts of Peru, such as the coastal valleys, the cultivation of coca seems to have ceased almost completely.[41]

The mass production of coca to supply a market economy also had a number of noticeable side-effects on the forms of labour which were common in the coca-producing districts. Under the old redistributive system, the labourers down in the sub-tropical valleys which produced coca had always been semi-permanent settlers, persons who had time to adapt themselves to the changed climatic conditions, and who knew that they would be able to return eventually to their own native villages. The Inca state had introduced a new practice, that of the permanent colony located on state-owned coca plantations, and these groups had been inherited by the Spanish conquerors, being known administratively under the collective name of *coca camayos*.

During the colonial period, the *coca camayos* did not have to do any of the coca picking themselves, but only attended to the general well-being of the bushes and packed the baskets of coca leaves once these were dry. The main body of coca pickers was provided by highland Indians who came down to the lower valleys for a month every year to pay part of the labour tribute exacted of them by the Spanish institution of *encomienda*. Though a small amount of migratory labour does seem to have existed on a localized scale in the pre-Hispanic period, it is also clear that it was the Spanish who first made a migrant system into the dominant form of labour in the coca plantations, with the direst consequences to the health of the highland Indians who were pressed into this service.[42]

Such factors as heat, humidity, and undernourishment had a terrible effect on the Indians used to a more temperate climate, and many of them returned home very sick and weak, if they ever returned at all. In addition, the coca plantations were a source of many ugly diseases which, although they rarely attacked the acclimatized local residents, were nevertheless absolutely deadly to the visitors from the mountains. One of these, *verruga peruana*, was transmitted by a mosquito and caused warts, eruptive nodules and anemia. Another, called *uta* or *mal de los Andes*, produced a sort of leprous cancer which ate away at the nose, the lips and the throat.[43]

Spanish policy was not, however, applied with the same rigorous uniformity throughout the Andes, and in the *yungas* of Songo, for example, it appears that the permanently established colonies of certain highland groups were respected, and the traditional forms of labour and reciprocal exchange were maintained.[44] Furthermore, the application of a system of migratory labour may have contributed paradoxically to the maintenance of exactly the type of reciprocal trading it was designed to render obsolete. Throughout the colonial period, and right up to the present day, one feature of the trade remains a constant — namely, the participation of the coca pickers in the fruits of their labour. The migrant workers were allowed to return home with a share of the harvests, serving both to supply their own personal needs, and to provide a lucrative means of exchange back in their own native communities. It is quite possible that this type of participatory trade increased during the colonial period at the expense of the older forms of reciprocity and redistribution. Given the dismembering of many primary ties of ethnic identity by the Spanish, it could well be that such face-to-face exchanges took their place, cemented through the sharing of common agricultural tasks.

This much, at least, would appear to be supported by a number of contemporary parallels which still exist today. Notwithstanding the ready availability of legal — albeit taxed — coca through the government distribution system, a recent description of the community of Nunoa has uncovered evidence of the continued survival of private trading missions between the mountains and the warmer valleys where coca is produced. This circumvention of the formal supply network can be very profitable, and under ideal conditions the individual can realize an eight-fold increase on his original investment.[45] These desirable returns are not, however, merely the result of commercial speculation, as in fact a considerable amount of labour must also be expended on the undertaking. The paths down into the valleys on the eastern side of the Andes are often long, difficult and dangerous — sufficiently so to prevent most people from repeating their excursion more than once yearly. In addition, most private coca traders must pick and dry their own leaves, so what is at stake is not simply a commercial transaction, but a participation in the actual productive process itself.

Such a situation often engenders social alliances between families in the different ecological zones, and the type of reciprocal *compadrazco* obligations which would normally be reserved for kinsmen or close neighbours. It may be possible to uncover in this arrangement something of the original character of the system of intra-tribal redistribution suggested for the central Andes in the pre-Inca and pre-Hispanic stages of development. Though the traditional pattern may only have survived in a transformed and marginalized state, it does serve as an encouraging object lesson in the Andean people's resistance to dubious and alien blueprints of economic efficiency.

THE COCA TRADE IN THE CAUCA AREA

Mention has already been made of Cieza de León's seminal description of the chewing of coca in the 1540s, in the regions surrounding Popayán and Cali.[46] Considering how widespread the habit was in this area, it is perhaps surprising that there should be so few other written accounts of the use of coca in the colonial period. What documentation there is — generally of little worth, when compared with the extensive material on coca in Peru — has almost never been published, and exists solely in the form of yellowing manuscripts at the colonial archives in Popayán. One might, however, be able to judge the extent of coca chewing, and the possibility of its spread to many white colonists and minor members of the clergy, by the statement of the Bishop of Popayán at an ecclesiastical Synod held in July, 1617. He violently condemned the use of this '... most efficient instrument for communication with the devil ...', and threatened the very worst of fates, an excommunication *mayor latae sententiae*, for any clergyman found using the dreaded leaf, albeit simply as a tea.[47]

Clearly the use of coca must have been quite pervasive to warrant such a virulent attack, and it probably stretched to many groups who no longer consume the leaf in any form whatsoever. These would have included the black slaves imported to work the gold deposits of western Colombia, many of whom would have found coca to be an excellent stimulant, perhaps vaguely analogous to their own native cola nuts.[48] To this day, there are a good number of black coca chewers in the Cauca area, particularly in the Patía valley and in the Salado district of Tierradentro, and to a lesser extent on the fringes of the *valle* near Corinto, Caloto, and Santander de Quilichao. Furthermore, the chewing of coca must originally have appeared more widespread even among the Indian population, itself far more numerous in the past. A document dating from 1746 provides evidence of the payments of coca made to the Guambianos — a group which has abandoned the habit in recent years — and contains a number of complaints against the local missionary for his failure to provide any other form of sustenance for his labourers.[49] At the same time, however, in many other areas — such as the vicinity of Cali — the decimation of the indigenous inhabitants would soon have led to a virtually complete disappearance of the custom of chewing coca as well. A report of 1808, which describes the numerous ornamental coca plants to be found in the gardens of that city, could be speaking equally well of the present day when it states that these bushes were '... without any particular use or function ...'[50]

The consumption of coca, therefore, tended in the Cauca area to be something of a localized phenomenon, and the large market structures of the Central Andes seem to have been almost entirely absent. The scanty evidence which is available on the nature of the colonial coca trade would appear to indicate that, at least in remote rural areas, the system of production did not greatly differ from that which is still common today. An official report on the province of Guanacas — in what is now the municipality of Inzá — was drawn up in January 1684, and describes individual

Coca at La Parada, the wholesale market in Lima, Peru. Notice the blackboard advertising prices of coca and *tocra*, the alkaline reagent most commonly used in the Central Andes.

family plantations which commonly produced between one and five *arrobas* (25 to 125 pounds) of leaves at each of the three annual harvests.[51] This would imply that the size of the plantations were very much the same as the ones which still exist in the same area, with most families cultivating between a hundred and, at most, a couple of thousand coca bushes each.

The Guanacas document does also mention, however, that a certain surplus of leaves was being exchanged with white traders for such desirable articles as iron tools, and thus it is clear that a certain amount of localized trading was already beginning to emerge even at this early date. It is unlikely, though, that this trade ever significantly affected the adjacent, but more remote and intransigent Indians of the area, such as the Paez. It must be pointed out that the homeland of the Guanacas lay astride the major route between Popayán and Sante Fé de Bogotá, and for this reason, they were in an excellent position to participate in the broader markets of the Spanish colony.

Furthermore, the Guanacas formed part of the same linguistic group as the Indians of Guambia, Coconuco, and of the region immediately surrounding the town of Popayán itself. Characteristically less belligerent than the Paez, this group seems to have formed the main pool of native labour for the Spanish colonists in Popayán, and thus they were accustomed to dealing with the white settlers on a great number of different levels, among which the trade in coca would only have been a relatively minor detail. Indeed, the leaves traded in this way merely served, in the end, to supply the very same Indians themselves; for colonial law stipulated that all native labourers should be given a ration of one third of a pound of coca for every week spent tributing their work capacity to the Spanish *encomenderos.*[52]

Coca would thus have provided an excellent source of income for those Indians who were willing and able to make sales to nearby white landowners. A case brought in 1610 against a Spaniard for the burning of an orchard and coca plantations belonging to the *cacica* or chieftess of Timbío, a village located strategically close to the market in Popayán, estimated the annual worth of her harvest at 50 *pesos*, or the contemporary value of half a pound of gold.[53] A comparison with the prices paid for coca in Guanacas would allow one to estimate that the *cacica* was picking between ten and fifteen *arrobas* (250 and 375 pounds) of coca at each of the three annual harvests. This is a remarkably large quantity, more than twice the maximum reported from Guanacas, and thus one might assume that either she was defending a collective or tribal plantation — which would explain her designation as *cacica* — or that she had turned to reasonably large-scale production of coca as a cash crop for sale in Popayán.

It would not, therefore, be surprising to find that some of the white settlers should also have seen in coca the possibility of making a fast buck. Although there is no reference to any of the colonists in Popayán ever having engaged in large-scale coca production, it is more than likely that certain individuals — perhaps with an experience of Peru — recognized the economic potential of this crop and took not only to the trading of coca grown by the Indians, but also to the direct cultivation of their own supply. This much can clearly be demonstrated in at least one part of the Cauca area — the settlement of Timaná, across the Central Cordillera in the upper reaches of the Magdalena valley — and it would not be unreasonable to assume its extension to many other similar white towns. The accounts from Timaná speak of the great popularity of the coca leaf in that region during the colonial period, and describe Indian labour being used to work the white landowners' coca crop. They even provide an explanation of the manner in which these landowners had originally established their control of the local plantations, a feat which seems to have been achieved by fraudulently expropriating the heirs of Indian owners who were recently deceased.[54]

All the same, the absence of any really sizeable coca operation in the Cauca area, and the failure of the colonial aristocracy in Popayán to convert this crop into as big a source of earnings as it had become in Peru, requires a closer examination of the local economic conditions. Clearly the fact that the area's indigenous population was less numerous, and less accustomed to situations of massed labour, played an important role in keeping the production and commercialization of coca within more modest bounds. But underlying these more obvious factors, there also exist a number of clearly cultural and geographical considerations which give the coca trade in Cauca its distinctive features.

In the first place, local ecology concerns only two broadly defined climate zones: the *tierra fria*, or cool zone, located between 2000 and 3000 metres altitude, and the *tierra templada*, a sub-tropical zone between 1000 and 2000 metres. The greater humidity of the Northern Andes gives these mountains a very different aspect to those of Peru, and the cold, damp *páramo* or moor (above 3000 metres) has never been permanently settled by man, and mainly served the native population as an extensive reserve of wild game.[55] At the same time, a number of other geographical limitations also exerted some control over the type of settlement patterns which became characteristic of the area in pre-Hispanic times. Though the *tierra templada* did manage to support the emergence of dense populations and nucleated village settlements — notably in the flat alluvial valley around Cali (c.1000 metres altitude) and possibly also on the plateau surrounding Popayán (c.1760 metres)[56] — the *tierra fria* consists mainly of narrow valleys without any really significant flat spaces, running transversally down the main ridges of the Andes. It is true that a few of these high altitude valleys — such as those at Huila, Mosoco, Silvia, or Coconuco — did provide the occasional seats of ceremonial or military authority for the major chiefdoms of the Paez and Guambiano groups, but they do not appear to have witnessed the formation of true village structures, nor could they support any really significant density of population.

This point is an important one, for a comparison of the inhabitants of the narrow valleys of the Cauca area with those of the broad plateau of the Sábana of Bogotá (c.2450 metres altitude) makes it clear that small, quasi-egalitarian chiefdom structures were not always necessarily the most favoured forms of social organization among the different groups of Chibcha-speaking Indians in highland Colombia. On the contrary, the relatively simple chiefdoms of the Cauca area seem to have responded to the specific conditions of an extremely rugged and broken terrain, and in the same way, the large and far more hierarchical Muisca kingdoms can be seen to reflect the greater availability of arable land, and the consequently greater density of population, on the wide plateaux surrounding Bogotá and Tunja. Indeed, by the time of the Spanish Conquest, the situation in this latter part of Colombia was already beginning to approximate quite closely that previously described for the highland areas of Peru. In other words, a dense nucleus of population located at the higher altitudes — the grain-producing zone — does seem to have maintained peripheral colonies on the warmer sub-tropical slopes which lead down to the lowlands, and it would have been such colonies which assured the Muiscas of their own supply of coca leaves.[57]

An approximately similar picture is also reported from another area which bears certain similarities with Cauca. The most famous of the coca producing districts in Ecuador was Pimampiro, in the Mira river drainage in the extreme north of the country. An extensive description of the situation in Pimampiro was written in 1582, and describes a labour arrangement which in all respects is very similar to that which had been pioneered by the colonial authorities in Peru. Highland Indians from Otovalo in northern Ecuador, and from Pasto in southern Colombia, were accustomed to make periodic visits to the lower altitudes to assist in the picking of coca leaves, in return for which they received a share of the harvest. By 1631, even the Jesuits were being accused by the Inquisition of making huge profits on their coca plantations in Pimampiro.[58]

What emerges from these comparisons with the situation in Cauca, is the crucial importance of the large concentrations of population in such localities as the Sábana of Bogotá, and the plateaux surrounding Pasto and Otovalo. Whether or not these groups were organized in nucleated village settlements is not itself the prime consideration in the present argument, since the important point is that these mass markets were located at some considerable distance from their nearest supplies of coca. Either by the maintenance of peripheral colonies, in the pre-Hispanic period, or by the institution of a white-controlled market structure in the colonial context, both the Pasto/Otavalo and the Bogotá regions experienced an organization of the coca trade which was not significantly different from the typical forms observed in Peru.

The Cauca area therefore remains, due to its specific cultural and geographical conditions, one of the few stretches of the Andes where notably different economic forces have prevailed in the coca trade. Where dense populations did exist, as on the valley floor around Cali, the coca supply lay immediately at hand. In all the other, narrower valley systems of the Cauca area, it would be impossible to state that any particular altitude was necessarily the 'nuclear' occupation zone, or that any other altitude was necessarily 'peripheral'. In keeping with the local topography, the Indians of Cauca seem to have occupied in a continuous fashion all the more favourable lcoations at any altitude between the valley bottoms (c.1000 metres) and the edge of the *páramo* (c.3000 metres). Even today, the routes of communication which run up and down each valley are much more heavily travelled by the local people than those which connect various valleys at the same altitude. The primary flow of rural produce would appear to lie between adjacent eco-niches, rising in a sole continuum from the warm sub-tropical valleys to the cold moorland above the tree-line.

Within each valley, the population is usually small enough to allow a series of reciprocal exchanges based primarily on face-to-face alliances, ties of close kinship, and a broad, enveloping concept of solidarity within the tribal or linguistic group.[59] These exchanges can be repeated virtually whenever need dictates, since the distance between the 1000 and 3000 metre extremes seldom implies more than a single day's journey on foot. Indeed, many Paez families still maintain cultivated fields in both the sub-tropical and the temperate zones at the same time, travelling from one to the other as required by the agricultural round. This kind of intimate and self-sufficient economy is also arguably the norm which characterized pre-Hispanic Cauca, and as a result of this, the supply of coca leaves to even the very highest altitude groups need never have involved more than an extremely localized form of trading. The inherent strength of this system resides, above all, in its resilience and independence; a fact appreciated even by the Guambiano Indians who — unlike most of the Paez — have long since lost all their warmer climate lands to the white population which colonized the route between Cali and Popayán. Reinvesting the profits derived from the commercialization of their potato and onion crops, the Guambianos have recently — in the last twenty years or so — begun to buy back a substantial amount of land in the sub-tropical zone, most notably around Piendamó and Morales. A good deal of the produce from these new farms is traded exclusively within the Guambiano community, and more often than not, with close kinsmen who have maintained their home in the cold valleys of Guambia itself.

Coca at a small rural market in southern Cauca. The scales have weighed out *un huevo* — an egg, or one tenth of a pound. The three circular pieces are blocks of white lime or *mambe*.

With a recognition of such patterns in the organization of local trade, it is not difficult to explain why a large coca business should never have flourished in colonial Popayán in the way it did in Peru. Localized exchanges could never be effectively intercepted or monopolized by the Spanish commercial classes, who would thus be left to supply only the demand for coca produced by situations of massed labour. These all depended ultimately on the *encomienda* — an institution which extracted work from the Indians as part of the tribute owed to the Spanish crown — and while it is true that Indian labour was often put to use on the large estates surrounding Popayán, it was nevertheless the mining operations which led to the greatest single concentrations of the native work-force. It is therefore not surprising to find the best evidence for a flourishing coca trade in the colonial settlement at Almaguer, the town in southern Cauca which served as administrative and commercial centre for the most important gold mines of the area. The collection of more than a dozen Indian labourers in the same place would have been a relatively rare phenomenon in the agricultural enterprises of Popayán, but in Almaguer large teams of miners were a regular feature, and provided the coca traders with a huge captive market whose purchases were paid for in gold, the most precious commodity of all.[60]

Though itself above the coca growing zone, Almaguer (c.2300 metres) lies on the rim of the San Jorge valley, still to this day the most important coca-producing region in all of the Cauca area. It literally takes only a couple of hours to climb from the best coca plantations to Almaguer, and clearly the importance which coca retains in the district is to some considerable extent a legacy of its crucial role in the colonial mining system. At the height of the gold rush, even the San Jorge valley was not sufficient to supply all the local demand, and a commercial attraction was exerted right over the Central Cordillera to San Agustín and Timaná, at least four days' journey away. A system of long-distance trade seems to have emerged, almost in miniature reproduction of the Peruvian colonial scheme, with drastically disruptive effects to the native subsistence economy of southern Cauca.[61]

It has been mentioned previously that the Timaná district has provided the only documentary evidence of large-scale coca plantations ever having been owned and operated by white colonists in the Cauca area, and now it should be clear that this exceptional phenomenon was probably produced as a result of the demand for large shipments of coca in the gold mines of Almaguer. After the rapid decline of the mining economy in this area in the eighteenth century, the coca trade also suffered a reduction in the size of its markets, and thus it is likely that white landowners lost interest in the bulk production of this crop, and trading became once again a small-scale, localized undertaking. Furthermore the abolition of obligatory Indian labour tributes after Colombia's independence from Spain must have further contributed to the reduction of the demand for coca by the large agricultural employers. With the collapse of this broader market, many of the coca-producing districts in southern Cauca — such as La Herradura, in the San Jorge valley — reverted to a pattern of reciprocal trade with neighbouring high-altitude communities, a pattern still observable today in the Sunday market at the Indian reservation village of Caquiona.

The decline of the gold mines did not, however, completely eliminate all the long-distance trade in coca. One group of Indians in the Cauca area would still have provided a captive market for the leaves, as their close proximity to the white capital of Popayan had led to the loss of most of their lower altitude lands, and thus to the interruption of the traditional sources of coca which they must have enjoyed in the pre-Hispanic period. Accounts written at the beginning of this century certainly show that the reservations in Coconuco, Puracé, Totoró and Guambia remained the major outlet for all the coca which entered the market economy. A group of white, reasonably small-scale traders would buy from the few villages which still continued to produce a surplus of coca, such as Timbío, Piendamó, and particularly the by now rather depressed communities in the vicinity of Almaguer. The leaves would then be retailed through the marketplace in Popayán and other neighbouring centres, but the quantity moved was never sufficient to interest the really large commercial concerns. For this reason, the coca trade has remained to this day in the hands of a few very small-scale operators, mostly lower middle class women from Popayán, who are the same group who control the marketing of many other minor vegetable products as well.[62]

In the 1920s, a new factor served to further discourage many coca growers, and contributed to the almost complete disappearance of coca production in certain parts of the Cauca area. The introduction of coffee plantations to the same ecological zone which had previously been dedicated to coca provided a substantial shift of emphasis in local agriculture, as coffee and its export market soon became the major source of cash earnings for many small farmers. The most heavily affected area was around Popayán itself, and along the railway line to Cali, which was completed in 1927. Today coca has virtually ceased to exist in all this region — from Timbío and El Tambo to Morales and Santander de Quilichao — and the occasional ornamental plants are all that remain of what was, even fifty years ago, still a major crop.

The switch from coca to coffee produced a certain scarcity of the leaves in the market at Popayán, and contributed to the emergence of two closely related side-effects. One was the decline of the coca habit itself, which began to be considered an 'uncivilized' form of behaviour by many of the more progressive Indians, particularly those of the Guambiano/Coconuco group who lived closer to Popayán, and were thus most directly affected by the shortage. In addition, the coca surplus from southern Cauca — a region whose soils are not suited to extensive coffee agriculture — soon began to find new buyers, and the San Jorge valley actually experienced something of an economic revival.[63]

Meanwhile the Paez Indians, whose supply of leaves had never been significantly dependant on the white-controlled market mechanism anyway, persevered in their use of coca with great tenacity, for even on the western side of the Central Cordillera they could still enjoy the use of much land which was suitable for its cultivation, such as that in the vicinity of Caldono, Paniquitá, Caloto and Corinto. Both here and in Tierradentro proper — on the other side of the Central Cordillera — they continued to practice the forms of localized exchange which had marked their history since pre-Hispanic times, and which had always allowed them such a marked degree of independence from the mainstream Colombian economy.

Nevertheless, even the Paez were finally to suffer the onslaught of pressures generated from outside by the ebb and flow of international commerce. Coffee gave the white colonists who bordered on Paez reservations a new reason to press the easily corrupted local authorities into an unconstitutional attack on the integrity of the Indian territories. A series of legal measures were passed by the governor in Popayán; some simply extinguishing whole reservations, while others chartered the establishment of white 'settlement areas' on favourable land located deep within the traditional boundaries of Indian *resguardos*. Once they had established this legal toe-hold inside these reservations, it was obviously not very difficult to use force or trickery to extend the settlement areas far beyond the limits which had been determined in the original charter.[64]

This invasion of Indian lands was to achieve its most notable successes in the warmer climate zone, where the economic solvency of the new colonists could be assured by sales of coffee. The importance of this crop as a source of cash earnings led many of the Paez themselves to reduce their coca harvests, and turn over some of their lower valley land to the cultivation of the bean. This marginal participation in a market economy clearly began to produce a number of detrimental changes in the traditional practices of reciprocity. While the sub-tropical zone took to trading more extensively with the white settlements which bought its coffee, a very similar process began to affect the higher cold zone as well, especially such reservations as Pitayó and Mosoco, whose proximity to the market centre of Silvia allowed a profitable outlet for such products as cinchona bark, potatoes, onions and wheat.[65]

The advent of a major civil war, the *Violencia*, which swept through Tierradentro on repeated occasions between 1949 and 1964, soon demonstrated the extreme fragility of the market economy in which the

Paez had begun to participate. The decimation of their livestock by the Army, the interruption of supplies to the white market towns, and the wild fluctuation in the prices paid for agricultural produce, all served to underline the undesirability of dependance on the whte man's economy, and consequently led to a renewed respect for traditional ways. A major economic study of the Paez conducted in the early 1960s showed an almost complete divorce between the cultural attitudes which characterize the cultivation of coffee, and those which control the production of coca and food staples. While coffee is produced by the Paez almost exclusively for cash sales — they hardly ever drink the stuff themselves — all other crops are subject to what amounts almost to a moral rule, which tends to discriminate against the sale of food or coca to whites, and attempts to limit the exchange of such resources to the circle of interdependent friends and kinsmen who constitute the basic solidary unit of Paez society.[66]

Given that coca is demonstrably such an intimate part of the native economy, it is surely of more than incidental interest that the reservations which have seen the most marked decline of the coca habit should be high altitude settlements, especially those whose links with the warmer zone are so tenuous as to be almost non-existent. While a broadly defined acculturation could certainly be considered a factor contributing to the classification of the coca habit as 'uncivilized', it is nevertheless the harsh economic reality of spiralling coca prices which has most significantly undermined the once universal use of coca by the Indians of Cauca. Quite apart from the pressures created by the new market economy, a cheap piece of electioneering by the then Minister of Hygiene — Jorge Bejerano, a medical worthy from Popayán — produced further restraints on the coca trade in the form of a complete legal prohibition. *Decreto* 896 of March 11th, 1947, rendered the cultivation, distribution and possession of coca in Colombia a criminal offense, and though the law was seldom applied with any real rigour in the Cauca area, it did serve both to put pressure on the indigenous economy and to justify a number of callous, punitive raids into the heart of Indian territory, a policy which continued unabated in the middle 1970s with the occasional burning of coca bushes in many parts of Tierradentro.[67]

As a result of both the legal and economic disruption of the coca trade by outside forces, it is perhaps not surprising that such communities as Guambia, Coconuco and Mosoco — which all depend on long-range supplies of coca, and on cash earnings to pay for their purchases of leaves — should have found that they simply could no longer afford to maintain the habit. Even despite their effective wealth, in terms of *pesos* cash, they were relatively less well off, with respect to coca, than many of the more 'backward' high altitude communities, those who spurned participation in the cash economy in favour of continued reciprocal links with

Paez woman picking coca.

La Herradura, southern Cauca. A bandit town: notice the absence of a church.

neighbouring coca producers in the warmer climate zone. It is surely for this reason that the coca habit has survived most in those reservations such as Lame, Suin, Chinas, Calderas and San Andrés (in Tierradentro), and Caquiona and Guachicono (in southern Cauca), where there is least participation in the white market economy, and where the greatest desire exists to retain traditional forms of exchange and reciprocity.

This point has been stressed considerably, because it has long been fashionable for anti-drug writers of all political persuasions to point to such ambiguous factors as 'education' or 'the raising of living standards' as the vital issues in the suppression of undesirable drug habits among peasant peoples throughout the world, and specifically among the Indians of Cauca.[68] The dubious nature of such assumptions, and the even more doubtful efficacity of the legislative approach to the 'problem', become even more apparent if one considers the manner in which the cocaine business has begun to affect the Cauca area. The early 1970s saw a rapid increase in coca prices occasioned by the huge purchases of leaves made by the clandestine cocaine laboratories, and thus still fewer Indians could afford to buy their coca in the marketplace. As if this were not enough, the police — itself little more than a watchdog for the vested interests in cocaine — began to further harass the traditional small-scale traders of coca leaves, imprisoning many of them to discourage any competition to the laboratories.

In a very short space of time, much of the trade mechanism which supplied coca to such market centres as Popayán and Silvia became starved of leaves, and the Indians dependant on the traders for their supply soon found it beyond their means to continue chewing coca. And yet this decadence of the coca habit was occurring precisely at a time when the acculturative process was suffering a considerable reversal, and many Indians were flocking to the banner of CRIC (Consejo Regional Indigena del Cauca), an Indian civil rights organization which stressed respect for the authoctonous culture of the area, including even — to the dismay of many rather orthodox radicals and other non-Indian adherents — the actual consumption of the dreaded coca leaf itself. It is fortunate that CRIC has begun to realize the vital importance of repudiating the addictive allure of a capitalist market economy. Hopefully this will provide an impetus towards regaining much of the economic independence that the Indians of Cauca have lost; for only a reapproximation to indigenous forms of reciprocal exchange — and an extension of similar practices to other class allies throughout the length and breadth of Colombia — is capable of building an authentically socialist future, of defending the use of coca, and with it the very Indian way of life as well.

IV. The Politics of Cocaine

'Lt. Fernández and four policemen, dressed in civilian clothes, came in a rented jeep looking for the cocaine factory. They only checked the house, and some strange things attracted their attention, such as the carbide for our lamps... They left making the remark that they knew everything and that we would have to deal with them...'

Ché Guevara's Bolivian Diaries.
Entry for Thursday, January 19th, 1967.

Though clearly a good many fortunes were made in cocaine during the period of its first great popularity (1884-1930) — including those of many highly reputable pharmaceutical companies — it is only in the last ten or fifteen years that the world has experienced again a really widespread revival of interest in the drug, producing in this short space of time a rapid increase in demand and a thriving, multi-million dollar industry centred on the Andean areas where the coca bush is cultivated. Some idea of the expansion of the market can be deduced from the dazzling statistics for seizures of illicit cocaine by the United States Customs: From a mere 8 pounds confiscated in 1961, the figures rises to 408 pounds by 1971, and peaks at a grand total of 1,125 pounds in 1976.[1] Although such figures can only provide, at best, an extremely approximate barometer of the total volume of the trade, it still remains arguable that the consumption of cocaine — at least in the United States — has increased roughly a hundred-fold since the early 1960s.

The economic forces generated by a boom of this kind could not fail to produce a number of alarming side-effects in the producing countries as well. In particular, the demand for raw material has seriously affected many of the traditional coca growers and coca chewers themselves, groups which are plainly at a marked disadvantage when dealing with the far more powerful cocaine industry. It should be obvious that small peasant farmers usually have precious little say in the kind of ruthless, self-perpetuating organizations which protect the continued operation of the cocaine business, even though they may benefit incidentally from the prices paid for their harvests. Indeed, the plight of the coca producers cannot be isolated from the plight of the peasantry as a whole in South America, for it is part of a class struggle which transcends the specific mode of production of this or that individual commodity. It is, however, in order to clarify the particular details of the manufacture and commercialization of cocaine that the present study has been undertaken; for it is hoped that an exposure of the links between the drug trafficking groups and their powerful local allies — normally, in the present historical context, reactionary politicians and the high commands of the police and Armed Forces — will serve to provide the reader with a useful insight into a few of the more ugly ramifications of the vicious neo-fascist technocracies which have recently emerged throughout the continent.

At the same time, while necessarily condemning the present structure of the cocaine trade, this would hardly be the place to unleash any flood of ill-considered invective against the supposed evils of the dread cocaine, the big C itself. Such an approach — so common among the gutless bureaucrats who daily ventilate their inane views on the drug 'problem' — serves only to deflect attention from what should be the really crucial issues, issues which reach far deeper than the rather limited and, in any case, self-inflicted dangers of cocaine abuse. The most pressing necessity remains that of unmasking the crass fiction of the narcotics agents' 'war on drugs', and by this means, to proceed to a more acute and realistic analysis of the economic structure of the international drug business, itself probably the single most dynamic growth area of contemporary imperialism.

Furthermore, it would in any case be virtually impossible to exclude the cocaine phenomenon from any serious consideration of the present-day ethnography of coca chewing in the Andes. The two subjects are so inextricably entwined that to consider them in isolation smacks of a scientific specialism as redundant as it is offensive to the dignity of the plant itself. In the specific case of the Cauca area, any such scholastic nicety could only be condemned as doubly unwarranted. Did not Nelson Rockefeller himself state that: 'Virtually all of the cocaine entering the United States comes from South America and principally from Colombia . . . '?[2] To ignore the harsh social and political realities produced by this situation, to imagine that such features are somehow 'irrelevant' to the pure anthropological study of coca chewing among the Indians and *campesinos* of the Department of Cauca, would seem to imply precisely the sort of ineffectual academicism which has itself permitted the continued portrayal of the cocaine business purely in terms of the paranoid delusions and often quite deliberate misrepresentations of the world-wide narcotics agencies.

In the first place, it must be pointed out that Colombia's prominence in the drug trade is only really a very recent development. The vast majority of the cocaine refined in Colombia is derived from crude 'base' smuggled in from the other Andean republics, and the relatively insignificant coca harvests of such areas as southern Cauca — the only part of Colombia to produce a traditionally large surplus of the leaves — cannot really begin to compare with the huge quantities of coca exported from the departments of Cuzco and Huánuco, in Peru, or from the Yungas valleys of Bolivia. Prior to the late 1960s, there appears to have been virtually no black-market cocaine available in Colombia at all, and the very small illicit consumption of the drug — mainly concentrated among the country's political and social elite — was usually supplied with a fine crystalline powder produced in official laboratories, and slipped through the fingers of the pharmacists and other members of the medical profession. As late as 1971, I was still able to purchase a small bottle of Merck cocaine — reputedly the world's finest — from an ordinary street dealer on the hillside alleys up behind the Hilton hotel in Bogotá.

Admittedly, pharmaceutical cocaine of this quality was already considered something of a rarity by this time, and the legal shipment from which it originated had reputedly been ripped off during a moment of chance carelessness by the Customs at the international airport of Bogotá. By the latter part of the 1960s, an illicit cocaine business had already come to dominate the market in Colombia, exploiting both the expansion of the North American market, and the country's strategic location as an intermediary stop in the northward flow of drugs. Business also benefited from the simultaneous growth of demand for marijuana, and a number of reasonably small-scale, fiercely competitive criminal organizations sprung up almost overnight to cater for the *gringo* need.

Initially, at least, the quality of the cocaine was often prejudiced by a severe lack of the requisite laboratory skills. The crude cocaine 'base', or *pasta de cocaína*, is usually produced in small rural 'kitchens' (*cocinas*) by means of a very simple process: the green or undried coca leaves are ground into a powder and put into a large vat — normally an empty oil-drum — which contains some dilute sulphuric acid to act as a leaching agent. To this must be added an alkaline reagent such as sodium carbonate, potassium carbonate or quite simply vetegable ash or industrial lime. A light petroleum or benzene is stirred into the solution, taking up the cocaine and other alkaloids. This benzene, in turn, is separated from the other chemicals and the leafy matter, then treated again with sulphuric acid and the alkaline reagent. This precipitates the mixed coca alkaloids, which can then be collected in a filter.[3]

In this form — a yellowish, greenish, or even greyish paste, with the consistency of nasal mucus — crude cocaine can be easily transported out of the coca-growing areas, and carried without risk of damage over long distances and through severe extremes of climate. Brought into Colombia through the Amazonian ports of Leticia and Mocoa, or smuggled across the poorly-controlled Andean border near Ipiales, the crude cocaine makes its way to the second-stage laboratories, normally located in the big cities — Cali, Medellín, Bogotá — or in the Caribbean seaports of Cartagena, Barranquilla and Santa Marta. The very multiplicity of routes makes surveillance or interruption of the trade a virtual impossibility, and this is true despite the fact that most of the second-stage laboratories are to be found close to the points from which the finished cocaine is sent out to the United States. Their localization is governed as much by reasons of practicality as of convenience, for the finished product — cocaine hydrochloride — is soluble in water and can easily be damaged by accidental exposure to the humidity common throughout Colombia.

The transformation of crude base into refined cocaine is one of the most profitable stages of the entire enterprise, for — unlike smuggling — it involves remarkably few really serious risks. An organic solvent such as ether or acetone is used to separate the pure cocaine from the other coca alkaloids such as ecgonine, which are insoluble in ether. Hydrochloric acid is added to the solution, followed by an alkali such as sodium carbonate which precipitates the cocaine in solid form, allowing it to be collected in a filter, and set in trays to dry by evaporation. Repeated washings with distilled water and the solution of ether and hydrochloric acid serve to remove any remnants of the other alkaloids, producing a progressively cleaner and more crystalline cocaine hydrochloride, with a degree of absolute purity which may rise from a low of 79% to the pharmaceutical standard, usually over 99%.

Though this process itself hardly requires the skills of an expert chemist, there are nevertheless a number of things that can go wrong in the laboratory. An excess of either hydrochloric acid or sodium carbonate can produce cocaine tending towards extremes which are either very sharp and pungent, or else unbearably 'soapy'. A good deal of the illicit cocaine in Colombia is often, therefore, of a rather inferior quality — even before it has been cut or 'stepped on' with lactose or synthetic local anaesthetics like procaine, a practice which is becoming increasingly common, even at the level of laboratory production. Furthermore, the ether or acetone remaining after the filtering process is often evaporated too slowly, and the cocaine remains with residues whose somewhat unsubtle properties predominate over the natural smell and taste of the drug, as well as producing an initially giddy reaction to the user which detracts from the clean, clear-cut rush of exhilaration normally produced by the drug in an unadulterated state. Indeed, not only are the laboratories quite often very sloppy, they are also dangerous; for should volatile substances such as ether be carelessly handled or overheated, they may easily ignite or even explode, destroying the whole laboratory and claiming the lives of its operators, as occurred in one famous case in Cali on the night of July 5th, 1974.[4]

Other than Colombia's strategic location between the main coca producing areas and the American market, however, one might also be able to identify a number of secondary factors whch apparently encouraged the emergence of a thriving local business in cocaine. In the first place, smuggling has long been an accepted, almost respectable way of life throughout much of the country's Caribbean coastline. An eighteenth-century manuscript in the British Museum makes explicit reference to its great economic importance all along the erstwhile Spanish Main, an impression whose present validity can readily be confirmed by the claim of the police chief in Barranquilla, who asserted that at least 300 clandestine airfields were in operation on the north coast of Colombia in 1974.[5] In recent years cocaine has been added to emeralds and marijuana and a great number of other classic articles of contraband, evolving into a trade which — with its infiltration of local government and the customs service — accounts for a great deal of the political and economic power wielded by the *mafia costena*, the traditional social elite which has always dominated public life in the coastal cities.

This well-established precedent in smuggling would have rendered the country's entry into the cocaine business a relatively easy process to accomplish. Initially, at least, the reputation of Colombia was ensured by a policy of 'wide-open' drug dealing; all buyers, big or small, were equally welcome, including large numbers of reasonably small-time, youthful independents from the United States. For them, scoring coke in Colombia was considerably less sweat than in the extremely paranoid, uptight atmosphere of Bolivia or Peru; and Colombia, furthermore, could also provide some of the very finest marijuana in the whole Western hemisphere. All in all, the attraction of doing business there was almost irresistable, so — with only a very minimal risk of official harrassment — large numbers of amateur *gringo* dealers began to hop over on the notorious Aerocondor flight from Miami to Barranquilla. This, at least, was still the situation when I first arrived in the country in 1971, probably the last year in which a genuinely open market existed on the drug scene in Colombia.

Little more than a year later, however, the old laissez-faire scenario was rapidly becoming a thing of the past, and within another twelve months large numbers of luckless *gringos* were beginning to find themselves languishing semi-permanently in the rather insalubrious penitentiaries of the state. The primary reason for this change of climate can be traced very clearly to the continental conference on the drug traffic held in Bogotá in

October, 1972, sponsored by American narcotics agents of the now extinct BNDD (Bureau of Narcotics and Dangerous Drugs), and intended to provide the impetus for a great continental offensive against the use of drugs. Such crusades, of course, serve mainly to draw attention, power, and research and enforcement money to the crusaders themselves, and the subsequent reality of this particular operation predictably bore very little similarity to the original pipe dreams about 'saving our youth' put out by the narcs. Instead, it would appear difficult to avoid the conclusion that the anti-drug campaign has only served as a smokescreen for ruthless and wide-ranging monopolization of the cocaine business, all the more alarming since undertaken by the very same organizations set up to combat the 'menace' in the first place. As a result, the period of the open market in Colombia — with all the colourful, free-for-all gangsterism, the droll, almost farcical rackets of the bad old days — is now little more than a memory, having given way increasingly to a new breed of sleek, highly efficient cocaine cartels. The dangers inherent in this situation — the dangers to coca growers, coca chewers, cocaine consumers, and Colombians and South Americans as a whole — clearly require the identification and exposure of the groups who can be seen to be benefiting from the new situation. It should come as no surprise that these are the same groups who have monopolized a great many other profitable enterprises as well — not least of which is the very ship of state itself.

THE COLOMBIAN SECURITY FORCES

Any account of the drug traffic in Colombia must necessarily begin with a consideration of the various outfits vying for overall control of the entire undertaking, namely, the narcotics agencies themselves. Traditionally the most powerful of these is the *Departamento Administrativo de Seguridad*, or DAS, a security organization that was originally set up to persecute the politically 'subversive' sections of Colombian society. As such, it received a rather inflated idea of its already very arbitrary powers, and by the early 1970s had penetrated a great deal of the Colombian underworld, including many of the more lucrative aspects of the cocaine business. It was common knowledge in Bogotá in 1971 that the 'fat fish' (*pez gordo*) in cocaine was General Ordónez Valderrama, the commander of DAS, but it was not until the change of government in 1974 that the real details of his involvement began to be made public.[6] Interestingly enough, investigations showed that he had not only used his official position as a shield to cover criminal organizations working outside his office, but had also actually turned DAS itself into a wide-ranging cocaine distribution network, controlling all stages of the illicit traffic and initiating the policy of ruthlessly victimizing its competitors.

In any case, the few established facts about DAS would seem to speak for themselves: In May 1972, June 1973, and November 1973, large stocks of apprehended cocaine disappeared from the official DAS safes. In May 1973 the chief of DAS in the Amazonian port of Leticia was arrested by Customs in the airport of Bogotá with nineteen kilos of cocaine in his suticase. The investigation which followed on this affair was carefully and deliberately obstructed by General Ordónez Valderrama. By November 1973, the uniformed national police force publicly accused DAS of being heavily involved in the drug business. At the beginning of 1974, forty-eight DAS agents were dismissed from the Medellín office for drug trafficking and other smuggling offenses.[7]

Most of the details regarding the corruption of DAS — the public exposure and subsequent 'retirement' of key figures — have only emerged through rivalries within and between the different Colombian security forces, and it would be naive to imagine that DAS is alone in its involvement in the drug business. The Policia Nacional — and especially its plainsclothes branch, the F-2 — are unlikely to have a much cleaner record than DAS itself. General Henry Garcia Bohórquez, commander of the Policia Nacional at the same time as Ordónez was running DAS, was also later the subject of a number of high-level inquiries into his underworld affiliations — including his links with the cocaine traffic — and his case was considered sufficiently serious to be taken up by the Supreme Court in Bogotá.[8] Another official body which has been very intimately involved in the business is Colombia's diplomatic service. An example of this was provided by the vice-consul in New York City, José Alvaro Córdoba Bojassen, who was arrested in October 1970 while attempting to introduce twenty-five kilos of cocaine into the United States. He fled back to his native Cali, and the U.S. served extradition papers on the Colombian government, which were approved by the Supreme Court in Bogotá. In April 1972, however, the Minister of Justice, Escobar Méndez, and the President of the Republic, Pastrana Borrero, both refused to lend their signatures to the order of extradition.

This type of action would seem to seriously compromise the 1970-1974 Pastrana administration, and led his successor to adopt a rather more cautious policy. On becoming president in 1974, López Michelsen was clearly a little upset at the state of corruption existing in his largely discredited security forces, and most notably in DAS. Rather than embarking on an embarrassing program of revelations, however, he simply dismissed Ordónez Valderrama and replaced him with General Matallana, an Army commander infamous for his bloody anti-guerilla campaigns in the 1960s. Matallana purged at least half of the higher ranking DAS officials, and went on a widely publicized drive to save the image of his department. The chief of DAS in Ipiales — a town on the Ecuadorean border long known for its keen participation in all forms of illicit commerce — was actually himself arrested in September 1974, and charged with a long list of abuses ranging from the forgery of passports to the inevitable smuggling of cocaine.[9]

Clearly the intended effect was to create a new media image of a pure and efficient DAS, engaged singlemindedly in the elimination of corruption on every level, and to this end Matallana began to attack his other rivals as well, accusing the Colombian judiciary and the Customs service of obstructing his investigations into the cocaine traffic.[10] His efforts earned him an excellent reputation with the American narcotics agencies, and he became a daily figure on the front page of all the newspapers, a knight in shining armour coming to the rescue of his country, a veritable ideal of traditional no-nonsense Colombian *machismo.* The grand theatrical gestures of Matallana, however, were hardly enough to dismantle the by now very well-established apparatus of the Colombian drug trade, and away from the headlines, outright participation in the traffic continued to be the norm of all the Colombian security forces.

There was, for example, the strange case of the American narcs in Bogotá who, in March 1975, had received information regarding an eleven-ton shipment of marijuana which was awaiting exportation, and had proceeded to the scene of the crime in a private plane, accompanied by Colombian Customs officers. On arrival, they were greeted by heavy gunfire, and a shoot-out ensued between the Customs and what were later to be identified as DAS agents.[11] The official story is that DAS thought the arriving Customs men to be the owners of the shipment, but in that case, why did they open fire, rather than waiting to catch them in red-handed possession of the weed? Indeed, since no third parties were arrested in the case, and since it is unlikely that such a large hoard would be left unguarded, the only logical conclusion is that the DAS agents were themselves in possession of the shipment, and hoped to scare off any potential assailants with their gunfire. Back in Washington, Senator Henry Jackson limited himself to describing this case of armed confrontation between two competing narcotics forces — both of them financed and assessed by the U.S.A. — as 'highly disturbing'. These were fine words, but they predictably failed to produce any major upheaval in the Colombian drug business. On the contrary, DAS was soon involved in at least one more shoot out — this time with the F-2 plainsclothes branch of the Policia Nacional — over the ownership of yet another big shipment on its way to the States.[12]

By the end of 1976, more than two years after Matallana had originally launched his campaign, the situation of armed conflict within the trade had escalated to the point where the chief of the American Drug Enforcement Agency (DEA) in Bogotá was actually assassinated in his own office, at a moment when the security net around him had somehow mysteriously failed to function.

Some sources state that the assailant — T.C.Cole, a Vietnam veteran and DEA informer — was in turn gunned down by the authorities as he tried to escape; while others claim that Cole shot himself when he found his route blocked by U.S. Marines. In either case, no convincing motive for the crime was ever established, and speculation has centered on the possibility that 'the hit may have been ordered from on high.'[13] Such a statement is, of course, intentionally ambiguous, but the fact that the DEA chief in question — Octavio González — had originally been posted to Bogotá at the time of the 1972/1973 offensive to 'control' the Colombian trade in illicit drugs would seem to suggest that he was not entirely the innocent hero he was made out to be. Likewise, his Cuban background and previous career on the Miami police force would also tend to imply a long history of links with the crime syndicates which control the bulk of the cocaine traffic. Whether such links were purely professional — straight-forward 'cops and robbers', like on TV — or whether they involved a number of more shady feedback loops, is a matter which cannot be isolated from the fact that, at the same time as González's mission, a major Cuban takeover was occurring within the cocaine business in the United States.

Scandals such as the murder of González are endemic in Bogotá, however, and even President López Michelsen — always anxious to keep a clean nose in such matters — found himself being embarrassed by members of his diplomatic corps, while on an official visit to Washington in September, 1975. Shortly before, his consul in New York City had been identified as a big wheel in one of the smuggling networks bringing cocaine into the United States, and very credible rumours identified the ultimate source of such shipments in Indalecio Liévano, López's minister of foreign affairs.[14] The truth, in any case, is that matters were — by this stage — quite largely out of López's hands, for he had already become that very strange political anomaly, an elected civilian president held virtually captive by the state of siege declared by his minister of Defence and the commanders of the Armed Forces. It would not be unfair to suggest that this disguised putsch in Colombian public life had more than an accidental bearing on the ongoing process of monopolization within the local cocaine business, and that it reflected a deliberate policy initiated with the Army's 1974 takeover of an equally profitable industry, the fabled emerald mines of Muzo, so long contested by the rival power groups in the Colombian underworld.

Though such a slide into racketeering may well have been one of the more immediately striking features of the new military consciousness, there was also a decidedly repressive twist to the generals' increasing prominence as well. The triumph of the extreme right in the Colombian Armed Forces — a process initiated in 1975, and finally sealed in 1976 — was much more than just a faithful reflection of the climate prevailing throughout the continent at this time. It coincided, for example, particularly neatly with a similar drift to the right in neighbouring Peru, the country which supplies virtually all the crude cocaine to the Colombian laboratories. Another aspect of the backlash was the violent bombing campaign to silence the radical press in Bogotá — notably the weekly 'Alternativa', sponsored by Gabo Garcia Márquez — which had become particularly outspoken in its accusations against leading members of the military and political establishment, especially with respect to their involvement in the cocaine business. Though terrifying enough in themselves such explicit acts of intimidation were only the outward signs of an even more crucial power struggle taking place within the Army itself, for a great deal of the ammunition used by the press had originally been leaked by an unofficial pressure group — the Military Brigade of Liberation and National Reconstruction — composed of the younger, more nationalist officers, and tacitly supported by a few of the less extreme generals as well.

The views of this group were essentially those of the career soldier, disgusted at the transformation of a professional institution into little more than a sorting house for political nepotism and corrupt patronage. Indeed, the alarm had first been sounded in 1975 by the assassination of General Rincón Quinones, who — the Military Brigade of Liberation claimed — had been liquidated by his brother officers on account of his uncomfortably thorough inquiries into the structure of the cocaine traffic.[15] Needless to say, the senior commanders publicly disclaimed the very existence of the Military Brigade of Liberation, and furthermore, vociferously denied that General Rincón had ever been involved in preparing a dossier on cocaine. Instead, they staged a show trial in which a number of radical activists were accused of the murder, and by means of a rich blend of trumped-up charges, sheer intimidation, and the spreading of wildly contradictory rumours — what the CIA likes to call 'disinformation' — they did eventually succeed in keeping the lid on the Rincón scandal. At times, however, publicity surrounding the trial threatened to backfire, uncovering a veritable chink in the armour of the right-wing generals, and rendering all too apparent their role in subverting and manipulating the wider political life of the nation. Fear of exposure drove them to an increasingly widespread use of the military intelligence apparatus — particularly the super-secret agency known as BINCI — to spy on officers suspected of moderate sympathies, and to a series of drastic purges which aimed at silencing the Military Brigade of Liberation and eliminating its supporters within the Armed Forces.

The high command was seemingly quite successful in this operation, for it became increasingly difficult to track down any really concrete proof of their direct involvement in the cocaine business. The last major mishap had been an accidental bust in January, 1975, on a Colombian Air Force plane which had been forced to land in Ecuador, and was found to be carrying fourteen kilos of cocaine.[16] One of the main obstacles to uncovering their participation was, of course, the generals' understandable reluctance to become involved directly in any observable transactions — to sit, as it were, with large quantities of illicit drugs in their offices or their homes. Learning from the mistakes of General Ordónez, the relatively amateur ex-commander of DAS, the new overlords realized the need to avoid any direct contacts with either the drug itself, or even the persons who normally handled the drug. A more diffuse, but no less efficient system was allowed to take the place of the older, direct organization; with those groups who wished to remain in business paying protection money and coming to a tenuous — and always mutually deniable — accommodation with the big guns on the general staff. One result of this system was the emergence of a class of civilian bailiffs who undertook the day-to-day liaison work with the actual manufacturers and smugglers themselves; 'Alternativa' identified one such figure as Carlos Obando Velasco, a political aide to the minister of Defence.[17]

In general, however, the only signs of overt corruption in military circles were provided by the almost hysterical sensitivity of the high command to any suggestion that it might be profiting from the drug trade, and using it to bolster its already obvious stranglehold over the farcical democracy practiced in Colombia. It was this political aspect which most troubled the generals, for the magazine 'Alternativa' had laid its accusations in early 1975 with amazing accuracy and foresight; identifying such figures as Varón Valencia — the minister of Defence — and his fellow generals Camacho Leyva, Sarmiento Sarmiento, Landazábal Reyes and Armando Orejuela as the 'hard line' within the Colombian military, the group which seemed most prone to invoking a Chilean-style solution to the unrest which simmered throughout their country. As it turned out, there was little immediate need for a formal military coup in Colombia, for by early 1977 this same group had effected an almost complete takeover of all the vital commands in the Armed Forces, even ousting the supreme commander of the Army itself, the more moderate General Valencia Tovar.

One of the more interesting aspects of this pre-emptive coup-without-a-coup was certainly its treatment of ex-commanders of the police force — those figures whose unashamed involvement in the drug business had already passed into the popular mythology of the back streets of Bogotá. The ex-chief of DAS, General Ordónez, had necessarily to be sacrificed — if only to placate the narcotics watchdogs in the U.S. Embassy — but it is significant that his arrest merely led to his being confined to comfortable quarters in the barracks commanded by Landazábal Reyes on the outskirts of Bogotá. Despite the gravity of the charges made against him, he was still able to continue enjoying such privileges as going out to society cocktail parties in the evenings.[19]

His successor General Matallana, 'Mr. Clean', the man who had been sent to expel all the bent cops in DAS and 'smash' the cocaine traffic once and for all, also suffered a minor contretemps in his otherwise illustrious career. Either his activities finally proved too much of an embarrassment to the vested interests in cocaine, or — as less sympathetic critics have suggested — he attempted to muscle in on too large a share of the action; but whatever the reason, in July 1976, less than two years after his appointment, he was relieved of his command and committed to the less troublesome position of chairman of the joint chiefs of staff. Here he came to be identified — rather ironically, considering his blood-curdling anti-insurgency record — with the moderate group of officers, and in late 1976 and early 1977 he was twice passed over in the new rounds of promotion.[20]

A careful reading of the overall implications of these labyrinthine struggles for power cannot fail to suggest that the widely publicized campaign against the drug traffic — an everyday feature of the Colombian press — has actually been used to conceal a far more dangerous process of gradual but inexorable monopolization within the illicit trade. Indeed, the very institution of courtmartial for drug-related offences — a legacy of the infamous state-of-siege legislation of mid-1975 — could itself be seen as one of the major moves of the military to arrogate the definitions of legality in the cocaine business, for by undermining the judiciary in this way, corruption would cease to be a matter of individual or private venality, and would instead become identified with the very process of justice itself. In such a context, the court-martial would serve simply as a means of settling internal disputes within the drug traffic, a truly cynical ploy whose token elimination of a few individual traffickers — be they police chiefs or minor stooges — could never alter the fact that, at least according to American statistics, the flow of drugs from Colombia to theUnited States has increased, and continues to increase, as if subject to an almost infinite geometrical progression.

Top-ranking generals may well succeed in covering up their participation at the actual centre of the decision-making process; but at the local level links between civilian politicians and the military, the police and the Customs service seem often far more intimate than they could ever afford to be in the rather self-conscious and scandal-prone capital city of Bogotá. It is, therefore, in the provincial *departamentos* that one must look for the clearest evidence of the everyday organization of the trade. In particular, it may be useful to consider the areas which serve as entry and exit points for the cocaine on its voyage northwards from the Central Andes to the United States. One of these is Colombian Amazonia, and specifically the town of

Leticia, Colombia's sole port on the main course of the river Amazon. The virtual impossibility of controlling air and river traffic in this area makes it a natural stop-over for crude 'base' cocaine on its way from the major coca-producing districts of Peru, and the easy route Tingo Maria to Pucallpa-Iquitos—Leticia is probably responsible for a substantial portion of the total flow. Leticia itself has long been a byword for corruption: the local DAS chief was arrested in May, 1973, by Customs in the airport of Bogotá, with a suitcase carrying no less than nineteen kilos of cocaine, and the private airplane of the local hotel and jungle-tours magnate, Mike Tsalickis — A U.S. citizen, incidentally — was also busted with eleven kilos of cocaine at the same place, in September, 1974.[21]

Nowhere, however, is the collusion of the authorities, local politicians and the illicit drug business any clearer demonstrated than in Santa Marta, traditionally the major outlet for drugs in the Caribbean. 'Alternativa' identified two main groups controlling the trade in mid-1975 — the Cárdenas and Valdeblanquez families — whose links with the local governor, the manager of the port, the president of the local council, and the members of the regional supreme court were all extensively documented in their study.[22] As even a very sober anthropologist was forced to note, in his study of the local production and consumption of marijuana:

> 'Members of the best families are involved in contraband activity . . . It is they who staff the patronage government customs posts and the smuggling operation. Cannabis traffic (and to this one may add cocaine as well — ed.) has been accepted as merely another contraband activity, one of the more lucrative specializations.'[23]

THE IMPACT OF THE ILLICIT DRUG BUSINESS IN THE PRODUCING AREAS

Perhaps even more significant than the evidence of corruption along the known smuggling routes, is the kind of phenomenon observed in many rural districts which actually produce the drugs in the first place. One example of this is noteworthy because it concerns the Cauca area, or more specifically, the 'militarized' region around Corinto, where a running battle between the Army and the left-wing guerillas of FARC (Fuerzas Armadas Revolucionárias de Colombia — an orthodox Communist Party group under the leadership of Manuel Marulanda, the legendary 'Tirofijo') has become a permanent feature of the history of the last twenty-five years. Unable to conclude the struggle with any resounding victory on the battlefield, the Army has taken to gratuitous intimidation and the occasional assassination of its many political rivals in the area, such as the native Paez Indians and other neighbouring *campesinos*. Given this rather volatile situation — and the pervasive criss-crossing of the area by helicopters and camouflaged patrols — it might seem strange that a plantation of one million marijuana plants, with a total area of 1,530 hectares, should have been planted, let alone allowed to grow, before being suddenly 'discovered' under pressure from the U.S. narcs.[24] None of the local inhabitants — neither guerillas nor small peasants — would have been capable of such an undertaking, and one must, therefore, necessarily consider the involvement of some large cannabis-exporting syndicate, an unfortunate outfit whose understanding with the local military commander must have suffered some untimely reversal shortly before harvest time.

Occasional mishaps of this kind are a functional part of the wider drug business, for they serve to maintain the public fiction of the 'war on drugs', and at the same time show those who are more intimately involved that they had better toe the line, or risk being sacrificed to the *gringo* narcotics agents instead. A similar case concerned a huge coca plantation in the Vaupés drainage, in Colombian Amazonia, which was burned down by paratroopers in February, 1974.[25] No less than twenty-seven thousand coca bushes were involved in this case, but predictably enough, the owner of the land had his identity maintained 'in reserve' by the military authorities, and no legal case was ever brought to court. Again, one is left with the impression that this bust — like so many others — failed to demonstrate any really effective assault on the cocaine business as a whole, and served little other purpose than an exercise in public relations, or at most, a settling of private scores between the various competing power blocs within the trade as a whole.

The hypocritical nature of official 'concern' regarding the illicit traffic is nowhere better demonstrated than in one small rural area known personally to this author, the valley of the San Jorge river, lying between the towns of Bolívar and Almaguer, in southern Cauca. For reasons explained at length in the preceding chapter, this is probably the only area in Colombia to produce traditionally a large, exportable surplus of coca leaves, and it is therefore here — rather than in the virgin forests of Amazonia — that one must look for the clearest evidence of the political and social changes produced by the growth of the cocaine business. Coca is cultivated in small family plots, rarely exceeding a thousand bushes per family, and huge plantations — such as the one discovered in the Vaupés, or those common in the 'industrialized' coca-producing regions near Tingo Maria, Peru — simply do not exist.

The production of coca in the San Jorge valley has always provided a small cash income for farmers who otherwise concentrated only on a very rudimentary exploitation of subsistence crops. The *campesinos* of the area — many of them of Indian descent, though Spanish-speaking, and liberally intermarried with whites and blacks — commonly brought out their harvests to the local markets and sold them in lots measured by the *arroba* (25 lbs.), or in times of scarcity, by the pound. Many small-scale white traders were attracted from Popayán and the lesser provincial towns to these markets, and most of them would usually deal in fifty or a hundred pounds of leaves a week. These traders report that it was in 1969 that they first became aware of the presence of clandestine cocaine kitchens in the area; and although the buyers for these kitchens could be distinguished principally by their preference for green, undried leaves, they could also be recognized merely by the very large size of their purchases. Undried leaves are no use for chewing, but they are reputed to be more productive of cocaine when submitted to chemical processes. Furthermore, the coca trading scene is really a very intimate affair in Cauca, and clearly anybody buying hundreds of pounds of leaves, without any recognizable retail outlet, would stick out like a sore thumb.

The very recent arrival of the cocaine industry in Cauca contrasts markedly with the situation in Peru, where by the 1890s laboratories were already well established in both Lima and Huánuco.[26] Local accounts would have it that the first kitchen in Cauca was erected on the outskirts of Popayán, by an Ecuadorean with previous experience of the business elsewhere. Not long afterwards, he was driven out of town and retired to Bolívar, where he taught a number of the local people how to complete the essentially very simple process of refining cocaine 'base'. Soon kitchens began to proliferate all over southern Cauca, and cocaine production increased astronomically throughout the early 1970s. The rising demand for raw material can be demonstrated in relation to the prices received for bulk transactions of the leaves, as reported by various reputable old-time traders. The seasonal cycle of scarcity and abundance causes a large annual fluctuation in coca prices, so the figures given represent both maximum and minimum values, in *pesos* per *arroba*. In 1971, the minimum was 50, the maximum 250; by 1974, this had risen to a minimum of 200, and a maximum of 1000. This represents a 400% increase in a mere three years, and even allowing for world inflation, and for a 40% devaluation of the Colombian *peso*, the absolute increase in the value of coca has been enormous. (1 U.S. dollar = 20 *pesos* in 1971, 28 *pesos* in 1974.)

Cauca achieved such rapid notoriety in the cocaine business that it was chosen to inaugurate a widely publicized campaign against the rural kitchens, starting at the beginning of 1973 with a bust on a small laboratory that produced base near La Vega. This is a very peripheral locality in terms of the coca production of southern Cauca, and soon it was deemed necessary that more strenuous and exemplary action should be taken. The village of La Herradura, in the municipality of Almaguer, had long been famous for its Friday market — source of both the largest quantities and the very best qualities of coca in all the Cauca area — so it was perhaps not surprising that in December, 1973, a major raid was mounted by DAS on a small laboratory in the immediate vicinity of the village.[27]

Even more predictable was the press coverage of the raid, describing it as a major victory in the war on cocaine. However, there were a number of good reasons why the official stereotypes failed to communicate the real nature of the drug business in southern Cauca. In the first place, harassment by the authorities had already destroyed the traditional openness of coca trading at La Herradura, even long before the December 1973 bust. Large quantities of leaves were still changing hands, but in a clandestine fashion, and the leaf traders were experiencing ever increasing difficulties in moving their shipments past the police checkpoints and out along the road which leads from La Herradura to Bolívar, and from there to the Pan-American highway at El Bordo.

Meanwhile, at least fifteen clandestine kitchens remained in full operation in this same region throughout the year of 1974. Since the kitchen operators bought coca leaves and reduced them to base on the spot, their supply was not significantly interrupted by police vigilance further down the road in Bolívar and El Bordo. Not only were there no seizures of cocaine base ever reported leaving the area, but also the laboratories themselves were rarely subjected to any official pressure, and were only 'discovered' when political circumstances dictated the need for some expedient scapegoat.

It is not as if these cocaine kitchens are at all difficult to locate. The leaf traders and local farmers informed me quite openly that the son of so-and-so had a laboratory up such-and-such a path, and the traders in particular greatly resented the competition of the more wealthy and powerful cocaine operators. The people who worked in the kitchens could normally be picked out by the greenish stain on their hands, which was said to result from their meddling with the extractive process. Furthermore, they were often so anxious to maximize their supply of leaves that they took to intimidating the farmers with gangster methods, in order to monopolize the harvest and wrest supply from the hands of the traditional leaf traders. So great was the explicit rivalry between the old coca trade and the new cocaine enterprise that — had the authorities been seriously concerned with eliminating the kitchens — they would have been able to do so very quickly and easily, and with the cooperation of most of the leaf growers and traders themselves.

One must, therefore, necessarily conclude that these same authorities were emphatically not interested in eliminating cocaine production in southern Cauca. Their attacks on the leaf trading scene could thus be seen as a drive to destroy an indigenous economic system, and replace it with yet another facet of the export-oriented cash economy centred on the

United States. In that case, what began to make sense was the fact that the hauls of cocaine base in these 'major victories in the war on drugs' had been so insignificant, reaching only a little under a kilo in the La Herradura bust. It also explained a number of other strange occurrences in the region in the year 1974.

Given the known degree of participation by the secret police force DAS in the cocaine business, was it not puzzling that *Comandante* Aldemar Vargas, the chief of the DAS office in Popayán, should have been purged in the mid-1974 change of government, but only to be given the really rather vital post of mayor in Bolívar, the town which is the commercial centre for the entire coca-producing region of southern Cauca? His appointment became even more dubious when he was quoted in a Bogotá newspaper as saying that his municipality had suddenly been 'invaded' by coca bushes. In complete disregard for the history of the region, he suggested that the local Indians and *campesinos* had 'all of a sudden' been possessed by the most voracious need to chew coca. Only the very casual reference was made to the production of cocaine, and it was implied that the real problem lay with the health implications of this strange and novel form of abuse being practiced by the poor, misguided peasantry.[28]

The communications media cannot really be held responsible for perpetuating this kind of gross misinformation, but there have been other occasions on which local journalists have been victims of a more pervasive form of control, amounting to the effective censorship of inconvenient or undesirable information regarding the drug traffic. One example of this serves well to illustrate the situation prevailing in southern Cauca. On November 20th, 1974, the radio station La Voz del Cauca announced that a helicopter had come down between La Vega and Almaguer, and that aboard it the local police had discovered many kilos of cocaine base. After the first sensational exposure, the story was so rapidly and completely suppressed that neither the radio station, nor any of the newspapers, ever made another single mention of the subject. On my going round to the station's offices a few days later and inquiring after their source, they flatly denied that such a story had ever been broadcast at all. Nevertheless, local information from La Vega fully confirmed the occurrence, and the chief of police in that town was transferred out of the area shortly afterwards.

It must be pointed out that southern Cauca is the only part of Colombia where coca agriculture has been geared traditionally to the production and export of a surplus of coca leaves, and that all other areas of Indian or *campesino* cultivation produce only small quantities for local consumption, and for a strictly limited system of barter and exchange. The fact that coca and Cauca can be clearly associated in the public mind has therefore provided a perfect smokescreen, a diversion of interest away from what are probably the more significant illicit commercial operations. It is likely that

Owner of a small cocina producing unrefined cocaine base near Bolivar, southern Cauca.

many of the really large contemporary coca plantations in Colombia are to be found in areas where this plant has only recently — and only under the impulse of the cocaine industry — become a really significant agricultural crop. Colombian coca (**Erythroxylum novogranatense**) has a far greater ecological tolerance than the main economic species in Bolivia and Peru (**Erythroxylum coca**) and almost unlimited land is available for its cultivation in the dense forests of the Western Cordillera, the northern lowlands of the Magdalena drainage, and especially in the Orinoco and Amazon drainages to the east. One has only to remember the case of the twenty-seven thousand bushes discovered in a clearing in the Vaupés, to visualize what huge undertakings may be possible all over Colombia, far away from the show-piece Indian areas in the department of Cauca. To understand why such developments are possible, or indeed, even likely to occur, it is necessary to consider the broader economic context of the cocaine business — its role in providing extra-official funds to a ruling oligarchy not only keen for any kind of easy money, but also driven by historical circumstances to ever more desperate measures in its attempt to stem the tide of an inevitable social revolution.

COCAINE: THE POWER AND THE MONEY

Underpinning the entire structure of the cocaine business is the often neglected fact that this drug is rapidly becoming the single major trading commodity of all the Andean republics, and at a time when traditional exports are suffering heavily from the protectionism and economic depression of their established Western trading partners. It should be said, of course, that such exaggerated importance arises solely from the structural abnormalities of the present situation, dependent in turn on the fact that the anti-drug laws have themselves contributed significantly to the overall viability of the clandestine trade. The point is an important one, for how else could a New York market price of fifteen thousand dollars be maintained for a mere pound of cocaine, itself produced very simply from leaves worth little more than a meagre two hundred dollars at source?

While the mark-up per unit — or the accumulation of surplus value — is probably greater therefore than that of almost any other single product derived from natural resources, it is also equally true that the total volume of the cocaine trade still remains virtually impossible to calculate with any real exactitude. Of all the countries involved in the production of coca, only Peru has been fearless enough to publish its statistics, but in this case alone the figures are sufficiently dazzling to put the matter into a stark financial perspective. Approximately four million kilos of coca leaves are consumed annually by the Indians of the Peruvian Andes.[29] Allowing also for a legal — though hardly legitimate — intake of 770,000 kilos of coca by the manufacturers of Coca-Cola, and another 66,000 for the production of cocaine for pharmaceutical purposes, one is left with a total accountable consumption of coca which verges on the five million kilo mark.[30] It is only necessary to compare this with the estimates of Peru's total coca harvest to understand how great has been the expansion of the world demand for illicit cocaine in the last fifty years: for from a harvest of five million kilos in 1926, the quantity rises to ten million in 1950, and to a full twenty million in 1974.[31] This latter figure leaves a minimum of fifteen million kilos — a staggering three quarters of the total — for the extraction of illegal cocaine. Even applying the extremely conservative (0.5%) estimate of the final yield of refined alkaloid, the 1974 figures would indicate the production of at least eighty thousand kilos of cocaine from the Peruvian harvest alone, worth upwards of 250 million dollars within South America itself, and at least two billion dollars on delivery in the United States.

The significance of these earnings can readily be underlined by a comparison with the statistics for legitimate exports in 1973, which neither in the Peruvian nor in the Colombian case greatly exceeded the billion dollar mark.[32] The situation in neighbouring Bolivia is probably even more remarkable, for it has long been assumed that the size of the Bolivian coca harvest is rather larger than that of Peru. The only reasonable published assessment of Bolivia's illicit earnings through the export of cocaine put the figure at about 50 million dollars a month, which compares more than favourably with the country's rather paltry legitimate exports, whose total worth only reached 268 million dollars in 1973.[33]

Indeed, the influx of black-market dollars to many drug producing countries has had the somewhat paradoxical effect of keeping down the official exchange rate while at the same time boosting internal inflation. Fully 564 million dollars were cashed in at the banks for Colombian *pesos* by drug dealers in the first nine months of 1976 — as against only 164 million in the same period of 1974.[34] Unmistakeably, the sheer scale of these 'invisible' earnings allows many supposedly 'underworld' economic groups to expand their legitimate capital holdings almost indefinitely — and often, as the Peruvian case has recently illustrated, at the expense of their own central banks and officially constituted governments, which hover characteristically on the verge of bankruptcy, and virtually at the complete mercy of the International Monetary Fund.

As a result of their newly won but unassailable financial position, it is unlikely that any of the smuggling groups should actually feel very cramped by the attempts of their respective governments at control, always assuming that government and the smugglers are actually still separate organizations — an unlikely possibility, as we will attempt to demonstrate. In Colombia, for example, it has even become profitable to smuggle quite legitimate products, such as coffee, in order to avoid official taxes and bypass the inevitably bureaucratic hassles involved in dealing over — rather than under — the table. In the year ending in September, 1976, illegal exports of coffee accounted for an astonishing 27% of all Colombian coffee reaching the United States. The sheer quantity involved — 670,000 sacks, weighing 60 kilos each — makes a few thousand kilos of cocaine, or a few hundred tons of marijuana, seem like child's play in comparison, and perfectly illustrates the unwillingness or incapacity of the Colombian authorities to stem the flow of the illicit trade. After all, the class interests of the bourgeois state and those of the country's exporting oligarchy have always tended to coincide, and the growth of the drug smuggling business cannot really have done too much to upset this traditionally close relationship. In such a context, to speak of a drug-trafficking 'underworld' can only be seen as a deliberate act of mystification on the part of a government already compromised to the hilt.

A sharing of common class interests, however, does not exclude a certain amount of armed confrontation between separate outfits vying for overall control of the entire illegal enterprise. Nor does it protect the smuggling groups from the occasional troublesome intrusion of members of the Colombian ruling classes with genuine moral scruples. The assassination of General Rincón in 1975 has already been mentioned as one case where the drug-trafficking organizations took the law into their own hands, and a similar case has occurred more recently, in July 1977, when the same groups murdered the chief of operations at the national civil aviation board in Bogotá, Colonel Osiris Maldonado, and through their contacts in the media had the crime attributed to the 'guerillas', in a repetition of the smear tactics used in the Rincón case as well.[35]

Such is the fate which awaits any investigator too keenly concerned with uncovering the specific details of the organization of the drug business. It is not, therefore, very surprising that few such details have ever succeeded in being openly discussed in public. In the absence of any inside information, the precise social composition and political profile of the smuggling groups can only be analyzed in terms of their economic power, a power virtually unparalleled in all the recent history of South America, and which is all the more dangerous since it operates within the context of autocracies which have always bent a more favourable and sympathetic ear to the demands of capital than to the modest aspirations of the common people. The whole elaborate farce of the war on drugs is itself part and parcel of a deliberate misrepresentation of political realities, for in stressing the threat to national institutions which is posed by the 'parallel' power structures of the underworld, the orthodox view seeks only to deny what is already patently obvious — namely, that the smuggling interests have already prevailed, already succeeded in penetrating, corrupting and subverting the entire fabric of the state. Indeed, the very idea of a 'parallel' power structure serves no other purpose than to lend credibility to the laughable notion that legitimate and illicit economic groups are still, in some sense, actually competing with each other.

In repudiating this fictional scenario, with its image of a criminal and marginalized drug-trafficking underworld, it should be stressed that in South America any industry as important as that of cocaine will inevitably tend to remain in the hands of the same political and social elite who control all the continent's other major resources. Rather than allow such a very lucrative undertaking to fall into the hands of mere petty gangsters and rebellious youths, the native oligarchy is driven to control the trade not only for the considerable pecuniary rewards, but also for straightforward motives of 'national security'. As the Palestinians have already demonstrated with regard to the Lebanese hashish trade, anybody with access to the sort of economic power created by illicit drug earnings could pose a truly significant threat to the already highly unstable equilibrium of the established order.[36]

It is in this light that sensationalist accounts of supposed high-level 'corruption' should be seen. Scarcely a single governing body in South America has not at one time or another been wracked by noisy scandals associating leading public figures with the drug traffic. Some are so sensitive to this kind of adverse publicity that the mere mention of suspicion on the part of a foreign journalist is often sufficient for the offending party to be expelled from the country immediately. Such was the fate of an UPI reporter who dared to ask the president of a new military junta about his alleged ties to the drug business at a press conference in Quito, Ecuador, in January, 1976.[37]

The truth of the situation is that no government can possibly afford to relinquish control of the drug trade, and in almost every case where broad publicity has been given to a particular instance of individual corruption, this publicity has obeyed the need to find a scapegoat, or to acquire some moral advantage over a political rival. Often the victims are entirely innocent; a case in point is provided by the arrest of Dr. Oswaldo Pérez, a Marxist academic who was later appointed Rector of the Universidad Nacional in Bogotá. On the morning of August 4th, 1973, Pérez was arrested on the street in broad daylight and charged with the possession of two kilos of cocaine. The fact that the incriminating substance had not been apprehended on his person was explained away by the F-2 police, who claimed that Pérez had thrown away the bag on being approached by law enforcement officers. The ageing scholar was forced to spend a considerable period in gaol before his name was finally cleared, and in the meantime the press had a field day tying his 'communist sympathies' to his 'known links' with the international drug-trafficking 'mafia'. The incidental detail of his arrest being planned under the active encouragement of an American narcotics agent was, of course, only made public after the case had been thrown out of court.[38] Two years later, under the state-of-siege provisions for court-martial in all drug offenses, Pérez may not have been so lucky.

Blatant scapegoating of this kind tends, however, to be the exception rather than the rule, and it is often possible to detect the real interests behind the drug business by taking careful note of the details which surface in individual cases of proven corruption and in the many accusations and counter-accusations which emerge in periods of heavy political in-fighting. A recent example is provided by the struggle for the Liberal nomination for the coming Colombian presidential elections of 1978. The ex-president Carlos Lleras Restrepo and his mouthpiece, the Bogotá daily El Tiempo, have dedicated considerable attention to exposing the links which their rival, Julio César Turbay Ayala, maintains with the smuggling groups on the Caribbean coast.[39] Such muck-raking, and the incidental information it provides on the organization of the drug business, is one of the advantages of the Colombian system of old-style bandit democracy, and similar exposés are unfortunately rather less common in the more monolithic military regimes which rule the roost in the other cocaine-producing or exporting countries further south.

In these countries, the already beleagured civilians have been almost completely excluded from any participation in the political process, and — in keeping with the model already examined in the case of the Colombian state-of-siege legislation it is the court-martial and the military high command which have themselves taken over the definition of legality in the drug business. Institutionalized corruption has become the very *modus operandi* of the authoritarian state, with the simple result that scandals are restricted to discussion only within the general staff, and are seldom, if ever, ventilated in public at all. In Lima, rumours regarding this or that general's participation in the cocaine trade are common currency in the polite salons of San Isidro or Miraflores, but hardly ever do these rumours appear in the press, and nobody with a concern for his own health and safety would ever dare investigate the accusations in any detail. Nobody even bothers to point out one obvious fact; that the legal precedent for a military take-over of the cocaine business was already enshrined in Decreto-Ley number 11046, the decree which set up the state coca monopoly on June 13th, 1949. The military junta of the time — led by General Odría — clearly specified that all the profits of the coca monopoly, under the terms of article 6 of the decree, were to be applied exclusively to 'the construction and maintenance of military barracks'. It is small wonder, therefore, that Peru seldom makes the headlines with anything like the impact that its crucial role in the cocaine business would seem to justify.

Woman helping herself to coca from her *pircha,* Caquiona, southern Cauca.

Something of a similar conspiracy of silence also operates within the dictatorship exercised by General Stroessner in Paraguay, a country which — although it produces little cocaine of its own — is virtually the continental crossroads for all forms of illicit commerce. Contraband is here the major industry, a national institution, and its control is divided between Stroessner himself and General Andres Rodríguez, the commander of the cavalry barracks in Asunción. Disgusted with American exposures of his smuggling empire, this latter figure even allowed himself the luxury of snubbing General William B. Rosson, commander-in-chief of U.S. Forces in Central and South America, refusing him entry to the cavalry barracks in Asunción in August, 1974, when the American was in Paraguay on an official visit. The *gringo* general left the country three days ahead of schedule, reputedly incensed at the off-hand treatment he had received from the smuggling king. Closing their ranks against the common external threat, Stroessner and Rodríguez decided to put an end to the conflicts and competition between their respective organizations. In April, 1977, Stroessner's son married Rodríguez's daughter, thus cementing a single monopoly over the entire smuggling operation in Paraguay. A humourous touch was given to the proceedings by the fact that the President's son, Hugo Stroessner, was at that time in Madrid trying to kick an unfortunate drug addiction, and the wedding had to be postponed until he returned.[40] A delicious, surreptitious titter spread through the embassy drawingrooms in Asunción . . .

In the case of many other countries, one must usually wait for changes of government before being able to uncover a retrospective view of events. The Chilean example is particularly enlightening in this respect, as a very different type of coverage was given by the bourgeois media to the frankly dubious evidence of drug trafficking by members of Allende's Unidad Popular administration, and to the much more concrete examples of racketeering by the subsequent neo-fascist junta of General Pinochet. In July, 1974, the Colombian conservative press indicated a good deal of space to a report from Washington which quoted a Chilean Embassy official as claiming before a U.S. Congressional committee that Allende had financed his election campaign with money made in the cocaine business. Other than accusing Allende of being a moderate user himself, the source also cited cases where his police had refused to cooperate with Interpol on occasions when Chilean couriers had been intercepted abroad with shipments of cocaine.

Given Allende's quite legitimate suspicions of foreign security organizations, these revelations were not in themselves terribly astounding, nor were they backed up by concrete evidence of the President's own direct involvement. Indeed, the most significant aspect of the case was that although the accusations had been made in Congress in May, they were only deemed worthy of release to the public precisely during this first week in July. The root cause of this was not difficult to ascertain. Three days previously, the press had reported what must have been one of the biggest and most embarrassing diplomatic busts of all time. The victims on this occasion had not been members of Allende's entourage, but rather, a number of diplomats and military attaches working in the Chilean embassy in Washington, this being by now almost a year since the puppet regime had taken power in Chile.

The quantity involved — no less than 162 pounds — was sufficiently large to warrant a number of categorical denials and shame-faced dismissals on the part of the Chilean junta. The United States gave their new political allies an opening to save face, and the chief narcotics supervisor, John Bartels, and the Chilean ambassador made a joint statement denouncing the fact that diplomatic bags and military planes had been used to smuggle huge amounts of cocaine from Chile to the United States.[41] Needless to say, the matter was quickly dropped by the media, the flimsy accusations against Allende were correspondingly widely publicized, and by the end of 1974 the American narcs were claiming that the flow of cocaine from Chile had been reduced to a small trickle. Considering how many brazen lies the U.S. Government was then perpetuating with regard to recent events in that unhappy republic, their claim could only be considered of dubious merit, to say the least.

It is, however, from neighbouring Argentina that the most astounding revelations of high-level involvement in the cocaine business have been forthcoming — not, admittedly, with regard to the highly paranoid, super-secretive present military rulers, but to the equally sanguinary thugs and gangsters who predominated in the latter period of Isabel Perón's presidency. The story was exposed by military intelligence in the lead up to the coup of 1976, and involved a number of leading figures on the right wing of the Peronista movement, including the infamous minister of social welfare, López Rega, the foreign minister, Alberto Vignes, and a host of secondary figures such as minister Raul Lastiri, senator Cornejo Linares, the director of the 'El Tribuno' newspaper, Roberto Romero, and the commander of the military 'intervention' in the provincial administration of Córdoba, Colonel Raul Lacabanne.[42]

Operating a series of well-equipped cocaine laboratories near Salta, on the Bolivian border, these figures controlled a wide-ranging network which made use of the Federal Police for internal distribution within the country, and the cover of the diplomatic service for the consolidation of a safe route for exports. In a seemingly labyrinthine web of intrigue and corruption, federal authority was used to silence the troublesome and inquisitive provincial legislature in Salta, members of the local judiciary were scared off by machine gun attacks, and eventually one faction of the Armed Forces themselves were enticed into taking a piece of the action. It would not, in fact, be unfair to suggest that the fall of López Rega and Isabel Perón may well have been occasioned — among other things — by the same type of military take-over of the cocaine business which has already been suggested for most of the other countries with access to the Andean coca harvest.

Another perfect example of this process was provided by General Hugo Banzer's coup d'etat in Bolivia in 1971. Emerging from a stronghold in the nouveau riche cocaine-manufacturing town of Santa Cruz de la Seirra, Banzer's command of crack anti-insurgency troops — the U.S.-trained Bolivian Rangers — were forced into bloody confrontation not only with the politically astute miners' and peasants' unions, but also with a considerable section of the more nationalist members of the Armed Forces. On finally capturing La Paz, Banzer proceeded to purge a large part of the officer class, and institute a system of government-by-mafia which is almost a caricature even among the already horrifying array of tragi-comic military regimes spawned in recent years throughout the continent.

Admittedly, I bear Banzer's dictatorship a very personal grudge, for I was myself arrested on the streets of La Paz in that same year of 1971. All the same, I can state without equivocation that the colonel seconded at that time to the local Interpol office in the Palacio de la Policía was very keen to point out to me that the Bolivian cocaine business operated under his own direct and personal supervision. Gesturing at his files and describing his system of 'approved buyers', he made the distinction between undesirable cocaine merchants — young, independent dealers, such as I aspired to become at that time — and the more acceptable and regular connections which he maintained with the security forces of other neighbouring countries. He must have felt reasonably secure in his position to make such a frank statement of his methods of doing business, or possibly he was just giving voice to an access of cocaine-induced megalomania. It was hardly surprising, therefore, to read in 1974 that one Alberto Sánchez Bello had been arrested smuggling cocaine into Canada while travelling on a diplomatic passport given to him by the private secretary of President Banzer himself. One could not help being reminded of the figure of the drug-smuggling ambassador of Miranda, played by Fernando Rey in Bunuels film 'Le Charme Discret de la Bourgeoisie.'

THE INFLUENCE OF THE CONSUMER MARKET

It is very easy, when confronted by the almost unbelievable extent of the corruption financed by cocaine within the South American political process, to imagine that the whole set-up is somehow part of an alien tradition — as pathetic and idiosyncratic as the continent's historic propensity for palace revolutions and blood-soaked military coups. To fall back on such stereotypes, however, only serves to obscure the fact that the militarization of the 1970s is quantitatively and qualitatively different to all previous manifestations of the same spirit. For it heralds not just another temporary hiatus in the political life of the people, not just another passing interval of what has been fondly described as 'stabilization', but rather, must be seen as the last ditch stand of a class determined to defend its privileges to the last bullet and the last torture chamber. The rapidly accumulating crisis of industrial capitalism, the stiffening resolve of all genuinely revolutionary and progressive forces, and the gathering impetus of a war of liberation which stands poised to spread from Africa and Asia into the very belly of America itself — all these are factors which distinguish the present context from that of twenty or even ten years ago. The oligarchy may have succeeded in defeating the mass movements of the 1960s, in scoring a tactical victory over the armed vanguards of one generation, but it has done so at the expense of a complete loss of political legitimacy and public credibility. As a result, the dominant classes have been cornered, forced into a permanent state of siege — their policies of brutal internal repression being mirrored in the economic field by a weak-kneed capitulation to the interests of imperialism, by an abject surrender of national resources to the voracious consumer needs of the overdeveloped industrial nations. In South America today, literally everything is for sale.

It is within this context of impotent dependence on external markets and foreign creditors that the rise of the military-dominated cocaine business must be seen. True, it is only the latest in a series of depredations which have included at different times virtually all the mineral and agricultural resources of the continent, but it is a particularly clear example of the process of neo-colonial pillage, and all the more alarming since it operates under the protective cloak of illegality. It is important to stress that the entire organization as it stands today — with its cast of vicious generals and two-faced politicians — has not been produced as the result of any indigenous evolution of the coca and cocaine business, but on the contrary, depends for its very life-blood on its market, the well-heeled cocaine users of Europe and North America. A few years ago many of these people probably imagined — and with some reason, for it was largely true — that they and their purchases were supporting a rather romantic bunch of smugglers and latter-day pirates, the last exponents of a vigorous tradition of entrepreneurial capitalism. In the present context such an attitude is plainly no longer tolerable or excusable, for it betrays a profound ignorance and irresponsibility, as well as contributing directly to the maintenance of a society in which fellow drug users are themselves victimized, and drug producers are subject to some of the most savage regimes in their entire history.

It would, therefore, be interesting to consider the manner in which pressures generated in the centres of consumption have come to influence the organization of the cocaine business overall, for it can be shown that there is more than an incidental similarity between the various different components of the scene. There is, indeed, an element of synchronicity in the developments observable in different parts of the Americas, some underlying current which binds the Colombian process already described above — its evolution out of an originally anarchic and diffuse situation towards the kind of increasingly militarized and monolithic organizations common today — with similar trends in other South American republics, and particularly with the reorganization which has taken place in the domestic cocaine business within the United States.

The clearest example of this is provided by the city of New York, probably the world's major centre of illicit cocaine consumption. During 1971, the period of my own amateur participation in the smuggling business, it seemed that a great deal of the coke available on the streets of Manhattan had arrived there as the result of basically small-scale endeavours, such as those with which I was incidentally involved. That this opinion is not merely a personal and biased interpretation of events could also be supported by reference to a study undertaken by Richard Ashley, a New Yorker who has written an excellent popular history of the use of cocaine in the United States.[43]

Though personally I have kept well away from the coke dealing scene in New York since 1971, it would appear from Ashley's account that a lot has changed since that time. He describes 'the virtual decimation of a whole class of dealers'[44] as a process which had already been effectively completed by 1973, as heavily armed hoodlums scared the amateurs off the market. He adds a significant detail on the ethnic identity of the groups who took over the business: 'I do know that it was the Cubans who drove out most of the white middle-class cocaine dealers in New York.'[45] As a result of the Cuban takeover, the situation by the time of his writing (1974) was one in which 'the cocaine trade is largely in the hands of organized crime . . . ', and where 'the product is inferior and the prices very high.'[46]

It would be tempting to consider what this preponderance of the Cubans in the East Coast cocaine business means, when seen in the light of the effective monopolization of the sources of cocaine by the security forces in South America. In the first place, one should examine the origins of the Cuban underworld itself, the organizations which have sprung up among the exile communities of Florida, New Jersey and New York City. Their own native island, tired of the corrupt practices which flourished under Batista's reign of terror, expelled most of the old Havana racketeers, the pimps, casino operators and drug traffickers who were known collectively as *gusanos*, or worms. It was these supposedly 'democratic' elements who were given a new home in the United States, and CIA cover under which to organize their eventual recovery of the island. Many had learnt invaluable dirty tricks from the Cosa Nostra family of Santo Trafficante Jr., who had once been the representative of the 'Lucky' Luciano/Meyer Lansky syndicate in Havana, and who continued to run his operations from Florida after the revolution.[47]

Like the Sicilian and Corsican mafias, the Cubans quickly learnt how to exploit the CIA's political sensibilities to their own advantage. The New York Times reported that 'among those who have moved into the drug trade are certain members of the ill-fated Assault Brigade 2506, which landed at the Bay of Pigs on April 17, 1961.' Military security, an unquestioned principle of Cuban amphibious operations off the coast of Florida, could equally well be used as a shield to ward off embarrassing searches from U.S. Coast Guard and Customs services. American narcotics officials have always been adamant in their assertion that most of the coke which enters the United States does so through the Cuban community in Florida.[48]

It is not in fact unusual that CIA cover should have been used to protect huge drug trafficking operations. Alfred McCoy published in 1972 an exhaustive treatment of this very theme, in which he described an astonishing degree of official American involvement in shoring up the organization of the heroin business in Marseilles and South East Asia. It would not be unfair to suggest that there exist a number of clear parallels to McCoy's argument in the activities of such outfits as the Colombian DAS secret police force, and in those of the various reactionary power-groups which have recently risen to pre-eminence in the Armed Forces of most other South American countries as well. It would be difficult, of course, to prove the direct participation of the CIA in the day-to-day running of the cocaine business, though individual suspected agents, such as Mike Tsalickis of Leticia, Colombia, have sometimes been indicted in the context of big-time smuggling.[49] In any case, direct circumstantial evidence of the CIA's support for cocaine traffickers is hardly necessary at this stage, for the simultaneous spread of the drug industry and right-wing terror throughout the continent is itself explicit enough with regard to the United States' key role in the affair, whether or not the initiative is being directly routed through the CIA.

Indeed, there are many indications that a good deal of the activities traditionally associated with the CIA are now being handled by that new monster agency, the Drug Enforcement Administration (DEA), whose activities in 'controlling' the flow of drugs to the U.S.A. have also inevitably expanded into other areas of political and economic repression, many of which are not even directly related to the drugs issue at all. The American narcotics forces have been marked by a far from illustrious history, and it is scarcely surprising that they are held in almost complete discredit even by their own fellow citizens and brother security officers. In the aftermath of a series of scandals in 1968, which uncovered the participation of the old Federal Bureau of Narcotics in the lucrative New York heroin market, the Bureau of Narcotics and Dangerous Drugs was formed, and placed under the relatively competent management of John Ingersoll. By 1972, the BNDD had scored a number of notable successes in their war on narcotics, principally in their much publicized offensive against the Marseilles heroin laboratories.

In the short space of 1973, however, the emphasis on heroin suddenly changed, and a number of wasteful exercises were directed instead at the far less threatening 'menaces' of marihuana and cocaine. In the meantime, Mexican syndicates began to flood the market with crude brown heroin, which was both more plentiful and much more dangerous than the previous supplies from the Near East and South East Asia. At the bottom of these events lay the administrative reorganization of the BNDD, which was reformed under President Nixon's initiative into a new super-agency known as the Drug Enforcement Administration.

The advent of this outfit effectively emasculated U.S. Customs of any drug-enforcement capability, and furthermore, gave the White House, then in a hey-day of absolute power, its own carefully groomed force within the rapidly mushrooming police superstructure at the Justice Department. Ingersoll resigned in the middle of this process, accusing Nixon of intervention and outright manipulation of his Bureau. The likelihood of any American narcotics agent ever embarrassing Washington's political allies in the drug-producing nations was countered by the formation of a Cabinet Committee on International Narcotics Control. Its policy was to be determined by such notably sensitive individuals as Henry Kissinger and the head of the CIA, neither of whom were figures particularly well known for their concern about the drug traffic.[50]

In other words, the year 1973 not only witnessed the reorganization of the domestic cocaine and heroin markets in the hands of known pro-*yanqui* racketeers such as the Cuban and Mexican mafias, but also demonstrated the complete subjection of the American drug problem to the crude interests of Kissinger diplomacy. The DEA offensive which began to bear down on Latin America could be identified as little more than a public relations front, a smokescreen directed at maintaining appearances while the bulk of the drug trade was concentrated in the hands of a 'security'-conscious native elite.

It is clear that this situation explains much of the implicit motivation behind the terrifying array of abuses practiced by the DEA, and reported to the Jackson sub-committee during its Senate hearings on the subject in the summer of 1975. Torture and outright assassination have been used by many of the CIA's local allies in the Latin American police and Armed Forces, and it is clear that such practices are becoming commonplace, even routine, in the narcotics cases handled by the DEA.[51] Furthermore, the misuse of drug surveillance as a means of political control has led to repeated suggestions that the DEA is simply a new spy agency, an alternative pretext for meddling in local politics, especially in the light of recent sensibilities about the activities of the CIA. At the beginning of 1975, the DEA announced that it was going to hire 53 ex-CIA agents, a public gesture whose intended significance it would be difficult to ignore. The logic behind such a move was expressed by the then vice-president, Nelson Rockefeller, in his White Paper on Drug Abuse: 'By providing additional training to U.S. agents abroad in intelligence collection needs and techniques, intelligence could be a more effective tool in deterring the flow of drugs to the U.S.'[52]

As a result, the DEA has stationed at least 287 agents in different U.S. Embassies around the world, and has trained upwards of 9,000 foreign narcs in an attempt to encourage 'greater cooperation between them and American enforcement officials'. The effects of all this have been predictable; an increasing victimization of drug users, cultivators and small-scale dealers, coupled with a marked increase in the total flow of drugs and in the power wielded by the few monopolies which the DEA dare not touch. Rumour would have it that the DEA has itself been involved in smuggling drugs into the United States in order to set up local buyers and entrap them, and the DEA's first director, John Bartels, was forced to resign in May, 1975, after blocking an internal investigation into one of his protégés intimate links with organized crime and the large dealing syndicates. The very administrative reorganization which produced the DEA in the first place had given it sole authority to collect foreign intelligence and orientate foreign police forces; a capacity which supplemented its internal operations, it is true, but which at the same time removed the right of the U.S. Customs to conduct its own overseas intelligence and domestic follow-up activities. With inconsistent coordination between DEA and Customs, the chief Congressional investigator, Philip R. Manuel, was forced to conclude: '. . . this method of operation has prolonged old interagency rivalries, created new ones and has thus far actually weakened this nation's capacity to interdict the flow of narcotics into the U.S.'[53]

Recent articles on the DEA's domestic activities have concentrated on its use of gratuitous violence and intimidation, its emphasis on 'head counts' and other facile statistics which reflect its almost exclusive concern with small-time busts, and in particular, its failure to deal effectively with either the heroin problem or the more powerful smuggling operations. These abuses are certainly bad enough in themselves, but perhaps even more horrifying has been the DEA's recent slide into an overseas role as the channel for official U.S. funds into the hands of extreme reactionary groups who have been specifically black-listed by the American people's representatives in the Congress and the Senate.

Events in Argentina over the last four years have demonstrated very clearly how the narcotics pretext can be used as a front to provide support to right-wing hoodlums whose overt association with the U.S. Embassy might otherwise prove embarrassing in Washington. By means of the loophole provided by the anti-drug campaign, the State Department's International Narcotics Control Program was able to take over the funding of a good deal of police equipment destined for Argentina, equipment which had been specifically blocked by Congress when it abolished the discredited Office of Public Safety. A total of twelve and a half million dollars were granted in this way to the Argentine police in 1974, mainly through the funnel provided by the minister of Social Welfare, the infamous López Rega. It will be remembered that it was this same individual — and his allies in the Federal Police force — who were later accused by military intelligence of being the single major beneficiaries of the export drive in cocaine which Argentina was beginning to launch on the world at that precise moment. All of this certainly did not disturb either the DEA or the American ambassador in Buenos Aires, Robert Hill, who appeared on Argentine television with López Rega in May 1974, and encouraged him to make the patently absurd assertion:

> 'We have caught guerillas after attacks who were high on drugs. Guerillas are the main users of drugs in Argentina. Therefore, the anti-drug campaign will automatically be an anti-guerilla campaign as well.'[54]

While making pious statements of this kind in public — and privately lining his pockets with the huge profits of the cocaine operation — López Rega applied the narcotics enforcement money to the financing of his own death-squad and terrorist organization, the Alianza Anticomunista Argentina (AAA), and encouraged the Argentine Federal Police to take on a much more active counterinsurgency role. Even the eventual fall of López Rega probably did little to change the nature of the winning combination he had made between the extreme right-wing security forces and the Argentine drug business. As recently as February, 1977, the foreign minister of the new military junta was quoted as repeating the by now familiar refrain:

> 'We attack its body through the war against guerillas, and its spirit through the war against the drug traffic, both carriers of nihilistic and collectivist ideas.'[55]

Such a deliberate and arrogant recourse to scapegoating — and the almost hysterical fear and obscurantism it betrays — can only be the justification for yet another major onslaught on the youthful, revolutionary forces in South America, and for the continued and deliberate use of the narcotics pretext for the sake of political control. The DEA-sponsored continental conference on the drug traffic, held in Cochabamba, Bolivia, in July, 1975, paved the way for the institution of a truly monstrous international repressive apparatus, one which undermines the most fundamental principles of human rights and international law — including, as it does, the recognition of the need for "hot pursuit" across national frontiers, the use of simplified regional extradition treaties for narcotics 'offenders', the creation of a regional communications network for the rapid exchange of 'actionable intelligence', and the reciprocal accreditation of 'narcotics attachés' between the various police forces throughout the continent.

Criticism of this horrendous package has always been couched in terms acceptable to the straight left and other 'concerned' sections of the liberal intelligentsia, stressing not so much the intrinsic terrors of any such excess of repressive zeal, as the rather more acceptable truth that the whole hideous machine is likely to get into the 'wrong' hands and be used for the 'wrong' purposes. In other words, could we be sure that the narcs were playing a straight game, the issues would be clear and everything would be alright. After all, the liberal argument goes, the only victims then would be hard-core criminals, drug dealers and other alienated undesirables, persons who in terms of current sociological orthodoxy have already forfeited any right to be considered human beings at all. Such an attitude deserves to be roundly challenged and exposed for what it is, little more than another odious example of the ethic of the strong State, the dictatorship of petit-bourgeois moralism.

The fact remains that the enforced denial of drug-taking is *itself* an act of political repression, itself an intolerable infringement of the dignity of the individual and, particularly, of his freedom to treat his body as his own. This is not to deny that drug abuse is often dangerous and socially disruptive, but the point is surely that not all use is necessarily abuse. Virtually the world's entire population employ drugs of one sort or another every day, with widely differing effects both to themselves and to society. In that case, what is obviously required is not so much a further tightening of demonstrably ineffective legal controls, as a positive orientation in the use of drugs, education which attempts to point out the advantages of informal — that is to say, non-authoritarian — controls of the drug experience, controls which arise spontaneously out of the experience of the drug-takers themselves, out of their own recognition of the limits to the usefulness of each particular drug in question.

In the present situation, however, any such enlightened orientation is entirely lacking, and it is precisely the drug-takers who are most consistently victimized and discriminated against, for — unlike the large trafficking syndicates — they are powerless to oppose the ponderous progress of the narcotics bureaucracy, without voice to unmask the fact that they are being used simply as 'examples'. Indeed, were the laws against drugs to be applied with any integrity and honesty, a considerable slice of the world's population would have to be maintained permanently behind bars. As a result, the laws are only applied *selectively*, and used to weed out trouble-makers who might be capable of organizing some resistance to the brutal structure of the drug business as it is presently constituted. A corrupt narc is rarely 'busted', he is merely 'retired' — and the same goes for most of the other big wheels in the drug business, be they generals, senators, or under-cover CIA operatives. Who carries the can is always the lesser figure, the peasant producer or the small-scale dealer, or the universally ridiculed stereotype of the 'pathetic' youthful drug-taker.

Nowhere is this selective definition of criminality more glaringly apparent than in the treatment accorded to the Coca-Cola corporation in its use of the leaves of Trujillo coca — **Erythroxylum novogranatense** var. **truxillense**. Virtually all of the 770 tonnes of coca leaves legally exported from Peru every year are destined to the Coca-Cola factories, where their de-cocainized' essence forms the principal ingredient of that much over-rated substance known as 7X, the magic potion which gives Coke its zing. Quite apart from the fact that Coca-Cola thus has access to an immeasurable quantity of cocaine — the inevitable by-product of its extractive process — one should also consider the irony whereby the leaf itself is legally banned world-wide to all but this immensely powerful soft-drinks monopoly, allowing its properties to be commercialized exclusively by those who have the unbelievable arrogance of calling their adulterated soda pop the 'Real Thing'.

The preferential treatment accorded to the really big dealers in Coca-Cola — an ex-president of the corporation, Charles Duncan Jr., is today Carter's Deputy Defence Secretary at the Pentagon — is entirely symptomatic of the sort of double standard which prevails throughout the drug business. It would be interesting to consider, by way of comparison, the plight of the small dealer, the petty villain whose main virtue — apart from an often frank and sociable disposition — must surely be his enviable capacity to inspire sheer paroxysms of implacable hatred from the smug and the self-righteous. Even the most humane of card-carrying socialists would probably find it difficult to come up with a good word for this figure; and yet, their attitude of moral repudiation is quite inconsistent with their own stated ideals, for the lower echelon employees and entrepreneurs of the illicit drug business may well be one of the worst exploited groups in Western society. They have no union structure to press for a greater share of the trade's enormous profits, they have little control over the major decisions which affect their working life, and they may at any time suffer betrayal, murder, or imprisonment. Few are genuinely independent any more these days, and the majority must operate within a stucture determined by superiors who can, at the drop of a hat, ensure that any rebellious tendencies go rewarded with life imprisonment or a bullet in the back.

In Bolivia, for example, a death-squad composed of off-duty policemen — the Camba Civic Command — has recently been given the blessing of the authorities to gun down all drug traffickers without mercy.[56] Inevitably, the intended victims are not the police themselves, nor the members of the cabinet and the presidential entourage — the real beneficiaries of the cocaine business in that country — but rather, only the small-time street hustlers who fail to pay their dues. Similar forms of selective victimization are the stock-in-trade of the drugs enterprise throughout the world, and this would seem to constitute a deliberate policy on the part of those in power, for to operate within such an atmosphere of fear can only produce a dealing class which is atomized, neutralized, and rendered harmless to the system.

A similar motive lies behind the assault on youthful drug-users, a group who might otherwise begin to take matters into their own hands, as was clearly beginning to happen in the late 60s and early 70s. In South America the favourite victims are *gringos*, foreigners whose subsequent hassling of consular staff is obviously intended to convince international opinion that the local governments are actually 'doing something' about the drug scene. Over five hundred U.S. citizens are currently serving time in Mexican prisons for mostly insignificant drug offenses, close on a hundred have suffered the same fate in Colombia, and scores of others are rotting behind bars in virtually every other country in Latin America. The lucky ones manage to bribe their way out, the less fortunate are tortured, raped, and subjected to an almost Kafkaesque series of legal manoeuvres and bureaucratic delays. Even within the United States, the DEA has the constitutional power to entrap individuals by offering to sell them drugs, and the government can convict you of a conspiracy to import drugs despite the fact that the seizure of the drugs, the agreement on the conspiracy and the arrest of the defendants never took place in the United States at all.[57] Prosecution evidence in these cases is admissible even if the foreign policy used torture to obtain a 'confession'.

In all probability, however, it is not the affluent drug-consuming public of the developed countries which is likely to bear the full brunt of the current offensive. They are, after all, the market on which the entire structure is based, and by means of a spurious 'decriminalization' of possession they can be coaxed into a condition of mere passive consumerism — while the long arm of the law can be flexed to increase trafficking penalties, thus eliminating the more modest dealers and concentrating all the business in the hands of a few unassailable monopolies. One can only suspect that this new, 'liberal' policy has two major underlying motives: one being to maximize present-day profits, and the other to build up the structure of multinational concerns which, once they feel sure of their grip on the world market, will be able to bring about complete legalization without fear of small-scale, independent competition. It is no accident, therefore, that one of the prime growth areas in the development of a streamlined, disciplined drug industry involves precisely its efforts to spread tentacles into the producing areas, repeating the neo-colonial pattern already tried and tested in the case of commodity booms experienced in the past — such as those which sprung up around the consumption of 'non-drug' drug plants like chocolate, tea, coffee, and tobacco.

As has already been demonstrated with regard to the coca-producing districts of southern Cauca, a disciplined industry of this kind requires undisputed access to raw materials — and, since drug plants such as coca and marijuana are generally pretty easy to cultivate, a necessary corollary of this is the elimination of any producers who still choose to sell their harvests on the open market. Means to achieve this end have included the use of napalm and defoliating agents to destroy large plantations from the air, and biological research into the breeding of new monster insects which will consume smaller groups of particular drug plants that would otherwise escape detection. Further to the threat which such techniques present to the livelihood of peasant cultivators, one should also consider the irreparable ecological havoc they can cause over large areas, destroying subsistence crops and poisoning the water, the livestock and ultimately the human inhabitants as well.

Were not such forms of economic warfare already sufficient herald of the increasing Vietnamization of Latin America, there has recently been another movement afoot as well, one which would actually use the drugs issue as a pretext for expropriating peasants of their land, without giving them any compensation. In Colombia, the Minister of Justice promulgated a series of arbitrary 'determinations' at the end of July, 1974, which were a foretaste of things to come. The most important clause read: 'Land which is used for the cultivation of marihuana, coca, or similar items (*sic*) will be confiscated outright. The property will be placed out of all commercial activity as soon as the crime has been discovered.'[58]

The common citizen, therefore, will not only have to suffer imprisonment for growing basically harmless plants, but he will also lose his land and have his entire source of income frozen as well. In other words, the state authorities have every legal right to utterly destroy such an individual as an active member of his society. And the stipulation on coca, in particular, can only be considered deliberately alarming, for it threatens the very territorial integrity of a good number of Indian reservations. Of course, one returns again to the point that such laws can only be *selectively* applied, for their universal application in such a country as Colombia could only usher in a period of blood-letting which would make the *Violencia* of the 40s and 50s look like a tea-party.

There are, however, those who would welcome a chance to extend their private empires by using the drugs pretext as a means of expropriation, whatever the ultimate cost might be in terms of human life. This much, at least, was suggested by Senator José Guillermo Castro, a member of the leading land-owning family of Valledupar, at the foot of the Sierra Nevada de Santa Marta. Smarting from a refusal by the Indians of the Sierra Nevada to give him their vote in the 1974 Colombian elections, he stated bluntly:

> 'It is known that behind all this there is a huge business in cocaine and marihuana, cultivated in the Sierra Nevada . . . This should be investigated, as should the landing each week of a light plane . . . which, it seems, takes away marihuana in order to leave, according to reliable information, guns for the Indians, who have been walking about permanently armed for some time now . . .'[59]

Needless to say, the Senators version of events hardly fits with independent reports from the same area, which describe the violent intimidation of the Indians by the police of Valledupar, anxious to defend the huge estates carved out of the Indian reservations by families such as the Castros. Nor does it tally with the known extent of the drug business in the Santa Marta area, whose key role in the trans-Caribbean traffic would tend to imply that it is in the hands of organizations considerably more powerful than mere rural communities of Indians and poverty-stricken peasants.

Indeed, the point is not to discover which of the conflicting parties are actually telling the truth at all, but rather, to examine the words which the people in power are using, to perceive the sort of values which they are assuming, to uncover the ultimate horror-show scenarios that they seem to be warming up for. Transparent paranoiacs that they are, the ruling classes in South America are nearly always driven to project and betray their own worst intentions — and therefore, when they speak of drugs, they speak also of guns, of violence, of the need for 'investigation' or 'actionable intelligence'. The drug issue merely becomes confused in their minds with all the other cutting edges of social conflict, all the other excuses used since time immemorial to justify crude totalitarianism and a dull, myopic imagination. It should come as no surprise, in that case, if the dope wars only turn out to be the prelude to a far more terrible conflagration; one which will only be avoided if drug users in the Western conurbations raise their collective consciousness regarding the business as a whole, and take a firm, unequivocal stand not only on the interests of the consumer, but on those of the voiceless, marginalized producer as well.

ABAJO EL IMPERIALISMO DE LA COCA
LA COCA PARA QUIEN SABE MASCARLA

POSTSCRIPT TO CHAPTER IV

Colombia's key position in the world drug traffic has continued to invite the attention of journalists both within the country and abroad. Articles that have come my way since this chapter was written include:

'Quién es la mafia?' in 'Alternativa' no. 106, 8th November 1976, which discusses an earlier report by Albert Goldmann, a lecturer at the University of Columbia, which had been published in an October, 1976, issue of 'New York' magazine. Comparing the 'monumental corruption' of Colombia with that which existed in Chicago in the 1920s, 'Alternativa' pointed out the proven complicity of Barrera Domínguez — a magistrate on the Colombian Supreme Court — and quoted the ex-chief of DAS, General Matallana, as saying that above a certain level the heads of the cocaine business were 'untouchable'. Another article in 'Alternativa' no. 111, December 1976, entitled 'El ano de la corrupción', listed a number of other examples of official corruption: the use of the Colombian flagship 'Gloria' and the Navy Destroyer 'Santader' to smuggle cocaine; the facility with which a military judge had released from prison a number of key figures in the Santa Marta drug business; the accusation from a leading banker, Copete Lizarralda, that 'mafia capital' was taking over the country's financial institutions; and the assertion of the Federación de Cafeteros that the Banco de la República (the State-owned central bank) was helping the drug smugglers by buying their black-market dollars through the 'back door' (*ventanilla siniestra*).

Even the normally spineless New York magazine 'High Times' saw fit — in their March, 1977 issue — to publish an article called 'The Rise of the Dope Dictators: How the Dope War replaced the Cold War — a study in U.S. Foreign policy' by Robert Singer. Despite the rather facile simplifications of its political analysis, the article must be commended for its attempt to drive home the point to the dumb, blue-eyed American consumer that: 'In the years to come, the rhetoric of the Dope War will replace the rhetoric of the Cold War as a justification for foreign military intervention. Instead of sending in the Marines, Washington will send in the narcs.' Citing the precedent of Operation Buccaneer in Jamaica (June to December, 1974) and the offensive currently underway in the dope-producing areas of western Mexico — where, among other horrors, the use of banned herbicides such as Agent Orange are likely to produce lasting birth defects in the local human population — Singer showed how the narcotics pretext was being used to unleash a new form of economic warfare in areas traditionally held to be vital to the interests of U.S. security.

Significantly, the extension of such a pattern to Colombia was announced at the end of August, 1977 (see 'Latin America Commodities Report', 2nd September 1977) with the news that special anti-drug helicopters with trained advisors were being given by the United States to aid local narcotics agencies in their 'War on Drugs'. The cold logic of the anti-drug campaign seems, therefore, likely to become a major component of the new, supposedly 'liberal' Carter doctrine towards Latin America. This much, at least, can also be demonstrated by the case of Bolivia, where an agreement signed with the U.S. Government on 6th April 1977 has paved the way for an USAID scheme to erradicate the cultivation of coca in that country. The local peasants' union — the Confederación de Trabajadores Campesinos — has already stated its intention of fighting the proposals, pointing out that coca is not only an important aid to the diet and well-being of virtually all the rural population of Bolivia, but also that it forms the major cash crop for a large population of peasant farmers in the *yungas* (see 'Latin America Commodities Report', 13th May 1977.) And it is encouraging that the lead against U.S. drug policies is being taken by peasant organizations, for — as the Mexican and Jamaican experiences have already proved — such policies will only produce an increasing victimization of those sections of the drug-producing peasantry who still remain independent, coupled with the continued strengthening and enrichment of those who enjoy the support of figures in high places, and comply with the political status quo.

One thing, at least, is certain; the yankee government's campaign against drugs is in no sense reducing the overall profitability of the business: In an article entitled 'Colombian drug smuggling outpaces coffee earnings', the Latin America Commodities Report (3rd June 1977) estimated drug earnings in that country to rise from US$1,200 million in 1976 to US$3,000 million in 1977, as against legitimate coffee exports of US$930 million (1976) and US$2,000 million (1977, estimated). Rather more alarming, there are indications that Colombia is beginning to follow the lead taken by Mexico five years ago, and will soon be growing large quantities of opium poppies for the production of crude heroin. It is not, therefore, surprising that the Report should have concluded:

'Drug exports are clearly a vital element in the Colombian economy, if not its mainstay. And while exports are officially deplored, many senior members of the military and the political leadership are involved in the business . . . Several Bogotá narcotics agents claim that high level harassment of campaigns to curb drug smuggling confirms suspicions of participation by their own commanders.'

Perhaps one of the most interesting developments of 1977 has been the emergence in Colombia of a strong lobby of legitimate business interests who defend the legalization of marijuana exports. Such action is seen as a means of strengthening the national economy, breaking the power of the drug mafias, and increasing state revenues through taxation, and finds its most vocal champions in such figures as Leonidas Londono, a representative of the coffee exporting sector (see 'Colombian coffee losing out to marijuana', Latin America Commodities Report, 21st October, 1977). With declining world coffee prices, many of the major coffee growing regions in the Cauca valley — such as the departments of Quindío and Risaralda — are said already to be switching to large scale marijuana cultivation in order to keep pace with the boom occurring in traditional marijuana strongholds such as the Guajira, the Sierra Nevada de Santa Marta, and the *llanos* of Vichada. The arithmetic of the business is persuasive: with an average yield of one tonne (1000 kilos) per hectare, and a mark-up per kilo from 20 or 40 dollars from the grower to as much as 1,000 dollars on the U.S. market, there are obviously strong motives for any government attempt to impose a centralized control of the trade — through a Federación de Marihuaneros, perhaps, organized on the same lines as the Federación de Cafeteros.

It was even reported recently that Colombia's Foreign Minister, Liévano Aguirre, had stated his willingness to talk to potential importing countries about legalizing exports of Marijuana. The Colombian Embassy in London vociferously denied any such possiblity — see 'Latin America Commodities Report', 4th November 1977 — and stuck adamantly to the by now rather hollow fiction that: 'The fight against the traffic in narcotics continues to be a major preoccupation of the (Colombian) government.' Other than the inevitable frowns from the narcotics watchdogs and the police — who must have sensed a threat to their lavish funding — this explicit anti-legalization stance must also have been prompted by the fact that the present situation continues to provide far greater profits for the members of the Colombian ruling classes, as individuals, than it could ever do once legalization were accomplished. Tax revenue, after all, must be accountable to the state bureaucracy, and the emergence of a powerful lobby representing marijuana growers could only have disastrous effects on the profit margins of the present smuggling élite.

This group is unlikely to relinquish its hold on Colombian public life, and discipline in the business continues to be exerted through a ruthless use of the gun. In Riohacha,the capital of the department of Guajira, no fewer than seventy-two lower and middle echelon drug dealers were killed in shootouts in a mere twenty days in the month of August ('Latin America Political Report', 4th November 1977). Bloody vendettas of this type also struck at some of the leading figures in the drug trade; one series of murders, which started with the slaying of Jaime Caicedo Caicedo ('El Grillo') in Cali on 22nd February by a police lieutenant — Nelson Carvajal, himself the son of a big-time smuggler — finally resulted in the untimely demise of one of the few genuine 'godfathers' of the drug traffic, Iván Darío Carvalho, who was shot dead on the streets of Bogotá on the 11th November (see 'Latin America Political Report', 25th November 1977). The growth of such lawlessness and officially-condoned banditry — and the simultaneous aggravation of social and political conflict, as evidenced by the massive general strike which took place on the 14th September — does not hold out much prospect for the continued survival of the national institutions of Colombia, at least not in their present, utterly corrupted state.

With the assimilation of drug-smuggling interests by the various fragmented power groups within the military and political élite, Colombia seems headed for the virtually complete collapse of constitutional authority, and a repetition of the same sort of crisis of legitimacy that has been such a constant feature of the country's history. A development of this kind will allow the concentration of drug production in certain regions where there is little organized opposition to the dominance of the smuggling mafias — Santa Marta, the Guajira, and certain parts of the *llanos* and the Western Cordillera spring to mind — and the simultaneous extension of the Army's repressive operations into those areas where the peasantry shows any signs of independence or self-determination, and particularly, to those where freelance drug production might threaten the profits of the monopolist organizations. In certain places, notably the department of Cauca, such a state of latent civil war exists already, and it requires but little imagination to see it escalating into *Violencia* on a scale even more terrible than that of the period between 1949 and 1958.

A backyard coca patch in southern Cauca.

PPS TO THE SECOND EDITION. (WRITTEN JUNE, 1978)

In the six months since the first edition of Mama Coca went to press, a number of sensational developments have succeeded in focussing a further round of attention on the Colombian trade in illicit drugs. Since the implications of such events have tended to confirm and supplement the analysis contained in the main body of this chapter, a further post-script has been added to bring the material up to date:

At the beginnig of December 1977, the power struggle within the Colombian Armed Forces between, on the one hand, General Matallana — 'Mr. Clean' while chief of DAS from 1974 to 1976, and subsequently Chairman of the Joint Chiefs of Staff — and, on the other, the less impeccable Minister of Defence, General Varón Valencia, came to a head with the surprise announcement that Matallana would retire from the Army at the end of the year, thereby cutting short his rather meddlesome career ('Latin America Political Report', 9 December 1977). In their desire to reactivate a dormant tradition of right-wing moralism in Colombian public life, Matallana and ex-general Valencia Tovar — a former Commander-in-Chief of the Army also ousted by Varón — had both consistently failed to take into account the political realities produced by Colombia's huge earnings in illicit drugs, realities which were underlined by Turbay Ayala's landslide victory over the contending Liberal faction of ex-president Lleras Restrepo in the congressional and local elections of February. This victory ensured the former's nomination as Liberal candidate for the presidential elections of 4th June — an election which he subsequently won by a narrow margin over the Conservative candidate, Belisario Betancur — and thus confirmed the political ascendancy of Turbay, a figure justly described as a 'despised political boss who is widely regarded in more traditional Liberal circles as the representative of the 'emergent class' of drug smugglers and racketeers . . . ' (Latin America Political Report', 3 March 1978)

The political weight of this 'emergent class' also produced its inevitable financial counterpart, with a spate of feverish activity on the Bogotá and Medellín stock exchanges reflecting the extraordinary liquidity of drug-derived capital within the Colombian economy ('Latin America Economic Report', 12 May 1978). The threat which this money posed to the continued domination of Colombia by 'straight' financial institutions had already been foreseen by the 1977 Wolff Committee report, which estimated that between 3000 and 5000 kilos of cocaine passed through Colombia every month, and admitted an advanced degree of 'ingrained high-level corruption' within the ranks of Colombian law enforcement officials ('Report of the Select Committee on Narcotics Abuse and Control: South American Study Mission, August 9-23, 1977.' U.S. Government Printing Office, November 1977.) The Wolff Committee report failed, however, to single out such officials by name, and — in keeping with Washington's currently ambiguous diplomacy — pressure on the Colombian government was only brought to bear by largely indirect means, the most important of which involved the 'leaking' of a confidential report to President Carter by Dr. Peter Bourne, the White House adviser on drug abuse.

Most importantly, the Bourne report had given voice to the opinion that Turbay might in some way be connected with drug trafficking, a suggestion which thoroughly incensed Turbay's close ally, President López Michelsen, and prodded him into giving the by now notorious interview to a CBS television crew at the beginning of April. The Bogotá magazine 'Alternativa' (no. 158, 10 April 1978) described the President's televised defence of Turbay, and of his Ministers of Defence, Varón Valencia, and Labour, Oscar Montoya — both of whom had also been cited in the Bourne report, and in 'Le Monde' (19 January 1978), as accomplices to the drug trade — as no less than 'cornered, trembling, and grotesque . . . ' Arguing that the effects of the illicit drug trade were only one of many aspects of Colombia's dependency on the United States, 'Alternativa' proceeded to pick at the wounded nationalistic pride of the Colombian establishment with the equally pertinent observation that: 'what is shameful is not that corruption should be exposed in public, but that it should exist at all.' By way of a solution to this problem, and in a move that may represent a radically new departure for the Latin American left — traditionally rather puritanical in its attitude to drugs — 'Alternativa' actually came to recommend the immediate legalization of the trade.

Meanwhile back in Washington, as the shit really began to hit the fan, the administration decided against proceeding with any open confrontation with the Colombian government. Bourne denied that he had ever suggested that Turbay and Varón might be involved in drug trafficking, and the US Embassy in Bogotá was instructed to accede to their requests for 'certificates of good conduct', assuring the Colombian politicians that it was certain that there was no truth in the scurrilous allegations of the press — see 'Colombian drugs: the high and the mighty' in 'Latin America Political Report' (5 May 1978), and 'La conexión colombiana' in 'Alternativa' (10 April 1978). The same 'Alternativa' article had, however, detailed at least one case where General Varón had been known to protect the interests of the smuggling élites — by ordering, in March of this year, the transfer of Colonel Absalón Guerra Rubio, the chief of police in the department of Atlántico, after the latter had authorized a seven kilo cocaine bust involving a number of well-connected citizens in Barranquilla. Another of the Defence Minister's subordinates — the former DAS chief in Santa Marta, Captain José Antonio Cárdenas — was also arrested by Customs earlier in the year for attempted cocaine smuggling at the El Dorado international airport in Bogotá.

Though apparently unwilling, therefore, to follow through their anti-drug campaign to its logical conclusion, the American authorities spared no pains in proceeding with the victimization of Colombians who — unlike the Minister of Defence, and the new President-elect — failed to protect themselves against the offensive of the US-financed narcotics forces. In early 1978, responsibility for drugs cases was transferred from the discredited DAS to the judicial police, a dependency of the Procuraduria General de la República, or attorney-general's office, where the DEA could exert more effective control of the campaign. Recent reports from the department of La Guajira — by now the centre of operations for many of the smuggling syndicates on the Caribbean coast — describe the intensification of helicopter raids by troops in this area, repeating the tragic experience of the US-backed 'Operation Condor' in Mexico, best known for its unrestricted use of banned defoliants and for its strafing of politically 'subversive' peasants with heavy bore machine-guns. In an impressionistic article for the April, 1978 edition of 'High Times', Albert Goldmann spoke of 'Indians on the warpath in La Guajira', and suggested that the present abuses were likely to be 'just the beginning of the troubles' in that area.

At the same time, the dope wars in neighbouring Santa Marta continued to claim scores of victims as the different exporting groups struggled for control of multi-billion dollar trade. In one particularly significant incident, two reputed American drug dealers, Martin and Barbara Karper, were murdered on their farm fifteen minutes outside the city centre. The fact that their white Toyota bore diplomatic plates from the US Embassy has fuelled speculation that the couple's contacts reached right into the State Department — whose representatives have, incidentally, declined to comment in detail on the case, claiming that the deaths were the result of a 'property dispute' (see 'Highwitness News', in 'High Times', April 1978). It seems likely that the death of the Karpers marked a further warning against freelance yankee initiative from the established organizations in the area, and from the secret police force (DAS) which has traditionally defended their interests against uppity *gringos*. Similar evidence of the tightening up of the coca and cocaine business came at the same time from Peru — with the news that all sales of the leaf in that country would henceforth be handled exclusively by the national coca company (ENACO), and with the introduction of a new, and singularly absurd, DEA-backed law banning the possession and sale of coca leaves at altitudes under 1,500 metres.

All in all, therefore, there seems to be little reason to alter the theory expounded throughout this chapter: namely, that the present process of militarization and monopolization of the drugs trade at its source will continue apace, and with the tacit support of the international narcotics agencies, themselves more interested in the rewards of mass-media sensationalism and the maintenance of corrupt pro-Western regimes than in any serious and critical appraisal of the economic and cultural deformities produced by the present structure of the trade. It is, understandably, only to drug users and producers themselves that one must look for indications of less brutal possibilities in the future, for the State has shown itself, in this issue as in so many others, quite incapable of overcoming the inherent paternalism and authoritarianism which determine relations with its citizens. The prospect, however, can hardly be a very comforting one for the anarchistic doper, the libertarian workers of the drug industry who — like 'The Confederation', a group who published a short manifesto in the 'Special Dealing and Smuggling Issue' of 'High Times' (April 1978) — 'oppose all attempts to legislate how marijuana will be sold', and who would 'tell the Madison Avenue potheads: We will not sell our birthright. We will not sell our souls to the Whore of Babylon.'

Indeed, the very same issue of 'High Times' provides ample evidence that Babylon is already here among us. Consider, for example, the far greater prominence given to a lead article entitled 'The Dope Industry', a nauseous apologia for new-age capitalism by one Leslie Morrison, whose more memorable lines I will take the liberty to string together here, for the greater despair and disgust of my readers: 'Pot is such big business today that we can truly say that what's good for American dope dealers is good for America ... modern business requires modern methods ... modern dope agriculture has been heavily influenced by the techniques of American agribusiness ... If the grower is a small landholder, he will spend most of his dope income on items of American manufacture ... Latin growers simply follow local customs of evading national revenue collectors and export their monies ... Thus the profits of foreign marijuana growers ... return to the service of American capital at reasonable rates ... Smugglers are notorious buyers of expensive cars, private aircraft, pleasure boats, lavish estates, various electronic toys, outlandish stereo outfits and *people* (stress added) — dealers often find themselves keeping stables of women, gurus, bodyguards, gofers and attorneys with expensive tastes. The real foreign beneficiaries of dope money, exclusive of bankers, are the producers of Italian sports cars, Beluga caviar and Dom Perignon champagne ... '

It is interesting to compare such truly execrable rubbish, and its transparent defence of imperialism, with Timothy Leary's historic 1968 article for the East Village Other, 'Deal for Real', which was reprinted in the same issue of 'High Times'. True, Leary spared us the corny business-speak, but his naivety could also sometimes plumb the very depths of self-parody, as in the line: 'Here was a guy who was announcing with his mere presence that he was a flipped-out dealer in some sort of wondrous magic.' All the same, Leary's ideal of dealing deserves to be considered seriously, for in his attempt to equate the dealer with the shaman he establishes a crucial moral dimension which is sadly lacking from subsequent texts: 'You can't be doing it for the money or the power and you can't do it on your own ... '

It is precisely these social implications of the drug trade that most deserve critical consideration, for it is in the realm of international solidarity — and not in the 'High Times' obsession with the glitter of easy money and the latest developments in flashy technological gadgetry — that the future of the drug business lies. Should dope consumers and producers not unite to create a radical change in the very nature of the global trade — in an attempt to revolutionize mercantile commerce and reinstitute the principles of reciprocal exchange — it is, sadly, inevitable that the dealing of coca and marijuana will eventually succeed only in repeating the trajectory of other commodity booms in the past. It remains to be seen, therefore, whether the groups involved in the campaign to reform the drug laws in the affluent Western nations can overcome the present cultural stereotypes of the grinning Mexican peasant growing rich off his dope plantations, and direct their attention and considerable political weight to the implementation of some sort of effective aid to the marginalized and victimized producers of the plants that get us high.

V. How to Chew Coca Leaves

'I was desirous to see that hearbe so celebrated of the Indians, so many yeres past, whiche they doe call the Coca, whiche they doe sow and till with muche care and diligence, for because they doe use it for their pleasures, which we will speake of... The use of it amongest the Indians is a thing generall, for many thinges, for when they doe trauaill by the waie for need, and for their content when they are in their houses, they use it in this forme. They take Cokles or Disters, in their shells, and they doe burne them and grinde them, and after they are burned they remaine like Lyme, verie small grounde, and they take of the leaues of the Coca, and they chawe them in their mouthes, and as they goe chawyng, they goe mingling with it of that pouder made of the shelles in suche sorte, that they make it like to a Paste, taking lesse of the pouder than of the hearbe, and of this Paste they make certaine small Bawles rounde... and when they will use of them, they take a little Ball in their mouthe, and they chawe hym: passing him from one parte to an other, procuring to conserue him all that they can, and that beyng doen, they doe retourne to take an other, and so they goe, using of it all the tyme that they have neede, whiche is when they trauaill by the waie, and especially if it be by waies where is no meate, or lacke of water. For the use of these little Bawles doe take the hunger and thurste from them, and they say that they dooe recieue substaunce, as though that they did eate. At other times thei use of them for their pleasure, although that they labour not by the waie... When they will make themselves dronke, and bee out of iudgemente, they mingle with the Coca the leaues of the Tobaco, and they doe chewe them all together, and they goe as they were out of their wittes, like as if they were dronke which is a thyng that dooeth geue them greate contentment to bee in that sorte. Surely it is a thyng of greate consideration, to see how the Indians are so desirous to bee depriued of their wittes...'

John Frampton, 'Joyfull newes out of the newe founde worlde, wherein is declared the rare and singular vertues of diverse and sundrie Hearbes, Trees, Oyles, Plantes, and Stones, with their applications, aswell for Phisicke as Chirurgerie, etc.' London, 1577.
(being a translation of 'La Historia medicinal de las cosas que se traen de nuestras Indias Occidentales que sirven en medicina.' by Nicolas Monardes. Sevilla, 1574.)

During the two years that I was living in Popayán, I often made attempts to introduce the local university students and other itinerant visitors to the habit of chewing coca. I cannot claim, however, to have convinced more than a small handful of the inherently outstanding qualities of the leaves; a surprising fact, perhaps, considering the widespread enthusiasm for the marihuana, hallucinogenic mushrooms and cocaine itself which abounded in that charming city. Initially, it is true, the taste of coca is not particularly appealing. Furthermore, the very act of chewing a quid and holding it in the mouth is culturally repellant to most young whites — both *gringos* and Colombians alike — a fact which has led some recent North American researchers to suggest the development of a coca 'chewing gum' more acceptable to urban tastes.[1] In any case, the chewing of coca leaves themselves is never likely to become a fashionable trend in the over-developed industrial world; it lacks the central features of easy consumption and instant satisfaction, and requires altogether too much care and application to be easily assimilated to the consumer life-style.

There is even a sense in which the 'chewing' of coca leaves is a misnomer, for all that is involved is a short preliminary chew to get the leaves broken up and moistened, prior to the first addition of the necessary lime reagent. Although there is an initial tendency for newcomers to continue chewing beyond this point — based on a mechanical reaction of the mouth, which is used to shredding and devouring any bulky matter inside it — this mistake should be avoided, and the wad of coca must be held reasonably still in the gap formed between the teeth and the cheek. The penetration of the alkaloid into the mucal surfaces is a slow process, and each wad should therefore sit in the mouth for a minimum of an hour, being sucked gently to release the potent properties.

Almost without exception, the major problem encountered by any novice coca chewer concerns the manner in which the alkaline reagent — normally, in the Cauca area, a white lime powder — is added to the leaves, for should it be applied carelessly or in excessive quantities, an almost certain damage will occur to the gums, in the form of a cauterization or 'burn'. This may extend over the tongue, the inside of the cheeks, and any other soft surface from the lips to the throat, and the soreness can often be

Paez coca chewer.

so extreme that the person may be discouraged from ever chewing coca leaves again. In order to prevent such accidents, and the resulting disillusionment of so many beginners, the Paez Indians often engage in a form of careful initiation to the coca habit, in which a mother transfers her own chewed quid of coca into the mouth of her child, having already added the correct amount of lime. This ensures that the active alkaloids are already flowing freely, so that the first experience of chewing coca is likely to be a pretty encouraging one.

The Paez also provide another very useful hint, which is that lime ought to be added in very small doses about the size of a pinch of salt — and on repeated occasions, rather than in a single batch. By and large, it seems customary to take a couple of pinches at the outset, a third about five minutes later, and then additional doses at intervals of ten to fifteen minutes. You can tell when the wad of coca is 'hot' — in Indian terms — by a sort of anaesthesia it produces in the mouth, paradoxically called a 'freeze' in our own culture. The difficulty I experienced at the beginning was that of finding the right balance of lime to coca. On adding too much of the former the 'freeze' could easily become a 'burn', and the next day I would wake up with a number of raw and uncomfortable patches on the cheek and gums. On the other hand, if not enough lime were used, I would be disappointed by a rather flabby and mediocre 'freeze', which must surely indicate a failure to extract the full yield of alkaloid from the leaves.[2]

It is also quite common to add a small number of fresh leaves at occasional intervals, thus reviving the wad which is already in the mouth; obviously this also requires an equivalent addition of lime powder as well, in order to correct the balance. Above all, it is of crucial importance to decide on a technique for mixing the lime and coca leaves together into a single homogeneous wad. The Paez simply pour out a dose of lime from a gourd into their palm, or onto the back of their hand, and then toss it through the air so that it lands smack dab in the middle of the quid of coca in their mouth. This practice is inadvisable for beginners, however, as any error in calculation will lead to a nasty burn on the soft buccal membranes. For this reason, the Paez suggest that novice chewers should take the coca leaves out of their mouth and mix them with lime in their hand, only returning the ball to their cheek once the lime has been well wrapped in leaves, and not merely stuck to the outside as a crust.

Unfortunately, coca leaves release a dark yellow stain once they have been leached by an alkaline reagent, and thus anybody using this system will always have dirty hands and fingers. In addition, it is extremely inconvenient and time-consuming to pull the leaves out of one's mouth every time it is necessary to add lime. In order to avoid these drawbacks, it may be useful to consider the way in which lime is mixed with leaves among another group of coca adepts, the Indians of southern Cauca. In this area lime is normally used in the form of a hard lump, and small pieces are bitten off and mixed directly into the leaves. These bitten pieces of lime can only be transferred by a movement of the tongue from the front of the mouth to the cheek, but — since the tongue-tip has a high concentration of taste buds — the repeated handling of raw lumps of lime is likely to be extremely damaging. For this reason, the wad of leaves is brought forward from its normal resting place in the cheek and, being carried on the tip of the tongue, is mixed directly with the bitten pieces of lime before being returned to the side of the mouth. This motion also allows the folding of the wad over the recently added lime, thereby reducing the possibility of a burn to the gums or cheek membranes once the leaves are back in place. I began to use this system not only for the hard pieces of lime, but also for the powdered stuff as well, recommending it to other prospective chewers as less tiresome than mixing in the hand, and less dangerous than a direct toss of lime through the air.

Nevertheless, there is something aesthetically displeasing about a coca chewer spreading his lips and rubbing a wad of coca into the lime held in his hand, and certainly the Paez — with their system of tossing lime precisely but nonchalantly through the air — consider it a habit beneath contempt, chiding its practitioners with abusive nick-names such as 'yellow hand' or 'slobbering calf'. This may help explain the great prevalence of spatulae in association with many of the prehistoric lime-containers found in the Northern and Central Andes. The spatula — a foot-long rod of wood or metal — allows a much more precise application of lime than is possible with the hand alone. It seems unlikely, however, that it was ever employed in the Cauca area, as it is entirely absent from the archaeological record, and was not mentioned by Cieza de León in his classic description of the habit at the time of the Spanish Conquest. All the same, it was once very common in other areas of Colombia, and its use survives to this day among the Indians of the Sierra Nevada de Santa Marta. There a long stick is carried in the lime gourd, and being dampened in the mouth and dipped into the lime powder, it is then used to rub this powder directly onto the wad of coca leaves in the mouth. In Peru a bone, shell or wooden spoon was also often used for the same purpose.

One of the major features produced by the mixture of lime and coca is a marked transformation of the taste of the leaves themselves. On their own, these have a rather bitter, unpleasant flavour, which is made very much sweeter and more agreeable by the addition of lime. Nevertheless, the attendant anaesthesia does have its disadvantages as well, as it temporarily deadens the taste buds and renders the gums insensible to damage from the sharp points of the leaf stalks. In Peru there have been reports of Indians stripping the midrib off coca leaves before putting them into their mouths, and though I never saw any active coca chewer do this in the Cauca area, I did often employ the system myself, finding that sore, punctured gums considerably detracted from the pleasure of chewing coca.

Apart from the alkaline reagent and the coca leaves themselves, the third most important element in mastering the art of coca chewing is constituted by the individual's control of his flow of saliva, as this forms the all-important solution in which the alkaloids are liberated from the leaf cells. In the first place, saliva must be used to achieve a preliminary dampening of the dried coca leaves as they are put into the mouth. Before adding the initial dose of lime the leaves must be chewed into a wad or ball, and at this stage it is quite usual to spit out the dust and harsh juices which may accompany the first taste of the leaves. Once the lime has been added, however, spitting is generally held to a minimum, as it necessarily involves the loss of any alkaloids present in the yellow-stained liquid. For this reason, it is more common to allow all excess saliva to trickle down the throat into the stomach, where some of the alkaloids are likely to be at least partially effective, producing a warm glow which spreads slowly across the abdomen.

The main problem encountered by the beginner, however, is that the mouth — unaccustomed to the constant stimulus provided by the mixture of leaves and lime — will always tend to produce quite a large excess of saliva. Even were this to be swallowed, a good percentage of its cocaine content would be lost, and the addition of fresh doses of lime and new handfuls of leaves would become necessary at relatively short intervals. The experienced coca chewer always learns to avoid excessive salivation and the concomitant 'washing' of the leaves' drug content. By maintaining the coca juices, lime, and saliva in the form of a very concentrated dark yellow syrup, he succeeds both in extracting the maximum yield of alkaloids from the leaves, and in assimilating them by the most effective means possible, which is to allow them ample time to penetrate the mucous membranes. So thick is an expert coca chewer's saliva that it will often leave a dried brown crust on his lips and in the corner of his mouth, and so efficient is his gradual absorption of the coca alkaloids that a single wad will often last him for as much as two hours altogether.

In other words, excessive salivation in the chewing of coca not only brings about considerable waste, but also actively prevents a more effective assimilation of the cocaine and other alkaloids. For many months, I encountered great difficulty in controlling my own saliva, and I was quite at a loss to discover some way of reducing its flow. The clue to a solution lay in the very pronunciation of certain Paez expressions which concerned coca, but it was a long time before I discovered this. Initially, I was struck by the very appropriate sound of *esh* — their word for coca — which conveys so well the rather frothy sensation of freshly dried coca leaves in the mouth, and by the hard, abrasive edge of *kuétan* — the Paez word for lime.

It has already been mentioned that the local perception of the 'freeze' produced by cocaine usually involves a recognition of its 'heat', and when a wad of coca has lost its potency it is said: *se esfrió la mambeada*, meaning in Spanish that the wad has gone cold.

I asked a number of Paez how the phrases 'this wad of coca is hot' and 'this wad of coca is cold' are rendered in their own language, and was told *na-esh-báhia* and *na-esh-fínse*, respectively. On saying *fínse*, the mouth narrows, air is blown out through the lips and round the tongue, as if to expel the used, played out wad of coca. *Báhia* ... the mouth fills, the air circulates inside it, down the walls on the inside of the cheek, and along the gums. *Báhia* ... *báhia* ... it was almost like the sound of a person who has been holding his breath too long, and suddenly comes up for air. More Air.

AIR! That was it, of course! I wondered why the idea had never struck me before. One has only to think of those air jets a dentist uses to dry out teeth ... Obviously, the way to keep the wad of coca 'hot' or *báhia* was to suck in a stream of air at the corner of the mouth, and then circulate it round the ball of coca in the cheek. In this way, the coca could be kept reasonably damp, but not aswim in saliva, with the result that the freeze could be maintained over a much longer period than would otherwise be possible.

The degree of care and delicacy involved in achieving the correct balance of lime, coca leaves, saliva and air, contrasts very notably with the misconceptions shared by many whites who have never tried the drug, and who somehow consider its use to involve merely a question of mechanical chewing, a chomping and swallowing of the cud, as if the coca chewer were little better than a cow. Indeed, some of the respect with which coca is treated by its adepts is made manifest in the very way a wad of exhausted leaves is removed from the mouth. In this quite private act — *esh-púmbia* in Paez — coca is never simply spat out on the ground, but instead is carefully placed in the hand, then tossed into a cultivated field, or smeared with an almost religious reverence onto a tree-trunk or a nearby boulder. This is accomplished preferably without being seen, especially if possible witnesses might include dangerous rivals and white men. The former could misappropriate the leaves for the purposes of aggressive witchcraft, while the latter would be spoiling the implicitly magical nature of the act simply by their very presence, if not even by their ridicule.

This respect for the coca itself is expressed in many other ways as well, and the Paez always take great care not to drop even a single tiny leaf to the ground when they are putting a fresh batch into their mouths. Perhaps the single most important tribute which is rendered to coca can be seen in the way they fit their consumption of leaves into the local cycle of scarcity and abundance. Under optimum conditions, a single individual will consume as much as two ounces or 56 grams of leaves a day, or — allowing for the occasional gift to friends — about a pound a week. In times of shortage, however, it is not uncommon to find Indians reducing their consumption to a quarter of this figure; that is to say, a pound a month, a quarter of a pound a week, or only half an ounce a day. Though this is felt to be something of a hardship, the disadvantages are expressed in terms of having to put up with a rather small, uncomfortable quid of coca in the mouth, and not in terms of any diminished stimulation to the body organism, or any lessening of the cerebral exhilaration.

It would appear, therefore, that the cocaine and other alkaloids — when assimilated in the gradual, constant flow which results from chewing leaves — still produce approximately the same effects despite a reduction of dosage to one quarter of the normal level. Indeed, a subjective awareness of the stimulation produced by coca is often dependant on some prior sensation of tiredness or lassitude. To this extent, the effectiveness of the alkaloids is dependant to a greater degree on the biological and mental state of the coca chewer, than it is on the actual pharmacological properties of the leaves themselves. If this is in fact the case, it is clear why the precise dosage of the drug is a far less important factor than the socially and culturally felt need to chew coca under certain ritual and working circumstances.

THE EFFECTS OF COCA CHEWING

Given the large number of variables involved in the chewing process, it is actually quite difficult to ascertain the precise effects of coca on those individuals who have become habituated to its use. None of the extreme, manic reactions reported for large, laboratory-administered injections of cocaine have ever been shown to bear any great similarity with the form of stimulation experienced by the habitual coca chewer. In Peru, a useful comparison was made of the physiological responses experienced by a number of Indians in a resting state, including both a group of habitual coca chewers — who chewed normal quantities of coca during tests — and a group who never used coca, neither in their normal round, nor in the tests themselves. Given a daily ration of 58 gms. of leaves — with a cocaine content of approximately a quarter gram — the results were not able to demonstrate any discrepancy between the two groups, nor any occurrence of the rather significant alterations of basal metabolism which are generally associated with large intravenous doses of cocaine, such as increases in heart rate, blood pressure, and oxygen intake.

It was only during work performance that the stimulating properties of coca became evident physiologically. In comparison with the group of non-chewers, habitual coca users showed a slightly higher heart rate under conditions of physical stress, and they also experienced a reduction in the perception of fatigue, both of which can be considered features of some importance to the individual concerned with prolonging his endurance.[3] The action of coca on the body of the habitual user would seem, therefore, to be on a par with the effects of caffeine, another powerful stimulant which for economic and cultural reasons has been whitewashed, watered down, officially classified as a non-toxic drug, and freed from the biassed scrutiny and adverse propaganda which so often informs contemporary studies of the use of coca.[4]

The point must be made, however, that coca and its alkaloids — even in very small doses — do have other noticeable effects on the human organism, despite their failure to produce any gross alterations in the basic metabolic processes. A very low concentration of cocaine in the blood is all that is needed to produce a quite remarkable sensitivity in the nerve terminals. This in turn leads to an overall acceleration of the neural responses, with a consequent increase in stimulation to the Central Nervous System and the brain. In the rather opaque terminology of modern bio-chemistry, cocaine can be said to inhibit the active reuptake of a neurohumour, norepinephrine, back into the presynaptic — or 'transmitter' — nerve terminals. This increases the concentration of norepinephrine in the synaptic cleft — the interstitial space between two nerve terminals — thereby potentiating the synaptic action of the norepinephrine, and resulting in a state of exaggerated responsiveness and supersensitivity in the postsynaptic — or 'receiver' nerve terminals.[5]

This stimulant property in coca is probably its single most important feature, for a more responsive brain and nervous system clearly leads to rapid increases in the speed of thought, and in the transmission of nervous impulses, which collectively produce a subjective awareness of being 'wired'. The electric analogy is in fact quite an apt one, as it implies an acceleration of neural transmissions which are themselves based on the flow of electronically charged particles from one neuron to another. It also expresses the extremely subjective nature of the experience of 'stimulation', which — in the absence of any major alterations of body metabolism — is clearly a phenomenon which can only be 'felt' in the brain and nervous system itself. Many individuals can feel extremely 'wired' with only tiny concentrations of cocaine in their blood, whereas others — such as 'virgins' experimenting with their first doses of cocaine — may fail to notice any really pronounced effects, even despite the sudden ingestion of large quantities of the drug. The subtlety of the stimulation resides in the fact that the cocaine itself is only a catalyst, facilitating sensual and conceptual connections which already exist anyway. In other words, it depends for its effect on an awareness which is at the same time personal and cultural, subjective and historical, and in spite of all the assiduous research of a legion of well-intentioned pharmacologists, its action will never be susceptible to isolation from its social context, or to any form of purely causal and mechanistic analysis. It is hardly surprising, therefore, if the effects of the very low concentrations of cocaine — such as those resulting from coca leaf chewing — should be to all intents and purposes 'invisible' in physiological terms, for the 'euphoria' or 'optimism' engendered by the drug simply cannot be measured in quantifiable units.

This is not, however, to deny the validity of the many serious attempts which have been made to discover other physical ramifications of the effects of coca, particularly those which have sought to differentiate the use of the leaf from that of the refined alkaloid of cocaine. At the turn of the century, Mortimer had already suggested:

> 'The action of cocaine seems more pronounced upon the central nervous system, while the properties of Coca appear to be controlled by its associate alkaloids to affect muscle as well as nerve. The influence of Coca to excite muscle to energy is probably due to a direct chemical action toward the construction of proteid, as well as through the excitation of the hypothetical ferment of the contractile element . . .'[6]

It would be easy enough to attack the rather nebulous definition of Mortimer's 'hypothetical ferment', were it not for the fact that he also implied that the coca alkaloids could actually eliminate uric acid in the blood, thereby attacking not only the nerve-transmitted 'sensation' of fatigue, but also the very biochemical 'cause' of tiredness in the body tissues themselves.[7] However, in the absence of any serious research on the effects of the coca alkaloids other than cocaine, it became fashionable to discount Mortimer's ideas, and with them the possibility of any of these alkaloids significantly moderating or complementing the action of cocaine itself. The erroneous theory that coca and cocaine were one and the same thing held sway for a great many years, and a number of illustrious careers were built upon the facile simplifications — among them, the myth of coca 'addiction' — promoted by this view.

It is all the more significant, therefore, that the pendulum has slowly begun to swing in the other direction, for the last ten years have witnessed a welcome revival of interest in the coca leaf itself, including a number of pharmacological approaches to the complex chemistry involved in the chewing habit. Peruvian investigators had already argued in the 1940s that in the specific case of high-altitude oxygen starvation — conditions shared by a large segment of the coca-chewing population — the effects of the leaf might assist human adaptation by accelerating the transfer of nutritional compounds in the blood.[8] The precise biological theatre involved in this process, however, was rather more difficult to ascertain. True, one of the clear-cut effects of cocaine is to relax the bronchial airways of the lungs[9] —

making it easier to breathe in rarified atmospheres where oxygen is scarce — but this alone did not seem sufficient to explain the full range of coca's influence on human metabolism, and particularly its action in raising or sustaining the glucose level in the blood.

It would be discourteous, therefore, not to welcome the investigations of the pharmacologists who have recently addressed themselves to the question of determining the effects of coca in the human organism, among whom perhaps the most outstanding has been the German researcher, Dr. Otto Nieschulz. Most significantly, he has shown that the alkaloid ecgonine — for a long time thought to differ from cocaine only by its failure to form regular, stable crystals — in fact possesses markedly different and rather less potent psychoactive properties than its more celebrated partner. Indeed, it produces very little stimulation to the sympathetic nervous system and appears to have practically no anaesthetic or euphoric qualities, with the result that it increases exertion capacity rather less than does cocaine. At the same time, however, by raising and sustaining the level of glucose in the coca chewer's bloodstream, it does assist many Andean Indians to overcome the problems of an inefficient nutritional metabolism, itself the effect of a protein-deficient, high-carbohydrate diet, and — in the case of dwellers at high altitudes — a shortage of oxygen in the atmosphere.[10]

The importance of this observation is further underscored by the many other positive contributions to the diet afforded by regular coca chewing. In a paper on the nutritional value of coca, a group of American investigators have recently stressed that the leaves contribute significant quantities of calcium, iron, phosphorus, vitamin A, vitamin B_2 and vitamin E, all of which might otherwise be deficient among the Andean population.[11] Dr. Carlos Monge, one of the few Peruvian doctors to have consistently defended the coca habit, had already pointed out that the use of coca could be significant in preventing the incidence of beri-beri, scurvy and pellagra among the least well nourished Indians.[12] Even the much maligned cocaine itself has a positive contribution to make to the health of the coca chewer, for at the cold temperatures normally characteristic of the high Andes its effects in constricting the blood vessels could also be considered a positive advantage, enabling the body to reduce heat loss quite significantly.[13]

Other than cocaine and ecgonine, and the minerals and vitamins present in coca leaves, there also occur a number of other alkaloids in coca whose action is only very poorly understood. They include both tropeine and hygrine derivatives and, in particular, a compound known as cuscohygrine, which is present in the Peruvian coca leaf in very large quantities, being exceeded in bulk only by the main alkaloid, cocaine.[14] Pending the clarification of the pharmacology of these substances, a good deal of speculation has centered on the possibility that they may contribute significantly to the overall effect of coca chewing, and could provide a chemical explanation for the personal preferences of individual coca users for particular preparations or geographical varieties of coca leaf. The point was first elaborated by Henry Rusby — an informant mentioned repeatedly by Mortimer in his book on coca — and has recently been given another airing by such popular authors as George Andrews and David Solomon.[15]

Their basic argument was stated by Rusby in the following terms: 'It is highly probable that the amount of cocaine forms no element in the Indian's estimate of the quality of coca . . . '[16] Essentially, he felt that the Indians' choice of fresh coca leaves was based on the recognition of a number of 'sweet', volatile alkaloids present in the leaf, alkaloids which tended to disappear after prolonged storage. The point was a good one, but unfortunately he clouded the issue by referring to the native preference for a variety of coca known as 'trujillo coca' — the species **Erythroxylum novogranatense** var. **truxillense** which in botanical terms is more closely related to the coca cultivated in Colombia than the standard economic species — **E. coca** — which is consumed by most of the highland Indians of the Central Andes. Now, the 'sweet' flavour associated with Trujillo and Colombian coca does not appear to depend on the volatile alkaloids at all, but rather, on the presence of an essential oil known in North America as wintergreen oil (methyl salicylate).[17] Furthermore, as Rusby himself had been the first to admit: ' . . . it is true that a greater percentage of these ('sweet') alkaloids is usually accompanied by a larger percentage of cocaine also . . . '[18]

It does not, therefore, seem feasible or justifiable to assert that most Indian coca chewers consciously select for a lower concentration of cocaine in their favourite coca leaves. This is not, however, to deny that the presence of associated volatile alkaloids — and other essential oils — does significantly affect the choice of the prospective buyer, for it is these very elements which distinguish the fresh leaves from the stale. It is a common practice to sniff the aroma of the coca one is intending to buy; this is a sure indication of the freshness of the leaves, and of their ultimate palatability on being chewed. Nobody, if they had the choice, would choose to employ stale leaves, despite the fact that they usually suffer no real loss of their cocaine or ecgonine content. The choice, therefore, is not a straight contest between cocaine/ecgonine or the other alkaloids, but between cocaine/ecgonine plus the other alkaloids and essential oils (fresh leaves) or cocaine/ecgonine without such volatile accessories (stale leaves). Until further research into the properties of these 'other alkaloids' is completed, it would be premature to suggest that flavour alone is the deciding issue, or that, on the other hand, the Indian coca chewer is consciously searching out a better-balanced complex of pharmacological agents in his favourite drug.

Such an observation, furthermore, cannot be restricted to coca chewers alone; for the very same overlapping of flavour and 'desired effect' is also observable among tobacco and marijuana smokers, and among tea and coffee drinkers, to mention only the most obvious examples.

In the specific case of the Cauca area, there exists one practice which deserves a mention in this context, since it has a direct bearing on the issues raised originally by Dr. Rusby. The Paez distinguish two kinds of stale coca leaves: *esh-ísh*, which are brittle, dried-out leaves, and *esh-wuáwua*, which are leaves that have already begun to turn mouldy, most often through prolonged storage in a damp place. Though the flavour of *esh-ísh* is rather harsh — lacking the volatile oils and hygrine-based alkaloids of the fresh leaves — it is nevertheless considered perfectly alright to chew, especially if no alternative is available. *Esh-wuáwua*, on the other hand, is described as *canja* — 'foul' or 'ugly' — and one might expect it to be thrown away. This is not the case, however, and it is common to see the Paez reviving mouldy coca leaves by first sprinkling them with a solution of water and *panela* — a form of crude molasses — and then drying them out a second time. Such practices would suggest that, in the absence of any naturally occurring oils or 'sweet' alkaloids, the Paez will adopt the expedient of using *panela* in order to improve the flavour and provide an artificial balance to the 'bitter' cocaine and ecgonine content of the leaves.

This is not to deny, however, that there do exist a number of people who use coca in such a way as to minimize the ingestion of cocaine, more often than not by preparing the leaves in the form of an infusion or tea. Often they are whites who would never use coca in association with a lime reagent, considering such a habit worthy only of barbarians, and who would also judge the sniffing of cocaine to be scandalous in the extreme. Though in fact coca leaves will release a fair percentage of their cocaine even in a plain water solution, this is compensated by the fact that the juices of the gastrointestinal tract appear to have the effect of degrading cocaine to ecgonine before it can be absorbed into the blood stream. By this means, the mental and nervous exhilaration produced by cocaine is kept to a minimum, and the beneficial properties of ecgonine and the other alkaloids and essential oils can be enjoyed without any euphoric side-effects. In this respect, it might also be significant that those coca-drinkers who have access to bushes of their own seldom use dried leaves for the purpose of making tea, preferring to pick fresh leaves for this purpose direct from the bush. This again reinforces the idea that they are consciously or sub-consciously selecting for the volatile, aromatic properties in coca, many of which are lost in the drying process.

The question of cocaine's fate when it reaches the stomach has long attracted the attention of pharmacologists. Most of the old-fashioned explanations of the action of coca — especially those which described a supposed 'deadening' of hunger drives in the stomach — were based on the since discredited idea that coca was mainly chewed by the Indian in order to swallow its juices, and that the resulting mixture efectively anaesthetized the digestive organs.[19] Until quite recently it was still being asserted that the combination of cocaine and lime was neutralized by the hydrochloric acid in the stomach, thereby producing a cocaine hydrochloride which could easily be absorbed through the intestines.[20] In the last few years, however, a number of clinical tests have demonstrated that cocaine itself is quite inactive when taken orally, its slightly alkaline composition becoming highly ionized by immersion in the acidic gastric juices, and its molecule being to a considerable extent broken down into benzoyl ecgonine and ecgonine itself.[21] Both of these substances may easily be absorbed through the digestive organs, but their effects — as has already been pointed out — are considerably less pronounced than those of cocaine, especially in the cerebral and nervous spheres.

As a result of these observations, a number of authors have been led to assert that '... ecgonine rather than cocaine is probably the central alkaloid involved in coca chewing...'[22] And it follows from this that: 'In the amounts ordinarily consumed by the Indians, coca produces no euphoric effects...'[23], since the euphoric properties are associated with the intact molecule of cocaine, and not with the alkaloid ecgonine. However, such suggestions are undermined by a very basic flaw, for though it may be true that cocaine does become degraded in the stomach, it is by no means certain that it suffers the same changes in the mouth itself, and — judging at least from personal experience — it is through the membranes in the mouth that most of the effects of coca are absorbed, and not through the stomach at all. Indeed, since ecgonine is said not to cause any anaesthesia, it must be the cocaine which produces the very noticeable 'freeze' to the cheeks and gums which normally accompanies coca chewing.

Furthermore, many of the laboratory pharmacologists do not even appear to have any clear idea of what actually is involved in coca chewing, substituting hypothetical models for direct experience, a flaw which leads to the all too common blunder of mistaking mice for men, with all that this entails. Dr. Otto Nieschulz, for example, uses the ambiguous phrase 'oral doses' for describing the manner in which coca alkaloids were administered in his tests; it is clear from the context that he does not distinguish the mouth from the gastro-intestinal tract, an oversight understandable perhaps when dealing with guinea-pigs, but utterly misleading when considering the Andean Indian.[24] The resultant confusion is doubly unfortunate, for it leads to a misunderstanding of one of the most fundamental elements in coca chewing, namely, the addition of an alkaline reagent to the leaves. Contrary to the popular idea, one group of laboratory experiments showed that '... the extractable amount of alkaloid is not influenced by adding lime . . . '[25] Is one to conclude, therefore, that the Indian coca chewer is labouring under a primitive misapprehension in using his lime? That he might just as well be chewing his coca without lime and be done with it?

This can only be true if one accepts the idea that cocaine is degraded into ecgonine and absorbed mainly through the gastro-intestinal tract. It is patently not true, however, if one considers the probably route of entry of cocaine through the buccal membranes. In this latter case, the lime powder plays a vital role, for it raises the pH level of the saliva, thus preserving the slightly alkaline molecule of cocaine in a mainly un-ionized state. In this form, it is still fat-soluble and can therefore penetrate the fatty membranes easily and pass into the blood. Were the lime not to be used, the low pH of saliva would ionize a large proportion of the cocaine, rendering it water-soluble, and incapable of penetrating the mucous membranes in the mouth.

It is this process which has led to the popular idea that the lime somehow 'releases' cocaine and other alkaloids from the leaves. Perhaps only intuitively, the coca chewer knows why he uses an alkaline reagent with his coca. The laboratory pharmacologist, on the other hand, is so far removed from the experience itself that he can only speculate wildly, isolating his variables and models to the point where they cease to have any bearing on the realities outside their own closed and carefully controlled frame of reference. Typical, in this respect, are the words of Dr. Montesinos, writing in that well-known organ of disinformation, the Bulletin on Narcotics. Though he admits that: 'It is quite possible that the addict (*sic*) may absorb directly through the buccal and gastric mucosa very small quantities of cocaine . . . ' he proceeds without hesitation to assert that these small quantities '. . . are disintegrated by the cocainesterase in the blood, without any appreciable quantities remaining in the circulation or the tissues . . . '[26] Ergo, any idea that coca chewers may be experiencing a cocaine-induced exhilaration is stricken from the list of pharmacological possibilities, the personal feelings of individual coca chewers notwithstanding. The very expressions 'small quantities' and 'appreciable quantities' are themselves loaded to render the contribution of cocaine insignificant; but what is the yardstick which actually measures 'appreciable' or 'very small'? Could it not be that cocaine produces exactly its most interesting effects when assimilated into the blood-stream in very small doses, and repeated constantly over a long period of time, precisely to counteract the effects of the cocainesterase?

The point cannot be too firmly stated, for in the rush to distinguish an 'ecgonine-model' for cocaine chewing from the 'cocaine-model' of urban, illicit use, the distinctions between different types of 'cocaine-model' have been blurred or even consciously ignored. Assuming that the dosage of cocaine in an average chew of coca leaves and average snort of coke is roughly speaking similar — about 50 milligrams[27] — the major difference between the two lies in the rate and route of ingestion, for the same quantity absorbed through the nose in a few minutes takes close to an hour to be assimilated through the walls of the mouth. If blowing cocaine can be likened to a series of up-and-down 'snowpeak' effects, the chewing of coca leaves would seem to demand some such metaphor as the sustained heights of a mountain plateau. The very point of coca in the leaf form — with both its cocaine and its myriad other qualities — is that it can be used to produce an even, regular, uninterrupted stimulation to both the body and the mind, a stimulation so accurate in its dosage that it can be maintained almost indefinitely, and without the 'jag' and nervous excitability which is inescapable in the habitual daily use of cocaine.

Indeed, the very process of adding lime — or failing to add lime — serves as a mechanism to balance the cocaine against the other, milder alkaloids in the leaf. When feeling excessively 'wired' — a condition which is certainly within the realms of possibility even for the most modest coca chewer — one has only to go easy on the lime, reduce the intensity of 'freeze' in the mouth, and concentrate instead on letting the coca juices trickle down the throat. By this means, the nervous and cerebral response engendered by cocaine can be brought under control, and subject to a corrective balance bringing the rest of the body's metabolism in line with the brain and CNS. The Paez Indians themselves rarely add lime to their quid of coca when sitting still; in fact, the very action of tossing lime into the mouth is interpreted socially as a signal for getting it on — that is, as a hint that the coca chewer is ready to continue working, and as an expresion of the desire to proceed immediately with the task at hand. To this extent, the alkaline reagent can be seen as a kind of throttle, an accelerator used to control and regulate the stimulation resulting from a chew of coca.

It is hardly surprising, therefore, that most coca chewers should be so concerned with ensuring as good a supply of lime as of the leaves themselves. Among the Paez, lime is produced domestically, and the activities surrounding its production are probably subject to an even greater elaboration than those concerned with the cultivation and preparation of the coca crop. Equally, it should come as no surprise to note that there do, in fact, exist a good number of Indians who actually prefer to chew coca always without any lime at all. Considering that they are mainly older individuals — more often than not, post-menstrual women[28] — this observation would tend to confirm the broad outlines of the pharmacology of coca described above. In other words, those persons who choose to chew coca without adding lime seem, by and large, to be characterized by relatively frail constitutions, and might be expected to sacrifice the cerebral and nervous effects of cocaine in the interests of experiencing solely the more moderate metabolic assistance afforded by ecgonine and the other alkaloids and essential oils.

In my own experience, I soon found that the gentle sucking on a wad of coca leaves — without the addition of lime — was able to produce a state of mind which was noticeably different from that encountered in the use of coca in the normal way. Not surprisingly, the difference seemed to be best expressed in terms of a greatly reduced stimulation to the brain and nervous system, and though a certain alertness was still produced by the drug, there seemed to be none of the almost compulsive muscular activity which often accompanies the consumption of coca with lime. Such a condition lent itself especially well to sedentary pursuits like reading or writing or travelling in a bus, where the resulting wakeful state helped dispel fatigue and any temptation to doze off to sleep. With time, I began to restrict my use of coca-with-lime to those occasions when strenuous physical activity of some kind was required, and found that in other situations I actually preferred to chew without.

The recognition of this desire for an occasionally more moderate form of stimulation was itself based on an increasing sensitivity to the sheer brute potency of coca leaves. Initially, and in comparison to refined cocaine, I had not considered a chew of coca to be anything to write home about; in fact, it seemed hardly more powerful than the average dose of caffeine contained in a strong coffee or a gourd of *maté* tea. It must have required more than a year of daily chewing until I first began to notice that a chew of coca leaves with lime was actually capable of quite powerful alterations of my mental and physical state, including the same kind of uncomfortable tension around the heart which is also occasionally produced by large doses of caffeine as well. On discussing this feature with the Paez, it became clear to me why the chewing of coca was usually restricted to the work situation, in which the expenditure of energy itself provided the escape valve for excess stimulation. It was very noticeable that — at least among the Paez — very few individuals ever sat around chewing coca purely for the state of euphoria it could produce. This was not — as some authors have erroneously suggested[29] — simply because they were uninterested in, or failed to recognize, the state of euphoria per se, but rather, it seemed to imply a recognition of the fact that the physical effects of coca chewing could, in a sedentary state, become sometimes really quite uncomfortable.

The clearest example of this concerned the night-time activities of the shaman. Ritual activities require the almost constant chewing of coca throughout the night, and the Paez shaman normally ingests much more coca on these occasions than is needed simply to maintain a state of wakefulness. Occasionally, the excess stimulation can be channelled into a form of divination known as reading the *senas* — involuntary muscular twitches produced by a conjunction of coca-induced supersensitivity and telepathic communications from divinites, spirits of the dead, and the disembodied souls of rival shamans. We will return to consider the crucial importance of coca in Paez divination and magical practice, but suffice it here to say that the shaman must learn to control his *senas*, to dampen them if need be, for otherwise they may become too insistent and distract him from his other tasks. One means of reducing these muscular twitches is clearly to neglect to add any more lime to the quid of coca, but this is often considered dangerous, since it tends to lessen the shaman's powers of resistance to external magical attacks. The only alternative, therefore, is to add another drug which can in some way reduce the nervous excitement produced by coca.

A great number of plants are often used for this purpose, but in the Cauca area, the preferred counterbalance to coca leaves is without any shadow of doubt tobacco. Large black cigars form part of the shaman's basic kit, and they are sometimes smoked and sometimes chewed together with the coca leaves, depending on the individual's preference. A number of Paez coca chewers carry strands of tobacco or leaves of the local semi-wild **Nicotiana rustica** along with the coca leaves in their pouch, and they normally state that they like the addition of a little tobacco because it 'warms the body' or 'clears the head'. Similar practices have been reported among the Uitoto of the Putumayo river and the Kogi of the Sierra Nevada de Santa Marta, both of whom use a liquid extract of tobacco and add it to their coca at any time.[30] Since nicotine is usually thought of as a neural poison, it seems clear that the use of tobacco in these cases may well serve as an antidote to the supersensitivity of the nerve terminals and general 'jumpiness' which can result from prolonged coca chewing.

Another popular combination among the Paez is that of coca and alcohol, the latter being consumed in the form of a fermented sugar-cane beer — *núsa*, also known as *beca*, which is strictly speaking the word for maize beer or *chicha*, a drink that is only prepared very rarely these days — or as a distilled cane spirit known by its Spanish names: *el chiquito*, should it be a bootleg brew, or else quite simply *aguardiente*, if it comes from the state distillery in Popayán. It is important to note, however, that it is most unusual to see any Paez drinking *núsa* and chewing coca at the same time, and the combination of effects is usually achieved by an actual alternation of the drugs, rather than by any kind of strictly simultaneous consumption. There is a general consensus of opinion that the chewing of coca after prolonged bouts of drinking serves both to clarify and sustain the experience of drunkenness, bringing it into sharper focus and preventing the inebriated person from falling to the ground in a stupor. Considering the fact that the Paez are very heavy drinkers, and that most of the drinking takes place during the afternoon in large collective work groups, coca must surely play an important role in helping them to sober up and return home at nightfall, a feat that often will require walking many miles along tortuous mountain paths. This would seem to be related to the fact that coca has almost the opposite physiological effect to alcohol, which is essentially a strong depressant of the Central Nervous System.

Something of the same pharmacological balance is also discernible in the combination of coca with marijuana, another drug whose physical effects are primarily sedative and depressant, despite the otherwise well-known psychedelic properties which produce its characteristic action on the senses and the brain.[31] Though virtually undiscovered by any except the very youngest adult Paez males, the *punto rojo* weed of the Cauca area is justly famous for the potency of its euphoric properties. Clearly it must be considered an excellent smoke to accompany sedentary or contemplative activities, but I did personally find it rather debilitating whenever strenuous physical effort was required. For this very reason, it seemed undesirable to smoke too much before engaging in hard work or walking long distances uphill. At the same time, however, coca and marijuana have the sometimes useful effect of cancelling each other out, and for this reason a chew of leaves is often an excellent antidote to too much smoking, just as a joint is usually a fine conclusion to long hours of coca chewing. Furthermore (mystery of pharmacological mysterics!) depending on one's mood they not only can cancel each other out but also actually add together, combining their rather different effects simultaneously, and producing in this way an admirable blend which includes the very best elements of each.

This section would hardly be complete without a few words of warning, especially with regard to the supposed 'damaging effects' of long-term coca habituation. The overwhelming majority of the physiological and psychological disturbances which have usually been attributed to the coca habit are little more than poorly disguised justifications for ethnocentrism, or even outright cultural imperialism. There are, however, a number of other aspects to the question of coca chewing which might prove troubling to new initiates, all of which can conveniently be limited to the immediate sphere of coca's action, namely, the mouth itself.

It seems more than likely that repeated anaesthesia in the mouth should lead eventually to a marked reduction in the sense of taste, but exactly how acute this may be is a matter still open to debate. In all honesty, two years of daily coca chewing did not significantly deaden my own taste buds. On the other hand, the thick solution of coca alkaloids in the saliva does tend to produce a distinct staining of the teeth. Paradoxically enough, this actually seems to keep the teeth rather healthier than would otherwise be the case, as it prevents the formation of caries and other sorts of dental decay. The stain itself can be removed very easily by scraping the surface of the tooth with a sharp instrument, or by brushing it with a powerful dentist's drill.

More significant is the damage felt on the gums and other mucous membranes, subject as they are to the constant abrasion of the lime reagent. Careless application of this lime may result in an unsightly staining and swelling of the lips. Furthermore, long-term habitual users of coca usually develop marked preference for holding their leaves on one side of the mouth — often the left — with the result that the cheek may become distended on this side. Superficial features of this kind are, however, unlikely to be of any great medical significance, and I met many Paez who actually took a great deal of pride in their baggy cheeks, considering them a mark of traditionalist status which set them apart from the more modern, progressive Indians and their dazzling fluoride smiles.[32]

In any case — and discounting purely aesthetic considerations — by far the most uncomfortable aspect of coca chewing is the irritation produced by the action of lime on the inside of the mouth. I noticed a distinct hardening of my own gums and of the tissues on the inside of the cheek, as well as the faintly disturbing emergence of a raw spot at the back of my tongue. In all fairness, this damage did not appear to be shared by any of the Paez who showed me their tongues, and I can only assume that I failed to master all the more intimate secrets of coca chewing, and particularly, of adding lime to the quid already in the mouth. It may be that the extremely fierce lime that the Paez use was itself at fault, for on visiting Peru a short time later, I found that the milder alkalis used in the Central Andes — particularly the delicious *tocra* paste — were not only more palatable, but also much less damaging to the membranes.

Future medical research on the health of habitual coca chewers ought, therefore, to concentrate its efforts not only on the broad physiological issues, but also on the specific possibility of coca producing some lasting scar tissue in the mouth. Whether or not such scar tissue could lead to strictly pathological conditions should also be investigated, for it seems likely that there do exist a number of techniques — one, recommended by the Paez, was to wash out the mouth with a solution of alum — which are employed by the Andean Indians to effectively reduce the impact of this damage. In all probability, one will be forced to admit that coca does, lamentably enough, lead to a certain amount of wear and tear in the mouth. But as one recalcitrant old Paez warrior once stated to me defiantly, doesn't walking produce just as much wear to the soles of the feet? Nobody has yet suggested that anyone should stop walking . . .

POSTSCRIPT FOR THE SECOND EDITION

Having neglected, in my own research, the possibility of finding new medical applications for coca, it was with great satisfaction that I learned of

Dr. Andrew Weil's recent paper on this subject: 'Coca Leaf as a Therapeutic Agent' — in American Journal of Drug and Alcohol Abuse, vol. 5, no. 1: pp. 75-86. (1978). The major conclusions of his study are here reproduced with the author's permission:

'On the basis of my observations of coca users, my studies of the coca literature, and my own clinical experiences with the leaf, I would recommend experimenting with it in the following ways:

1. In painful and spasmodic conditions of the entire gastro-intestinal tract. Coca appears to restore proper tone of the smooth musculature of the G.I. tract. It may be superior to belladona, atropine, and other parasympathetic blocking drugs in that it produces no uncomfortable side effects; in fact, the "side effects" of coca leaf are usually perceived as desirable.

2. As a substitute stimulant for coffee in persons who consume much coffee and suffer exacerbations of gastro-intestinal conditions from that drug. Coffee is strongly irritating to the gastric mucosa and powerfully stimulating to the intestines; coca can provide useful CNS stimulation yet is a traditional remedy for G.I. disorders. Moreover, coffee can produce serious dependence with physiological components. Dependence on coca may be less common and less serious.

3. As a fast acting antidepressant. Coca has definite mood-elevating properties, especially when set and setting are supportive. The effect comes on within minutes of administration and does not leave patients feeling drugged or intoxicated. By contrast, current antidepressant medications (the tricyclics) may not produce an effect for weeks, have significant toxicity, and may make patients feel drugged.

4. As a treatment for acute motion sickness.

5. As adjunctive therapy in programs of weight reduction and physical fitness. Coca is mildly anorexic and stimulating; unlike amphetamines, it provides some nutrients and does not produce toxicity or dependence.

6. As an energizer for persons engaged in heavy physical work, including certain athletes.

7. As symptomatic treatment of toothache and sores in the mouth.

8. As a laryngeal tonic in persons who must use their voices more than usual, such as professional singers and public speakers.

9. As a substitute stimulant to wean users of amphetamines and cocaine from those drugs, which are more dangerous and have much higher potentials for abuse'.

VI. On Growing Your Own Coca

'Of all the Plants that any Soil does bear,
This Tree in Fruits the richest does appear,
It bears the best, and bears them all the Year.
Ev'n now with Fruits 'tis stored — why laugh you yet?
Behold how thick with Leaves it is beset;
Each Leaf is Fruit, and such substantial Fare,
No Fruit beside to rival it will dare . . . '

Dr. Abraham Cowley. 'History of Plants'. (1662)

Walking past any plantation of Colombian coca bushes you cannot help being struck by the colour of the leaves, their tone blending from an almost lemon yellow through to a pale apple-green Chartreuse, their lively sheen standing out very noticeably against the more sombre background of the surrounding vegetation. Should the leaves be gently pierced by the horizontal sunlight of early morning or late afternoon, the combination of this yellowish hue and the virtually diaphanous quality of the leaf-cells themselves will cause the foliage to shimmer in the breeze like so many tiny jets of flame, trembling on the branch and threatening to take off. Only when the leaves are ripe for picking do they lose their gilded, rather ethereal brilliance — becoming suddenly opaque and curling over at the edges, then turning that characteristic dark green colour which ushers in the harvest.

Once picked the plantation gives a radically different impression to the eye — its naked branches drooping sadly, their grey lichens forming a stark contrast with the surrounding piles of rotting vegetation, the remains of weeds which are uprooted at each harvest and left to fertilize the soil. Under the preferred weather conditions — abundant rainfall — it is, however, rarely more than two weeks before the next burst of leafy shoots begin to appear on the branches, sprouting more profusely out towards the tips of each twig. Their bright yellow colour blends perfectly with that of a luxuriant golden moss which flourishes — especially under humid atmospheric conditions — on the thicker parts of the stem, its intense, fiery warmth cheating the rather paltry coca blossoms of pride of place, and enlivening the otherwise cheerless lichens and the dark gunmetal surface of the bark. The coca flowers themselves tend to bloom a few weeks after the onset of heavy rains, but given their somewhat undistinguished small cream petals, and their exceedingly short day or two-day lifespan, the coca plant — even in full flower — never really looks as if it is blossoming in any great profusion. More remarkable, perhaps, are the small berries which result from the self-pollination of these flowers, for they are often quite numerous and noticeable — especially after a growing interval of two months or so, when they turn from a dark olive green to a bright pillarbox red.

The aesthetic features of **Erythroxylum novogranatense** would alone recommend the introduction of the plant into domestic horticulture, as can readily be recognized by its use as hedging in countless gardens and public parks throughout the Cauca valley. How much greater, therefore, would be the pleasure of cultivating enough bushes — say, a couple of hundred — to provide leaves for one's own consumption, as in this way the delights of gardening could readily be combined with the worthy pursuit of self-sufficiency. It is clear that if the present nightmare scenario of the drug traffic is to be overcome, one must welcome and encourage the widespread proliferation of small coca plantations to supply the needs of independent, libertarian communities — groups who recognize at once both the qualities of coca itself, and the inevitable political and economic disadvantages of depending on monopolist industrial enterprises as a source of supply. After the rise of home-grown marihuana, the advent of home-grown coca cannot lag far behind.

It is precisely this situation which renders so important the precedent of the Colombian Indians, for it is the species of coca which they cultivate — **Erythroxylum novogranatense**, as opposed to the **Erythroxylum coca** of eastern Peru and Bolivia — which would seem most applicable to diffusion on a world-wide scale. After all, **E. coca** itself can only thrive in a very clearly defined set of environmental conditions — the well-drained soils, moderate temperatures, and the almost constant humidity which prevails on the eastern slopes of the central Andes. Colombian coca, on the other hand, will tolerate much drier conditions and rather greater extremes of temperature, making it far more suitable for cultivation both in the tropical lowlands, and in those sub-tropical regions characterized by seasonal droughts.[1] It was no doubt these features which, at the turn of the century, led the British botanists at Kew Gardens to encourage the introduction of Colombian coca into other equatorial regions outside of South America. Their lead could profitably be followed by present-day horticulturalists and home-growers as well. One difficulty is certainly that of finding adequate seed, for coca is accustomed to germinating very quickly, and will seldom resist storage for more than a month or so. Assuming, however, that seed is forthcoming, one must turn to consider in detail the way the plant is cultivated by the few people who still care for the plant in the traditional way, most numerous of which are undoubtably the Indians of the Cauca area.

The limits — both altitudinal and latitudinal — of coca cultivation are necessarily circumscribed by the plant's failure to tolerate frosts. Since it is a relatively long-lived perennial, this disadvantage would be felt even in those sub-tropical settings where frost is only an occasional hazard, as — for example — in Florida or California or the coffee-producing districts of southern Brazil. In the Cauca area, the range of coca cultivation — like that of coffee — encompasses basically the middle-altitude zone between 1000 and 2000 metres. Nowhere in Cauca do there exist the sort of highly organized coca plantations which have been described in certain parts of Peru, with their use of spray insecticides, their neat rows of bushes separated by long parallel furrows of earth, or their agricultural terraces built onto the steep hillsides by the use of stone retaining walls.[2] The typical Colombian coca plantation is an extremely modest affair, consisting of between a hundred and a thousand bushes, and often occupying an irregular sloping field of less than half a hectare. Most commonly, the coca bushes are not mixed with any other crop, and each plant is separated from the next by about two metres of untilled earth.

One of the most noticeable features of any coca plantation is the complete absence of anything even vaguely resembling a 'standard' coca bush. Individual plants may be either extremely tall and spindly, or they may be no more than one metre high, and thickly beset with branches. When arranged in a plantation, there are a number of considerations which must be borne in mind in order to produce the maximum yield from the available plants. Individual bushes will never grow into proper trees, that is, they will never form a strong enough trunk to hold themselves erect much taller than two or two-and-a-half metres. Beyond that height, they tend to fall over sideways, and end up forming a dense tangle with other nearby coca bushes. Certain cultivators believe that this sort of tangle is to be encouraged, as it is supposed to be highly productive of leaves. In other cases, either due to a preference of the cultivator himself, or possibly to some genetic feature or insufficiency in the soil, the bushes never progress beyond the size of erect shrubs between one and two metres in height.

Either in the form of tangled growth, or in that of simple erect shrubs, pruning is almost always practiced in some for or other, albeit often as an

Coca: showing unopened flower buds.

involuntary side-effect of careless picking. Pruning of the lateral shoots tends to produce the long, fallen-over, tangled type of coca shrub; while pruning of the terminal buds on the main trunk usually results in a short, erect, and many branched coca bush. In either case the object of the exercise is essentially the same: namely, the most uniform and efficient distribution of light, so that the plantation does not appear to carry all its leaves at the same height from the ground. Nothing is more indicative of lazy coca cultivation than the occurrence of patchy leaf distribution, with wide empty holes contrasting with dense clusters of leaves. It is also sometimes asserted that coca bushes must be pruned in order to become more convenient and accessible for picking, but the flexible nature of the branches usually allows even the highest leaves to be picked once the branches have been bent towards the ground, and so this factor cannot really be considered of any overriding importance.

Occasionally, it is true, coca bushes are scattered among other crops, such as maize or sugarcane or, more commonly still, bananas and plantains. All these plants, however, have a much shorter lifespan than a coca bush — which often survives for a full thirty or forty years — and thus the chance juxtaposition of coca with another crop cannot always be considered a deliberate feature of the original coca plantation. Most cultivators explain the presence of other intrusive food plants as a situation which has resulted from the demise of some of the original coca bushes, leaving small clearings which have been replanted with new crops. In any case, the shading provided by these plants is seldom considered sufficiently important to either benefit or seriously impede the growth of the coca bushes themselves.[3]

At the same time, it is commonly believed that heavier shading — such as that provided by the high *cachimbo* trees used in the Colombian system of shaded coffee cultivation — is not very beneficial to coca bushes, as it reduces the yield of leaves and gives them a rather flimsy consistency, which may even indicate an absolute decrease in their alkaloid content as well. It is worth noting that the original wild progenitor of cultivated coca probably grew in just this kind of environment, as a member of the subtropical forest undergrowth. In this case, it can readily be appreciated that the 'domestication' of coca probably involved a transfer of the bush out of its natural habitat and into the open, thereby achieving an increase in the yield of both leaves and alkaloid, and probably without affecting the genetic features of the plant to any very marked degree.

The Paez have a bewildering number of terms to describe the various categories of coca leaves — the word *esh* (coca) being combined into compounds such as *esh-shúte* (coca-grown-in-the-shade) which demonstrate their keen perception of the effects of micro-environmental variables on the quality of the coca they chew. If *esh-shúte* refers to the conditions under

Coca: in flower.

which coca of this kind grew originally, *esh-ménshcue* describes the fact that they are 'thin-leaved' and basically disappointing to the palate of the coca chewer, who usually prizes the more tasty, thick-leaved coca — *esh-lépi* — which is grown in an unshaded place and is thus also known as 'sun coca' or *sek-esh*.

Another factor is concerned with the altitude — and hence the temperature — at which a particular variety of coca is grown. Confirming reports from Peru, which claim that coca produces an optimum yield of alkaloid when cultivated at an average temperature of 18°C., it is noticeable that most of the better coca plantations in Teirradentro and southern Cauca are to be found in the altitude zone between 1500 and 2000 metres, whose average temperatures are respectively 20°C. and 17.5°C., thus straddling the 18°C. isotherm. Even within this range, there can be little doubt that the most highly prized coca is that grown on the upper slopes, on rocky soils close to the limit of the plant's tolerance. Of course, coca bushes do grow much more luxuriantly at lower altitudes, thriving particularly well around the 1000 metre mark, but the Paez consider these warmer climate leaves to be too large and heavy, and not all that potent, according them the disparaging epithet *esh-átcha*.[4]

Other conditions are also clearly involved in the determination of the quality of coca leaves, for coca does appear to produce the finest harvests on steep, broken hillsides which would be unsuitable for more demanding crops such as coffee. This is partly related to the fact that the root system of the coca bush is not fond of waterlogging, and partly due to the influence of more strictly geological factors. It is no accident, for example, that the excellent quality of the coca of the San Jorge valley, in southern Cauca, should be largely dependant on the local occurrence of soils very rich in iron. Formed from the erosion of widespread deposits of pyritiferous schists, they have a telling resemblance with the soils which predominate in other famous coca-producing areas in Peru.[5]

A further feature affecting coca harvests is the frequency of rains, but this appears to have less to do with the yield of alkaloid than with the seasonal nature of the production of leaves in bulk quantities. During a drought, no coca bush will bear enough leaves even for local consumption, let alone cash sales. On the other hand, only three months of abundant rainfall are required in order to produce an excellent crop. With this in mind, some of the observed irregularities between harvesting time in different parts of the Cauca area become easier to explain. On the western side of the Central Cordillera — such as in the San Jorge valley, and along the Rio Ovejas, between Cali and Popayán — there are usually dependable dry periods between June and August, mid-December and mid-February. Harvests in these regions, therefore, tend to take place especially in late November, and then again — depending on the duration of the New Year

Coca.

dry spell — at staggered intervals from March through to June. Obviously the amount of rainfall will determine whether two full crops can be collected in the first six months of the year, or only one or one-and-a-half. Coca prices at those times when harvests are abundant are often less than half what they might have reached in September, which is usually the month of greatest scarcity.

By way of contrast, in the Paez districts on the eastern slopes of the Central Cordillera the rainfall is more evenly distributed, and only an occasional maverick drought interrupts the almost constant supply of water on the ground. The drier periods which characterize January and July do not have the same intensity as on the other side of the mountains, and thus most of the coca plantations in Tierradentro have at least three full harvests a year. These are held at the irregular intervals dictated by need, so that there rarely exists any marked alternation between periods of scarcity and abundance, nor any really wild fluctuations of prices either.

The impact of such climatic features serve to explain a great deal of the immediately noticeable differences in the flora which flourishes on opposite slopes of the Central Cordillera of the Northern Andes, and may also suggest the possibility that distinct geographical races of **Erythroxylum novogranatense** have emerged on either side of this mountain range. The differences in climate could also lend a certain amount of environmental support to the radically distinct economic practices of the San Jorge and Tierradentro regions. The former, with an historical tradition in making bulk exports of coca leaves, is characterized by two or three major annual harvests which take place with reasonable regularity. The latter, which features a largely self-sufficient economy based on face-to-face exchanges, is marked by irregular and modest pickings which seldom allow for the production of any large surplus.

The dependance of the coca crop on rainfall is so great, that many rural producers in the Cauca area often maintain a small stand of coca bushes in some well-watered spot in order to assure their own personal supply even in times of general scarcity. In the San Jorge valley, considerably more care is lavished on these domestic coca patches than on the larger hillside plantations, and during the most severe annual drought — between June and August — it is not uncommon to find irrigation ditches being used for the maintenance of an emergency supply of coca.[6]

Protracted drought of several months duration is also an occasional feature of the Cauca area, and though no large harvests of coca are feasible during such periods, the local species **Erythroxylum novogranatense** is highly resistant to the strain and — along with sugar-cane — is much esteemed by the peasant cultivators for this reason. Coffee, in comparison, is seriously affected by extended periods of dry weather, and coffee plantations often have to be replanted after very severe droughts. The coca plant's resistance is so great, in fact, that it can survive even major fires, and within a year of being burned to the ground will have produced a new stem and fresh branches. Should a bush ever become infested with a common breed of yellow coca-eating caterpillar — known simply as *uk* in Paez, which means 'death' — it is common to cut the bush down to a short stump. In this coppiced state, it will not delay more than a couple of growing seasons before producing a new spread of branches and yields as abundant as before.[7]

Though the propagation of coca by means of stem cuttings has been described in certain areas of Peru, and particularly in the Amazon basin, it does not appear to constitute even an occasional practice in the department of Cauca. The yield of bright red berries — particularly in conjunction with the main harvests in November and April/May — provides more than enough seed material for the needs of even the most eager cultivators. The berries are usually buried in a shallow seedling bed right away, for in general they do not maintain their fertility for more than two or three weeks. The seedlings grow very slowly, and it takes them a good two months after being layed in the ground to grow a stem, shed their dicotyledons, and expose the first pair of true coca leaves.

Thereafter, the growing speed is to some extent decreed by such conditions as temperature and altitude, but in any case it is most important for the seedlings to receive some shading from the midday sun, and to enjoy an adequate water supply. By the time they are twenty or thirty centimetres tall, they are considered ready to be transplanted to their ultimate destination, being planted out with a space of one or two metres between the bushes. Among the Paez Indians, it is still a common — though rapidly declining — custom to hold a large gathering known as a *minga* whenever a large new coca plantation is being sown. Feasting quantities of food, drink and coca are provided to all those who come and share in the work, and — since coca is considered a plant with magical attributes — the more traditional Indians engage the services of a shaman, who performs the necessary cleansing rituals, purifying the field of malign influences and encouraging the abundant yield of future harvests. The transplanting of coca seedlings usually takes place at the time of a new moon, for it is considered that the waxing influence 'pulls' the bushes and causes them to grow tall and strong.

THE PREPARATION OF COCA LEAVES FOR CHEWING

In the past, it was also common to hold *mingas* and cleansing rituals every time a large crop was gathered in, but this practice has accompanied the gradual decline of a great number of the older forms of cooperative labour.

It is unlikely, in any case, that the adult males — either in Tierradentro, or in southern Cauca, for that matter — should ever have contributed a great deal to the picking of coca leaves, as this is an activity considered more appropriate for women and children. Like spinning and weaving it is a long, laborious process, not requiring brute strength so much as considerable patience and the tireles repitition of the same movements. The coca branch must be grasped firmly in one hand, while the other picks each leaf individually and places it in a bag or basket. To merely run the hand along a branch in one fell swoop, pulling off all the leaves in a single movement, is considered a sign of laziness and bad technique, as it often results in the damaging of the extremities of the branch. These tips — the *cogollos* in Spanish — contain the potential for a new growth of leaves, and therefore bad picking will result in a significant decline of future yields from the same bush.

There are a number of ways of telling when coca is ripe for picking, most obvious of which is the already mentioned tendency of the ripe leaves to curl at the edges and turn a darker shade of green. Simultaneously with these changes, the leaf itself becomes more brittle, cracking at right angles to the midrib should it be rolled between the fingers — a test that is often used to determine the right moment to begin harvesting. It is important that the leaves should be picked when exactly ripe — *esh-téh* in Paez — for should they be allowed to grow over-ripe they will tend, once dried, to turn a dark brown colour and taste very bitter, a condition referred to in Paez as *esh-téche-úmbuiah*. At the same time, very pliable, unripe leaves — *esh-chácha* — are quite unsuitable for chewing, and good coca pickers will let them remain on the bush even though the rest of the leaves have already been picked.

The unprocessed coca leaves, *esh-kuitimé*, are taken to the house in large bags or sacks made form netted sisal fibre, and are often allowed to ferment in this state overnight before being dried. The Indians and *campesinos* of the Cauca area always toast their leaves over a slow wood fire; this being essentially the same system as that used by Indians in other highland areas of Colombia — such as the Sierra Nevada de Santa Marta — and in the Amazonian lowlands as well.[8] An earthenware dish is employed for this purpose, preferably with a wide diameter and reasonably thick walls, as this allows the most even distribution of heat. A narrow aluminium pot is most unsuitable, precisely because it tends to concentrate the heat on a red-hot metal surface at the bottom of the pan. Depending on the width of the bowl, anything between a quarter of a pound and five pounds of leaves may be dried at one time, though quality does seem to be better when larger quantities are toasted in a single batch. The leaves are turned constantly so that those at the bottom do not burn, a wooden paddle often being employed for the purpose. As much as 60% of the original weight is lost in the drying process.

It is debatable, of course, whether this system is as kind to the leaves as the common sun-drying method used in the Central Andes; and it is obviously less efficient than the use of modern drying sheds, such as those reported recently from the Tingo Maria area in Peru.[9] Both the sheds and the more primitive fire-drying methods have emerged, however, through a similar need being felt by the coca producers; for sun-drying requires fine weather — seldom a dependable feature of coca-growing regions — and it has been common in Peru for large crops to spoil through lack of the requisite amount of sunshine. Furthermore, drying techniques tend to be related to other factors as well, and in Peru it is clear that a quite exacting standard is required if the leaves are to resist many months of storage and travel over long distances. In Colombia and the Amazon, on the other hand, Indian coca chewers usually have access to fairly localized sources, and are therefore able to replenish their supplies with fresh leaves at reasonably short intervals.

In any case, freshly dried coca is seldom very palatable, since it has a green, leafy taste and a tendency to break up in the mouth through excessive crispness, a condition described by the Paez as *esh-pípi* or 'hard-leaved coca'. It is for this reason that coca is normally piled up or sacked again after drying, being allowed to rehumidify and become soft and pliable, what the Paez call *esh-lúpe*. This secondary 'sweating' of the coca brings out its heady aroma, and may even allow some secondary fermentation to take place within the leaf cells, altering their alkaloid composition.[10] Once ready for consumption, coca is normally pressed into bags, sacks or bales, as in this way the leaves are preserved in their optimum conditions. Such bales, however, will only remain in good shape if kept free from damp, and for this reason, the coca of Peru is immediately shipped out of the humid *montana* where it is cultivated, and placed in storage deposits located at considerable altitudes in the *sierra*, where the climate is much drier.

Unfortunately, storage of this kind is not feasible either in the Amazon nor in the wet highlands of the northern Andes, providing the inhabitants of these areas with yet another reason to consume their supplies reasonably quickly. In the Amazon, coca is pulverized and — in the absence of any source for mineral alkalis — the ashes of the leaves of the *yarumo* tree (**Cecropia** spp.) are added to the powder as an alkaline reagent. In contrast with Andean usage, this powdered coca has the advantage of not requiring the addition of any abrasive supplements once it has been placed in the mouth, with the result that the usual dangers of cauterizing the mucous membranes of the mouth are almost entirely eliminated. Furthermore, since the powder is finely sieved, it lacks the stems and midribs of the coca leaves, and therefore can be swallowed gently and gradually — rather than removed from the mouth after chewing, as is the custom in the mountains.[11]

Throughout the Cauca area itself, the basic system of coca chewing is similar to that of the Peruvian highlands, with a major difference being discernible only in the difficulties of long-term storage which are presented by the normally high atmospheric humidity which prevails in this part of Colombia. Once dried, coca leaves probably retain their original flavour and aroma for only two or at most three weeks; a fact which is no great problem if you have a plantation immediately outside your door, but which can be a major disadvantage to those Indians who live at altitudes too high and too cold to cultivate their own bushes. Short of stashing one's bales of coca in an artificially dry environment, a virtually impossible undertaking, there seems to be no way of avoiding the inevitable deterioration of the leaves; for either — by exposure to warm air and sunlight — they will become very brittle and dried out (*esh-ísh*), or — by allowing them to remain tightly packed — the dampness of the climate will cause them to turn mouldy (*esh-wuáwua*).

In either eventuality, the result is unlikely to satisfy the palate of the conoisseur coca chewer, and most Indians will simply refuse to use such leaves unless there is really no other alternative. Even plastic insulation is of little use in this case, as coca must be able to breathe while in storage, or it will turn mouldy simply from the humidity contained within the leaves themselves. Small wonder, then, that most coca sold in markets distant from the centres of production — such as those seen by tourists in Popayán, Silvia and San Agustín — is usually of a pretty dismal standard. It would also explain why practically all the most inveterate coca chewers in the Cauca area are also their own producers as well. In the kind of situation which prevails in Colombia — with both climate and the law militating against the survival of a dependable long-distance coca trade — the adept of the coca leaf must clearly be prepared to become self-reliant if he is to be sure of access to the best quality leaves. Ideally, he will replenish supplies every week or two, probably entering into some arrangement with another neighbouring coca farmer so as to spread the intermittent harvests over as large a number of bushes as possible. In this way, a single field of coca can be divided up into a series of small clumps, each ripening in succession to provide a constant source of fresh leaves.

THE MANUFACTURE OF A LIME REAGENT

A similar ideal of self-sufficiency is also observable in other, subsidiary aspects of the coca habit as well. During my period of permanence in the Cauca area, I often expected that the coca drying process should be the object of certain ritual observances, and that the precise technique employed should be shrouded in a certain amount of secrecy. Nothing could be further from the truth, and I never experienced any hesitation at all to show me how to toast the leaves. Slowly I came to realize that — at least among the Paez — the truly esoteric aspect of the habit lay not in the coca at all, but in the process of preparing a lime reagent. Though whites could be expected to use coca leaves — as tea, as medicine, to make cocaine, etc. — it was not normally considered fitting for them to have any business knowing how to prepare lime. Since it was assumed that white people never used coca for chewing, if followed that they could never possibly find any proper use for the lime either.

Like coca picking itself, the actual business of preparing lime powder consumes an amazing amount of effort. It is almost as if the speed and acceleration produced from the drug must be backed up by an equivalent investment of energy, so that men should not imagine that they can exploit the 'divine gift' with impunity, or without being obliged to recycle their work output. It is a telling paradox that the world's most potent aid to sheer velocity mut necessarily be approached through such a slow and laborious expenditure of energy. The lime of the Cauca area is made from limestone, which is heated until it is red-hot then subjected to a reaction with water, which causes it to fissure and produce a fine white powder. In chemical terms, limestone is a calcium carbonate, which on being heated gives off carbon dioxide. This has an exothermic reaction with water, which gives off heat and produces calcium hydroxide, which is a powerful alkali.[12]

The Paez have two different techniques for producing this chemical effect, and the choice between them is dictated by the size of their requirements. A small quantity is made in an ordinary wood fire, preferably of some long-burning hardwood, such as that of a guava tree. The pieces of limestone, usually no more than ten centimetres wide and two centimetres thick, are placed in the fire to warm up. After an hour or so, a pair of hollow bamboo canes are brought out. These are about one metre long and, having openings only at either end, they serve as bellows, being known by the name of 'flutes' or *yuta* in Paez. Usually two people puff on the fire together, but in very rapid alternation, and after an hour or two the stones are finally raised to a sufficiently high temperature being turned over once every fifteen minutes so that they are evenly heated all the way through.

This process is called 'blowing' the lime — *soplar el mambe* in Spanish; *kuétan yútia* in Paez — and it requires the establishment of a rhythm of inhalations and exhalations which can allow small, quick, and indefinitely repeated puffs on the stones. Every so often one of the participants gives a long and sustained blow on his flute, and then rests for a minute or two while he replenishes his mouth with coca leaves and lime. The whole business takes on the marked character of a discipline, with regular breathing and a patterning of body rhythms which add notably to the unique aura of the occasion. The judgement as to when the stones are ready to be removed from the fire is always taken with considerable seriousness and deliberation, and seems to depend far more on a subjective appraisal of 'balance' — between the fire, the stamina of the participants, and the stimulation produced by the coca — than on any clearly defined external characteristics of the stones themselves. Indeed, the practice of *kuétan yûtia* is a perfect example of the kind of social behaviour on which the intimate solidarity of the Paez is based, for although on the explicit level it is nothing more than a chore — and an extremely boring one at that — it contains within its confines a whole complex range of shared emotions, and involves the painstaking transformation of stone, a feature of the hard and hostile cosmos, into lime powder, obviously one of the most important cultural products in a society which uses coca.

The system used for the production of larger quantities of lime is much less common, but many of the same observations can also be made regarding the implicit ritual nature of the occasion. Four stones are used as a base, set in a square with sides of approximately half a metre, and upon these rests a superstructure composed of seven layers of bamboo, cut in strips ten centimetres wide and as long as one side of the square. Each layer is laid at right angles to the previous level, and the chips of limestone are placed in the middle of the upper layer. Two strips of bamboo are then set on either side of the limestone, and the underlying seven layer bamboo sandwich is repeated above. The resulting pile is probably as much as one metre high and, being lit at the bottom, it burns furiously for about an hour. Finally, when all that is left is a pile of hot embers, the flame is fanned for a further hour by stiff leaves set on the end of bamboo sticks. At least two people, and often more, take part in this stage of the process, and many of the remarks made regarding the flute-blowing system are also applicable here. The participants must likewise engage in a very long, drawn-out and repetitive action, which in this case is undertaken by standing on opposite sides of the fire and fanning the flames with a sweeping motion not unlike the swing of a broom.

Towards the end of either of these lengthy processes, an old piece of broken pottery is heated in the fire. The limestone chips are removed from the embers and placed in this receptable. Using the lip of a spoon, or else simply a finger, single drops of water are dropped slowly and carefully onto the stones. As they hit the white-hot surface there is a loud sizzle, and gradually the stones begin to swell, cracking along their lines of fracture and finally crumbling into powder. Since — even after ten minutes of this treatment — there are always some parts of the stone which do not crumble completely, the whole mass is put through a cloth sieve and only the finest powder retained. Small fragments may be ground in a stone mortar, and then put through the sieve as well, but larger pieces are kept to be reheated on another occasion.

The Paez make a distinction between various grades of lime, and these are clearly related to the different geological deposits of limestone in Tierradentro. It is generally recognized that the light brown lime (*kuétan kútchi*), which is extracted from the dark reddish stone in the cliffs at La Muralla, is probably the finest of all. Though very hard, and therefore difficult to process, it is nevertheless sweeter and more effective than any other. Many Paez, however, consider it too abrasive, and prefer the plain white lime (*kuétan ch'ijmé*) which is made from the scintillating black limestone found all over Tierradentro, and most especially at Cohetando — whose very name is a Spanish rendering of *kuétan* — and La Mesa de Togoima, Segovia and San Andrés. There are, furthermore, various other limes which appear greyish or even yellow in colour, but although these are less compacted and easier to 'blow', they are not a very potent reagent, and their use is generally considered the sign of a lazy coca chewer.

It is clear that in pre-Hispanic times a brown lime similar to the Paez *kuétan kútchi* must have been quite a common feature throughout the Cauca area, for Cieza de León spoke specifically in the 1540s of '. . . an earth which is like lime' when describing the use of coca in the vicinity of Cali and Popayán.[13] It is also the more traditional form of lime consumed by many of the non-Paez coca chewers today, especially those of Coconuco and Paletará, and to a lesser extent a few of the more remote groups in southern Cauca. In all these areas it is known by the Spanish name *mambe negro*, and although in a few places it derives its colour from the naturally ruddy tints of the local limestone, in many other parts it is given a brown stain by the addition of cane juice or crude molasses (*panela*) mixed with water.

Unlike the Paez *kuétan kútchi*, however, this *mambe negro* is seldom kept in a gourd in the form of a loose powder, being pressed instead into small round balls of about thirty grams in weight, which are buried in the ground for a few weeks to develop their flavour. Given that sugar was absent in the New World before the Spanish Conquest, it seems likely that the Paez *kuétan kútchi* most closely approximates Cieza's description, and the pressed balls of *mambe negro* must represent a colonial development, a sophistication designed to sweeten the palate of the coca chewers of Popayán. There are even reports from San Agustín that have described, in this century, the addition of other substances such as ash and ground chili peppers (**Capsicum** spp.) to the *mambe negro* of that district.[14]

Nevertheless, it is sad to note that very few non-Paez coca chewers in fact still make their own lime, or even buy it from the small *mambe negro* factory near Paispamba, which is the source of the brown balls sold in the markets of Coconuco and Paletará. In southern Cauca, the vast majority of coca adepts all use the same mass-produced lime — *mambe verde* or *mambe común* — which is pure white (not green, as its name suggests). It is produced at El Carmen, on the flanks of the San Jorge valley, in a major quasi-industrial plant located next to a limestone mine. Sold in large round cakes the size of a pound of cheese, the product is rather harsh, being little better than the industrial lime used as whitewash. When fresh it is damp and friable, when old it turns dry and as hard as stone. It is best when 'matured' underground, wrapped in banana leaves, and then allowed to dry out slightly, so that it is neither damp and volatile nor very chalky.

Discounting the crude *mambe* from El Carmen, one cannot fail to be somewhat impressed by the extremely wide variety of alkaline reagents used in the Cauca area. This feature of the coca habit is also borne out by comparisons with other parts of South America where coca chewing is a traditional cultural trait. The archaeological record would suggest that most of what is today highland Colombia always used limestone derivatives for this purpose, and the present day Tunebo Indians, who live in the cordillera between Bogotá and the Venezuelan border, also employ a system of production very similar to that of the Paez. One variant exists for Kogi, of the Sierra Nevada de Santa Marta, who make their lime from sea-shells called *yotínwe*, which are collected on special expeditions made annually to the shores of the Caribbean.[15]

This shell reagent is in most respects similar to ordinary lime powder, but in addition, it contains slight traces of organic potash, which may account for the preference manifested by the Kogi. By way of comprison, the vegetable ashes used in the Amazon yield only 25 to 30% of lime and 0.5 to 3% of potash, which would seem to suggest that the Indians of that area must employ rather larger quantities in order to achieve the same effects as the stone and shell preparations.[16]

In Peru, certain Indians also prefer a plain white *cal* or *llipta* — for instance, those in the valleys near Trujillo — and there are other types made from sea shells or snail shells which provide an interesting parallel to the customs of the Sierra Nevada de Santa Marta. By far the most popular alkaline reagent used in Peru, however, is the *tocra de montana* produced in the main coca-producing zones hear Huánuco, Ayacucho and Cuzco. This is usually moist, black and reasonably crumbly; it is made from the ashes of banana leaves or cocoa pods, often mixed with a little white lime powder, and bound together with a paste of desiccated, powdered potato mixed with water. In the sixteenth century, at least, it was also quite common to use an ash made not from a vegetable base, but from burned and ground animal bones. The Indians of southern Peru and Bolivia also have another reagent — known generically under the Spanish name *lejía* ('lye') — which adopts a number of very localized characteristics in different regions. The bulk of this substance usually comes from a mixture of potash and lime, derived in the main from the ashes of the stalks of *quinua* — an Andean cereal — or from other plant sources such as the *quenua* tree, bean stalks, banana stems, cacti and various other shrubs which may be found to hand. These are mixed with a number of flavouring substances — anise, sugar, cinnamon, salt, potato broth, and even human urine — then set in greyish or black and brown sticks and cakes, sometimes stamped with a figure of some favourite saint, and dried in the sun until hard.[17]

LIME GOURDS AND COCA POUCHES

The harder forms of alkali used in the chewing of coca — such as the plain *mambe* of southern Cauca, and the *lejía* of Peru and Bolivia — can obviously be carried loose, but the powdered forms would seem to require the use of some container. Throughout the Andes, archaeological sites have yielded a great number of these implements, and in the absence of any actual leaves, their presence has served to mark the extent of prehistoric coca chewing. They were made of horn or bone, gourds, pottery, and even gold, and their careful decoration attests to the singular importance of the coca habit in the ritual and ceremonial life of a great many pre-Conquest societies.

In Colombia today, there are two varieties of gourd used for the purpose of carrying lime powder. One is the *yubúru* (*popóro* in Spanish) which was once employed extensively all over northeastern Colombia and Venezuela, and whose use survives still in the Sierra Nevada de Santa Marta. It has an hour-glass shape and is quite large (15 to 25 centimetres long), being identified botanically as **Crescentia cujete** L. In the Cauca area, the Paez Indians prefer a smaller (5 to 10 centimetres long) lime container, which has a simple pear shape and has been classified as **Lagenaria siceraria** (Mol.) Standl. It grows on the ground like a marrow, and the Paez call it *kuétan tuka*, while in Spanish it is known as a *mambero*.[18]

Both the gourd and the daily ration of coca leaves are normally carried in a special bag, which is slung acros the chest or tied around the waist. In Peru, these commonly have a square shape and are made from finely woven wool — or, in the past, from feathers as well. In Colombia and the Amazon basin wool did not exist before the Spanish Conquest, and thus vegetable fibres were used for this purpose. These could have included cotton (**Gossypium** spp.), various types of sisal or *cabuya* (**Agave** and **Fourcroya** spp.), and other exotic tree fibres, such as that used by the present-day Tunebo Indians for making their coca pouches, which is known as *pita* (**Schoenobiblus cannabinus** Cuatr.)[19] In any case, both the Indians of the Sierra Nevada and those of Cauca have adopted the use of wool coca bags since the arrival of the Spanish and their sheep, most probably because they conserve the freshness of coca better, and prevent it becoming too crisp and dry from the loss of humidity.

Within the Cauca area itself, there are at least four kinds of coca bag still being made, all capable of carrying at least a quarter of a pound of leaves. These are immediately distinguishable from the cotton and sisal bags which are also sometimes bought in the market for the same purpose, for the home-made bags all have a rounded base, whereas the commercial products are square. The Paez use a single needle crochet system to knit what they call a *kuétan yáha* — a 'lime bag', notice, and not a coca bag — and some of the wool is dyed red, blue or yellow, and more recently, purple and green as well. The colours are arranged in one of two decorative techniques: either a simple zig-zag or chevron reaching the full length of the bag, or a more complex pattern which, although maintaining the basic zig-zag idea, breaks up the motif into a number of diagonally placed squares, framed in turn by a double row of inverted triangles. Together with their woven ponchos — *ruanas* in Colombian Spanish — and the long strips of cloth which make up the women's skirts, these *kuétan yáha* bags are undoubtably the finest and most carefully made elements of Paez material culture.

The neighbouring Guambiano Indians have almost entirely abandoned the coca habit, and with it the elaboration of their coca bags — whose name, *war'sh* (with an open 'a', as in 'march'), is the same as that used for the male scrotum. They have continued, however to make reduced versions of this bag as wallets for their cash, and increasingly — in recent years — for the sake of sales to the tourists in Silvia. It is produced by the same crocheting technique as the Paez *kuétan yáha*, but the design is rather different, and involves the juxtaposition of large equilateral triangles in red and blue, inverted next to each other, and running in a continuous band around the middle of an otherwise plain white wool pouch.

The fourth and last type of coca bag in the area is the *pircha* or *peesha* whose use was once a common feature of all the Indians of southern Cauca. It has largely speaking disappeared today from the more acculturated communities in the San Jorge valley, but survives among the older coca chewers of remote reservations such as Caquiona. It is made from the undyed wool of brown and black sheep, and, unlike the system employed further north, is manufactured by knitting with two needles. This produces a denser and more elastic bag, rather narrower than the Paez *kuétan yáha*, and not at all unlike a very thick wool sock. While not wishing to deny the aesthetic merits of the Paez geometrical designs, it nevertheless became clear to me after many months of comparative use that the *pircha* is undoubtably the most practical of the coca bags made in the Cauca area. Its thickness and ability to stretch help keep the ball of coca leaves in the bag well pressed, thus preserving their freshness and humidity much better than the thinner, flatter and looser weave of the Paez *yáha*. Anybody who has had to chew very crisp and dried out coca leaves will immediately appreciate the advantages of a bag which can maintain the original heady aroma and pliable texture of freshly dried coca, and even under the very hottest and most sunny of working conditions.

It would be appropriate to conclude this chapter with a consideration of the way in which the coca bags of the Cauca area are actually worn, for this forms a convenient link with the sexual themes to be discussed in the next section. The fact that the Guambianos use the word 'scrotum' to identify their coca bags is hardly accidental, for it would seem indisputable that such pouches have always traditionally been worn by men tied around the waist, and hanging between their legs directly over the sexual organs. The carrying of a distinctly phallic lime-container inside the bag further reinforces the symbolism, of course, but it is also true that this fashion of wearing the coca pouch does have a more strictly practical function as well, allowing the coca chewer the easiest possible access to leaves and lime gourd, clearly an important feature in the course of heavy agricultural work. Women, however, are also well aware of the sexual undertones, and — eschewing convenience in the interests of propriety — always carry their coca bags discreetly at the hip, its strap tied around the waist, or slung over one shoulder and across the chest.

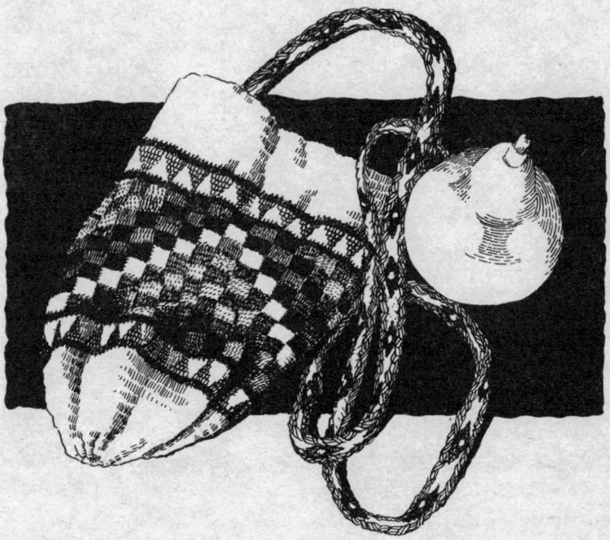

Paez: *kuétan yáha* and *kuétan tuka* (coca bag and lime gourd).

Paez woman with *kuétan yáha*.

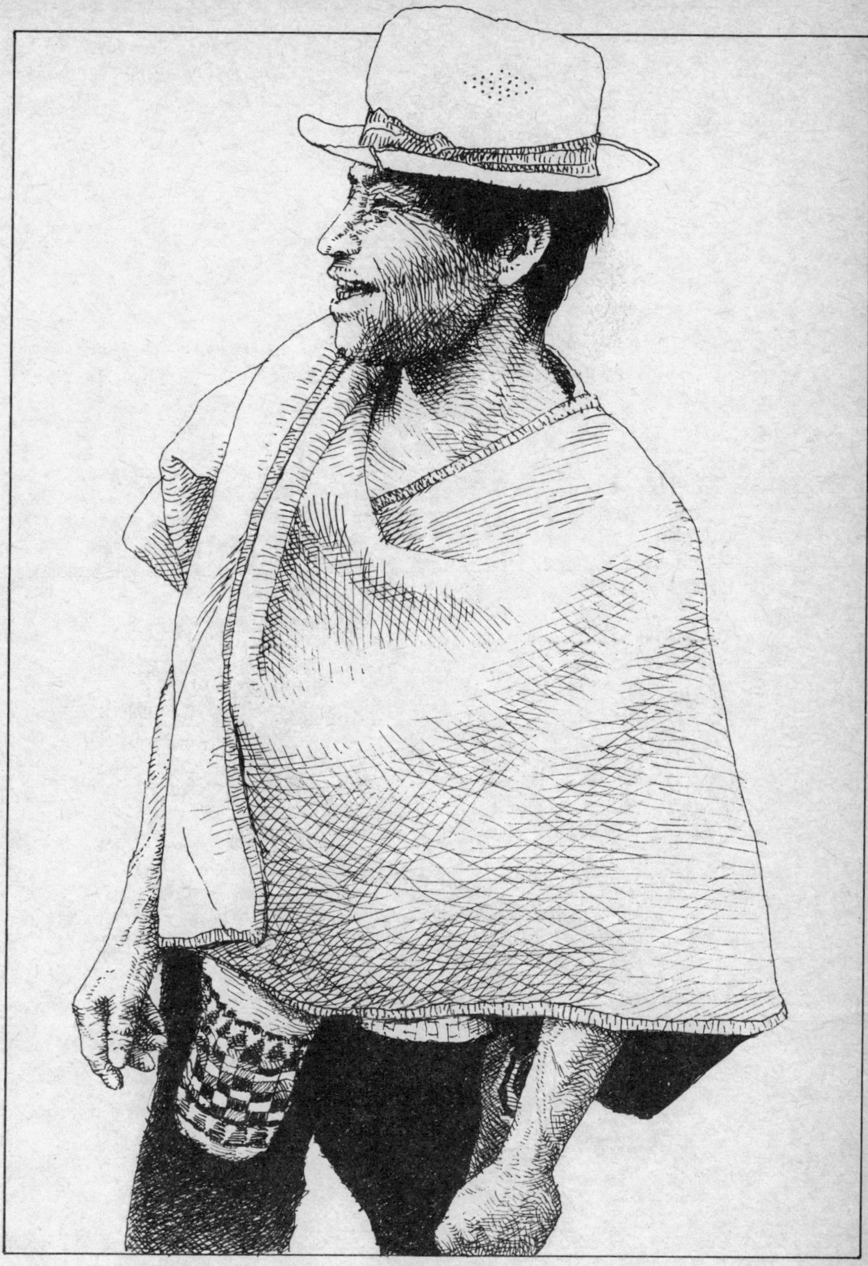

Paez man with *kuétan yáha*.

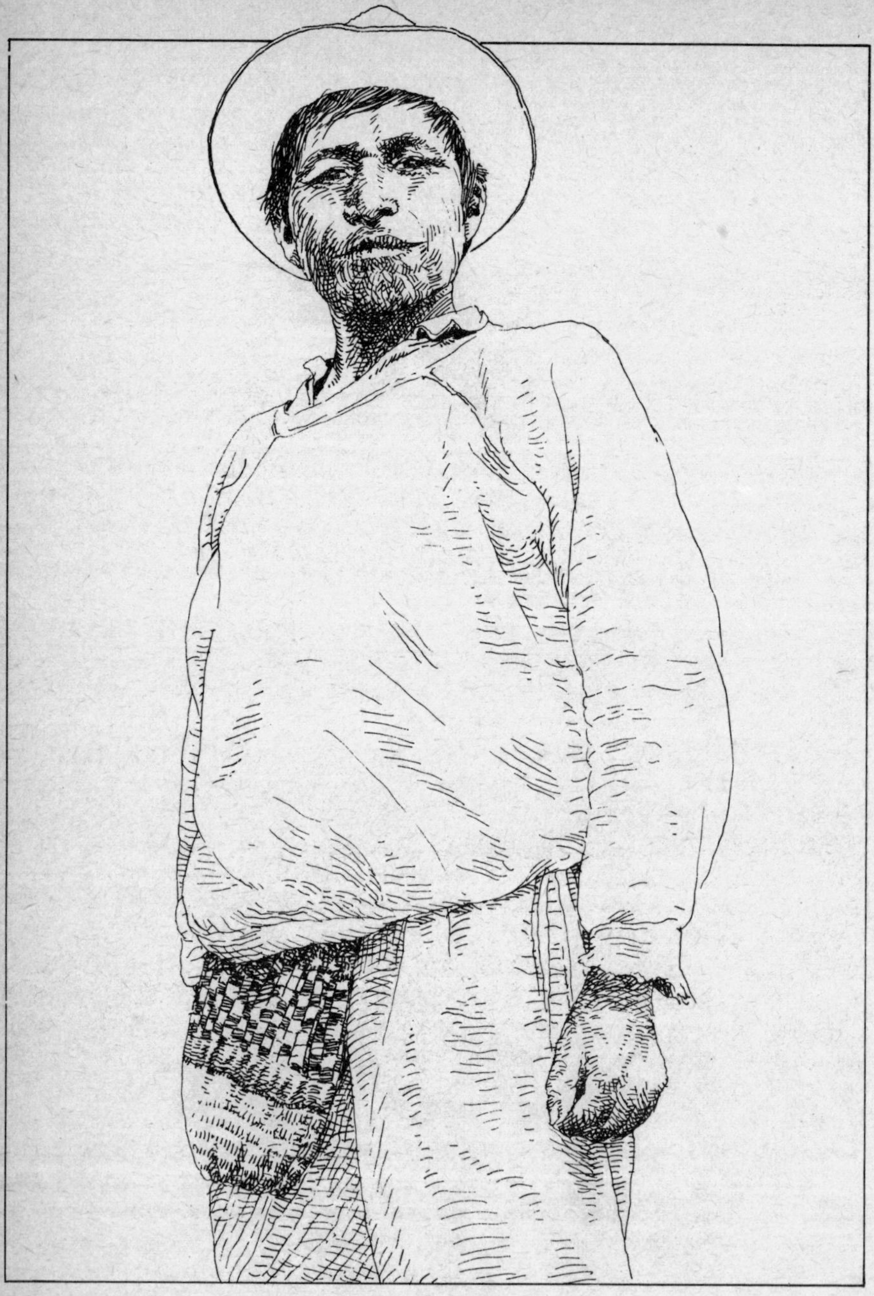

Paez man with *kuétan yáha* slung around waist.

Paez woman from Tumbichuque, Tierradentro. Notice the coca bag over her right hip.

Man playing flute, Almaguer, southern Cauca. Notice the modern type of square coca bag over his left hip.

Paez man adding lime to his coca. Notice the open gourd in his left hand, and the two *kuétan yáha* bags.

VII. Mama Coca Revisited

A preliminary definition of the *figura* of Mama Coca has already been attempted from the mythological point of view, and I would now like to consider her female character in terms of a more explicit sexual politics. Betraying perhaps greater respect for *macho* stereotypes than for the subtle nuances of the original Indian concept, it has long been common in our own culture to reduce the ambivalence, the very polymorphous perversity of Mama Coca to the role of a simple symbol of eroticism, and to assume that her material manifestations — be they coca leaves or refined cocaine — should be considered in some absolute sense an 'aphrodisiac'. The words of Sigmund Freud provide a typical case in point: 'The natives of South America, who represented their goddess of love with coca leaves in her hand, did not doubt the stimulative effect of coca on the genitalia . . . '[1]

Physiologically speaking, it seems indisputable that any stimulant will tend to improve sexual performance in the short term — and in much the same way as it will improve work performance of any kind. Furthermore, the direct action of the alkaloid cocaine in heightening the sensitivity of the nervous system will obviously be most effective — or will be 'felt' the most — in such areas of the body as the genitalia, which are characterized by a relatively dense concentration of nerve-ends. Even in Indian cultures, the most common and popular association has always been that between coca and male potency; clay figurines of the pre-Columbian period — particularly from the rather exuberant sexual cultures of Ecuador and the north coat of Peru — often show a grossly exaggerated phallus in association with pronounced, coca-induced swellings in the cheek.[2] In more recent times, the same general idea has surfaced in the widespread habit of applying cocaine to the more sensitive parts of a man's glans penis, where its pronounced local freeze can serve to sustain uncertain erections and to prevent premature ejaculation.

The fact that such titillation is most commonly associated with the male rather than the female sexual organs is probably no more than a faithful reflection of our society's pervasive sexist bias. It could readily be challenged by the observation that — at least in modern Babylon — it is women rather than men who most commonly report the efficacity of cocaine as an aphrodisiac, albeit perhaps because it reduces certain inhibitions and allows many a shy lady to adopt a more aggressive sexual role. All the same, it would be tempting to stand the whole cocaine-as-aphrodisiac argument on its head, pointing out that — at least among men — the sharp fluctuations of metabolism produced by cocaine may often lead to states of temporary impotence and sexual indifference. The point — in any case is hardly worth pursuing in too much detail, for we are dealing here with coca and not cocaine and, especially in the context of sexual behaviour, the difference between their respective pharmacologies would appear to be quite significant. And it must be pointed out that — at least among the Indians of Cauca — such extremes as impotence or rabid lust seldom, if ever, result from the chewing of coca leaves, if only because sex and coca chewing tend to be associated with different places, different moods, and different times of day.

Coca, then, can only be considered an aphrodisiac really insofar as it is a stimulant and an euphoriant. For this very reason, it would be preferable to remain with the idea of coca as 'feminine' not in the physical sense of something sexually arousing to a man, but more in the symbolic sense of a complement, a disciplinary counterpoint to the brute force of an aggressive masculinity. A perfect example of this kind of complementarity can be seen in the attitude of Paez women to coca chewing. As might be expected, it is extremely rare to find the younger women ever engaging in this habit, and normally they only begin to do so once they are finished with the business of bearing children. Many do not seriously take up coca chewing until they have stopped menstruating altogether, for there is a clear sense in which a woman's menopause alters the community's perception of her status, allowing her to adopt many of the more dominant male roles and activities, including the unrestrained use of coca.[3]

From such uses of coca as a complement to the essentially masculine functions of men and post-menstrual women, it is, however, but a short step to the idea of using coca as an actual substitute for sexual relationships of a more intimate kind. This is certainly the case among those very rare Paez males who elect to live alone — either as widowers, or as the result of some basic incapacity to deal with women — for such individuals are often the most voracious consumers of coca leaves. Nevertheless, it is among the Kogi Indians of the Sierra Nevada de Santa Marta that the idea of coca as surrogate for sexual indulgence finds its most elaborate expression. Here it becomes the central feature of an esoteric discipline whose aim is to sublimate or channel the pursuit of purely genital gratification into activities — such as dancing, myth recitation and music making —

considered more pleasing to the gods and more in keeping with the memory of the 'Ancients'.

According to the unashamedly neo-Freudian account of the Kogi published by Gerardo Reichel-Dolmatoff, a young man's initiation to the coca habit includes the ritual 'piercing' of a large lime gourd or *popóro* which, possessing the shape of an hour-glass, can readily be seen to represent a woman's body. At the same time, the long stick or spatula used to pierce the gourd plays the role of the male member, and the young man is taught to express all his sexual desires and frustrations by means of an almost constant rubbing and rattling of the spatula on the mouth and insides of the gourd. In the process of doing this, the Kogi coca chewer also licks his spatula and deposits a crust of yellowish, coca-stained lime around the mouth of the gourd, a crust whose prominence gradually increases with the passage of time. Since the size of the crust is considered an important indication of personal status, it is only very occasionally trimmed with a knife, and any accidental breakage is considered an extremely bad omen.

Through its association with coca and with collective myth recitals, the lime gourd eventually comes to mean not only 'woman' but also 'food' and 'memory'. Little wonder, therefore, that — unless he happens to be eating or working in the fields — no Kogi will ever be seen without his lime gourd and spatula in his hand. Most important for the present argument, the Kogi assert that — once a short period of adolescent stimulation has been overcome — the long-term effect of coca chewing is to produce an accumulating sexual indifference, amounting finally to an almost total impotence. In a culture which considers genital sexuality to be dangerous, a mere distraction from the really crucial areas of experience, this outcome cannot fail to be considered extremely welcome and desirable.[4]

I have stressed this point considerably, because there was a sense in which my own obsession with Mama Coca also finally came to be transcended only through a very similar, albeit temporary, repudiation of the delights and pleasures of genital sexuality. And so, given the theoretical weight which I had originally attributed to the idea of Mama Coca, it can readily be understood why this repudiation was not simply of sex — itself an entirely neutral factor — but also, more significantly, any kind of narcissitic 'romance', any sort of yearning or longing for the Other in terms which merely mirrored the Self. Here I would include not only Mama Coca, but all idolatrous 'images' of the godhead, all alienating scientific 'models' and the like; for the eventual subordination or exorcising of Mama Coca provides a good illustration of the way in which the structure of an inquiry can be radically altered by the very process of investigation itself, by the irruption of reality into the carefully controlled frame of reference demanded by a theory.

The matter clearly requires some explanation, for it may not be obvious to the reader how personal relationships can come to affect the outcome of anthropology, an edifice whose traditional foundations have always rested on the unquestioned principle of observation-through-detachment, that is to say on the shifting sands of an illusory conceit. It will be remembered that in the first chapter I described my initial meetings with *misiá* Eleonora, the widow who showed me how to prepare lime from the limestone which abounds in Tierradentro. With the benefit of hindsight, I can now see that — being without any female companionship at the time — a feeling of vague amorous longing had gradually come to be identified with my concept of Mama Coca, and that both had finally come to rest on the person of *misiá* Eleonora herself, the woman with whom I shared the closest affective bonds while in the field. In this I was very fortunate, for it was she who pointed out the confusion between these two components, she who had ultimately disentangled the knot by sending me to see her brother Don Elizondo, one of the most highly regarded shamans in the district.

Truth to tell, I hesitated for a month or two before I went to visit him, for I felt a strange unwillingness to become involved in what all the Paez — with their carefully veiled remarks and surreptitious winks — had always assumed to be my single major preoccupation, the 'night-time' coca chewing involved in their system of magic and witchcraft. I justified my reticence with the excuse that it was more important to come to terms with the ordinary context of day-time chewing first. But, as I was forced to recognize, with a growing sense of alarm gnawing at my more rational, sceptical self, the more I attempted to deny the path pointed out to me by *misiá* Eleonora, the more insistent became the hints and the prods of what — for the sake of argument — I will continue to call Mama Coca.

Despite all the most assiduous mental hygiene, manifestations of this figure appeared almost nightly in my dreams, no longer exclusively tied to the image of *misiá* Eleonora, but instead a shadowy, subliminal presence whose indistinct features sometimes invaded my thoughts even in a perfectly conscious, waking state. Often she would manifest herself simply as a gut sensation — the warm rush, the electric buzz off a chew of coca leaves. On other occasions she adopted more troubling forms, her presence marked by the low moan of a woman's voice over an empty landscape, by the sudden heady smell of freshly toasted coca, just as if a large sack of leaves had suddenly been opened right underneath my nose. An olfactory hallucination? Such phenomena could always be explained away, of course. *Calma*, I told myself, it was simply a case of the investigative model getting out of hand, producing emotional feedback between the material thing — coca itself — and its ideal category, the image locked away in the investigator's mind. A simple case of conceptual endocannibalism, I thought, well pleased with my ability to dismiss in intellectual terms what

I was so obviously incapable of exorcising from the real — that is to say magical — life of the spirit, the subconscious, the soul.

Needless to say, when I did finally come to visit Don Elizondo, I did so in bad faith. I had, of course, done a little preliminary reading on the subject of Paez shamanism, but — to judge at least from the somewhat mechanical, mid-century treatments of the theme — the esoteric practices of this particular group of Indians were unbelievably tedious and ritualistic, hardly credible in fact, and dominated by a rigid dualism between nice, 'good' magic, and nasty, 'evil' witchcraft.[5] The whole thing reminded me uncomfortably of freshman anthropology courses and stuffy lecture halls, and that was a memory I could certainly do without. The various sources had pointed, however, to the great importance which coca, tobacco, and other herbs shared in the shaman's pharmacopeia, and thus it was that I first went to Elizondo's house with a number of tidy and strictly 'medical' questions to ask him about the use of his various plants.

It was a sunny, pleasant afternoon, and Elizondo was sitting in the middle of a pile of *bagazo* — the remains of crushed sugar-cane — more than a little drunk from the *núsa* or *guarapo* — fermented cane juice — which he had been imbibing with some distant cousins who had come to the valley to trade for coca leaves. They were all in far too good a mood to be irritated by my eager questions, my collecting of samples and compulsive note taking, but all the same, I often had a sneaky suspicion that they were simply taking the piss. Only when I offered coca leaves to the assembled company, and started chewing myself, did the conversation take a more personal turn, with my awkward questions giving way first to an almost disconcerting amount of back-slapping and shoulder-hugging, and then to the question which, on Elizondo's lips, was the last thing I wanted to hear: 'My sister has told me that you have seen *la duenda*, and want to talk to me about her. Is that true?'

A deathly hush fell over the half-dozen men collected in the dusty backyard. All eyes were on me — inquisitive, challenging. Sucking hard on my wad of coca leaves, I blurted out: 'Some other day, perhaps?' There was a chorus of hollow laughs from the men as they shifted uncomfortably on their stools, a sense of unresolved tension and disappointment hanging heavy in the air. Elizondo shook his head and retired back to the other side of the sugar-mill, observing me cautiously, prepared to bide his time. I avoided any further mention of the subject, and it was already dark by the time I dragged myself away and stumbled home with one of Elizondo's cousins leading me along the path. 'Dangerous for a man to walk alone at night,' he said, 'especially if he has seen *la duenda* . . .' He sniggered in anticipation of the horrorshow to come, the echoes of his voice resounding off the hillside, heightening the menace which lurked in every shadow. Mirror eyes — or so they seemed — peeping through the lace outlines of the vegetation. Shades of paranoia lysergica . . .

There was nothing here, however, that I had not learnt to deal with — and deal with successfully — before; and I was damned if mere insinuation would be enough to unhinge my mind, to succeed where so many chemical toxins had failed to prevail in the past. Accordingly, my next few meetings with Elizondo would always repeat more or less the same pattern; I would ask a few questions about medicinal herbs, he would answer them with great candour and politeness, and inevitably, he would point out that the plants themselves were quite powerless, that they depended for effect on the magical contexts in which they were used. This observation always led up to the same question regarding *la duenda* — my Mama Coca — the spirit whom he always gave the Spanish name, presumably in deference to my still rudimentary grasp of the Paez language and Paez cosmology. Still unwilling to enter into any consideration of what could be easily dismissed as the 'nebulous', the 'supernatural', I continued to ignore or evade his question, hoping that with time he would grow tired of it and eliminate it from his repertoire completely.

It took a major accident to finally bring me to my senses. On the afternoon of the 23rd December, 1973 — more than six months after I had first come to the valley of Pisimbalá — I mentioned to Elizondo that I had read in a newspaper some days previously that there would be a solar eclipse the next morning. He looked at me in some surprise, then muttered angrily: 'The moon covering the sun . . . this is the work of your *duenda*. She is a dangerous, rotten, filthy old hag. You will be well advised to stay at home with your doors closed. Above all, do not try to look at the eclipse . . . ' There was a challenge, almost a threat, implicit in his words.

On waking the next morning, there was obviously no alternative but to go out and face the test resolutely and without any fear for the consequences. Filling my coca bag to its full capacity, I set out without breakfast on a two-hour climb to the top of the highest promontory in the district, the Filo del Aguacate, a narrow ridge dotted with countless small prehistoric burial chambers, many of which — incidentally, but hardly accidentally — contained a number of curious representations of crescent moons (or could they be eclipses?) In any case, the astronomic event — a partial eclipse at this latitude, not a complete one — was hardly very remarkable, as it remained shrouded in thick cloud most of the morning. Tamely, almost timorously, I made the best of the occasional clear patches to look at the heavenly bodies through glasses especially smoked for the occasion. Dumbly, cynically I sat blowing joint after joint, chewing my coca leaves and waiting for the avenging sword of the vindictive goddess to smite me dead. Nothing so dramatic occurred, nothing so spectacular. In the end, the eclipse had come and gone and the world continued just the same. A little depressed by such a complete failure to hook up with Fate, I descended once again into the valley of my own imminent fatality, arriving back on the farm where I lived by the middle of the afternoon. Danger? What danger . . .

It was only after forgetting about the whole matter that disaster finally struck home. I had decided to take a shower outside, at a small cascade fed from the stream by a long and complicated system of pipes made from split bamboo. There was a blockage somewhere in the system, and it required clearing if I was to enjoy my shower. I found the cause of the trouble in a mass of dead leaves, which had collected in a place hidden in the middle of some thick undergrowth, right on a corner where the bamboo pipe crossed over a small, but deeply eroded gully. Apparently it often blocked at this point, for someone had toppled a thick tree trunk just below so as to provide easy access to the pipe. I climbed onto this trunk without the slightest apprehension, and walked out to the middle of the makeshift bridge. At this moment — with all my defences down, a prey to complete insouciance — the trunk suddenly shuddered and broke, leaving me to fall three metres to the bottom of the gully, cracking a couple of ribs on a jagged boulder as I landed. The agony was intense, my head rested on a rotten fragment of the tree trunk — so soft — and I passed out.

The period of convalescence was long and tedious, and it must have been more than a week before I returned to Elizondo's house and showed him my bruises. Not surprisingly, he interpreted my misfortune in terms of what he considered to be an obsession with the wicked bitch goddess, and he admonished me for my continued dependence on the female spirit, the female model — be it Mama Coca, *la duenda*, or indeed, his sister *misiá* Eleonora herself. 'These are things of a child,' he said, with scarcely concealed derision, 'a man cannot spend his life suckling his mother's breast.' Then he turned and smiled warmly, almost exultantly, and added: 'Tonight, it just so happens, I am going to *work*. Wouldn't you like to stay and *accompany* me?' Clearly, by this stage, I could hardly refuse . . .

COCA AND PAEZ SHAMANISM.

Thereafter our relationship carried on from strength to strength, and throughout 1974 I must have maintained closer and more intimate contacts with Elizondo than with anyone else in the entire Cauca area. Though he often sent me to study with other Indians in the neighbouring valleys — many of whom were older and more respected, and more traditional in their practices — it was nevertheless with him that I learnt practically all the basic principles of night-time coca chewing as it is practiced by the Paez. From the outset, he emphasized that it would be impossible to learn things 'about' shamanism without a serious commitment to actually working as an initiate myself, and thus it was that I came to be introduced always to his family and his patients as an 'assistant'.

I cannot say that I was entirely happy with this role, for it threatened to expose a number of inconsistencies underlying the very nature of my field work. After all, the simple descriptive or historical approaches to the coca phenomenon were very much easier to handle; all they implied was a bare modicum of research ability, and a willingness to travel under what were sometimes rather uncomfortable conditions. To tackle shamanism, on the other hand, seemed somehow to be a much less enticing prospect altogether. In the first place, there was little doubt that it would demand a much more thorough, substantial appraisal of my own supposed 'participation' in Paez society and culture than I was really able to envisage at the time. By extension, any immersion in the world of shamanism also threatened to call into question the entire sustaining myth of anthropology itself — the idea that one can investigate the 'structure' or the 'function' of a given system of beliefs without becoming a party to those beliefs oneself. The choice is always stated in the most coercive terms: either you must accept the conventional wisdom of science and persevere with a purely rational inquiry — in which case, inescapably, you usurp the role of the gods, arrogating for yourself their own purpose, which is to suffuse life with a divine meaning or you just abandon the cloying certainties of academe forever, actually making that qualitative leap of faith which renders any further sociological inquiry a largely superfluous undertaking.

We would do well, however, to ask ourselves whether blind faith or ineffectual cynicism are really the only possible alternatives. It is difficult to avoid the conclusion that the terms of such a choice are based essentially on a false dichotomy — materialism *or* transcendence — whose only real object must be to deny the unifying, purposeful vision which animates both the best of mysticism and the most courageous of innovative science as well. The political dimension of this task is cemented through recourse to an orthodox scientism, a mish-mash of meaningless theoretical constructs which reduce every individual to an arithmetic of sterile role playing, and which reflect nothing so much as the mechanistic categories of Western professionalism itself. Instead of the shaman in all his glory, we are taught to think in terms of some unlikely cross between a herbalist/doctor/priest/psychotherapist/actor/charlatan/mystic; we are taught to separate his functions so that we do not have to consider him a whole person, capable of conflicting and often contradictory responses.

Precisely in order to avoid such a very mistaken impression, the present chapter emphatically will not attempt to resolve the tension between the reverent and sceptical approaches to the subject of shamanism. On the contrary, it will seek always to maintain the tension and develop it, for the aim here is to expose the parameters of choice and not to justify any particular conclusion, any definitive or final solution to the question. Not only is this faithful to my own (mixed) feelings on the subject; but also it seems to be the only real tribute I can make to Elizondo and the Paez people as a whole, whose culture is mercifully so free of either extreme — gratuitous esotericism or hard-bitten cynicism. Elizondo would have been the first to admit that the social functions of his practice were just as important as any amount of communications with the gods, but he would not, for all that, ever attempt to treat sickness or witchcraft without the active assistance of his tutelary deities. They were, in a very real sense, seen both to represent and reinforce the principles of natural justice; they were considered an effective part of the bio-sphere, active in the ecological politics of destruction and regeneration, a real force, suffusing all of creation with meaning and purpose.

Often Elizondo would put his hand over my heart, literally, and ask me if I believed in 'god' — *diós*. Since I knew it was not the Christian trinity that he was on about, I felt no qualms about answering in the affirmative, but all the same, I could not help finding his questioning of my faith a little disconcerting. Certainly, I was aware that his aim was to provoke in me some perception of the palpable reality of his gods, but I was not very sure that such a transformation — the step from a rational acceptance of the supernatural as an idealization of the natural world, to a sublime experience of the actual immanence of the deities themselves — was entirely within my grasp, at least in the initial stages of the inquiry. We will return to consider this question of being able to 'see' the gods again later, for it is obviously of crucial importance in being able to understand the real springs of the shamanic vocation. At the outset, however, my own inclination was to try analyzing the question of faith in terms of consciousness itself.

A fruitful point of departure was to be found in the rather obvious differences between the shaman's and the anthropologist's views of the function of magic and witchcraft. One might, perhaps, see fit to adopt the cautious perspective of conventional social science; claiming that the outside observer is alone capable of perceiving the 'objective' role played by the shaman, since his own understanding is necessarily wrapped up in an egocentric or entirely 'subjective' view of events. The problem with this approach is that it presupposes some sort of unequivocal definition of what constitutes the difference between objective and subjective forms of awareness. In other words, it seems to ignore the fact that both objectivity and subjectivity are part and parcel of the same intellective process. As Jean-Paul Sartre has been fond of pointing out:

> 'There are two ways to fall into idealism: the one consists in dissolving the real into subjectivity; the other in denying all real subjectivity in the interests of objectivity. The truth is that subjectivity is neither

The late Juan Penkue — a famous shaman of San Andrés de Pisimbalá. This photograph was taken only a week or two before his death; the result of a witchcraft contest.

> everything nor nothing; it represents a moment in the objective process (that in which externality is internalized), and this moment is perpetually eliminated only to be perpetually reborn.'[6]

To truly 'participate' as an anthropologist, therefore, means to accept that subjective experience will modify and yes, even distort the tidy objectivity of the sociological approach; it means to admit that any understanding of objective social processes is itself dependent on an antecedent moment of subjective awareness in the field. In a sense, I felt that this was the 'faith' that Elizondo was demanding of me — not, perhaps, to 'see' his gods, but rather to see the events which unfolded before me with an open mind, and without any recourse to any preconceived models of behaviour. All this may seem perfectly straightforward, and the more significant point surely must be that the implications of the objective-subjective double bind cannot be limited simply to the person of the anthropologist, but must also be made equally applicable to the figure of the shaman himself. He is not operating — as many 'scientists' would want us to believe — in a well of hopelessly alienated subjectivity, he is not merely a psychic automaton capable of 'projecting' forces and energies of an extrasensory kind. In order to project successfully, he must know what he is up against, and the discipline of shamanism is concerned precisely with opening up the perception of the initiate to communications from the external world. He must learn to 'internalize' these messages accurately, so that his (subjective) reading of events forms an accurate reflection of the wider, objective social reality in which shamanism is practiced.

In Western culture, the transfer of information is largely considered to be a question of language and graphic images, elements whose neat form finds a sympathetic echo in the structure of our own rationalist intellectual apparatus. The Paez have, perhaps, rather less reason to place their faith in the powers of reasonable argument and logical debate. The shamans, in particular, appear to lend far greater credence to a form of communication which uses the body itself as its medium. Herein lies the singular importance of coca chewing in the night-time context, for it alone is capable of promoting — by means of a 'magic' which the West would see, perhaps more prosaically, in terms of simple pharmacology — the *senas* (signals) or involuntary muscular twitches which serve as the basis of almost all Paez divination. The very verb 'to divine' — *peijúia* in Paez — usually implies that the shaman remain seated outside for long hours during the night, interpreting the sudden involuntary spasms which a potent, coca-induced stimulation must almost inevitably produce in his motionless body. In day-to-day practice, therefore, the divinatory 'trance' of the Paez shaman has little to do with any visionary state or any actual 'possession' by a given spirit, but rather, depends to a very large extent on a carefully orchestrated state of 'automatic' communication which uses the coca-stimulated body itself as its vehicle.

Similar systems of body-mysticism were also at one time quite common among a great number of other Colombian Indian tribes, particularly those whose languages belonged to the widespread macro-Chibcha group. Chronicle sources report that the twitching of fingers and the movement of the joints were considered to be 'omens' by the sixteenth-century Muiscas of the Bogotá plateau. Their contemporaries, the Tairona of Santa Marta, are also described as practicing divination by means of muscle twitching and fingernail tapping. To this day, the neighbouring Kogi Indians of the Sierra Nevada de Santa Marta still engage in very similar practices, thus providing close parallels to the Paez case, and — since all these societies are well known for their use of coca — stressing the importance of this drug in determining the use of *senas* as a system of divination.[7]

'Divination' is itself, of course, a very nebulous term, and one would do well to consider the precise applications which the Paez have found for their *senas*. Often they serve merely to determine the right moment to perform a given ritual — be it a cleansing ceremony or the repudiation of a witchcraft attack — and sometimes they are used to determine which particular herbs should be used in curing a given patient of his illness. For this, the shaman sits with his trousers rolled up to the knee and his herbs piled beside him, passing them — one by one — up his right leg from the ankle to the knee. Those herbs which cause a twitch in the calf muscles are the ones which should be used to treat a particular case, and the others are thereafter discarded.

In some cases, however, the stimulation brought on by coca — when taken in an immobile state — is so great that the nervous reaction may become excessive, and the *senas* are then too numerous and insistent to be effectively interpreted. The Paez consider only the single twitch to be an authentic *sena*, and any trembling or repetitive twitching is not given any magical connotations. Indeed, the necessity of controlling the *senas*, and maintaining their frequency within acceptable bounds, may be the real explanation for the widely reported use of tobacco and other herbs as masticatories consumed together with coca leaves. In the Cauca area, tobacco in the form of cigars is commonly chewed or smoked along with coca, and the combination of the two plants — and of a third, the *chayuts* herb, whose tranquilizing powers further reinforce the tobacco effect — are usually considered essential in achieving any significant evocation of the *senas*.

The actual *senas* themselves are subject to a considerable amount of personal interpretation, and the long ten or twenty year process involved in becoming a respected shaman in the Paez community involves a patient, gradual attunement to the meaning of one's own body symbolism. Too rigid a definition of the precise connotation of the *senas* in each major muscle would obviously be an oversimplification, but it may, nevertheless, be possible to establish certain general guidelines regarding their interpretation.[8] Any real meaning seems to depend a great deal on the context in which the *senas* occur, and thus they must be seen in terms of answers to specific questions posed by the shaman. Very few *senas* have any absolute or irreversible meanings, even within the experience of a single individual, and certainly there is no one pattern held in common by all the Paez.

The key to the reading of *senas* lies in their dramatic potential, and a twitch in one particular muscle has as many meanings as that muscle has movements and uses. The case of the limb muscles, which could be used for a great number of different actions, provides an excellent example of the variety of possible interpretations. Depending on the attendant circumstances, different muscular *senas* could mean going or coming, lifting or dropping, stepping or slipping, or any other set of mutually exclusive movements associated with the limbs. Other muscles have fewer dramatic connotations, and therefore their meaning is rather more clearly defined. A case in point would be that of the heart muscles: *senas* affecting this organ are considered an interruption of its normal involuntary action, and by analogy with the effects of a heart failure, they are universally thought to indicate the imminence of some mortal accident or homicidal attack. In many other cases, it is not the muscular capacity for action that is involved at all, but instead, a dramatic event that rubs on the body surface from without. Examples of this would include a *sena* running down the cheek — indicating tears, and by extension, a death or misfortune in the family — or one encircling the wrist — signifying the use of a rope or handcuffs, and therefore, the imprisonment of an individual by the authorities.

This dramatic or imitative aspect of the *senas* cannot, however, always provide an entirely adequate explanation of their meaning. Another interpretation would see the *senas* as points of resistance produced along the course taken by psychic energy as it flows through the body of the shaman. This energy — conceived as a current analogous to that of an electric circuit or magnetic field — is considered to enter the human organism from the ground and through the right foot, circulating up the right-hand side to the crown of the head, then down the left-hand side, and finally leaving the body again at the left foot. It is in order to promote an uninterrupted flow of this energy that herbal remedies and the shaman's *tama* wand are passed from right to left across the patient's body during treatment. Predictably, one very effective act of offensive witchcraft is to place a chewed wad of coca and magical herbs under the right foot of a rival when he is not watching, thereby 'blocking' the flow of energy into his body and rendering him virtually impotent. It is clear that the crown of the head must be thought of as a crucial point in the total flow — since it is here that the incoming energy is reversed, and becomes outgoing — and so a *sena* on this spot is taken to mean interruption, disaster, or the imminence of a witchcraft attack in the form of a bolt of lightning to the brain.

Any *sena* which runs counter to the normal direction of flow, that is to say, a *sena* in the thigh, calf, ankle or toe which runs down the right-hand leg, or up the left-hand leg, is usually considered to be indicative of a worsening condition. Any *sena* which runs in the same direction as the flow of energy — up the right leg, or down the left leg — is considered to be indicative of an improvement. The actual extremity of the toes is the most important point; should a *sena* run from the instep to the point of the toe on the right foot, death is unavoidable and the shaman will refuse to treat his patient any longer. In the left foot, however, the same *sena* usually means that a definitive cure is at hand. It is the combination, then, of the dramatic aspects of the *senas* with their explanation as points of resistance along the path of this psychic energy, which together allows of such a bewildering variety of interpretation. Thus a calf muscle may indicate with a *sena* the arrival of a friend — if on the right hand side — or of a stranger — if on the left. Twitches on the sole of the foot suppose that a journey will be undertaken shortly by the shaman himself, either as a quest — right foot — or as an escape — left foot. If *senas* should occur in the same organ on both sides of the body, it is usually taken as a sign of some impending confrontation or witchcraft contest. The organ itself serves to determine the ground on which this contest will take place, whether it be agility (foot *senas*), strength (arm *senas*), vision (eye *senas*), or any other physical or mental capacity.

The Paez use of *senas* as a system of divination — with its indirect, but substantial reliance on the pharmacology of coca chewing — differs notably from the kind of divination practiced by the Indians of the Central Andes, who tend to use the coca leaves themselves in a more explicit fashion. Bertonio's 1612 Aymara dictionary used the phrase *cocana ulljatha* — meaning 'to divine by means of looking at coca' — and this must be the system recently described by La Barre, in which a handful of leaves are thrown onto a cloth. Again, the interpretation of the throw is situational or contextual — being mainly employed in order to assess the desirability of some future action — but in general, the upper sides are taken to indicate good fortune, whereas the underside of the leaves usually mean bad luck.[9] The Quechua, on the other hand, normally practice their form of divination by means of chewed leaves. Two different systems are reported; one involves the interpretation of coca juice spat out onto the hand, and the other requires the chewing of a single good leaf into a ball. When this is removed from the mouth, a favourable outcome may be indicated by the fact that the leaf stalk sticks out of the chewed ball, whereas misfortune would be suggested by a projection of the opposite tip of the leaf.[10]

Another notable feature of the Paez is their unwillingness to use coca leaves as any form of 'offering', a practice which has been very widely reported elsewhere, even among other Chibcha-speaking groups such as the Kogi of the Sierra Nevada and the Muiscas of Bogotá and Tunja.[11] The only possible exception to this would be provided by the Paez custom of burying coca with the dead, but even this would seem to be less an 'offering' in the strict sense, than a case of providing provisions for the deceased in his coming voyage to the next world. The reticence of the Paez to use coca as an offering may be due to the fact that they consider magical power — like the *senas* — to emanate not from the coca itself, but from the actual chewing of coca by an individual shaman. In other words, within the Paez scheme it would seem that coca leaves themselves are quite devoid of any innate potency, and depend for their effect entirely on the specific context in which they are employed. Not only does this indicate a surprising coherence with the latest views in pharmacology — those that stress the importance of cultural 'set' and environmental 'setting' in determining the effects of a given form of drug use — but it also implies the recognition of distinctly non-material cosmology, in which the purely chemical attributes of coca are themselves subject to far greater forces, capable of either blocking or releasing the plant's yield of alkaloid, and of denying or potentiating the forces solicited by the shaman from the leaves.

The underlying principles are not difficult to grasp — at least not in their basic outline — and not surprisingly, they bear comparison with many other religious systems of a similar type. Living in close contact with the natural world, the Paez recognize that all of creation is subject to an inescapable cycle of growth, destruction, and transformation, and furthermore, they stoically accept the fact that the human body cannot itself be excepted from these biological processes. Within the context of this predatory order — the daily business of eating and being eaten — only two points may be said to represent lasting values, and it is around these twin pillars that the entire logic of Paez shamanism is based. On the one hand, there exists the idea of an ultimate Creator: *Diós* or *Agnus*, his name possibly derived from the colonial missionaries' Agnus Dei; whose immobility and permanence is complemented by a more dynamic divinity, *El Trueno* or *Peeshím* ('Thunder'), the culture hero of the more traditional, unashamedly heathen shamans. At the opposite pole there lies the irreducible spirit of the individual, the soul — normally seen as the 'pulse' or heartbeat — which leaves the body after death. Everything else is considered to subsist in a state of flux, and nothing is more liable to sudden upsets than the body, the human frame itself. It would not, therefore, be unfair to say that Paez shamanism functions principally as a means of reestablishing communication and solidarity between the individual and his gods, lending strength and conviction to a faltering 'pulse', and thereby enabling each person to overcome the parasitic forces which would deprive him or her of life on earth — be they natural forces and natural impurities inherent in the environment, or more importantly, social forces within the community at large.

Paez shamans rarely choose their profession by means of a conscious act of will, but instead have it forced upon them by a mixture of insistent, unsolicited *senas* and visionary experiences which leave them with no other choice. Often a young man will try to resist his vocation — knowing that it is unlikely to bring him much material prosperity or peace of mind — but there comes a stage when he risks angering the gods by such behaviour, and courting disaster and eventual madness through a failure to heed his visions and come to terms with his *senas*. Understandably, he tends to transfer the attributes of these initial visionary experiences to the character of his own tutelary deities, and it was in this way that Elizondo interpreted my descriptions of Mama Coca, assimilating her to the general class of spirits known as *duendes* (or *duendas*, in the feminine form) in Spanish, and as *kályim* in Paez.

Kályim are closely associated with particular natural features such as riverbeds, springs and caves — or coca bushes, for that matter — and they also sometimes appear in an anthropomorphic form, a diminutive puckish spirit normally described with semi-bestial atributes such as a very hairy body. Generally considered to be morally neutral or indifferent, they only pursue and harm those individuals who have neglected their vocation as a shaman, or who have failed to perform the necessary rituals of cleanliness about their person or their house. The early discipline of the initiate shaman consists mainly of acquiring a working familiarity with the *kályim*, defining which particular manifestations are most in keeping with his own personal disposition, and getting used to calling on these spirits as allies or messengers in shamanic practice.

Elizondo often alluded to the necessity of seeing the *kályim* in their traditional guise, and he went to great lengths to point out that my version of a female *kályim* — Mama Coca — was necessarily a very dangerous one, as the Paez consider women, and female forces in general, to be almost entirely 'lunar' and destructive in the context of shamanism. Above all, he stressed that the content of a particular visionary experience — a dream, an hallucination, a sudden perception of divine immanence — was itself accessible to discipline, that one could learn to recognize specific manifestations of the *kályim* in the weather conditions, in the flight of birds, even in the shimmer of a leaf held in the dying rays of sunset. He suggested, therefore, that I concentrate my efforts on measuring my response to the various different outward forms of the *kályim*; including, of course, that of the coca plantations, but even more importantly, that associated with the rainbow — *kitus* in Paez — a phenomenon whose almost daily occurrence in Tierradentro provided the perfect metaphor for an ascent from the terrestial spheres into heaven.

'Heaven' itself, however, was quite literally a nebulous entity, the cloudy home of the god *Peesh* or *Peeshím* or *Kapish*, referred to in Spanish simply as *El Trueno* or 'Thunder'. Once liberated from the scene of their terrestial lives, the souls of the dead were supposed to retire to the perpetual snows high on the flanks of the volcano of Huila (5750 metres altitude), for this is a peak shrouded in an almost perpetual cloud cover. *Peeshím* himself is only at home in a cloudy sky — using his creative energy to release water, the physical source of all life — and when the sky is clear, he returns to his resting place below the surface of the freezing, desolate lakes which lie high in the *páramo* moorland, astride the main ridge of the Central Cordillera. Being an all-pervading god, different Paez reservations identify his 'home' in different lakes, and in the past these were often the scenes of many important ritual activities, such as the formal initiation of new shamans and the washing of the rods which denote political authority in the *cabildo* of each reservation. On the rare occasions when he is actually seen in human form, *Peeshím* appears in the guise of an old man of remarkably small stature, occasionally with pendulous, exaggerated genitalia and a large green hat made from banana leaves, and almost invariably with one or more coca bags slung around his neck, symbolizing his mastery of the shamanic arts. It should, therefore, come as no surprise to note that his fashion of carrying the coca bag — hanging simply like a bib over the chest and stomach, rather than over the shoulder or across the hips, as it is worn during the day time — should be one of the most distinctive traits of any Paez shaman engaged in magical undertakings.

It is important, however, to take a closer look at the type of situation in which the vision of *peeshím* actually appears to the shaman, for it is significantly different to the highly conscious, wide-awake state which normally accompanies the sensual 'blaze' produced by manifestations of the *kályim*. Unlike these lesser spirits, *Peeshím* cannot ever be summoned or manipulated. He has a will of his own and announces his proximity always by casting the shaman into a state of extreme drowsiness, showing his power precisely by overcoming the stimulating effects of any coca that the shaman may be chewing. In this dozy state, usually described in terms of having the eyelids closed, the shaman is suddenly 'awoken' by *Peeshím*, who delivers his message or advice, then closes the shaman's eyes again before leaving. On account of his power over coca, and his ability to utterly 'possess' the shaman in this way, *Peeshím* is usually considered the master of all Paez magical practitioners — a beneficent deity, a defender of traditional practice — and his position is quite the opposite of the morally neutral, subservient *kályim* spirits, those who can be controlled or manipulated by the shaman's use of coca and other herbs.

The point here cannot be too lightly stressed, as it is unusual for the Paez to speak of more than two or three encounters with *Peeshím* in a lifetime dedicated to shamanism. These occur characteristically at extremely crucial points in the individual's career — such as during his long period of initiation, or shortly before his death — and they emphatically do not form part of the daily experience of the Paez shaman. Though everyday practice is often characterized by states of trance or dissociation, these can only be seen as a form of indirect communication with *Peeshím*, sometimes undertaken through the medium of *kályim* messengers, or more commonly, routed directly through the medium of the body *senas* themselves. The intervention of *peeshím*, therefore, his ability to block or release the flow of *senas* in an individual, can thus be seen as the principle of divine purpose which pervades the entire structure of Paez shamanism. He who emerges triumphant in a witchcraft contest, does so ultimately through an appeal to *Peeshím*, since it is only this divinity who can finally override the use of poisonous herbs or the manipulation of *kályim* spirits by an unscrupulous rival.

All shamans tend to have at least one meeting with *Peeshím* in the initiatory stages of their career, but any individual who has gone on to suffer one or more major magical defeats — and lived — is often thought of as maintaining an especially close contact with this god, of being one of the 'chosen', in other words. His reputation, therefore, may in fact paradoxically increase as the result of these reversals rather than decline, for a major magical defeat is seen as a passage through the topography of chaos — often apprehended in the form of temporary madness, or as a journey into the land of the dead. This usually involves a period of some months' duration in which the shaman abandons the inhabited valleys and retires to 'live like an animal' off whatever wild foods he can find in the dense forests of the high Cordillera.

Elizondo himself claimed to have been 'lost in the forest' (*perdido en el monte*) at least three times in his twenty years experience as a shaman. He described how on all these occasions his cure had been effected by the sudden appearance of a bag of freshly-toasted coca and a lime container; twice they had been given to him by *Peeshím* in a vision, and the third time he had merely found the bag hanging from a tree beside a waterfall. In the latter case, he supposed that the *kályim* of the waterfall was acting as an intermediary of *Peeshím*, and he took this to mean that the god was angry at his excessive fondness for the techniques of aggressive witchcraft. He had, accordingly, eliminated from his repertoire all the more vicious symbols and poisonous herbs, and had learned to deal with magical conflicts by means of the purely defensive rituals alone. This development, he claimed, was quite typical of most shamans reaching full maturity; by the age of forty, more or less, they had succeeded in dominating the full range of magical practice, and the more unpleasant tricks no longer seemed necessary or desirable. It seems more than likely that a couple of severe magical defeats — close brushes with death — are sufficient to restrain the malice of even the most impetuous and over-confident young shamans; and certainly any individual who persists with unilaterally aggressive or 'paranoid' shamanic behaviour is widely considered ripe for an early grave, and few would mourn his demise.

The Paez do, in any case, distinguish very clearly between natural and social foes, and rather different forms of ritual activity are directed towards maintaining them in check. The idea of a basically pitiless and indifferent natural environment finds expression in the concept of ptansh (el sucio in Spanish, or 'dirt') and a great number of cleansing rituals are commonly employed to counter its malefic influence. The basic form of cleansing a given geographical space — a house, a field, a path — is again based on the use of coca, but in accord with the principles established for the interpretation of the *senas*, it is always chewed coca rather than whole leaves which are used for this purpose. The action involves spitting a fine spray of coca — often, but not always, supplemented by tobacco, *aguardiente*, and other magical herbs — and this is achieved by rolling over the tongue and pressing it hard against the teeth, so that only fine particles are released, and not a solid jet. This spitting or spraying action is known as *pútia* in Paez, and rendered into Spanish by the verb *soplar* (to blow). The more traditional Paez will *pútia* every time they have to negotiate virgin forests, deep banks of mud, fast flowing rivers, or any other natural hazard. It is also customary to *pútia* on trees that are about to be cut as timbers for the construction of houses or bridges, and to *pútia* on any land which is being planted to a new crop, or where a house is going to be built.

The *pútia* action is also employed to clear the environment in a great number of life-crisis rituals, such as those which accompany any birth, death, or marriage. The actual social formalities of these occasions seem to differ a great deal, and they are no doubt undergoing constant modification. When Segundo Bernal Villa did his field work in the early 1950s, the effects of the *Violencia* had still not been felt in their full severity, and there was obviously enough livestock in Tierradentro to allow the sacrifice of whole pigs by the participants. The shaman often received a full half of the animal for his services, and this was an important reward, for traditionally magical services cannot be payed for in cash, and the shaman otherwise only demands a certain amount of coca, tobacco, and *aguardiente*. The conditions of economic scarcity produced by the military 'pacification' of Tierradentro in the early 1960s has largely halted the practice of making sacrifices, except perhaps for a chicken or two, and the coffee economy has affected many of the shamans in the more acculturated zones, many of whom have become more cash oriented and now demand a straight payment for their services. Nevertheless, important cleansing ceremonies still are considered occasions meriting lavish entertaining, at least by today's standards, and large pots of *mote* (a soup of maize, beans, potatoes, onions, cabbage, etc.) and of *nûsa* (fermented cane juice) are always provided for the use of all the guests and participants.

The principal cleansing ceremony — the only time when large groups of people are gathered together for distinctly magical purposes — is the wake held to release a dead man's spirit, and to allow it to travel away unencumbered into the after-life. It is considered extremely dangerous to allow the ghost any excuse to remain in the localities that he frequented while alive, and within nine days of the actual funeral — itself a simple affair — the family must engage a shaman to clean out the house where the dead man lived and the fields that he cultivated. This involves a good deal of *pûtia*, not only of the house and fields, but also of the actual death bed of the deceased, and the shaman must suck on the crown of the head of each and every member of the dead man's family, freeing them of any residual *ptansh* caused by the close proximity of death. The clothes of the deceased are usually washed, subjected to *pûtia*, and then either burned or abandoned in one of his favourite outdoor haunts. Often his house is also left empty after being cleansed, and allowed to fall into ruin. If the man was a shaman himself, his coca bag and lime container are laid out by the place where he was accustomed to sit and read his *senas*, and this spot is studiously avoided by his heirs for many years afterwards.

Though the Paez are acknowledged throughout Cauca to be the foremost experts in these matters, it should be noted that similar cleansing rituals are also shared by the neighbouring Guambianos, and even by the more acculturated Indian groups in southern Cauca and Narino, who use the *pûtia* technique in much the same way as the shamans further north.[12] Indeed, given the fact that the Guambianos have almost entirely abandoned the chewing of coca in the daily working context, it is perhaps significant that their terms for a shaman — *pi'ij mavi* or *maase mavi* — mean literally 'lime eater' and 'coca eater' respectively. Furthermore, the Guambianos often have recourse to visiting Paez shamans, especially when major cleansing rituals are required, and they obviously consider their own mastery of coca chewing — and with it the shamanic arts of *pûtia* — to be insufficient on such occasions.

Such cases, involving as they do the suspension of deep-seated ethnic hospitalities, underline the crucial importance attached to the correct observance of traditional ritual practices in many parts of the Cauca area. Should one fail to cleanse the *ptansh* successfully, jealous *kályim* spirits — or the ghosts of the dead — will be angered by the resulting state of disorder, and further retribution will inevitably follow. A classic example of this is provided by the case of female menstruation. In the more remote Paez reservations, each family still maintains a special menstruating hut, where women are isolated from contact with the crops and their own male kinsmen. The women are fed only by other female kin, and they must bathe themselves and sprinkle their clothes thoroughly with chewed coca and magical herbs after each menstruation.

There is not, however, *pace* the feminist reader, any real sense of guilt attached to menstruation; it is, after all, an entirely natural and unavoidable function, and the *ptansh* which it produces is no more virulent than that, say, which accompanies a man's failure to cleanse his house and fields after a prolonged absence in another valley. This kind of *ptansh* — 'natural *ptansh*', it could be called, since it results entirely from the action of biological processes — only becomes really dangerous if allowed to fester without the requisite ritual cleansing. In no way can it be considered as severe as the more strictly malicious *ptansh*, the 'social *ptansh*' which springs from interpersonal envy, jealousy, and covetousness.

This, in fact, is seldom referred to as *ptansh* at all, and it is normally given the distinctive names of *dji'ij* in Paez and *el maleficio* in Spanish. It can either be produced by an explicit act of aggressive witchcraft, or more commonly still, can result from the accumulating social animosities which are almost inevitably produced by the strains of living in a small, egalitarian community. In either case the final outcome is the same, first ushering in sickness and misfortune, and then ultimately death itself. Not surprisingly, it is in dealing with these forms of social conflict that Paez shamanism shows its greatest strength.

Any serious onset of illness — or even a plague on crops or livestock — is usually dealt with by consulting a *té ué* ('shaman'), even though there exists today a marked tendency to resort initially to white man's medicine, at least in the case of certain specific and identifiable complaints. The *té ué* receives the patient in his house at night and proceeds to discuss the details of the case, before retiring outside to consult his *senas*, normally in a private meditation spot — *káchi* in Paez, *sentadero* in Spanish — known only to himself. Then he may discover that the illness is due to some negligence on the part of his patient, some failure to clean out natural *ptansh*, and he will then simply return to the house and give the person his verdict. Together with a good deal of general counselling and quite explicit morale boosting, the shaman may recommend the use of certain medicinal herbs or the *pútia* cleansing of the patient's house. In most cases, however, the emphasis is not on the medicinal prescription nor even on the *pútia* observances, but instead concentrates on a very dramatic form of body cleansing, whose impact is obviously a fundamental aspect of the patient/healer relationship.

The first of these techniques concerns the pulse — which, as has already been pointed out, is normally taken to symbolize the 'soul' — and it bears many similarities with the *pútia* exercise. In a sick person, the pulse is said to become weak, and its throbbing descends from the wrist towards the points of the fingers. Should it 'escape' out of the end of the fingers, death will inevitably occur. It is therefore necessary to compell the pulse to return up the fingers, across the palm of the hand, and back to the wrist itself. This is done by the shaman holding the three middle fingers of the patient's hand, and — with his mouth full of coca and other magical herbs — 'blowing' on the pulse and driving it back.

The removal of such *ptansh* impurities as may have become lodged inside the body requires a rather different approach, normally expressed in terms of a sucking out of *ptansh*. This is a dangerous exercise, as the shaman may incorporate into his own body the impurities that he has received from his patient. In order to prevent this he fills his mouth to full capacity with strong herbs and coca, thereby producing a mass which acts as a recipient of the *ptansh*, and which can then be removed from his mouth and buried. In the case of an actual physical illness, the affected area of the body is sucked in this way. In the case of a death in the family, the shaman sucks all the surviving relatives on the crown of their heads to remove any residual *ptansh* caused by their close proximity with the deceased. A really accomplished *té'ué* will often vomit when he is spitting out the herbs that contain the *ptansh*, in order to demonstrate that he has rid himself of any possibility of contagion.

The reason for these precautions must necessarily bring us to a consideration of the fundamental dynamic of Paez shamanism — the witchcraft contest — beside which all the *pútia* cleansing and all the sucking, blowing and washing rituals must necessarily pale into relative insignificance. We have seen that *djï'ïj* can certainly be considered the latent, underlying cause for a given case of illness, but it is not an active form of ceremonial witchcraft so much as 'possession' of a passive, almost unwitting kind, and it does not necessarily imply the intervention of a shaman nor the unleashing of any formal witchcraft contest. One must, therefore, introduce the new concept of *ech* or *echím* to account for the kind of individual magical attacks normally encountered in the practice of Paez shamanism, since it is *ech* alone, and not *dji'ij*, which is seen to be capable of sudden displacements and fulminating blows, especially those direct strikes which are themselves indescribable, but which might perhaps be likened to our idea of a bolt of lightning.

Earlier authors have often seen fit to describe *ech* as 'the devil', but such a crude simplification does little justice to the Paez sense of the word, not least because there are a great many guises for *ech*, each of them dependent for their meaning on a precise context, on a specific dramatic situation. In the course of everyday activities, for example, *ech* is often used as an exclamation, in order to express the sudden arrival of some unexpected thing into a space occupied by a particular group or individual. A man may shout '*ech!*' when a stray dog or any other animal approaches his house, and often this cry will be accompanied by the throwing of a stone as well. *Ech*, therefore, seems to be clearly associated with any hostile or potentially disruptive being; it is seen as an invader, capable of producing disorder in an area 'cleansed' by the ritual behaviour associated with human habitation. Since the area in which a shaman does his magic has also been ritually cleansed at the outset of every ceremonial undertaking, it is easy to understand why *ech* should come to be used as a general, all-inclusive term for magical assaults on the area in question.

In the very simplest outlines, then, the witchcraft contest first requires that the shaman define his area, establishing a 'clear space' around his patient by means of a number of reasonably standard ritual observances. These are performed outside, and preferably on an entirely moonless night, since too much light is not usually considered very conducive to the flight of spirits. The rituals themselves include placing a sprig of the *cháyuts* herb on the crown of the patient's head — sealing him or her to external attack — the *pútia* of coca, tobacco, and *aguardiente* to the four corners of the globe — thus clearing the immediate vicinity of *ptansh* — and a combination of sucking and pulse-blowing to initiate the purification of the patient's body. Having completed the initial cleansing, the shaman then sets up an 'altar' as the focal point of the seance. This consists of his *tama* wand stuck into the ground and hanging with bags of coca and other magical herbs; a combination which is in turn flanked by a gourd of *aguardiente* (with *cháyuts* floating on the surface) on one side, and a foot-deep hole on the other.

In an atmosphere of increasing seriousness and concern, the shaman and his patient wait for the *senas* that announce the arrival of the aggressive *ech* into their pre-established 'clear space'. Once identified, the *ech* must be captured, an action which is normally accomplished with a sudden and dramatic flourish, expressing to the patient the vital turning point in his cure. The type of capture obviously depends on the type of *ech* encountered on that particular occasion. It may involve a collective 'hallucination' which hovers in the air above the altar, and in this case the shaman will seize his *tama* wand and beat the spirit down into the hole. Alternatively, the *ech* may be manifested as an animal, or more commonly still, as a kind of red firefly known as *echimbé* (red *ech*), a distinct species which is easily recognized since it has a smooth flight and emits a constant source of light, as opposed to the jerky movements and flashing light of the ordinary white fireflies which abound in Tierradentro. Animal or *echimbé* are seized by the shaman and wrapped in banana leaves, together with

A Paez shaman: Tumbichuque, Tierradentro.

some strong magical herbs and a symbol of penetration such as a thorn or a claw or a snake's tooth. The captured *ech* is buried in the hole and covered with repeated layers of earth and herbs; then the patient is cleansed once more, his or her body sucked and washed and rubbed with herbs, all of which — together with the coca and tobacco used by the shaman himself — are buried in the same hole, and again sealed with numerous layers of hammered earth and fresh herbs.

The complete cycle — preliminary discussion, divination by *senas*, first cleansing, capture of *ech*, and final cleansing — normally occupies the whole night, and the shaman does not rest until dawn has begun to shew on the eastern horizon. There may be cases, however, when the shaman wishes to call off the seance, probably because he has received a *sena* on the crown of the head or on the heart, indicating that he is in danger of suffering a major reversal at the hands of an *ech* spirit which he is incapable of mastering. He may wish to sleep under such conditions, and — since sleep is normally considered the most vulnerable condition of man — there are precautions which he can take to protect himself, precautions which emphasize the role of the altar which has already been described. When sleeping, the same combination — *tama* wand, *yáha* bags of coca and other herbs, and a gourd full of *aguardiente* and *cháyuts* — are set up beside the shaman's bed, and all *ech* are said to be deflected or absorbed into the coca, herbs, and *aguardiente*. In the morning, these are all formally buried and the hole sealed in the manner outlined above.

Under whatever circumstances it is achieved, the capture and burial of an aggressive *ech* spirit implies that its mischievous potential be reverted to the sender, who receives a *sena* indicating the failure of his attack. This *sena* will cause the rival to redouble his own defensive and offensive measures, for the failure of one specific *ech* attack does not necessarily remove the underlying reasons for social animosity, and a continuing state of mutual bad blood, or *dji'ij*, may easily lead to an emission of *ech* attacks from either side. Elizondo and my other informants often contradicted themselves on the question of whether all *ech* attacks necessarily required the use of formal aggressive rituals, the most common of which involve putting thorns or poisonous herbs in contact with the ground once trodden by the rival. Indeed, under certain circumstances an *ech* attack is thought of as arising spontaneously or unconsciously, within a situation characterized by a dangerous accumulation of *dji'ij*, and the boundaries I have established between *dji'ij* and *ech* — seeing the former as the antecedent condition of social animosity, and the latter as the actual ritualized magical attack — are often considerably less clear-cut.

If this is true, it would seem to be rather difficult to assign ultimate responsibility for starting *ech* attacks to any one side in a given witchcraft contest, just as it would appear rather simplistic to assign 'blame' to one or other individual for initiating the kind of social animosity known as *dji'ij*. Human relationships in a small, traditional community are often based on a very long and complex history, and they cannot usefully be reduced to the kind of boxing-ring model of social conflict which is common in many larger and more faceless communities, with their legal concern to assign guilt by determining who hit whom first. It is for this reason that the clear distinctions between 'good' magic and 'evil' witchcraft — such as those asserted by the Colombian anthropologist, Segundo Bernal Villa, in his study of Paez shamanism — would seem to be more than a little blurred in practice, and probably betray an excessive reliance on the cultural certainties provided by the Christian precedent. After all, the Paez word for 'evil' — *eumet* — really means simply 'not good', for the particle *met* is often used as a negative postfix on a great number of other nouns and adjectives as well. To separate Paez shamans into 'good' and 'evil' practitioners has, therefore, very little absolute meaning, for one's perception of these dual values obviously depends on one's affective position in the conflict concerned.

A very clear-cut, black and white illustration of this could be provided by the case of the Paez assault on the mission station at Huila, on the night of 4th June, 1945.[13] Having set fire to the priest's house and burned it down, the men of the vicinity then gathered triumphantly to *pûtia* with herbs and chewed coca all over the smouldering ruins. Such action constitutes only the most extreme case of a good deal of aggressive, 'evil' witchcraft which is still directed at the Lazarist missions and the local white landowners, groups who only in this century have begun to occupy Tierradentro effectively and disinherit the Paez of their lands. The 'evil' aspect of this Indian behaviour — 'including even the desecration of the Holy Sacrament', as one horrorized priest once claimed to me in Belalcázar — must clearly be balanced against the Paez perception of the same events, which unmistakeably identifies its own 'evil spirit' in the religious and secular groups dedicated to the invasion of their territory and the annihilation of their culture. Of course, the example provided by this kind of inter-ethnic conflict may tend to place the whole ethical question into an excessively stark perspective, but it does serve to underline the fact that the moral implications of witchcraft are dependant not on some universal scale of values — the good/evil paradigm — but on the precise position held by each individual participant in a particular confrontation of wills.

It would seem impossible to overstress the point that Paez shamanism — in both its aggressive and defensive dimensions — must always be seen to function within the context of a given set of social relationships, and what may appear from one point of view as the capture and immobilization of an *ech* attack, will be interpreted from the opposing position as simply another turn of the screw, another escalation in the reciprocal flow of *dji'ij*. Of course, total conflict between individuals can only, in the final instance, really be resolved by the demise of one of the participants, and in fact, most deaths are usually seen by the Paez to occur in this way. Nevertheless, morbid preoccupations are hardly characteristic of the society at large, and the normal experience of the shaman is definitely not that of 'killing' his foes, so much as that of 'saving' his patient from the aggressive action of a rival.

In a sense, therefore, the magical 'contest' — the capture and subjection of an aggressive *ech* spirit — does not even require the actual or objective existence of two hostile camps, for the emphasis is usually on the dramatization of the cure, rather than on some explicit trial of strength between two competing shamans. Indeed, the 'projection' of envy or jealousy onto the person of a rival is often no more than a subterfuge used by the shaman to point indirectly to the fact that the envy or jealousy in question could, in fact, be lodged exclusively in the mind of his patient himself. By searching out a 'rival' — a possible source of *dji'ij* — the shaman attempts to discover the underlying sources of the patient's own affliction; and then, with his cleansing rituals and the repulsion of an orchestrated *ech* attack, he succeeds in bringing the problems to the surface, symbolically exorcising them and removing their subconscious hold over his patient's mind.

Most Paez shamans, furthermore, tend to show a profound disrespect for the niceties of ritual practice, often inverting or confusing the order of specific actions, and engaging in strange, idiosyncratic behaviour which is quite unlike the pious demeanour common to doctors and priests in our own culture. The apparent nonchalance of the shaman — his frequent lapses into humourous anecdote or transparent self-glorification — is an integral part of his performance, for it stresses his ambivalence and humanity, his desire to demystify the sacred traditions and render them understandable to mere mortals. Rather than relying on an aura of illusory 'expertise', the shaman operates through a profound empathy with his patient — an intimate sharing of the same hopes and fears — and through the application of a cathartic psycho-drama whose impact in the deep black night cannot fail to be profoundly moving.

Observations of this kind would seem to suggest certain limitations to the tangible extent of social conflict which is involved in many Paez witchcraft contests. Though there do exist occasional instances of two shamans becoming involved in a truly life-or-death struggle, this is by no means as common as one might suppose at first sight. There is a marked tendency for relatively weak individuals to become involved in indirect witchcraft accusations — 'indirect' because they are confided to a shaman, and not to the rival in question — as a means of attracting attention to their distress, and forcing some conciliatory action on the part of their better adapted neighbours and kinsmen. The supposed rivals in such cases — those who have been accused of initiating the bad blood, or *dji'ij*, in a given social relationship — are more often than not individuals marked by good health and material success, persons who have grown rich and failed to redistribute their wealth, thereby renouncing their commitment to the fiercely egalitarian ethos of Paez society. This kind of individualism — a sell-out to the white man's concept of private property — is clearly a character trait which must be harshly penalized by the Paez people as a whole. Indeed, the very fact that witchcraft attacks or accusations encourage the more 'progressive' Indians to have recourse to the generally poor, 'backward' shamans can itself be seen as a major triumph for the Paez social traditions, for in this way criticism of what is considered *mooshka* ('foreign') behaviour can be rendered very much more direct, intimate and effective than would ever be possible in a formal political gathering.

The levelling social impact of Paez shamanism is also paralleled by that of a number of other closely related factors, all of which militate forcefully against the formation of any political or religious hierarchy, and any kind of personal status other than that determined by an individual's own talents and capabilities. The Paez have no hereditary elite, and their kinship terminology emphasizes the nuclear family above all, having few of the formal structures normally associated with ancestor cults and complex geneological descent systems. A generally patrilocal or neolocal residence pattern — and an unwillingness to marry persons with the same patronymic — may possibly indicate the previous existence of strictly exogamous patrilineal clans, but such suppositions would have to be balanced against the conflicting evidence provided by numerous chronicle references to the *cacicas* or chieftesses who led the Paez in their first struggles against the Spanish. All in all, therefore, there seems to be no good reason for assuming that the Paez should ever have employed anything other than the quite straightforward classificatory and bilateral kinship system still in use today.[14] Not only does it seem excellently adapted to their fissiparous political organization and their small-scale, family-based practices of economic reciprocity, but also — given the very large gene-pool available to one valley and its immediate neighbours — there seems to be no real need to subject the community to any very explicit sanctions on endogamy.

Furthermore, both the Paez kinship system, and their political, economic and magical practices are all the result of a long period of adaptation to the limitations imposed by a specific environment. The broken terrain of Tierradentro seldom allows the concentration of large population groups in a single place, and the Paez settlement pattern is one of scattered individual homesteads, normally located in extremely inaccessible places, such as high ridges well away from the main paths. Population pressures in one valley often lead to a splinter group setting up a new colony elsewhere — usually further back into the cold, misty rainforest of the high Andean cordilleras — and thus authority is constantly being fragmented, leaving individual *cabildos* with responsibility for reservations or *resguardos* whose number seldom exceeds two or three hundred *macaneros* ('war-club carriers', or adult males), all of whom are able to resolve their differences on a strictly personal basis. The very bellicosity of the Paez — especially when compared with the more docile character of their neighbours, the Guambianos — provides a fertile ground not only for the indirect aggression observable in their witchcraft practices, but also for a good deal of wrestling and hand-to-hand *machete* duels as well.

Physical violence, however, is a tactic employed mainly by the younger men, those with an insufficient mastery of the more subtle arts of the magical contest. It is hardly surprising, therefore, that Paez shamanism should play such a very crucial role in the resolution of internal social conflict for, as we have seen, there are few other legal, political or economic sanctions — other than a straight knife fight — which could reasonably be expected to take its place. In a sense, the Paez people's repudiation of all forms of constituted authority — the very trait which gives them such an immeasurable advantage when dealing with the Colombian state and the opportunist politicians from surrounding areas — would seem to actually *require* the institution of shamanism, and not only for its medicinal and religious functions, but for its strictly politico-legal contribution as well.[15]

Particularly interesting, in this respect, have been the attitudes adopted towards the Paez shamans by the often non-Indian activists of CRIC, or Consejo Regional Indígena del Cauca, the Indian civil rights movement in the Cauca area. Initially, at least, recruitment to CRIC involved mainly marginalized or dispossessed Indians living on the fringes of reservation society; in this situation, there existed a definite tendency for the movement's white sympathizers to repudiate 'primitive' traits such as coca chewing, and the kind of 'mystification' and 'obscurantism' supposedly involved in shamanism. As CRIC continued to expand its field of influence, however, the organizers clearly found themselves being led to reassess their position, shedding a good deal of their earlier intolerance, and coming round to a recognition of the fundamental role played by the shaman in the physical and moral well-being of the community. Such trends have sometimes led to a considerable amount of friction between CRIC and its other class allies — specifically the white *campesino* organization ANUC (Asociación Nacional de Usuarios Campesinos) — who would normally see fit to dismiss such practices as coca-chewing and witchcraft as little more than the tools of repression, the pernicious results of ignorance, backwardness, and despair.

Admittedly, conflicts of this kind are only very rarely brought out into the open, being understandably avoided in the interests of a more wide-ranging solidarity. But the absence of a frank debate also has its price, and predictably, the position of many white militants with respect to their Indian allies is often characterized by a large degree of latent paternalism and thoughtless ethnocentrism, the inevitable products of a mistaken reading of the words 'progress' and 'progressive'. More often than not, this is expressed through the twin poles of an ambiguous rhetoric which at once glorifies the vaguely defined and poorly understood 'communalism' of Indian society, and at the same time clamours for the 'educating' of that same society in the interests of a crass 'development' which will itself — more than any other factor — eventually destroy the self-reliance which is such a crucial feature of that original communalism itself. An obvious potential for sheer heavy-handed chauvinism lies implicit in this approach, and it is the political and moral task of the anthropologist — despite the threat of being stigmatized as a 'romantic', or worse, an agent of the CIA — to forcefully challenge the assumptions of those who would seek to impose a mainly urban and industrial perspective on the needs of the Indians, and indeed, of all the inhabitants of rural Latin America.

In the present historical context, therefore, the most pressing need is hardly that of 'educating' the rural masses to the realities of power; in the eyes of the Paez, for example, such realities are already perfectly self-evident. Far more important is the task of educating the urban intelligentsia to the real economic needs and cultural values of the people whose interests they are supposed to be defending, providing a perspective on those needs and values which is not so much 'ethnographic' — in the sense of merely colourful and folkloric — as clearly explanatory and sympathetic, and non-coercive in its ultimate application to social and political change.

This book has attempted, in its own way, to provide this sort of analysis with respect to one particular element of Andean life, the chewing of the coca leaf. In a sense, the restrictions involved in narrowing the field of inquiry to a plant, rather than a particular people, have pointed to the inadequacies of this kind of comparative approach. It was my own experience, while living in the Cauca area, to find my attention being constantly drawn away from the generalities of coca chewing, and attracted to the single most notable feature of the Paez as a people: their tenacious and relentless resistance to cultural and territorial absorption by the white man, a process sustained uninterruptedly for more than four centuries, and with a success which is truly remarkable in the historical record of the indigenous Americans. To the Paez themselves, their struggle is eternal — a gut reaction, requiring no formal, written History to give it meaning — but it might interest the non-Paez sympathizer to examine the very different forms their courageous endeavour has taken over the years. An annotated bibliography on this question has been included as Appendix C, and hopefully this will provide an impetus to a further understanding of the manner in which at least one group of South American Indians have succeeded in surviving first the bloody sword of Conquest, then the more insidious catechism of a colonizing, missionary Church, and finally — though hardly definitively, as yet — the pitiless bulldozers and machine guns of a neo-colonial industrial technocracy.

THUNDER OVER THE COCA FIELDS

'. . . it is not for the anthropologist to attempt to usurp the role of the gods whose worship he studies.'

A quote from a standard text-book on the sociology of shamanism.[16]

The path seems to wind uphill forever, a thin drizzle laying its damp hand across your shoulders, as you stagger uncertainly over yet another bank of eroded clay, slipping into a dark grove of sodden banana plants. The surface of the path turns from a hard, compacted orange subsoil to a thick black mire mixed with jagged pebbles and rotting leaves, churned by the hooves of a thousand stamping horses which have passed this way before. You cast off your shoes and plunge knee-deep into the ooze, the *barrial*, toes squirming as you are sucked down to a narrow stream and through the flow of its icy waters — your body one transient slick of mud and sweat driving relentlessly through a slipping universe. Shooting star or retinal flare, after image fading . . .

Slime climb the next rise, grabbing hold of roots which slack and slap back, your butt-end falling through endless space to a single, solid curse: 'What the Fuck am I doing *here*?' The gods thunder without lightning. Clouds sunder, yielding shaft-rays of luminous afternoon sun, pouring gold across the open valley. Flame sparkles on the leaves, tanager birds come out to strut, prance across and twitter, pearls of water casting reflections from their yellow feathers. The scent of sodden leaves, a curtain pierced as you break out across the open hillside, long grass itching, pricking, as it wipes blood and blister from your feet, shirt heaving in a cloud of steam.

And then — you hit that picture of a house, the first one since five miles back, since before the rain began. Brown mud walls, thatched roof, small out-houses made of split bamboo and rushes. A wooden mill, the sugar cane crusher, set in the middle of a patch of horse-shit and vegetable debris. Dog barks, hens cackle. A couple of kids' faces, covered with soot, loom out from the darkness at the door. Alarm. Man appears, leans against the wooden door-frame, feigning nonchalance. He greets you with a suspicious smile. *Eucha*, you reply, careful to put the stress on the first syllable. You inquire as to the state of the path further on, you mention the names of some mutual friends. *Esh guéninga*? You offer some coca leaves, a little tobacco. You are asked indoors.

Enter one large square room with an open wood fire set on the floor over to one side. The smoke makes your eyes water. It has long covered all the rafters with a thick layer of the blackest grime, but you can make out a few net bags hanging above the fire, preserving dead meats, suspending cobs of red, black and yellow-speckled corn beyond the reach of hungry rodents. Beaten earth floor covered with cow-hides, large dented pans and the occasional bundle of tattered woollen blankets. Maybe a half-dozen stools placed around the hearth, small blocks of wood a foot long by half across, carved anatomically to hold the body in a squatting pose, no more than three or four inches from the ground.

You sit — women and children retire to the other side of the fire and eye you with amazement. You are presented with an enamel bowl filled with about a pint of steaming soup — *mote* — containing maize and beans and cabbage, tasting strangely of a light wood ash used to dehusk the grains of corn, the whole effect somehow rotten and fermented, as if the vegetables have been sitting in water for a few days. Then, the inevitable questions: Where from? And what for? But most of all, why here?

Why, indeed. Hardly the right time to trundle out a string of platitudes about scientific models and methodologies, about the need for an abstract Mama Coca as a prop to structure your research. Your answer, therefore, comes out direct and to the point, measured with a blade of tempered absence: 'To learn how to chew coca . . .'

Your words are greeted with a smile. A knowing smile. A friendly smile, even. (You think: 'See how nice it is to contribute to a people's respect for its own traditions? Full marks for the *participant* anthropologist . . .') And yet. An edge of doubt, of disbelief suspended only through cunning, a flash of mockery in the Indian's eyes. (He seems to say: 'All anthropology is imperialism, buster, let's get it straight. *Participant* my ass . . .')

You spring forward — metaphorically baring your chest — preferring some direct, explicit repudiation to the dead weight of misunderstanding, hoping that some final encounter will at last shake off that ghostly academic identity carried with you like a shield, *muy estimado doctor*, allowing the field of inquiry to strike back and finally gobble you entire. Phrases like: 'No more trying to become something while maintaining a critical distance from the process of becoming . . .' — or even, curse the thought, 'A rich confrontation between the thing itself and one's own awareness of it . . .' *Lógico, hermano, ni hablar* . . .

Personal bees in your bonnet swatted, brought down by sudden hits of the specific. The next morning you may awake with a terrible rash spreading up your arm from the fingers to the elbow. You could rush out to smother the fact with some timely explanation, only to find that the tools of such a deliverance are no longer in your own hands — that in Tierradentro it is the Paez *té'ué* who calls the shots. Rash on the right arm; that is, a sign of something coming in. On the hand, notice, meaning that you have touched on things you would have done well to leave alone. Things like *sena*-magic? The coke business?

Or, wait a minute — the horror, the thrill, the dawning realization — could not these trips be entirely tame in comparison to the overbearing Pride, the sheer aggressive witchcraft, underlying your belief in the scientific endeavour itself? The evidence is conclusive — so you take it, your itch, and show it to Elizondo:

'A *caspi* rash. An *ech* attack. Either you must leave Tierradentro for ever, or . . . '

Accept that the *persona* of the mere rational scientist is dead — yes, dead, deaded, dead.

You add a final word in the margin of your field notes: Anthropology as participation? Why anthropo-*logy* at all? Reflection, description, a terminal discourse spoken to a mirror-full of stuffy seminars, an empty gesture describing only the parameters of your own loss, our own and everybody's loss. To respect a primitive — that is to say, an original and primary — form of humanity from the comfortable distance of the Faculty is only tourism, no matter how learned the travelogue. A true anthropology, in order to have any meaning at all, must reintegrate its discourse into action, must reapply the lessons learnt from men more attuned to their environment and more sensitive than ourselves — mining the bastions of an alienated expertise, the assumptions of a much debased Civilization, and *recreating* the primitive in the everyday life of the libertarian groups of the future, the white Indians of the post-industrial age.[17]

In order to do so, anthropology must also, inescapably, sever all connections with the kind of Science practised by the Great Universities, particularly those all-consuming *gringo* institutions who make it their business to monopolize the intellectual life of Latin America. Individual anthropologists must forsake a professionalism already compromised beyond any possibility of redemption, fleeing the ghetto of academe for ever and returning into the field — not as a visitor this time, nor as an observer of any kind, but as a feature of the landscape, a permanent resident. For what is permanence if not a rejection of the elsewhere/later scheme of the bored careerist, what is it but a real commitment to your own unguarded, excited presence, to the actuality of being here and now. . . .

Elizondo sits in a menacing huddle in the dark, moonless night, the thousand muscles of his body in *sena*-communication with the spirit legions of the rainbows, riverbeds, the springs and caves. Maybe he sees them in the flesh, hairy bodies moving in and out through the lace outlines of the undergrowth, their presence in his vision sending a crackle of reciprocal machine-gun *senas* echoing through your body. Your I dissipates into a twinkling of an eye to eye. The earth, the sky no longer simply up and down, but curling over at the edges, a drunken swirling round the dead point you call observation.

A rush of cold fear and nausea breaks across you like a wave. You take a long, hard suck on your wad of coca leaves — but you get no freeze this time, no substance, no hard edge with which to draw the line. Coca dissolves into a vortex of spinning head and swoon — a clammy sweat on the body, a final panic of bubbles as you go down and out — your choking voice from off-stage blurting out a desperate 'Hey, wait a minute . . . ' The axis of your sense perception spiralling down, telescoped into an empty hole — black, still, a vacuum . . .

You wake up to the perfect stillness of the dead. All is a play of light on darkness, everywhere a timeless sleep. A long, hollow roll of thunder. In front of you an old man with half a dozen coca bags slung around his neck. You croak. 'Are you?'

A green smile. Ground shudders, trees bend without any wind. Feel the tongue, frozen, speechless . . .

Awe and wonder as you are forced to recognize

THUNDER OVER THE COCA FIELDS.

Appendix A.
'Dope, Mushrooms and Yajé'

No account of the drug culture in the Cauca area would be complete without a few words on those plants most sought after by *gringos* and other foreign travellers in this part of Colombia; namely, marijuana (**Cannabis sativa**), the local variety of *hongos* or hallucinogenic mushrooms (**Stropharia cubensis**), and — to a lesser extent — *yajé* (**Banisteriopsis** spp.).

MARIJUANA

The very varied ecology of Colombia has led, over the years, to the emergence of a fair number of quite distinct local types of marijuana, a plant characterized by a marked degree of long-term genetic plasticity. At the same time, the pursuit of improved quality and the rapid diffusion of the drug have both encouraged frequent exchanges of seed between different areas, a fact that would suggest a certain degree of botanical uniformity throughout the country, as the **Cannabis** plant is known to reproduce quite faithfully the character of its immediate parent stock. While not wishing to ignore the significance of this sort of hybridization, the truth remains that the plant does usually yield the highest concentrations of cannabinoids under certain quite narrowly defined climatic conditions. It is this fact which, despite the widespread trade in seed material, explains the clear prominence of a few reasonably circumscribed areas in the popular mythology surrounding Colombian marijuana.

What is commonly referred to as 'Colombian' on the world market can conveniently be sub-divided into at least three major types: *la mona* or 'gold' (literally 'blonde') — a very stimulating, light tan or golden coloured weed known principally from around Santa Marta; *el mango viche* or 'green' (literally 'unripe mango') — a more average dope, produced mainly in the Cauca drainage and the tropical savannas or *llanos* east of Bogotá; and *el punto rojo* or 'red' (literally 'red spot') — a very psychedelic smoke, the pride of all the Western Cordillera, and of the Cauca area in particular. In addition, there exist a number of very dark green varieties, whose almost blackish or purple tints, and lesser degree of psychoactive potency, both normally result from the climatic extremes in which the plant is cultivated — whether they be the low altitudes and very heavy rainfall of the Amazon basin and the Chocó, on the Panamanian border, or the high altitudes and rather low temperatures which prevail on the upper slopes of the main Andean cordilleras (see 'Silvia Purple', below).

With respect to the more important commercial varieties, the 'red' in *punto rojo* would seem to be derived from two quite different factors. One involves the concentration of cyanins in the pistils of the plant, that is to say, the thin, hair-like stigmas and other parts of the female flower — a condition which is occasionally given the distinctive name of *pelo rojo* ('red hair'). The other, more common, identification of *punto rojo* results from a clear spotting of the bracteoles (seed coverings) and other leafy matter in the flower, a condition marked by a profusion of tiny brilliant points which are clearly visible to the naked eye, and which result from an accumulation of the cannabinoid-containing oil in the multicellular glandular hairs which form on the plant's skin or epidermis. In either case, since the 'red' is a quality independent of the colouring of the main parts of the plant, it is clear that some kinds of *la mona* or 'gold' may also be considered 'red'; that is, they may show red stains against a light tan or golden background, like the famous Panama Red. The *punto rojo* of Cauca, however, is distinctly red-on-a-green/brown background, and cannot therefore be confused with the lighter coloured weeds of Santa Marta and Panama.

All this would seem to indicate that there are two main varieties of marijuana in Colombia — a light tan 'gold', and a distinctly darker 'green' — and that the 'red' quality is a separate feature, applicable to both the green and the gold types. The distinction between these two types might involve genuine genetic and morphological differences, or alternatively, might simply result from the rather different drying and curing techniques used in the Santa Marta and Cauca areas. A more accurate breakdown of the commercial brands of Colombian marijuana would, therefore, tend to look something like this:

simple light tan — *la mona*, or 'Santa Marta Gold'
red-on-light tan — 'Panama Red', 'Santa Marta Red'
simple green/brown — *mango viche*, 'Llanos Green', 'Cauca Green'
red-on-green/brown — *punto rojo*, 'Red Spot'

Since it is clearly the green/brown varieties of marijuana that concern us more specifically in the Cauca area, it would be interesting to consider the differences which set the more potent and highly esteemed *punto rojo* apart from the milder, less valuable *mango viche*. It may be that they represent distinct genetic types of the plant or, more probably, it could be that they indicate the same plant harvested at different stages of its growth. Being considered the lighter smoke, it seems likely that *mango viche* should be cut rather earlier than *punto rojo*, before the plant has had time to develop the cyanins and the cannabinoid-containing glands which together give the flowering extremities their marked red 'hairs' and 'spots'. In support of this idea, dealers in Popayán often pointed to the fact that *mango viche* tended to contain rather light coloured, undeveloped seeds, whereas those of *punto rojo* were usually found to be much darker and more mature.

Local techniques of drying and curing marijuana are also another element clearly influencing the final appearance of the weed. Many knowledgeable dopers, for instance, argue that the 'gold' quality of Santa Marta results not from any genetic or ecological differences between that weed and the green/brown types of inland Colombia, but from the use of a distinctive technique of preliminary drying — in which an inch-wide strip of bark is cut off round the trunk of the marijuana plant, often as much as two or three weeks before the final harvest. This blocks the sap and allows the buds to start drying in the sun, so that they turn sticky and begin to produce their characteristic light tan or golden colour while still in the ground.

In the Cauca area, this preliminary sun-drying method seems to be resorted to only very infrequently, and this may account for the absence of 'gold' weed in this part of Colombia. Nor is it very usual to cut the plants and leave them drying in a pile or spread out on the ground outside — a custom reported in many drier dope-growing countries, such as those of the Middle East — for the extreme humidity and heavy rainstorms of the Western Cordillera could severely damage the quality of the final product. *Mango viche* is usually dried in the simplest way possible, which is to cut down or uproot whole plants and hang them in the shade ('So that the sap drains down to the buds', as the growers put it), producing a distinctly green coloured weed with an almost 'home-grown' smell to it. *Punto rojo* is also often dried in this way, though at least two other methods are also used.

One of these is resorted to more commonly in the Cauca *valle* proper, and in other areas where there is a dependable amount of sunshine, and involves laying out the half-dried female flowers in the midday sun for an hour or two every day, allowing the heat to burst the cuticle of the glandular cells — the 'spots' of *punto rojo* — and release the cannabinoid-containing oil, thereby producing a very sticky and rather more tightly shrivelled bud than is possible by air-curing alone. The other process involves a principle very similar to the sweat-curing of tobacco, that is to say, a gradual and controlled fermentation of the green plant material so that it 'matures', breaking down the chlorophyll and acquiring a richer aroma and much darker colour than weed dried by more straightforward means. The female flowers are normally detached from the main stem of the plant and laid on a wooden or bamboo rack — a couple of feet off the ground and under shade — usually in bundles or piles as much as eighteen inches thick, requiring turning every couple of days to interchange the buds on the outside for those in the middle of the pile. Though in some areas it is common to dry marijuana in this way without the use of racks — laying it simply on the ground, or on top of a few layers of newspaper — the growers of Cauca point out that rack drying prevents the accumulation of excessive moisture, and thus stops the weed from over-fermenting and turning into rotten compost.

At the same time, a small amount of mould — marked by a sort of whitish froth on the buds, and a distinct stench of ammonia — is often thought to be conducive to good maturation, as is the addition of various boosters to the natural sugar (carbohydrate) content of the weed, such as cane-juice, *panela* (molasses) or honey mixed with water, or even strong spirits (*aguardiente*). As with all curing processes, however, it is possible to overdo the amount of fermentation; and thus, when the crop is deemed sufficiently well cured, the drying is speeded up by a short spell in the sun, or by separating the buds and hanging them up inside. Obviously, there must exist an ideal temperature and degree of humidity in which to accomplish this fermentation process, and in the future exacting standards will probably become as mandatory for marijuana as they already are for tobacco. A quick glance at the section on flue-curing in Frank and Rosenthal's recently published 'Marijuana Grower's Guide' (And/Or Press 1978) indicates that the first steps in this direction have already been taken by the more discriminating producers/consumers.

Once the marijuana is packed into sacks for shipment, a certain amount of rehumidification is inevitable, especially in the damp conditions of the Western Cordillera. Not rarely, the mould begins to form again, and in Popayán it is quite usual for wholesalers to undertake a second drying of the weed before retailing it on the street. By this time any argument about the different means used to produce *punto rojo* and *mango viche* become quite largely academic. To most discriminating dope smokers, after all, the main distinction between these two kinds of marijuana lies not in any appeal to genetics or esoteric drying techniques, but in a subjective appreciation of the rather variable physical and cerebral effects of each particular smoke. It is this that would serve to explain the rather puzzling fact that a *mango viche* which has been stored for a while often finds its identity on the street being transformed into a *punto rojo*, even despite the fact that it has little observable 'red' in the buds. Not only has it become rather darker and browner in colour, but also its smell has lost its original freshness, and the effect has turned more 'heavy' and somniferous. Indeed, the degree of freshness or staleness in marijuana is a factor often overlooked by the casual observer, and yet it is clear that some notable transformation of its chemical structure does occur with prolonged storage.

A recent book by Michael Starks, 'Marijuana Potency', goes a long way to explaining to the average layman why this should be so. The main active principle in marijuana — delta 1, also known as delta 9, tetrahydrocannabinol (THC) — degrades with time into Cannabinol (CBN), a compound with considerably less psychoactive potency than THC. Starks also discusses in detail the influence of various environmental factors on the growing plant, and their importance in determining the yields of THC, CBN, and Cannabidiol (CBD) — the biosynthetic precursor to THC in the plant cells. His observations have a direct bearing on the question of the regional variability of different races of **Cannabis** in Colombia. The less interesting marijuanas — such as the lowland crops of the Chocó, the lower Magdalena drainage, the Amazon basin and the *llanos* — are all cultivated in areas of high temperatures, and this would seem to encourage the growth of a luxuriant but understrength weed, with relatively high yields of CBD and CBN, which together detract from the high and produce a 'heavy', soporific or debilitating physical effect. Starks cites controlled experiments which showed that the THC content of marijuana was maximal when the temperature was maintained at 24 degrees C — conditions which are best approximated in the Colombian Andes at altitudes between 800 and 1200 metres.

It is no accident, therefore, that it is precisely this belt which — both in the Western Cordillera, and in the *valley* of Cauca around Cali — seems to produce most of the best-quality weed in south-western Colombia. The plant continues to do reasonably well right up to the very edge of the subtropical climate zone, but attempts at cultivating it in the temperate country above 2000 metres are undermined by low night temperatures, and have only succeeded in producing a stunted, sterile crop. A certain amount of this high-altitude marijuana was available from a grower near Silvia during 1974, and it was known in Spanish as *la negra*, and to the *gringos* as 'Silvia Purple'. These names referred to the fact that the local plant, being cultivated at around 2500 m., suffered a major change in its pigmentation, with the result that its profoundly green tints verged on a purple colour, which turned deep black on being dried. The cannabinoid content of this weed was significantly lower than that of an average middle-altitude plant, but on the other hand, the cerebral high had the advantage of being untramelled by any of the more acute physical side-effects — such as nervous trembling and heart palpitations — which sometimes result from the use of excessive quantities of full-strength *punto rojo*.

There have also been suggestions that moderate altitudes not only ensure a suitable range of temperatures for the marijuana plant, but also reduce the atmospheric screening of ultraviolet rays, thereby encouraging *Cannabis sativa* — an extremely heliotropic (sun-loving) species — to grow rather better and stronger than it would do in the lowlands, particularly in the tropical rainforest, which is notoriously overcast. Furthermore, the equatorial latitudes of Colombia also permit the country to enjoy two major annual crops of marijuana, a clear advantage when compared with the essentially single crop potential of producing areas located further away from the Equator — such as Mexico, at one extreme, and Paraguay at the other. In the Cauca area, seeds are normally sown at the beginning of the rains; that is to say, in February/March, and again in September/October. In this way, the plant is able to make the most benefit of the water for its early growth, and will mature in a relatively dry season — a fact which has often been noted elsewhere to be beneficial to the production of the desirable psychoactive resins — yielding the finest harvests at the end of the 'summer' dry periods in January and August. The popular explanation of this fact shows that the growers are keenly aware of the effect that strong sunshine has on their crop, for it is considered that the sun has the capacity to 'pull' the alkaloid-bearing resins into the flowering extremities of the plant. Marijuana is always planted in large, unshaded clearings, and it is rarely mixed with any other crop except maize, which alone among domestic plants seems incapable of adversely affecting its requirements in terms of light and soil conditions.

At the time of my stay in the Cauca area (1973-1974), no well-established forms of cultural intervention had yet become at all generalized in the local folklore of marijuana cultivation. Individual growers resorted to a great number of private techniques in order to improve the quality of their harvests; for example, animal manure or human urine and feces mixed with water were sometimes used to fertilize the soil, though in truth the rich humus of the recently cleared forest areas used for clandestine planting seldom made this necessary. More often there was a need to balance the virgin earth with ash or construction lime, as an excessively acid mixture usually produces a very harsh and bitter smoke.

The male plants in a plantation were often eliminated as soon as they could be identified, as too many seeds in the final crop were considered undesirable by the consumer. On rare occasions, special care was taken to produce a seedless (*sinsemilla*) crop, as this seemed to encourage the production of cannabinoids more strictly cerebral than physical in their effects, obviously a positive advantage when competing with the more debilitating, 'heavy' varieties of seeded, over-ripe *punto rojo*. In these cases, small stands of pollinated female plants were usually maintained for the supply of seeds necessary to ensure a future crop. At the same time, however, it was frequently stated that a plantation — once established in a particular field — did not really require any further replanting at all. Marijuana normally has a short, 5 or 6 month growing cycle, and thus it would be assumed that such a plantation could only maintain itself by means of a casual dispersal of seeds. It is this which renders so interesting the claim of many growers that their plants were capable of seedless reproduction or perpetuation through their roots and stems, for it seems to lend support to the idea that cannabis may become a perennial under certain very favourable circumstances.[1]

Another motive in removing the male plants from a marijuana plantation may lie in the fact that the female appears to decrease its secretion of resin once it has been fertilized. Such an interruption of the natural reproductive process could be seen as the first step in the torturing or traumatizing of the cannabis plant, a practice which has been widely reported elsewhere as a means of increasing the yield of desirable psychoactive resins.[2] In the Cauca area, it is usual to trim off the leaves from the plant, as they are of little market value, and — since such pruning also forces the plant hormones to concentrate their action on the flowering tops or buds — this could also be considered an elementary form of plant 'torture'. None of the more complex traumatizing techniques — such as repeated pruning of the flowering buds themselves (rather than the trimming of the leaves), or stem twisting, stem cracking, and stem piercing — appear to be anything more than a very occasional practice in the Cauca area. Nevertheless, one grower claimed that he twisted the flowering tops of his plants at the point where they became a naked stem, and left them hanging for a week 'with their necks broken' before proceeding with his harvest. On the other hand, this practice — like that of stripping off a ring of bark around the stem of the plant, a trick which is very popular in the Santa Marta area — was simply explained by the grower in question as constituting a very efficient means of accomplishing a preliminary drying of the weed.

Other than the occasional weeding and pruning, a marijuana plantation requires very little care, and can therefore be hidden in a *roza* located at some considerable distance from human dwellings, so as to render its discovery more difficult for the occasional marauding sorties by the uniformed authorities. The only labour intensive part of the production cycle is the harvesting and drying of the finished article, and large groups of landless peasants travel up to the hills behind El Tambo at harvest time to find work of this kind. Once dried, the buds must be cut off the stems and packed in sacks for transport, care being taken not to press them too tight, as this tends to affect the quality adversely. The sacks are of one, or more commonly, two *arrobas* (25 or 50 pounds), and are normally carried out of the growing areas on mules, or more simply, on the backs of specialist porters who know the more secretive mountain trails. One of the most interesting routes taken by the Cauca marijuana harvest is by canoe down the rivers which drain into the Pacific Ocean, where it is transhipped onto fishing boats or cargo vessels on their way from Tumaco, Guapi or Buenaventura to the coast of California.

Before leaving the subject of marijuana, social historians may find it interesting to examine the way in which this plant has acquired its present prominence in Colombia. The precise details of the arrival of **Cannabis**, at least in the vicinity of Popayán, remain something of a mystery; and it is not rare to hear local people claim that the use of this drug was virtually unknown in the town until the middle 1960s. It would, therefore, be instructive to consider the broader context of the history of marijuana in the New World.

It seems clear that the plant was first introduced to this part of South America by the Spanish in the colonial period, largely in order to stimulate the production of cordage and rope for the use of their navy.[3] Faced by competition from the indigenous *cabuya* fibre — **Fourcroya foetida** (L.) How., or **Furcraea macrophylla** (Hook.) Baker — the introduction was not a great success; and considering that the seed came from the European stock of **Cannabis**, better known for its yield of hemp than for its psychoactive properties, it seems highly unlikely that the plant was ever smoked at this early date. This was not true all over South America, however, and in Brazil linguistic evidence points convincingly to the ritual and medicinal use of *maconha* by slaves introduced from Angola as early as the sixteenth and seventeenth centuries, and to the subsequent spread of the habit to indigenous groups such as the Canela Indians of Maranhao.[4]

The real question is that of ascertaining whether marijuana smoking ever spread out of a reasonably restricted area in north-eastern Brazil. The evidence, on all accounts, is not convincing, and recent studies in the Caribbean area suggest that the habit had not become established in this part of the New World until the mid-nineteenth century, largely as the result of the introduction of indentured labourers from India.[5] Even in such a haven as Jamaica, *ganja* had not become really widespread until the beginning of the present century. It seems likely, therefore, that it was only in the early 1900s that the weed spread to the coast of Colombia, possibly via Panama, where work on the canal brought together the varied cultures of a work force which had come from all over the Caribbean.[6]

Whatever its ultimate origins, marijuana had soon become a noticeable feature of the people of the coastal lowlands of Colombia — William Burroughs, for example, writing in 1953, reported: 'A little weed among coast side Negroes.'[7] It was probably these black groups who provided the initial impulse for the introduction of marijuana into the inland regions of

Colombia, particularly to such areas as the middle Cauca valley — the *valle* around the city of Cali — where a large black population enjoyed close links with the bustling Pacific port of Buenaventura. In the rural setting, cannabis came to be used most commonly as a stimulant in the context of cane cutting and other forms of hard physical labour, reflecting the type of usage described both in Jamaica and on the north coast of Colombia. In 1973, I had the opportunity to visit a black community in the vicinity of Corinto, Cauca, whose traditional herbal lore and respect for the cannabis plant had, as yet, been little affected by the pressure of recent events. Here adult males commonly smoked as many as half a dozen cigarette-sized joints during the course of the working day — claiming increased vigour and concentration as a result — but, what is equally significant, this was not the only way that the drug was used. Even other members of *valley* society who smoke rarely or not at all — such as black women or children, and elderly whites from the neighbouring towns — used the infusion of cannabis leaves as an all-purpose panacea, and even more commonly resorted to marijuana crushed in *aguardiente* as a poultice for arthritis and other inflammations of the joints and muscles.

One other notable aspect of this traditional type of marijuana culture is its virtual self-sufficiency, and the unwillingness or incapacity of its members to become engaged in any large scale production for the illicit trade. The press coverage of the mid-1940s, denouncing the existence of an urban black market and clandestine marijuana plantations in the Cauca valley and on the Caribbean coast, shows that this latter scene had developed quite early on in Colombia.[8] Predictably, the media were little concerned with describing the traditional context of well-balanced marijuana smoking, and — probably under pressure from U.S. narcotics officials — limited themselves to churning out the standard propaganda about 'reefer madness' and the abuse of the 'killer weed' by petty criminals and other members of the urban underworld.

It was, however, the civil war known as *La Violencia* (1949-1958) which saw the first widespread adoption of marijuana by a significant proportion of the non-urban and non-black population, particularly those members of the irregular guerilla armies who found a need for an easily produced and easily transported substitute for their usual high, *aguardiente*. It is this fact that would explain the introduction of cannabis into such predominantly 'white' or *mestizo* rural areas as the *llanos* — the hot savannas east of Bogotá — which witnessed what were probably some of the most savage campaigns of the civil war. And it is for this period that Germán Guzmán — the outstanding historian of the *Violencia* — has produced the first really reliable published reference to the use of marijuana in the Cauca valley:

'There was some use of drugs, especially in the west of Caldas and in the department of Valle del Cauca. Marijuana is easily found in these areas, and was used as a daily stimulant by the *bandoleros* of *capitán Venganza* ('Captain Vengeance'), who was also known to smoke. The visitors to the jail in Caicedonia took the damned weed (*sic*) to their imprisoned friends and relatives with the same regularity as their daily lunch.'[9]

At the same time, the movement of population groups displaced as the result of the *Violencia* — and the simultaneous growth of demand for marijuana in the urban consuming centres, and subsequently, on the international market — also led to the emergence of a very novel phenomenon in Colombia, the non-smoking farmer who produced his weed exclusively as a cash crop. In the foothills of the Sierra Nevada de Santa Marta, for instance, it is such groups — often known generically as *cachacos*, which refers to all war refugees from the highlands of central Colombia — who are today responsible for the vast bulk of marijuana produced for the export market. The *costenos*, on the other hand, the traditional marijuana smokers of the coastal lowlands, are usually only very small scale producers, and tend to consume most of their crop themselves.[10]

It would be interesting to see how far the situation in the Cauca area mirrors that observed in the vicinity of Santa Marta. The parallels, at least on the surface, appear to be quite close; for the black population of the Cauca *valle* around Cali are consumers of marijuana and small scale cultivators — the equivalent of the *costenos* — while the really large commercial plantations are mainly concentrated in the Western Cordillera — notably, as far as supplies to Popayán are concerned, in the *municipios* of Morales and El Tambo. Like the major producing areas near Santa Marta, these mountain valleys have only been extensively occupied and colonized in the last couple of decades, and principally by refugees from the *Violencia*.

It is not clear, however, how long this tidy situation will continue to last. Already in 1974, it was obvious that many new marijuana plantations were springing up in the Central Cordillera — both on its western slopes between Cali and Popayán, and in the east-facing valleys which drain through the department of Huila into the Magdalena river. Furthermore, it is surely too simplistic to continue supposing that — at least in the Cauca area — there still exists any very definite and clear-cut divide between non-smoking bulk growers and the small scale producers who only smoke their own crop. This may have been true until quite recently, but by 1974, at least, many of the large growers in El Tambo were definitely not adverse to taking a hit or two on an occasional joint. This would seem to be related to a number of factors: firstly, the generalized impact of a hip youth culture on young people throughout Colombia; and secondly, the fact that many of today's more youthful growers actually grew up in the areas where they have their plantations, losing the distinctive *paisa* (from the department of Antioquia) or *cachaco* identity which has traditionally set their parents apart from the local community.

One cannot fail to note, however, that this development has seldom led to the adoption of marijuana as an everyday stimulant or aid to hard work, at least not in the classic pattern described for the Jamaicans, the *costenos*, or the blacks of the Cauca valley. Young white peasants in the Cauca area normally use marijuana in much the same way as it is used in the cities of the industrialized nations — as an euphoriant, a drug used to relax, to unwind, to kill time or to 'meditate'. Often it is consumed together with *aguardiente* at a party or a Saturday night dance. Nowhere is this more striking than in Tierradentro, an area where there has never previously been even any small scale production of marijuana, and where the habit of smoking dope was only just beginning to become common among young people as recently as 1974. Ironically enough, many had first smoked while suffering through their period of obligatory conscription in the Army. The local anti-insurgency barracks at La Punta (near the *páramo* above Belalcázar) was, for instance, well known in the district for its pioneering role in stimulating the local production of weed, for most of its underpaid, underclothed and underfed soldiers were brought in from other areas of Colombia where dope-smoking is far more widespread, and they obviously preferred getting stoned on patrols to tangling with the elusive and battle-hardened guerillas of the FARC liberation army.

In terms of the local farmers themselves, most of the new generation of dope smokers seem to have come initially from among the sons and grandsons of the white coffee growers who colonized the warmer valleys of Tierradentro in the early part of this century. Subsequently, the habit has spread into the Indian community as well, and a number of young Paez have been known to ask their neighbours for seed so that they could begin to grow their own. It must be pointed out, of course, that marijuana smoking is very definitely looked down on by the more traditional Paez, many of whom have only the very vaguest ideas of the plant's properties. Even a relatively young shaman — such as Elizondo, who was still in his 30s — considered it a plant to be used exclusively in the context of aggressive witchcraft, in order to *adormecer* ('to put to sleep') a rival. I witnessed a tussle between him and one of his nephews — a man in his early 20s — over the latter's recent adoption of the habit of smoking marijuana. In reply to accusations that the weed would make him lethargic and forgetful, the younger man replied (in Spanish, a gesture not entirely for my benefit, as by this time I understood Paez reasonably well): '*Dices que la marihuana le deja a uno trava'o, pero la verdad es que me siento más torcido que trav'o . . .*' (You say that marijuana makes a man feel 'blocked', but the truth is that I feel more 'twisted' than 'blocked' . . .).

Having travelled a few times to Cali and Popayán, he was using terms taken from the hip slang of those cities, terms which were obviously untranslatable into Paez. In any case, the point he was making was a good one: stereotypes about the debilitating effects of dope smoking are usually founded on a good deal of ignorance, and they betray a profound misunderstanding of the qualitative effects of marijuana on human consciousness. In any event, the pugnacious attitude of such individuals as Elizondo's nephew may serve indirectly to reduce or counteract the often chronic alcoholism of so many of the Paez, providing a far less damaging alternative to bootleg *aguardiente*, and — at the same time — eventually encouraging a positive reassessment of the coca habit itself. Indeed, given that a certain amount of cultural change is inevitable in Tierradentro, the addition of cannabis to the shaman's pharmacopeia could not fail to be a much more beneficial development than an abject sell-out to, say, aspirin or broad-spectrum antibiotics. All power to the herbs!

HONGOS

The local species of hallucinogenic mushroom — **Stropharia cubensis**, sometimes identified, erroneously, as **Psilocybe cubensis** — emerges in large quantities during the rainy seasons (September/December, February/May) and provides a major focus of attention for *gringo* travellers in the Cauca area. It has also been adopted enthusiastically by a number of youthful Colombians from the cities, but — as yet — seems to have made little or no impact on the local rural population. **Stropharia** ranges in size from 2cm. across to as much as 15cm., from 2 to 10cm. high, and in shape it can vary — depending on its age — from a closed bell to a wide platter curled up at the edges. Its distinguishing characteristics are an orange-brown stain at the apex fading to a dirty beige at the edges, a deep purple collar on the neck, and bluish-brown gills on the underside.

On being broken open and allowed to remain in contact with air for a few minutes, the flesh takes on a marked blue colour, this being held in popular credence to give evidence of the presence of the main active alkaloid, psilocybin. Each specimen lives about three or four days before beginning to wither and be eaten by insects. During this time it progresses from being very resilient and full of moisture, to a much drier and more friable state, and the brown colouration on the cap tends to darken considerably with age. It is advisable to consume only the fresher mushrooms, as the older ones often contain worms and other parasites. A moderate dose (8 to 12 mg. of psilocybin) can be obtained from roughly five medium sized mushrooms; but — since the drug produces tolerance — the dosage must be increased geometrically each time it is used, or a few days allowed to elapse between one trip and the next.

Stropharia appears to do well in a great variety of different climate zones, and its only basic requirement is the presence of a reasonable amount of humidity on the ground, and — more crucial still — a matrix of cow dung on which to grow. The spores do not germinate directly when they reach a suitable environment, but must be ingested with forage and pass through the complex digestive system of ruminants, such as the cow and the deer. Prior to the arrival of the Spanish in the New World, the distribution of **Stropharia** must have been very closely tied to the pastures frequented by deer, and in the sixteenth century the Mazatecs of Oaxaca — whose very name means 'people of the deer' — observed a strict prohibition on the killing of these animals. In the Cauca area today, the mushroom is most abundant in cattle pastures at altitudes of 1000 metres or less, and it is relatively uncommon higher up. This does not, however, prevent it from being easy to find both in Popayán (1760 metres) and Silvia (2450 metres); and many old-time *hongo* users claim a 'cleaner head' on the high mountain varieties, which may indicate some variation in alkaloid structure.

It is worth pointing out, at this stage, that **Stropharia** may be sometimes mildly toxic in its effects, particularly when the lower altitude mushrooms are being used. Other than the visual hallucinations common to a great many hallucinogens and psychedelics, the *hongo* eater may also suffer a feeling of very high body temperature, a constriction of the throat, headaches, stomach disorders, and occasional bouts of sudden nausea. The only area where **Stropharia** is still consumed by the indigenous Americans is in Mexico, where it has been reported among the Mazatecs of Huautla de Jiménez, and among the Lacandon Indians of the Chiapas lowlands. The Mazatecs call it *el honguillo de San Isidro Labrador*, and hold it in less esteem than the various smaller mushrooms of the genus **Psilocybe**. My own experiences of **Psilocybe** — both of **P. semilanceata** (the 'Liberty Cap' of the British Isles) and of **P. caerulescens** var. **mazatecorum** (the Mexican derrumbe or 'landslide' mushroom) — would certainly tend to confirm that the members of this genus are somewhat preferable to **Stropharia**, as they lack the occasionally unpleasant physical side-effects of the latter mushroom, while retaining all the more positive aspects of the psilocybin high.[11]

Though **Stropharia** does not yet appear to have been adopted by any Indian groups outside of Mexico, its wide distribution has allowed it to become very popular with a great number of young people throughout Latin America. Originally identified in Cuba at the turn of the century, it is now known all the way from Florida to Argentina. News of its properties spread like wildfire in the late 60s and early 70s. For example, in 1971 it was already a common feature of cattle pastures in Central and Southern Brazil, and yet very few people there had ever seriously considered trying to eat it, as its properties were not generally recognized. By 1973, however, this situation had changed suddenly and dramatically, and its potential recognized to the point of being included on the list of health 'problems' requiring the attention of the police. *O cogumelo subversivo* . . .

It seems, somehow, strangely appropriate that such a widely appreciated contemporary hallucinogen should have a history whose mysterious lack of outline should be perfectly in keeping with the almost instantaneous and telepathic diffusion of its consumption in the last few years. One is reminded of the mushroom folklore of many young South Americans, who view it as erroneous to enter a field actually 'looking' for the little beauties. Just as individual *hongos* are supposed to present themselves spontaneously to the seeker — as if guided by the superior wisdom of the mushroom spirit — so also it may be argued that **Stropharia** merely 'appeared' of its own accord, at a time and in a place where it could be sure of an enthusiastic welcome.

As a scientifically recorded species, it was only identified in 1906, and prior to this date there are no written descriptions of even its existence, much less of its use. Reports from the area surrounding Oaxaca were the first to describe its actual consumption, and these were only published in the 1950s. Whether news of its properties diffused from this centre, or were simply discovered by means of independent experimentation, is obviously a matter open to considerable dispute, but the likelihood of diffusion is certainly enhanced by the clear pattern connecting the use of this mushroom with the hip cosmopolitanism of the 1960s and 70s, and not with the traditional drug cultures of the native South American Indians.

In the Cauca area, its use does not appear to significantly antedate the mid-60s, but it must be stressed that this threshhold indicates not the arrival of the species, but only the actual recognition of its psychedelic properties. However, the fact that it is a matter of absolutely no interest to the local Indians would certainly tend to suggest that it is not an original and native member of the flora. After all, **Stropharia** propagates itself with extreme facility — scattering huge quantities of spores to the wind — and its spread throughout tropical and sub-tropical America has, therefore, depended principally on the availability of cow dung, and consequently, on the vast increase in the extension of land dedicated in this century to the pasturing of cattle.

This association has been clearly and graphically recognized in the Mazatec identification of the **Stropharia** mushroom with the figure of San Isidro Labrador. San Isidro is the patron saint of Madrid, and as such his image has long been revered all over the ex-Spanish colonies of the New World, being portrayed in all standard iconography as a heroic ploughman held between a pair of oxen. Clearly it was this link with Spain, and with cattle in general, that brought about the identification of **Stropharia** with the figure of San Isidro, for — other than the deer — no ruminant animal existed in Mexico before the Spanish Conquest, and it is, therefore, impossible that the dung-loving **Stropharia** could have had the same wide distribution that it enjoys today. One cannot fail to notice a potent irony in the fact that an expatriate European civilization should have both created the environmental conditions for the spread of **Stropharia** and indeed, ultimately become the principal exponent of its use; while it remained the indigenous Americans who were the first to discover and utilize the bizarre properties of this mushroom. *Una onda de la más sollada . . .*

YAJÉ

Though not used by any of the highland Indians of the Cauca area, *yajé* (**Banisteriopsis** spp.) is very popular among the lowland Ingano Indians who live along the banks of the Caqueta river — closer to Mocoa than Popayán, but still within the south-eastern boundary of the department of Cauca. Furthermore, the Cholo (Embera) Indians who live in the rain-forest inland from the Pacific coast of Cauca employ a hallucinogen known as *pildé*, which also appears to be a member of the genus **Banisteriopsis**, and thus a close relative of *yajé*. Most travellers tend to follow in the steps of William Burroughs and Allen Ginsberg, looking for the drug either in the Putumayo district of Colombia, or in the area surrounding Pucallpa, Peru. It is also, however, occasionally available through the itinerant herbalists — mainly Sibundoy Indians — who carry their wares to the markets in Silvia and Popayán, offering either whole lengths of the stem of the *yajé* plant (a jungle creeper), or more commonly, selling it in the form of a pre-prepared brownish liquid contained in an old bottle of *aguardiente*. The problem with this preparation is that it cannot always be guaranteed effective, as *yajé* quickly loses its potency when stored as a liquid. Any sign of fermentation, such as bubbles in the bottle, is a sure indication that the drink will be next to useless.[12]

On the few occasions when I did have access to reasonable doses of *yajé*, I found it an admirable drug in every way; like a cross between opium and psilocybin, at once psychedelic and narcotic, tranquillizing and sublimely euphoric. True, there is a distinct tendency for a rather severe nausea to set in occasionally, coming in waves which have to be fought off with a terrific effort of the will, but I found that this could best be countered by using a method of *yajé* drinking reported from the Vaupés. Rather than sinking a single large dose all at once — the obvious temptation for most beginners — this method involves taking repeated small doses of the preparation at hourly or half-hourly intervals, so that the cumulative effect of the drug is staggered in time. In this way, one can usually avoid the sheer agony of feeling poisoned and thoroughly fucked-up — the Burroughs syndrome — and instead approach that more desirable state of mind which anthropologists often mistakenly describe as a 'stupor', a result of their paying greater attention to a mere objective state — the material fact of a man lying slumped in a hammock — than to the less obvious subjective realities of his inner mindscape.

Hallucination? Dream? Whatever it is, the voyage of the soul under the influence of *yajé* is quite different from the mushroom or acid trip. Above all, it seems to deny any further pretence at control, dismantling that residual paranoia, that self-consciousness which lurks with watching eyes behind the visual fireworks of so many other psychedelic experiences, *yajé* seems to take you, quite literally, outside or beside yourself. The ultimate fix? All ultimates dissolving . . . nothing left to fix . . .

Appendix B. Magical and Medicinal Herbs in the Cauca Area

NATIVE MEDICINAL PLANTS

Cinchona spp.
local names: *cascarilla, quina, quinaquina.*

An evergreen tree growing wild between 1500 and 3000 metres altitude. Source of quinine and a number of related alkaloids, the ground bark is prepared in an infusion and used to treat fevers, neuralgia, and *la gripa*, the common 'flu. In the second half of the nineteenth century, the *quina roja* (red quina) of Pitayó and Mosoco was one of the most highly prized products of the Paez reservations, and attracted a large group of foreign buyers who organized their operations from a base in Silvia. Within twenty or thirty years, however, indiscriminate exploitation of the wild plants brought about the virtual disappearance of *Cinchona* throughout most of the Central Cordillera. Since there was never any attempt to plant new trees — and since the Paez themselves benefited little from the extraction of *cascarilla* from their lands — the Cauca area experienced only a very short-lived boom as the result of this flourishing export trade. Today's domestic supplies are mainly brought in by Indian herb dealers from Santa Rosa, Descanse, and other parts of the upper Caquetá drainage.

See also Patino (1967, pp. 331-346). Douay (1890) provides an excellent first-person account of the exploits of one French *quina* buyer of the last century.

Chenopodium anthelminticum Bert.,
syn. **Chenopodium ambroisiodes** L., var. **Antihelminticum**.
local name: *paico*; in English, 'American Wormseed'.

A very efficient vermifuge, the seeds and a decoction of the fresh plant are widely used in the Cauca area against tapeworm (**Ascaris**).
See also Patino (1967, p.179).

Jacaranda caucana Pittier.
local name: *gualanday*.
The local species of a very widely distributed pantropical genus; its leaves, bark and fruit are prepared in an infusion, highly valued for its depurative action on the blood and its tonic effect on the liver and the kidneys.
See also Patino (1967, p.330).

Juglands neotropica
local name: *nogal*, the Spanish name for the Old World walnut tree, which is of the same genus.
A strong decoction of the leaves is prepared, usually mixed with salt, and applied in the treatment of skin troubles — scrofolous diseases, eczema, etc. — as well as for healing skin ulcers, infections, contusions and inflammations.

Nicotiana rustica L.
local names: *um-wêh* in Paez, *tabaquillo* in Spanish.
The local wild or semi-domesticated tobacco plants are prepared in infusions or decoctions and used to treat dysentery and afflictions of the liver.

Portulaca oleracea
local name: *verdolaga*; the English 'Green Purslane'.
The leaves are prepared in an infusion, or as a compress to the forehead, for the treatment of headaches and fevers. Also used to balance the often toxic effect of **Chenopodium**.

Spondias purpurea L., **S. mombin** L.
local names: *ciruela, hobo*.
Leaves and inner bark possess strong astringent qualities, which would account for their widespread use in tropical America as dressings for infected flesh wounds. In the Cauca area, the young shoots and leaf buds are also prepared in an infusion and used to reduce fevers. Sometimes they are made into a compress, which is applied to the forehead in the case of extreme headaches.
See also Patino (1967, p.239).

INTRODUCED MEDICINAL PLANTS

The Spanish introduced a number of Old World plants to the Cauca area, most obvious of which are perhaps the various members of the mint family, the Labiatae, and such common cure-alls as garlic and ginger. The Labiatae include:

Melissa officinalis.
local name: *toronjil*, the English lemon balm.

Mentha viridis.
local name: *yerbabuena*, the English spearmint.

Ocimum basilicum.
local name: *albahaca*, the English basil.
All three are prepared in infusions and used as *frescos* — that is, refreshing drinks — to relieve headaches and fevers.

Other European introductions in the Cauca area include:

Apium graveolens.
local name: *apio*, the English wild celery; leaves are used in an infusion for heartburn and stomach swelling.

Verbena spp.
local name: *verbena*, the English vervain; used as a poultice for headaches and in a decoction for the treatment of liver complaints.

The Spanish were also responsible for the introduction of at least two important Oriental plants to the Cauca area — see Patino (1969, p.134).

Citrus aurantium var. **bigardia.**
local name; *naranja agria*, the English bitter orange. The leaves are prepared in a decoction with fresh coca leaves for the treatment of extreme cases of diarrhoea.

Cymbopogon citratus.
local name: *limoncillo*, the English lemon-grass. The infusion is universal in Tierradentro for the treatment of colds and influenza, and is also reputed to calm the chills felt by a woman in labour.

MAGICAL PLANTS

The herbs mentioned above tend to be used by all the rural inhabitants of the Cauca area — both white and Indian alike — and they are usually considered to be exclusively therapeutic. The plants used by the Paez shaman, on the other hand, are seldom if ever resorted to by whites, for their potency is seen to reside in their magical, rather than their purely medicinal qualities. Generally speaking, these magical plants are chewed together with coca and used to suck and to blow in the *pûtia* rituals, and as such their use stands out quite clearly from that of the medicinal plants, which are normally prepared as infusions, decoctions or poultices. Indeed, the practice of chewing other herbs together with coca is not restricted to the Cauca area, and both La Barre (1948, p.102) and Rostworowski (1973, p.194) have reported the widespread use of the bitter *akhana* — **Werneria poposa** Philippi, or **W. ciliolata** A. Grey — as an additive to coca among the Quechua and Aymara Indians of the Central Andes.

The Paez magical herbs include:

Scutellaria racemosa Per.
local names: *cháyuts* in Paez; *contento* or *alegría* in Spanish. The plant is of the same genus as the European and North American skullcaps.

The nervine and antispasmodic qualities of this drug are due to the presence of a volatile oil, Scutellarin, and they obviously explain the widespread chewing of the fresh herb as a check and balance to the stimulant action of the coca leaves themselves. Like tobacco, *cháyuts* is used in this way by Paez shamans in order to control the divinatory *senas* and, if necessary, reduce their intensity. It also forms an essential part of the 'altar' used both in ritual cleansings and in the witchcraft contest — a sprig of *cháyuts* being floated for this purpose in a gourd of *aguardiente* — and the herb is also commonly placed as a protective talisman on the crown of the head of all those who participate in such undertakings.

Being the basic Paez panacea, it is also often prepared in an infusion or a poultice for common complaints such as headaches, coughs and convulsive twitching, and it is sometimes employed to bathe inflamed eyes. The best *cháyuts* grows in the cold valleys above 2000 metres altitude, and it is often traded among Paez shamans for the coca leaves of the lower, sub-tropical climate zone.

Myrcia acuminata.
local names: *umsim* in Paez, *yacuma negra* in Spanish.

The plant grows abundantly in Tierradentro between 1000 and 2000 metres, and its elliptical black seeds — 7mm. long by 3 mm. diameter — are chewed together with coca during *pûtia* rituals. It must not be confused with the thin, white, sweet-tasting roots of *yacuma blanca* — or plain *yácum* in Paez — which is a different unidentified species growing down in the hot country near La Plata at about 1000 metres. Supplies of this latter herb imported from outside Tierradentro are more highly prized than the rather weak examples found growing in the warmer parts of Tierradentro itself, and these Paez home-grown varieties are given the distinctive name *yacuma de pena. Yácum*, however — whether local or imported — is considered by the Paez to be one of the most powerful of magical herbs, and it has a very pleasant taste when combined with coca.

Hibiscus abelmoschus L.
local names: *ush ni'in* in Paez; *culebrina* or *pepa de arco* in Spanish; known in English as musk seed.
The small kidney-shaped seeds have a pungent perfumed taste which combines well with coca, and they are considered to contain a potent magical charge perhaps related to their stomachic and nervine qualities. The shrub flourishes throughout Tierradentro in the sub-tropical zone between 1000 and 2000 m.

Scleria cattarinensis Boeck.
local names: *yuts-kái* in Paez; *curíbano* in Spanish.
A tall grass with a strong-tasting root which is often chewed with coca. A variety — or, more likely, another species altogether — is distinguished by a more swollen root and a rather more pleasant and musky flavour, being known in Paez as *chinda-alco* and in Spanish as *pata de perro*. Both seem to grow throughout the 1000 to 3000 metre range occupied by the Paez in Tierradentro. They are also used in an infusion for treating stomach disorders. It is interesting to note that different shamans often have conflicting opinions on the virtues of *yuts-kái*; for though it is considered a positive element — adding to the shaman's power — in the reservations of Calderas and Togoima, it is thought to be 'dangerous' in San Andrés, and is only used there in offensive witchcraft.

Chundur (not identified botanically).
The tuberous root of *Chundur* is covered with short brown hairs and punctuated by occasional swellings, which are the part of the plant that is chewed in magical practice. A distinction is often made between the more swollen variety — *chundur núsha* in Paez; *chundur de Castilla* in Spanish — and the thinner, more fibrous type — plain *chundur* in Paez, or *chundur de arco* in Spanish. It is possible that the former variety has developed as the result of a process of conscious selection, for *chundur* — like *cháyuts* and *yácum* — is considered one of the most important plants used in Paez magical practice, and is often found growing in what is clearly a semi-cultivated state, in the vicinity of human habitation.

Peperomia spp.

Two species, or sub-species, are distinguished by the Paez names *shugués* and *shupenín*, and both are commonly chewed with coca in a fresh state. A third plant, *shulape*, has not been identified botanically, but is normally used with the other two. The use of a fourth, called simply *shu* — a moss of the genus **Sphagnum** — seems to be falling into decadence as a masticatory, though it is still widely employed as a dressing for flesh wounds. It is significant that none of the first three plants have Spanish names, and their use in shamanism seems restricted to the more remote, higher altitude Paez reservations such as Calderas, Chinas, Lame and Tumbichuque. This may reflect the fact that many of the standard plants of the magical pharmacopeia — such as *chundur, yácum* and *ush ni'in* — are natives of the lower, sub-tropical valleys, which tends to make them rare and difficult to obtain at the higher altitudes. As a result of this, the shamans in the higher zone often prefer the fresh herbs taken straight from the ground — the *shulape/shugués/shupenín* group, plus *cháyuts, chinda-alco*, and *yuts-kái* — whose supply is more localized and dependable. It is important for the shaman to have access to his own sources of magical herbs, for — quite apart from the financial considerations — he simply cannot afford to depend on supplies which could be blocked by an unscrupulous rival. It is this which accounts for the virtual absence of a long-distance Paez trade in magical herbs, and in the few cases where such a trade does exist, it is nearly always to be found in the hands of whites or other non-Paez Indian traders who characteristically do their business in the mixed ethnic context of the marketplace. One drug plant in particular provides an excellent example of how this trade is organized:

Myroxylon balsamum (L.) Harms., **sensu latu**.
syn. **Myroxylon Pereirae** Klotsch.
local names: *ta'atsa* in Paez; *tache, olor* or *balsamo* in Spanish; the English 'Balsam of Peru'.

The resin of this plant was much used in Popayán during the colonial period to make an insect-repelling incense; but it is the almond-sized seed of the plant which today serves the Paez shaman as a masticatory. Wild *tache* trees occur in many parts of the Cauca area, but I have never heard of any being exploited in Tierradentro itself. All supplies of the drug to the Paez are provided by a group of ambulatory Indian herbalists whose own native valley of Sibundoy is located close to the rain-forest of the Putumayo, traditionally the source of most of the *tache* used in and around Popayán. The Paez maintain an uneasy relationship with the Sibundoy Indians, for the latter also have a formidable reputation as shamans, and thus represent more of a potential threat than any other Indian neighbours of the Paez, such as the relatively quiescent Guambianos. The differences between the Paez and the Sibundoy lie not only in mutually unintelligible languages and cosmologies, but also — perhaps more importantly — in their very choice of drugs: the Sibundoy are *yajé* drinkers and never chew coca, whereas the Paez are basically coca chewers and would never touch *yajé*. Predictably, then, it is only the shamans operating on the fringes of Paez reservation society who show any willingness to adopt the use of the powerful *tache* or *ta'atsa* seeds. Indeed, as little as twenty years ago — at the time of Bernal Villa's (1954a) study of Paez shamanism — the use of *ta'atsa* in Tierradentro seems to have been completely unknown.

See also Patino (1967, pp.185-193).

PLANTS USED IN OFFENSIVE WITCHCRAFT

These plants are never consumed or ingested in any way by the Paez shaman, but they are often handled in the witchcraft contest and their toxic qualities projected onto the victim by an act of 'imitative' magic. Usually they are combined with a claw or a snake's tooth, or any kind of vegetable thorn, in order to more effectively 'penetrate' the enemy.

Fourcroya foetida (L.) How.
syn. **Furcraea macrophylla** (Hook) Baker.
local names: *cabulla, cabuya*.
Apart from using the sharp point of the leaves as a thorn, the caustic sap is also said to 'rot' the body of a rival.

Euphorbia cotinifolia L.
local name: *lechero*.
Used as hedging all over the Cauca area at altitudes above 2000 metres, this plant has a very poisonous, rubbery sap which may cause a rival's body to 'burst'.

Urtica sp.
local names: *guepekás* in Paez; *ortiga* or *pringamoza* in Spanish; a plant of the same genus as the English 'stinging nettle'.
The weakest of the offensive herbs, and probably the one most commonly used. Its power of stinging the skin is seen to encourage an unwanted rival to keep away from a particular place marked out by the shaman by means of the *pútia* ritual. The plant is also sometimes used as a remedy, prepared in an infusion and drunk by those suffering from disturbances of the bladder.

Toxicodendron striatum Kuntze.
local name: *caspi*.
Contact with this bush or its sap produces a terrible rash which itches uncontrollably for many days. *Caspi* is often used in witchcraft to produce inflammations and swellings in the victim. Its action can be countered through the external application of the sap of the new buds of the common *yuca* (*Manihot esculenta*).

Datura spp.
local name: *borrachero*.
The active alkaloids of this plant include a significant amount of hyoscine (scopolamine), together with smaller quantities of atropine and hyoscyamine, which render it similar in effect to the thornapples, deadly nightshades, and henbanes of the Old World. The leaves and seeds of the South American tree datura were once widely employed as a medicinal and magical drug by the Indian inhabitants of the Andes, and in many areas this plant was the only really well-known and easily available native hallucinogen. Chronicle sources describe its widespread use around the early Spanish settlements in Quito and Bogotá, and it seems likely that Cieza de Leon's triple mention of the local Indians' habit of 'speaking to the devil' must also refer to the use of **Datura** in the vicinities of Cali and Popayán. (Cieza, 1962, pp.95, 99, 109.)

A study by Piedrahita (1973) could also be cited in support of this idea, since it provides well-documented details of a Synod held by the Bishop of Popayán in 1617. In the instructions imparted to his clergy there figures a section on the native fondness for getting drunk, and though the good bishop felt powerless to prevent the manufacture of alcoholic beverages, he does state very specifically:

> 'We give consent . . . to make fermentations of cane juice and ground maize beer, on the condition that no herbs or violent things be added to give them greater strength . . . nor mixed in any root, leaf or flower that may produce a greater degree of drunkenness in those that imbibe the said drinks . . . '

The reference to a 'root, leaf or flower' containing strong properties clearly suggests that **Datura** continued to be employed quite extensively by the Indians of Cauca at this time. This impression is confirmed by another report dating as late as the second half of the nineteenth century, in which Douay (1890, p.755) was still able to speak of the use of an hallucinogen among the Paez which he called 'stramonium' — the name of the European thornapple, another member of the same genus **Datura**. He describes it being used as a fish poison in the rivers of the Central Cordillera, as well as '. . . to give hallucinations, during which one is said to acquire the gift of second sight.'

By the time Bernal Villa (1954a) made his classic study of Paez shamanism, however, the custom of actually ingesting **Datura** in any form seems to have died out completely. Nor was I able to find any Paez shaman still alive in 1974 who had ever used — or ever heard of anybody else using — **Datura** for the sake of achieving any kind of 'second sight' or divinatory trance. At the present time, the application of the drug seems to be restricted to the context of aggressive witchcraft, where it is usually employed in order to drive a rival shaman insane. In handling the plant, however, it seems likely that the shaman should absorb at least some of the effect of **Datura**, for its alkaloids are known to be capable of penetrating the body quite simply through the skin. The magical 'projection' of its qualities onto the person of a rival may, therefore, paradoxically involve a real, though relatively mild, experience of the drug's effects by the very shaman who has resorted to **Datura** in the first place.

This would explain, perhaps, why tampering or even remaining in close proximity with the plant is usually considered so extremely dangerous. A Guambiano myth reported by Hernández de Alba and Tuminá (1965, p.91) speaks of the agreeable scent the **Datura** flowers give off in the evening, but warns that a spirit resides inside the plant, an evil spirit who takes the form of an eagle. He jealously guards the plant where he lives and pursues anybody who tried to cut it down, ruining all the offenders' harvests and visiting a plague on their livestock.

The bush is also seen to be capable of causing forgetfulness in any person — man, woman or child — who rests too close to its enveloping smell, carrying them off into a strange dream-world where they are confronted by visions of the now virtually extinct Pijao Indians, a cannibal people who were a terrible scourge on the Guambianos and the incipient Spanish colonies of the sixteenth century. All these associations would seem to indicate that the Indians of the Cauca area are perfectly aware of the powers of the **Datura** plant, and strongly suggests that it has long been recognized as one of the more potent psychoactive agents provided by the native Andean flora.

Two species of **Datura** are found in the Cauca area, both of them 'tree daturas' — that is, shrubby perennials, as opposed to the annual, herbaceous **Daturas** found in Europe and Mexico. The more common one has white flowers, grows up to four metres in height, and seems to be most at home in the cooler climate which in the Cauca area is found between 2000 and 3000 metres; it is usually identified as **Datura arborea** L. — see Patino (1967, p.273) or **Datura candida**, or possibly even **D. sanguinea** — see Bristol (1970). Vawell (1974, p.208) describes the use of the fresh herb in Popayán in the nineteenth century as a 'narcotic' to induce sleep in humans and dangerous snakes. The plant was considered a menace by the white population, as it had sometimes been used by slaves to drug their masters and lay venemous snakes in their beds, often with mortal results . . .

Another rarer species is known in the area of the Puracé volcano, and does best under the *páramo* conditions which prevail around the 3000 metres mark. The bushes in this case are smaller, being seldom over one metre tall, and the flowers are of a reddish-purple colour, which has earned it the local name of *borrachero colorado*. It has been given the botanical denomination **Datura vulcanolica** by Barclay (1959). The common occurrence of this latter species near archaeological sites in the upper reaches of the valley of Coconuco, would certainly suggest that the plant was once used quite extensively by the prehistoric inhabitants of that area — perhaps in some association with body washing rituals, as so many of these sites are located close to hot sulphur springs.

Appendix C. Paez Resistance and the Land Struggle

Most travellers usually come to this part of Colombia not to chew coca leaves or fraternize with the Paez Indians, but in order to visit the archaeological park in the valley of San Andrés de Pisimbalá. The local sights — which include the unique painted burial chambers of Segovia, El Filo del Aguacate, and El Alto de San Andrés, as well as the large stone sculptures of El Tablón, which were dug out of the ground and rearranged in a very pleasing (though artificial) circle a few years ago — have been described, with varying degrees of competence by Burg (1936), Perez de Barradas (1937), Hernández de Alba (1938, 1946b), Silva Celis (1943-1944), Patterson (1965), Reichel-Dolmatoff (1966), and Long and Yanguez (1971). Perez de Barradas, the first to address himself seriously to the problems of chronology in this region, argued that the culture of the painted tombs of Tierradentro should be accorded a rather later date than the statues at El Tablón. These latter show remarkable parallels with the lithic art style of the nearby site of San Agustin — itself undated, though usually supposed to have reached a climax in the period between 100 and 500 A.D. Patterson, on the other hand, suggested that the pottery of the large painted tombs in Segovia is much older than that associated with the San Agustín style — and hence, by extension, with the statues at El Tablón — and proposed that the painted tombs may date as far back as 700 B.C.

Long and Yanguez, despite the assiduous excavation of a number of habitation sites, were unable to confirm or disprove Patterson's sequence by reference to any concrete stratigraphy; nevertheless, they too suggest a relatively later date for the statues at El Tablón, and would even support the idea that this site was still being occupied at the time of the Spanish Conquest. The stylistic affinities between the coca bag represented on one of these statues, and the contemporary Paez *kuétan yáha*, would certainly tend to support this hypothesis, and may even lend weight to the provocative suggestion that the Paez are, in some general sense, the descendants of the men who carved the amazing statues at San Agustín. As pure conjecture, such an idea does seem to have greater credibility than the rather ludicrous 'invasion' theories of so many earlier historians of the Cauca area, who — seeking a justification for the white man's intrusion in Tierradentro — always sought to dismiss the Paez as mere upstarts, barbarians who had entered the area only just ahead of the Spanish, destroying the high cultures of the previous inhabitants, and leaving their romanticized, and conveniently extinct civilization to be cynically appropriated as part of the 'Colombian' national heritage.

It is to be hoped that recent, as yet unpublished excavations by Alvaro Chaves and Mauricio Puerta will, at last, overcome the old racist antiquarianism, and cast a new light on the sequence and chronology of the prehistoric cultures of Tierradentro. Given the inconclusive nature of most archaeological research — particularly in the vicinity of Popayán — it must be recognized that all attempt to clarify the impact of the Spanish Conquest in the Cauca area have long been hampered by the absence of any first hand chronicle describing the action. It seems likely, however, that Castellanos' (1944) blow-by-blow account of the first expeditions which drove north from Quito in 1536 and 1537 was based on eye-witness reports — according to Arroyo (1955, p.187), those of two soldiers called Serrano and Minderos — which were recorded at a later date. The early history of the new colony, and the conflicts between the various field commanders and the man who ultimately directed the Conquest — Sebastián de Belalcázar (or Benalcázar), a companion of Pizarro's who, disappointed at his failure to hold on to Ecuador after leading the Spanish troops in the Quito campaign, broke away to establish an independent *gobernación* of Popayán — is very competently analyzed in Jijón y Caamano's (1936-1938) cxccllcnt biography of thc conquistador.

The policy of virtual genocide initiated in the Popayán and Cali regions by the leaders of the advance guard, Ampudia and Anasco, and later perpetuated by Belalcázar himself, produced an extraordinary amount of hardship to both Indians and white settlers alike. Andagoya's (1938) description of the situation when he arrived in 1540, although politically motivated against Belalcázar, contains a savage indictment of this early stage of frontier anarchy, and provides ample explanation of the Paez people's total and uncompromising rejection of any accommodation with the invaders. Significantly, Andagoya himself lost several men in an attempt to subdue the Paez on the western flanks of the Central Cordillera. At the same time, the incipient colony at Timaná — on the other side of this mountain range, in the upper Magdalena drainage — was hard put to survive the onslaught of the Paez and their allies, united under the leadership of a fiery chieftess known as La Gaitana. Despite the use of blunderbusses and man-eating dogs, both Ampudia and Anasco — seasoned veterans who had fought through all the campaigns of Peru and Ecuador — lost their lives attempting to occupy Tierradentro, a 'tragedy' recorded at length both by Castellanos (1944) and Cieza de León (1918), and summarized in Jijón y Caamano (1938, pp.46-77). It is not surprising, therefore, that the early descriptions of the Paez all tend to concentrate on their prowess as warriors:

> 'They are very brave, very strong, skilful in the art of war, of good physique and very clean... They fight with long lances made of a hard black wood, often longer than twenty-five hands each, and many large slings... They have killed so many officers and men — such brave, dedicated Spaniards — that it causes great distress and not a little fear to see that these Indians, being so few in number, should be capable of doing so much harm...' (Cieza de León, 1962, p.109).

On his return from Spain in early 1541, Belalcázar sent a series of small punitive raids against the Paez, all of which were rapidly defeated. Finally, in mid-1543, he led the first really large military expedition into Tierradentro, a force composed of 120 men, 50 horses, and numerous Indian porters. It was greeted by a policy of scorched earth which left the Spanish without any food or shelter, forced to make their way on narrow tracks where they were subject to the threat of rolling boulders, and pinned down by almost constant guerilla attacks from the Indians who had taken refuge on the steep hillsides. A decisive engagement was fought against a Paez stronghold above the cliffs of Tálaga, and for the first time in his long career Belalcázar was forced to concede defeat, losing his lieutenant Tovar and many of his best troops in a suicidal attempt to scale the high mountain ridge. He struggled back to Cali through the misty thickets of the *páramo* of the Central Cordillera, being forced to abandon all his horses and many stragglers, and thereafter only organized small containing operations to keep the Paez from cutting communications between Cali and Popayán. Jijón y Caamano's (1938, pp.225-241) account of this period is taken largely from Castellanos (1944); and from a series of letters written to the Spanish King by Belalcázar himself, and by his Treasury officials Guevara and Magana, which have recently been edited by Garcés (1936; see especially Belalcázar's letter from Cali on 20th December, 1544).

A situation of effective stalemate persisted for many years after the Spanish defeat at Tálaga, and throughout this time the colony in Popayán lived in constant fear of sudden Paez attacks on isolated farms, mines and supply convoys. Other Indian groups, however, were less fortunate, and their surviving members received such inhuman treatment that Bartolemé de las Casas (1946, pp.131-133) felt obliged to pen a virulent condemnation of Belalcázar's bloodthirsty zeal as a conquistador. A humanitarian response came from Spain in the figure of Don Juan del Valle, the first bishop of Popayán. His attempts to counter the excesses of the colonists have been admirably charted by Friede (1961), whose account covers the crucial period between 1548 and 1560, in which the foundations of a stable colonial administration were laid down in the area. It was perhaps due to his influence that the Paez were left pretty much to their own devices during these years, and it was not until 1562 that another great expedition was sent into Tierradentro, this time under the leadership of Domingo Lozano, whose objective was that of founding a permanent settlement in the fertile and densely populated valley of the river Paez.

Though under permanent siege by the surrounding population, this nucleus — San Vicente de los Paez — seems to have survived for at least six or seven years. Fortunately — at least for our purposes — one of the Spanish colonists must have lived to tell his tale to the chronicler Pedro de Aguado, for it is this author's 'Recopilación Historial' which provides by far the best of the early historical records regarding Paez society. He dedicated seventy-five pages to Lozano's expedition — pp.487-561 of the second volume in the 1956 edition — and the account provides a truly astonishing wealth of detail not only of the military engagements between the Indians and the Spanish forces, but also of the Paez people's own social, political and economic organization, and of their rivalry with the neighbouring Guambiano Indians from Silvia, who — pursuing a policy of peaceful collaboration with the Spanish — were used on occasion as a native auxiliary force against the Paez. In recognition of his singular contribution to the understanding of the early colonial period, Aguado's sources and the history of his manuscript have been extensively documented by Friede (1956) and Fals Borda (1956).

At least initially, opposition to Lozano's colony seems to have been hampered by the internal dissension and lack of cooperation between the various Paez 'chiefs', all of whom — significantly, since it would seem to deny the possibility of any indigenous ruling caste, and reinforce the idea that Paez leadership has always been 'situational' rather than formal or hereditary — are referred to simply by means of place names. Perhaps even more important, Aguado repeatedly points to the intervention of the Paez shamans in stiffening the people's resolve to fight, thereby reducing inter-valley conflicts and producing a unified repudiation of any attempt by the Spanish to impose a 'negotiated settlement'. The colonists were left empty-handed inside their stockade, isolated to the point where precious lives had to be risked even to ensure supplies of such basic commodities as salt and water. Cornered in this way, the settlers committed savage atrocities which — rather than cowing the Paez into submission — only led to a strengthening of the old warrior traditions. Indeed, once San Vicente had been abandoned and the Indians began to realize their strength, they swiftly moved onto the offensive, laying siege to a number of other white settlements which encroached upon their territory. In 1577 they massacred the inhabitants of the silver-mining centre of La Plata, and from 1582 to 1589 they repeatedly sacked the gold-producing town of Caloto. Unlike San Vicente, neither of these were located strictly within the geographical confines of Tierradentro, but the ferocity of the Indian attacks ensured that both were subsequently resited further down their respective valleys, a tactical retreat which effectively ensured the territorial integrity of the Paez lands until the beginning of our own century. Other than the chronicle of Aguado, other sources on this period include the rather fanciful Arroyo (1955, II, pp.127-132, 142-148, 160-170); Sendoya (1964); and Otero (1952, p.56).

It is important to stress that — among the Indians of the Cauca area — the Paez were almost unique in their successful resistance to Spanish domination. Trimborn has written a comparative ethnography of the various different groups living in the area at the time of the Conquest, but his analysis can provide no real explanation of why this should be so. Local histories written about other specific regions — such as Arboleda (1956) for Cali; Romoli (1962) for southern Cauca; and Romoli (1965) for the Western Cordillera and Pacific coast of Cauca — all describe the rapid collapse of Indian independence in geographical settings which do not differ significantly from Tierradentro. And even the fierce cannibal Pijaos — who occupied the Central Cordillera north of the Paez — were finally subdued by a campaign of pitiless genocide unleashed between 1605 and 1613. If anything, the cultural context of Pijao resistance — the subject of two excellent ethnohistorical studies by Lucena (1962, 1965) — was even more intransigent than that of the Paez, though it could perhaps be argued that their fondness for cannibalism, and especially their impudence in attacking quite large Spanish towns such as Ibagué, Buga and Cartago, would have been likely to produce a more virulent response than the Paez policy of limiting armed action to the defense of their own traditional frontiers. Garcés (1935, p.571), for example, has transcribed a Cédula from the King of Spain, dated July 8th, 1598, which instructs those responsible for the war against the Pijaos to consider all captives as slaves — a treatment commonly meted out to cannibals. It is surely of some significance that such instructions were never made extensive to the Paez as well.

After the initial period of the Spanish Conquest, the Paez seldom ventured near Popayán, and the more subservient Indians of the Guambiano-Coconuco group provided an excellent buffer between that city and Tierradentro. A fort was built in Silvia to ward off any Paez incursions accross the Central Cordillera, and the route from Popayán to La Plata, and on to Santa Fé de Bogotá, was routed through the territory of the Guanacas — neighbours of the Paez on their southern side, and apparently less belligerent, being linguistically related to the Guambianos and Coconucos. Furthermore, since Tierradentro was not particularly rich in gold, the Spanish saw no major economic reason to proceed with its occupation, and — given the failure of their attempt at forcible intimidation — the business of 'converting' the Paez was, during the seventeenth and eighteenth centuries, left in the hands of a small and largely impotent band of missionaries.

The best history of this period is a manuscript written by Rev. David González — a Lazarist priest who lived in Paez territory from 1922 to the early 1950s — which is in the jealous keep of *Monsenor* Vallejo, the patriarch who runs the church mission in Tierradentro. González had the opportunity to compare his excellent knowledge of the terrain with the various published historical sources, and drew much of his original information from the parish records of the first stable Spanish church in Tierradentro — San Juan Bautista de Tálaga, which survived from 1682 until the War of Independence caused it to be abandoned in 1816. Earlier Jesuit missions (1613-1640) had met with little success, and the 'barbarity' of the Paez — and their custom of 'laughing' uncontrollably at the priests' attempts at conversion — had supposedly reduced one of their number, a father Ignacio Navarro, to a state of complete and catatonic speechlessness. Records from the later colonial period — such as the Paez dictionary written by the eighteenth-century missionary, Eugenio del Castillo I Orozco (1877) — echo the impressions provided by Aguado's earlier chronicle, again stressing the role of the shamans in resisting the penetration of Christian civilization. A manuscript in the colonial archives in Popayán (ACC — Sig. 607, dated 1686) also seems to indicate that the priests themselves often tired of their thankless vocations. Furthermore, though actual open warfare against the Spanish seems to have ceased throughout most of the seventeenth and eighteenth centuries, it was replaced by a wall of sheer indifference to missionary overtures, and the numbers of Christian baptisms in the parish records cannot possibly represent more than a very small minority of the total Indian population in Tierradentro.

More important to the Spanish, in any case, than questions of spiritual well-being, was the fact that all Indians who were subject to the Crown should be obliged to pay a fixed annual tribute for every adult male aged between 18 and 50. The economic background to the *encomienda* system has been analyzed by Colmenares (1973) and the *encomienda* institution itself explained in detail by Juan and Ulloa (1918), Arboleda (1948), Ots (1957), and Smith (1967). Since the Paez were not divided up into *encomiendas* until well into the seventeenth century, they had the good fortune to be spared the rigours of *servicio personal*, the system of serfdom which had been the original type of *encomienda* applied in the first stages of the Spanish Conquest, both in Mexico and on the north coast of Colombia. The later laws governing the institution allowed the *encomendero* — the holder of an *encomienda* — only to collect tribute, which he could do either by gathering up 'products of the land' and selling them in the market, or by demanding labour from the Indians which — being remunerated at a rate fixed by the Crown — could be deducted against the tribute owed. The *encomendero* did not have the right to make use of the Indians' land, nor to make permanent demands on their labour, nor to live near his Indians and sit in judgement over them in criminal offences, as had originally been the case in the very early *encomiendas*. Furthermore, a *corregidor* — normally the local missionary — had to be appointed to care for the Indians interests, and a complex system of legal checks and balances instituted to prevent the emergence of any new abuses by the *encomenderos*.

All this was fine in theory, but the practice of the *encomienda* system in Tierradentro was complicated by a number of local factors which were little understood by the legislators in Spain. In the first place, the extraction of tribute depended on the drawing up of a complete census in each encomienda, and — to judge at least from the rather incomplete tribute lists still surviving in the archives in Popayán — this was seldom a process completed with any great degree of success. Not surprisingly, since the Paez were still in open revolt, neither of the late sixteenth-century sources on the *encomiendas* in Popayàn — Descobar (1938) and López de Velasco (1894) — made any reference to the tribute produced by the Indians of Tierradentro. Even the *Ordenanzas* decreed by the *Oidor* of Quito, Don Diego Inclán y Valdés, on an official visit to Popayán in 1668, state specifically that no comprehensive census of the Paez had yet been taken at this date — see Olano (1910, Appendix p.31). The tribute lists which do exist, ably summarized by Arboleda (1948) and Otero (1952), show that the offensive to complete a census and begin seriously extracting tribute from the Paez had only really got under way in the last two decades of the seventeenth century, reaching a peak in the period 1698-1719. With the legal demise of the *encomienda* system in 1740, this initiative rapidly ran out of steam, disappearing completely with the death of the last *encomendero*, Capitán Polo Nieto of Toez, in 1761, as recorded by Castillo I Orozco's entry in the Tálaga parish records (González, mss., p.57).

Even in the two or three generations in which the *encomienda* was actually in force in Tierradentro, it seems to have run into considerable difficulties in fulfilling its tribute obligations. First and foremost, the material poverty of the Paez — as noted, for instance, in ACC — Sig.4296 — caused their annual tribute to be calculated at a rate so low that many of the smaller *encomiendas* could not afford the cost of a journey by the *encomendero* or his representatives every time a census had to be taken or the biannual tribute collected. As a result of this, many of the *encomiendas* operated at a loss, their debt to the Crown exacerbated by the fact that the Indians very often ran away when they were supposed to turn up for work — a fiasco recorded with not a little irony by the *corregidor* of Suín, in a statement dated 1696 (ACC — Sig.971). In cases where the debt became too outstanding, the Crown's representatives would place an embargo on the *encomendero's* further use of Indian labour, or — in a few cases, such as that recorded in 1715 by the corregidor of Vitoncó (ACC — Sig.2827) — the *encomienda* would simply be declared 'extinguished'.

The problems of administration were compounded by the very cultural traditions of the Paez themselves, for — unlike the situation in the Central Andes, or even in the neighbouring *encomiendas* of Guambía and Coconuco — there was rarely any individual leader in the Indian community who could be held solely responsible for the correct observation of the tribute laws. The example of San Andrés de Pisimbalá shows the absurdity of Spanish attempts to impose the idea of hierarchy in a society which is, and always has been, essentially egalitarian. In their efforts to produce a responsible leadership the *corregidores* in this area nominated *caciques* ('chiefs') purely in function of the numerous *encomiendas* into which the valley's population had been split, and without any reference or respect for the indigenous social structures. A community of rather less than a hundred adult males was thus provided with close on a dozen supposed *caciques*! (ACC — Sigs.2545, 2907, 2910, 2911).

It is hardly surprising, then, that the *encomienda* was almost as disheartening an experience for the *encomenderos* of Tierradentro as it was for the Indians themselves. Time and again the colonial sources describe the pressing need to collect the Paez in nucleated villages — an aim still pursued by the Church today, with a marked and continuing lack of success — so that they could be more effectively catechized and disciplined in forms of agriculture deemed more 'productive' (see Olano, 1910, Appendix p.2). Beating their heads against a brick wall in this way, it was inevitable that some of the *encomenderos* should have been tempted to take matters into their own hands. The Marqués de la Vega, governor of Popayán from 1707 to 1713, felt constrained to take away the *encomienda* of the Palomino family in Calderas and Togoima 'for excesses committed against the Indians . . .' (ACC — Sig.8363). On visiting Tierradentro in 1721, the Bishop of Popayán inveighed against the *encomenderos* for two main abuses: that of absconding Paez women and children to work as domestic servants in Popayán, and that of using adult males as beasts of burden to carry loads across the treacherous *páramo* of Guanacas (González, mss., p.51).

This raised an important question, for it is clear that the Indian work force must have been of little use to the *encomenderos* in Tierradentro itself,

Paez woman at work.

an area where they had neither land, nor mines, nor any other profitable enterprise requiring a large captive team of labourers. Indeed, numerous documents — ACC — Sigs.8960, 8527, 1896, 7856 — speak of the seasonal migration of Paez workers onto the great estates surrounding Popayán, and particularly to those owned by the Mosquera y Figueroa family in Coconuco (ACC — Sig.1984; and González, mss., pp.48 and 108.) This was no accident, for the original *encomienda* of Don Cristóbal Mosquera was, at the beginning of the eighteenth century, reputedly the largest in Tierradentro, including a major share of all the Indians in Vitoncó and Huila, two of the most densely populated valleys in the whole district. Only families with the political weight and economic power of the Mosqueras could successfully coax a sufficient number of 'their' Indians away from Tierradentro to make the whole business of organizing an *encomienda* worthwhile — for undoubtably, at least in the initial stages, they had to use considerable coercion.

The smaller *encomiendas* on the other hand, collapsed along with the very institution itself in the mid-eighteenth century — giving way to a system known as *repartimiento*, whereby the Indians were still forcibly obliged to labour on behalf of the white colonists, but in return for a straight wage, rather than for the payment of tribute. Though the law regarding this work levy stipulated that no Indian was to be taken more than ten leagues from his native homeland, the conditions were altered to take into account the special case of the Paez, who had to travel rather further, but who 'are accustomed from time immemorial to work in the city (Popayán)...' ACC — Sig.3207 — see also Sig.8462 and Arboleda (1948). Undoubtedly, a good number of the Paez resisted the *repartimiento* just as they had the *encomienda*; and Father González, for one, believes that the latter half of the eighteenth century saw a distinct lessening of missionary activity and administrative zeal in Tierradentro. No further baptisms were registered in the parish records after 1756, and the priest in charge of Tálaga at this time abandoned the church and went to live in Vitoncó, where the influence of the Mosqueras continued to be felt.

In a sense, it was this link — this unlikely collaboration between a paternalistic, patrician family in Popayán, and the proud Indians of Vitoncó, at one time called *chamba-guála*, the Paez 'capital' or 'big house' — which was the sole surviving bequest of the colonial period in Tierradentro. The death knell of Spanish rule in the Andes had already been sounded as early as the 1740s by the splendidly subversive 'Noticias Secretas' of Juan and Ulloa (1918), which had thoroughly condemned the tyrannical rule of the Indians by the old *corregidores* and *encomenderos*, and which — as if in recognition of its explosive criticism of the old regime — had been denied publication and thoroughly buried and forgotten by the courtiers to whom it had been submitted in Madrid. The Paez themselves were among the first to rally to the cause of Independence, and — under the leadership of an Indian from Vitoncó, one of the few genuine *caciques* of Paez history, called Agustín Calambás — provided vital support to the patriots cause in the early years of the war.

At the outset of hostilities, a missionary working in Tierradentro, Andrés Ordónez, organized a system of communication between the revolutionary sympathizers of La Plata, Caloto and Cali, spying on royalist movements across the *páramo* of Guanacas, and finally leading a group of Indians in the first armed action of the Guerra Magna in the Cauca area — the capture of a small Spanish garrison in Inzá in February, 1811, (see Otero, 1952, p.22; and Olano, 1910, p.182). Paez volunteers also provided a vital back-up force to the first large battle of the Independence campaign — at Bajo Palacé, on 28th March, 1811 — and subsequently fought with distinction at Alto Palacé (30th December, 1813) and Calibío (15th January, 1814) — see Aragón (1939, p.196) and Arboleda (1952, pp.121 *et seq.*) Narino, the republican commander in this latter engagement, was known to value the assistance of the Indians particularly highly, and went out of his way to demonstrate friendship for a Paez leader known as Astudillo. The ambiguity of the *criollo* aristocracy's new found sympathy for the Indians was, however, perfectly captured by a contemporary eye-witness, José Maria Espinosa, who — describing Narino's relationship with the Indian — felt constrained to write:

> '...and in the end his (Narino's) trust was such that he kept him (Astudillo) constantly on his staff, taking him out every afternoon for a spin in his coach; a fact that caused no little scandal to the assembled company, who — not understanding the aims and political style of Narino — could not understand this intimate friendship between two persons with such different backgrounds and positions.'
> (Espinosa, 1971, p.49).

Clearly, Narino had good motives for adopting such a liberal attitude, for it was the Paez — and not the local slave owning élite — who eventually provided the necessary porters to help take his artillery south to the historic capture of the royalist stronghold at Pasto.

Shortly afterwards, however, the tide turned against the revolutionaries, and despite another minor victory within Paez territory at Rio Palo (5th July, 1815) — their main army was massacred at La Cuchilla del Tambo (29th June, 1816). The Paez leader, Agustín Calambás, was among those captured in this engagement and subsequently shot by firing squad in Popayán. The tattered remnants of the rebel force fled into hiding in Tierradentro, where they were assured immunity from further Spanish attacks. Though effectively 'liberated' by this time, no further pitched battles were fought on Paez soil until the main Cauca and Neiva battalions reformed in La Plata in June 1820. Here — together with a number of Paez irregulars and British volunteers of the Albion regiment — they proceeded to march up to Vitoncó, across the *páramo* of Moras, and down to Pitayó, where they roundly defeated the royalists in a decisive battle which finally sealed the independence of Popayán (16th July, 1820). A first hand account of this campaign was written by a British officer who took part in the action at Pitayó — Richard Vawell (1974, p.194).

The later efforts of the war were all concentrated on Sucre's offensive in Pasto, Quito and Peru, and as the battlefront receded from the northern Andes, so also the internal dissension within the new Republic began to make its presence felt. Even the *Libertador*, Simón Bolívar, was himself obliged to start using force in the Cauca area in order to recruit an army of conscripts to fight in the south. His sympathy for the local aristocracy — the Mosqueras, Arboledas, Caicedos *et al.* — soon provoked an understandable indifference to the new régime among the less favoured sections of the population — see Aragón (1939, p.209). The Paez themselves, having freed Tierradentro, were already enjoying a welcome emancipation from the wider context of white man's politics; Bolívar's decree of 5th July, 1820, and a subsequent law of 11th October 1821, had between them abolished all colonial tributes and labour obligations, and stipulated that Indian lands were to be returned to their rightful owners. Missionary activity in Tierradentro decreased substantially, and — with the Colombian ruling class fragmented into countless warring factions — the Paez in the nineteenth century probably benefited from a greater degree of effective independence than they had done at any point since the drive to set up *encomiendas* in the 1680s.

There were moments, of course, when the Paez surfaced onto the wider stage of official History, but it would be misleading to imagine that they were of any real consequence in deciding the political fate of the new nation. León (1969) has provided an excellent analysis of the social indifference shown in this period by the Colombian élite; and such a total marginalization of the masses could not fail to produce — at least among the Paez — a sentiment that their territory, Tierradentro, was somehow quite separate from the geographical fiction known as Colombia, a state whose boundaries and very name, not to mention the constitution, changed over a dozen times in the course of the century. Of course it is true — and largely due to their age-old ties with the Mosquera family in Popayán — that the Paez normally took the federalist or liberal side against the centralists or conservatives, championed in Popayán by the Church and such families as the Angulos and Arboledas. But a detailed examination of their involvement in what was probably the single most important engagement to be fought in Tierradentro in this period — General Tomás Cipriano de Mosquera's triumph at Segovia (19th November, 1860) over an army sent from Bogotá to subdue his 'Independent State of Cauca' — shows to what extent these occasions were viewed in terms of traditional ethnic hostilities, as a pretext for the Paez to engage in a little salutary looting, to settle old scores with the encroaching white population.

The battle itself, fought on the plains between Inzá and San Andrés de Pisimbalá — for a blow-by-blow account, see Arboleda (1935, pp.445-489) — was not a particularly significant affair from the Indian point of view, and the real importance of the Paez guerillas lay in the constant harassment they maintained on the conservative forces both during the two or three months prior to the main confrontation, and especially, throughout the following two years, in which the whole of Cauca was plunged into a particularly savage and bloodthirsty civil war — see Aragón (1939, p.262) and Arboleda (1952, pp.186-189). Mosquera himself had gone on from Segovia to capture Bogotá (18th July 1861), but in the meantime the Conservative leader, Julio Arboleda, had retaken Popayán and most of the Cauca valley. The Paez, therefore, armed to the teeth by the Liberal general Obando, were given a free hand to vent their spleen on the Conservative elements in Inzá, Pedregal, La Plata, and particularly, in the prosperous town of Silvia, which they sacked on 11th January, 1862 — see Caro (1952, p.61). Furthermore, their allegiance to the Liberal or federalist cause was always conditioned by a good deal of enlightened self-interest; and Mosquera's supporters experienced considerable frustration in trying to recuperate the arms they had handed out to the Indians in the preparations for the battle of Segovia. On 27th November, 1860, Colonel Hurtado was asked to try convincing the Paez to join Mosquera's main force at La Plata; clearly, however, there was little hope that the Indians would be willing to fight so far away from home, and the instructions continued:

> 'If it is not possible to persuade the Indians to leave Tierradentro and offer their services at this headquarters, you will collect . . . the arms already referred to. . . . Avoiding the occurrence of robbery, looting or any other kind of excess by the militia of Tierradentro, and endeavouring that respect and obedience to the authorities become the basis of the service given by the villages under your command.'
> (ACC — Paquete 78, legajo 22, Comunicación 21.)

Once armed, however, the Paez were understandably unwilling to be subjected to any form of external discipline, and a state of latent insurgency persisted in Tierradentro until well into the twentieth century. An attempt to set up a seat of local government in Vitoncó in 1872, under a General Guevara Cajiao of Popayán, failed dismally despite the use of considerable intimidation; and a conservative revolt in 1876 provided the Paez with a new reason to besiege the white settlement of Silvia — see González (mss., pp.64, 78). A French *quina* collector resident in the town at that time made the following admiring commentary on the Indians' bravery: 'We have witnessed a battle where 300 badly armed Paez . . . put 1200 Colombian soldiers to flight . . . ' (Douay, 1890, p.784). In 1885, the Paez again took the Liberal side in a revolt against central authority in Bogotá, and as a result suffered the bloody consequences of the Conservative backlash which produced the Constitution of 1886 — see Aragón (1939, p.282).

The following fifty years saw the pendulum swing definitively in the direction of the reactionary elements in Colombian political life, and consequently, Tierradentro began to experience for the first time a determined and concerted attempt at occupation by land-hungry white colonists. Initially, the process of penetration was very slow, being further delayed by the civil war known as La Guerra de Los Mil Dias (1899-1902) — the last major effort of the Liberals to resist the increasing authoritarianism which emanated from Bogotá — in which the Paez ran riot all over the Central Cordillera, defeating and killing the Conservative Colonel Lorenzo Medina at the bridge in Avirama — see González (mss., p.109). Unlike the Liberal oligarchy, however, the Paez could not be bought off by the élitist compromise which ended the war, the infamous Pact of Wisconsin, which ushered in the humiliating secession of Panamá, and the golden age of the banana companies such as United Fruit. Although faced by ever more disadvantageous circumstances, the Paez have provided a shining example of resistance to the rapacious spirit of a century that has been — to put it mildly — unsympathetic to the political and economic autonomy of their traditional culture.

It is important, however, before considering the different forms their struggle has taken in recent years, to understand that the very first permanent occupation of Paez lands was occasioned not by coffee, the cash crop which sustains most of today's white colonists, but by the need for a very much more basic commodity — salt — which was always in short supply in colonial Popayán. As early as 1663, powerful interests in that city had managed to establish limits to the Paez community of Togoima which allowed them the right to exploit the saline waters of a river called El Salado. Shortly afterwards they established an *hacienda* — Pueblito de la Sal de San Antonio de Ambostá — with a church and slave quarters which finally gave rise to today's black communities in El Salado, Araujo, and Rio Negro de Narváez — see González (mss. p.75). The long permanence of the slaves' descendants in Tierradentro has produced a rural culture which, perhaps not surprisingly, has shown a far greater degree of adaptation to local conditions than has ever been achieved by the white colonists — including both the adoption of the coca habit and a fusion of magical and shamanic techniques, a specifically afro-Paez syncretism.

Other than the occasional missionary and the blacks of Pueblito de la Sal, however, no outsiders had ever managed to settle permanently in Tierradentro until the beginning of this century. In 1885 a *municipio* had been formed with its capital in Inzá, but this remained strictly speaking outside Paez territory, in the land of the neighbouring Guanacas Indians. It was only after the Guerra de los Mil Dias, under the proto-fascist dictatorship of Rafael Reyes, that a new *municipio* of Paez was formed, by means of Decreto 1510 of 18th December, 1907. In order to get round Ley 89 of 25th November 1890, the basic charter which was supposed to protect the territorial integrity of the Indian reservations (*resguardos*) in Colombia, the capital of the new *municipio* was located on ground already owned by the big landlords in Popayán, namely, the old Pueblito de la Sal, now renamed Belalcázar, in honour of the conquistador who had been so roundly defeated in 1543 by the Paez in nearby Tálaga.

The crude symbolism of such a gesture was not lost on the native inhabitants of the area, but much worse was in store than mere historical insults, no matter how offensive these might be. Soon a Lazarist mission established its headquarters in Belalcázar, and proceeded to operate unashamedly as an agency to spy on the Paez on behalf of the Conservative party, as well as to direct the spearhead of a cultural and political offensive aimed at breaking the spirit and stealing the land of the Indian people. One missionary of this period wrote: '... the Indians are stubborn and incorrigible; only the mixing of their blood, the splitting up of their communal land into private plots, and the building of roads through the area, can possibly make their territory into something worthwhile ...' (González, mss., p.221). Racist sentiments of this kind were also echoed by the local political worthies in Popayán, such as the Secretario de Gobierno, himself officially responsible for protecting the Indian resguardos: 'A grave obstacle to the exploitation of the land and the increase of livestock and agricultural wealth lies in the special institution of community to which the Indians' resguardos are subjected, and in the fact that many reservations have much more land than they need or are able to cultivate ... Here one might introduce a modification (*sic*) by way of permitting the leasing of the remaining fields, with certain guarantees ...' (Medina, 1916, pp.113-115).

Indian opposition to this sort of treachery was understandably intense, and open rebellion again broke out in Tierradentro in 1916, under the leadership of Manuel Quintín Lame, one of the great Colombian folk heroes of contemporary times. His famous assault on Inzá is still the subject of many contradictory accounts, but it is clear that — on or around the 12th November of that year — he both looted the town, lost a piece from one ear as the result of a sudden tempestuous machete blow from the crazed local mayor, and suffered a cowardly ambush in which six of his supporters were gunned down in cold blood — see Castillo (1971), Castrillón (1973), Quintero (1955) and González (mss., pp.66, 109), for a number of widely differing versions. There can be little doubt, however, as to the overall significance of the encounter, for it must be accepted that Quintín Lame's rallying cry of 'All whites out of Tierradentro!' was a very real and live issue at this time, less than ten years after the foundation of the town of Belalcázar. The Conservative authorities in Popayán, however, grossly and deliberately exaggerated the threat to life and property, putting the entire department of Cauca into a state of alarm and sending a flood of troops into Tierradentro from all points of the compass. General Palacios proceeded to apply the law of conquest all over again — killing a good number of Paez in the field, pillaging their homes and destroying their crops, and taking many of their leaders, such as the stoic Rosalino Yajimbo, away to prisons from which they never returned.

All in all, the period was a bleak one for Indian activists of any kind, for — unlike the Paez guerillas of the nineteenth century — they could no longer depend on Liberal arms, or on exploiting the internal dissensions within the Colombian oligarchy. All the more significant, therefore, was the way in which Quintin Lame's subsequent career developed, for he soon realized that force alone would never be sufficient to check the fury of the modern bourgeois state. He turned instead to the business of reinforcing Indian cultural traditions — visibly disintegrating all around him under the impact of a banal conception of 'progress' — and concentrated particularly on defending and, in some cases, even reviving the collective land ownership of the Indian *resguardo* system, as defined in Ley 89 of 1890. The practical aspects of this struggle slowly led him to adopt a political strategy which remains the basic formula of Indian civil rights action in the Cauca area right up to the present day, and which is remarkable for its deft use of the wider arena of Colombian public life — be it the courts, the legislature, the press, or even the organisms of corrupt local government itself. No longer could the Paez be dismissed by the authorities as a group of barbarians only interested in looting and killing for their own sake, no longer could the convenient fiction that they were 'tending to disappear, and gradually blending into the common mass of the Colombian population' (Medina, 1916, p.116) be used as an excuse for their marginalization, expropriation and ultimate genocide. The development of Quintin Lame's philosophy marked the end of the Indian cause as 'savage', and its emergence as a banner worthy of the respect and support of left-wing intellectuals, a sort of national conscience, a healthy antidote to the cess-pit Age of the Plastic Yankees and their unsavoury puppet régimes. Quintin Lame, the man who worshipped Nature as the only true source of knowledge, actually wrote a book in 1939, published posthumously as 'En Defensa de mi Raza' (1971) — as well as a number of short essays (Lame, 1973) — which must surely rank as one of the most significant texts to have ever come out of Latin America, a fine mixture of polemic, fiery prophecy and mystical abandon to the palpable, physical realities of life in the Central Cordillera. Let his memory be praised!

The example of Quintín Lame was all the more important in the light of the increasing ridicule to which the Indian population in Colombia was subject during the course of the twentieth century. In 1924, the first *monsenor* — a Frenchman by the name of Emile Larquère, best known for his habit of wearing kidskin gloves whenever he had to touch the beastly dirty natives — arrived to take charge of the newly formed Prefectura Apostólica de Tierradentro. This was a semi-autonomous fiefdom which, by the terms of the Concordat signed in 1887 between Rome and the Colombian government, was invested with sole and exclusive control of all local education, and the power of veto over members of the Indian *cabildo* — the representative group elected annually within each *resguardo* — and over the mayors and other civil authorities appointed inside mission territory. Such high-handed paternalism towards the 'savage and barbarous tribes' — as they were defined in the Concordat — was also reflected in further pressure on the territorial integrity of the *resguardos*; Ley 19, signed by the governor of Cauca in 1927, established nuclei of white colonization (*areas de población*) on choice pieces of land located well within the Paez reservations of Ricaurte, Guadualejo, Cohetando, Tálaga, Tóez, Huila, Mosoco, San Andrés, and Yaquivá — see Iragorri (1962, pp.55-61) for a detailed account of local legislation referring to the *resguardos*. The Paez resisted these measures with not inconsiderable tenacity, but their neighbours, the Guanacas Indians, were rather less fortunate: in the 1930s and 40s their remaining reservations were simply extinguished by laws which, at the stroke of a pen, established the reign of 'civilization' and brought with it the blessings of private property — see Otero (1952). This move opened up the valley of the Rio Negro, east of Inzá, to increasingly unscrupulous penetration by white coffee farmers, who — by the time of my visit to the area in 1973 — had succeeded in expelling all but a small handful of the original Indian inhabitants. Similar processes of 'de-collectivization' of Indian lands have been documented in detail in other parts of the Central Cordillera, such as San Agustín (Friede, 1943) and particularly the coca-producing valley of the San Jorge river, in southern Cauca (Friede, 1944).

Wherever this policy has been applied in Colombia, the object of the exercise has always been the same — to destroy the political, economic and cultural independence of the Indian *resguardos*, and 'integrate' the remaining Indians into Colombian society at the very lowest level, that of marginalized, and preferably landless peasants. In Tierradentro, the resentment caused by such a wilful disregard for the people's own interests was to surface repeatedly in the last fifty years, and as the struggle itself deepened, so also did the need to find concrete allies for the Indian cause. The first of these were the local white Liberals of Belalcázar, who in 1932 — under the leadership of Pío Collo — successfully besieged the mission station in that town, which had long been plotting with the Conservatives all kinds of petty obstructions to the policies dictated by the new Liberal administration in Bogotá. Soon other civil rights organizers from Popayán — such as Alfonso Paz and Manuel Tránsito Sánchez — began to encourage active Indian resistance to the missionaries in the reservations of Vitoncó, San José and Huila, basing their campaign on an opposition to any form of subdivision of the collective lands of the *resguardo* into private farms or *parcelas*.

The conflict between the Paez and their supporters, and the Church and landowning interests which supported *la parcelación*, rapidly escalated — to the point where, on 14th April 1934, the Indian Jacinto Julián was brutally murdered by an assassination squad in the pay of the large landowners. The University of Cauca rallied to the support of the Paez, sending a lawyer — Gerardo Cabrera Moreno — to put their case at an international *indigenista* ('Indianist') meeting in Pátzcuaro, Mexico. By the middle 1940s, an organizer by the name of Víctor Merchán had popularized the idea of peasant leagues in Tierradentro, helping to form a Comité de Propaganda to defend Indian interests in the reservation of Huila, which brought together the efforts of many combative Paez families in the area — such as the Chindicués, the Teres and the Chapenos. The cabildo of Huila directed the Indians to boycott mass and the missionary schools, and — faced by the complete intransigence of the priest assigned to the reservation — finally forced all the clerics to evacuate to Belalcázar, then burned down the school, the priest's house, and the mission station of the nuns. See González (mss., pp.208-222) for a detailed account of these events, doubly interesting since it is written in an attempt to justify the Church's position — González was the priest in charge of Huila at that time (mid-1945).

It seems clear, then, that the basic impetus of the present-day land struggle in the Paez *resguardos* had already been established as a dynamic force all of thirty years ago: there was already a militant movement in defence of the integrity of Indian lands, sometimes assisted or — more often — undermined by the political opportunism of the left wing of the Liberal party, and faced by the implacable opposition of the Church, the Conservative party, and the white landowning interests which formed the bulk of the mainstream Liberal party. Before considering the subsequent course of events, it might be worth examining the position taken by the ethnographers who studied the Paez in this period, for their work provides an object lesson in how a certain brand of uncommitted 'science' can fail utterly to reflect the real needs and aspirations of the people subject to its jaundiced scrutiny. Leaving to one side the rather romantic idealization of the Paez warrior evident in Douay (1890), all subsequent accounts have been marked by an unaccountable, but surely deliberate attempt to deny that any real social conflict was actually taking place at all in Tierradentro.

Earlier reports — such as Pittier (1907), Cuervo Márquez (1920), and Lunardi (1934) — were unmistakeably racist and ethnocentric in tone. More frightening, perhaps, is the fact that the grand generation of mid-century social scientists usually managed to avoid taking any explicit position whatsoever, shielding their sensibilities behind a spurious 'objectivity' that could not afford to dirty its hands with anything that might detract from the well-wrought mediocrity of their respective ethnographies. To judge from the accounts of Hernández de Alba (1944, 1946a) or Pérez de Barradas (1937), the Paez would seem to be living in a complete political vacuum. Even Bernal Villa, perhaps the best informed student of the Paez, dismisses the period of the *Violencia* — in which he himself was doing his field work in Tierradentro — with scarcely a single mention, as if the heat of actuality were somehow to undermine the scholarly tone of his work. On one occasion, he identified the parties to the conflict simply as 'armed subversive groups' (Bernal, 1954a, p.241) and left it at that; a ploy echoed by Ortiz (1973, p.33) who lumped together Communist and Liberal guerillas — and, presumably, their Paez supporters as well — by means of the conveniently vague, but hardly neutral term 'bandits'. Equally unwilling to discuss contemporary political conflict was Otero, who — despite an obvious sympathy for the Indians' land campaign — still saw no contradiction in perpetuating the old missionary intransigence, the Christian horror of heathen gods, referring to the tutelary divinity of the Paez shamans as an 'evil spirit' (Otero, 1952, p.92).

It is not, therefore, at all surprising that the Paez should view most anthropologists with a certain amount of suspicion, even hostility, for they have so notably failed to provide them with any really effective support. Like medics and big-wig politicians they are considered *doctores* — members of the professional classes or the urban oligarchy. Furthermore, their field work has almost always been concentrated in a very restricted area of Tierradentro, the *resguardos* of San Andrés, Santa Rosa and Calderas, where they have been able to enjoy a safe haven at the *Parque Arqueológico*, a tourist trap owned and operated by the *Instituto de Antropología* in Bogotá. Don Teófilo, who administers the *Parque*, was a well-known gunman or *pájaro* for the Conservative assassination squads during the *Violencia*; and Calderas — alone among the Paez *resguardos* —

always voted Conservative in the past, largely as a means of reasserting its isolation from the other Paez groups, a trait already noted by Aguado in the sixteenth century. At the same time, American anthropologists — some of them ex-Peace Corps, and reputedly CIA — have normally given the Paez a wide berth, preferring to test their models and sharpen their functional analyses on the more easy-going Guambianos. And even the theoretically well-meaning bureau of Indian affairs (the *División de Asuntos Indígenas*, of the *Ministerio de Gobierno*) has found that its Indian 'training' centre in Tóez has been totally incapable of bridging the enormous gap between government agencies and the local communities. The harsh fact is that *all* official and scientific bodies in Colombia are identified with the powers-that-be; and the Paez have excellent cultural and historical reasons to suspect the motives of *anyone* associated with Authority.

They are, moreover, quite justified in repudiating any compromise with the State called 'Colombia', as it is presently understood. The events of the last thirty years have shown conclusively that nothing good or worthwhile can be expected of a system whose very raison d'être is that of suppressing popular culture and any genuine desire for political self-determination, of sustaining ad nauseum the infra-human system of exploitation which weighs over the land, like the gold-plated, bald-headed vulture which shits above the door of the U.S. Embassy. As we have seen, the Paez had — by the mid-1940s — organized themselves to the point where they were beginning to strike back at the Church and the white landowners who had invaded their land, and what is more important, were doing so at a moment when their struggle was paralleled by a great upsurge of revolutionary sentiment throughout Colombia. This feeling had peaked in a spontaneous insurrection in Bogotá — the *Bogotazo* of 1948 — but, deprived of leadership by the assassination of Jorge Eliécer Gaitán, and further undermined by the vacillation and salon intellectualism of the Communist Party, the initiative had rapidly passed back into the reactionary camp. By 1949, the Americans had armed a newly-appointed Conservative president (the Liberals did not contest the election) called Laureano Gómez, who proceeded to send out his para-military terror squads into the countryside, with instructions to carry out a policy of virtual genocide on the mainly Liberal peasantry.

The man in charge of the campaign of intimidation in Tierradentro was one Santos Rincón, a soldier from Boyacá who was appointed mayor of Belacázar by the new Conservative governor of the department of Cauca, a member of the Angulo family from Popayán. The account of Rincón's excesses in González's manuscript makes truly horrifying reading, and — apart from explaining the Church's reluctance to have the book published — is especially significant when one considers that the author, a priest and ardent Conservative, was bending over backwards to justify the repression.

Rincón began by beating up the head of the local Liberal party offices in the main square of Belalcázar — a town almost entirely Liberal in sympathy — then imprisoning the local magistrate and generally aggravating and intimidating anyone who got in his way. With police and troops brought in from La Plata he succeeded in forcing almost the entire population of the town to flee into the hills, dynamiting their houses and forcing — with a revolver in one hand and a wooden cross in the other — all those he met to kneel and swear allegience to the Conservative party.

On 2nd November, 1949, the Paez and the Liberals from Belalcázar met in Taravira and settled their differences; and for the next two or three months they proceeded to arm themselves and prepare for an eventual counter-attack. This finally came at 3 a.m. on 28th January, 1950: ten men were killed in the action, and the town of Belalcázar was entirely sacked, including the mission station, which was found to be harbouring explosives for the Conservatives. Rincón himself had escaped, however, and on the 29th he returned from La Plata with three truckloads of government troops. The mixed force of Paez and Liberals retreated back into the mountains, and within a few days the long and savage war of attrition had begun. In the following years, the Army went repeatedly on the rampage through Tierradentro, particularly at El Salado and La Símbola — in the vicinity of Belalcázar — and in those reservations where Paez activism was strongest such as Huila, San José and Toribío. On more than a few occasions the soldiers were guilty of the rape and cold-blooded murder of women and children; and many of the men captured on these raids were taken down to the bridge at Cohetando and shot — as many as 112 in a single day, according to Guzmán (1968, p.83) — their bodies being disposed of by the river Paez, a grim warning to those who lived further downstream.

The officially condoned violence of 1949-1950 was itself only the beginning of the civil war. It was followed in 1954 by a second wave of government terrorism — the supposed 'pacification' of Tierradentro by the Armed Forces loyal to Rojas Pinilla, who had taken over from the now largely discredited Conservative leadership. In truth, the *Violencia* never really stopped at all, it merely had moments of greater or lesser savagery which came and went with the different military commands assigned to the area. Fluharty (1957, p.270), for example, provides an account of one battle in March, 1955, between the Army's Rook batallion and a band of Liberals and Paez irregulars, in which at least six Indians were killed by the troops. Furthermore, the united front of the Paez and the local Liberals had itself been subject to a process of endless fragmentation; and throughout the decade of the 50s a number of mutually antagonistic Liberal guerilla groups ranged all over the Central Cordillera doing battle with the authorities. Driven initially by necessity, and thereafter by convenience, these columns rapidly degenerated into pure *bandolerismo* (banditry), often stealing their supplies from isolated Indian families in the more remote mountain areas.

The Paez, therefore, whether faced by the Army or by Liberal *bandoleros*, obviously found themselves being forced to adopt the same tactics they had employed in similar situations in the past — be they as diverse as Belalcázar's invasion of 1543, or the punitive raids of General Palacios in 1916. First they would lie in ambush and attempt to drive back the invading force, then — if out-numbered or out-gunned — they would retire to the high, inaccessible ridges and forests of Tierradentro, allowing their houses and fields to be burned, but at least preserving their lives, and those of their families as well. In the end, the intruders would inevitably get tired and go home, and there would be nothing to prevent the Indians from returning to their land again. Many Paez still alive today — especially those of Huila and Toribío — remember going through this process once or twice a year throughout the period of the *Violencia*. Drawing on past experience, they learned to conceal crops in small clearings that would provide them with a minimum of food; and — central to the argument of this book — came again to recognize the irresistible vitality of the coca bush, which could be cut or burned to the ground (it is difficult to pull out, given its mass of very fibrous roots) and still, within a period of a few months, produce another abundant growth of new branches and leaves. The Paez were fond of pointing out the parallels with their own situation: 'Like the coca bush, you can cut us to the ground and we will still spring up again, from the roots . . . ' A perfect expression of the nature of their defensive war, of the rearguard/vanguard action which the Paez have been fighting for four hundred years or more — the defence of their communal *resguardo* system as a form of social organization not only of the past, but also, even more importantly, of the present and of the *future*.

The point, then, of the *Violencia* in Tierradentro was that it marked the definitive transformation of the ethnic conflict — Paez against white colonists — into a situation much closer to the classic model of class conflict. The Indians were engulfed in a civil war whose cold logic was determined in Bogotá, by the oligarchy's need to abort and deny the Colombian people's efforts to produce a social revolution. The impotence of the Liberals — their failure and lack of leadership in the armed struggle, coupled with their humiliating sell-out to the imperialist-sponsored 'peace' of 1957 — showed that the old two party system was now effectively little more than a farce, a dead letter. The brutality of the Conservatives and the 'moderate' compromises of the Liberals could now be identified as simply two sides of a single coin — both merely reflected the desire for vertical hegemony by a political class entirely unrepresentative of the population as a whole. The Paez grasped this point intuitively; as far as they were concerned, there could be no return to the patronizing, highly centralized form of politics which had always been the hallmark of the old Colombian bandit democracies. Institutional reformism — to put it bluntly — could only appeal to the lame-brained, to those Indians who are always polite to the priests, to those laughed at by their fellows. In future, therefore, the Paez would have to choose their non-Indian allies with great care, and — above all — they would learn to rely increasingly on their own organizational skills, on their own direct forms of political action and cultural resistance.

Initially, they had very little choice in the matter. With the defection of the Liberals, almost the only outside source of support lay in the *Repúblicas Indepentientes* of Marquetalia and Rio Chiquito, guerilla-held zones which bordered on the northern and northeastern limits of Tierradentro. Respectively under the leadership of Manuel Marulanda Vélez (*Tirofijo* or 'Sure Shot') and Ciro Trujillo Castano (*Mayor Ciro*), both of whom owed their ultimate allegience to the orthodox Communist Party of Colombia, these areas nevertheless managed — due to the Central Committee's ambiguous stance on guerilla warfare — to administer their territories in almost complete independence from outside interference. The *Repúblicas Independientes* had welcomed large numbers of peasant refugees from Tierradentro and all over the departments of Cauca, Huila and Tolima; and rather than engage in the gratuitous violence of so many of the Liberal guerillas, they had concentrated on the construction of an exemplary society in the liberated areas, distributing land to all, and organizing a genuinely responsive and self-regulating structure of local administration which put the surrounding government-held areas thoroughly to shame. A priest from Belalcázar who visited Rio Chiquito in 1959 felt constrained to write, despite his lack of sympathy for the guerilla cause:

> 'Among all these people I did not find either cruelty, nor brutality, nor malice of any kind. There is a marvellous foundation of uprightness, sincerity and good will . . . The people do not seem bitter or oppressed . . . they sincerely believe themselves to be engaged in a war of national liberation . . . if we compare the crimes of the guerillas with those of the men who hide behind the national flag, the balance of guilt would surely weigh against the latter . . . ' (Guzmán, 1968, p.448).

Furthermore, and most importantly from the point of view of the Paez, the guerillas were practising a form of land colonization which did not threaten the neighbouring Indian *resguardos*, but rather, made a deliberate attempt to respect their traditions of independence and communal land ownership. The guerilla command at Marquetalia had made a clear and unambiguous statement of policy:

'. . . the Indian communities will be protected, granting them sufficient land to develop, returning to them the farms usurped by the large landowners and modernizing their system of cultivation. At the same time, the autonomous organization of the communities will be stabilized, respecting their *cabildos*, their way of life, their culture, their own languages and internal organization . . .' (Documentos Políticos: Revista del Partido Communista de Colombia. no.47. February/March, 1965.)

Clearly, 'bad examples' of this kind could not long be allowed to flourish in the Central Cordillera. After 1957, the guerillas had actually ceased to engage in any further armed action against the authorities, and were winning over the peasants purely on the basis of their proved capacity for organizing a more equitable distribution of the area's resources. Dismayed at the events then taking place in Cuba, the CIA began in 1961 to stress to the Colombian government the need to wipe out such 'threats to freedom' before they had the chance to spread, offering all the new technological hardware which was currently being perfected in Vietnam. Attacks on Marquetalia began in 1962, and — after a few 'experiments' with bacteriological warfare — the offensive finally came to a head with the napalm-bombing and helicopter-borne assaults of May, 1964. The guerilla force itself, however, managed to escape the encirclement of the Army, and by September, 1965, the onslaught was extended to Rio Chiquito, where the same pattern was repeated as elsewhere: bombing with napalm and aerial strafing of any visible buildings, followed by massed infantry assaults and the torture and terrorization of any peasants found in the area. Again the guerillas escaped, this time into the untracked forests around the Nevado del Huila, but by now the main tactical object of the exercise had been achieved — the destruction of the menace to State hegemony posed by the peaceful, self-governing *Repúblicas Independientes*. General accounts of these operations include Guzmán (1968) and Gott (1973) but the only detailed eye-witness report of the operation in Rio Chiquito has been taken from the diary of a student, Hernando González, who lost his life in action on 23rd September, 1965, and published in 'Documentos Políticos: Revista del Partido Comunista de Colombia.' (no.54. October, 1965.)

Almost inevitably, these repressive operations overflowed into the Indian reservations of Tierradentro, particularly those — such as Huila, Tóez, San José and Toribío — which were closer to the guerilla strongholds, and which were therefore considered to be harbouring refugees and other potential 'subversives'. In July, 1964, for example, twelve Indians were gunned down by the Army in La Símbola on their return from work — they were unarmed. A military presence, most noticeably at the base in La Punta, has been a constant feature of the last ten years in Tierradentro, and the forms of popular resistance have had to evolve accordingly. In April, 1966, the guerillas of Marquetalia and Rio Chiquito re-grouped to form the *Fuerzas Armados Revolucionárias de Colombia* (FARC), a mobile column which has struck back at the Army with impunity in many parts of Huila, Cauca, Valle and Tolima. After ten years of operations, this group and the Ejército de Liberación Nacional (ELN) — operating further north, in the department of Santander — represent the sole surviving guerilla fronts in action anywhere in rural Latin America, a record which is in itself something of a major feat, given the appalling tide of reactionary militarism which has recently swept the continent.

To a considerable extent, the success of FARC has depended on the fact that it commands widespread support among the peasantry in many areas of the Central Cordillera, and has been able to coordinate purely tactical operations with a good deal of broadly-based political activities as well. There is even a sense in which the military side of FARC has been made very deliberately low-key, for the guerillas are anxious to avoid the stigma of *bandoleros* associated with the private armies of Liberals which criss-crossed the area during the *Violencia*. In this, they have a distinct moral advantage, for the inhabitants of Tierradentro — both whites and Indians — are perfectly aware of the fact that it was *la tropa* (the Army), and not the guerillas, who brought war back to the area again in the mid 1960s. '*Tirofijo*' is himself already a legendary figure in Colombian history, and the exploits and lifestyle of his guerillas have been widely popularized in works of a very high literary quality, such as 'Las Muertes de Tirofijo' by Arturo Alape (1972).

At the same time, the recognition of the Army's almost infinite capacity for bloodshed has led to remarkable evolution of political consciousness among the Indians and *campesinos* of the Cauca area. Faced by the vastly superior, U.S.-financed fire-power of the Armed Forces, most activists no longer see immediate armed resistance as a viable alternative — for the Paez to rise up today in open rebellion against the government in Bogotá, for instance, would be an invitation for the state to visit genocide upon the *resguardos* of Tierradentro. The experience of the *Violencia* and the 'anti-insurgency' campaigns of the 60s has left deep scars on the collective consciousness of the people, and a realization that the final Paez uprising — for, inevitably, there will be one sometime — must, in order to succeed, be synchronized with revolutionary action on a broad front throughout Colombia. It is in this sense that the localized ethnic conflict has — in the last ten or twenty years — become absorbed into the greater continental drama, the repudiation of imperialism. And though many individual Paez would welcome the opportunity to meet the Army in a latter-day battle of Tálaga, they also realize that the present situation allows them the opportunity to take certain political initiatives, which — being effectively exploited — may ultimately be of far greater service to their cause than any hurried recourse to *la lucha armada*.

The ground-work for such forms of political action had already been laid down in the 1930s and 40s, with the organization of peasant leagues and self-defence committees in many of the Paez *resguardos*. Support from lawyers, journalists, and students in Popayán and Bogotá ensured that the Paez struggle could be carried through to the courts, where — as Quintín Lame had pointed out — any just application of Ley 89 of 1890 would result in the immediate devolution of most of the land illegally separated from the Indian reservations. After the institutional hiatus caused by the Violencia, the return of 'democracy' — in the form of an alliance of the Liberal and Conservative oligarchies — meant that, in theory at least, the legal battle to defend the Paez *resguardos* was once again a feasible possibility. The publication of a study by the *Comité de Solidaridad con los Presos Políticos* (1974) shows, however, to what extent the institutions of the period of the 'National Front' (1958-1974) were riddled with nepotism and corruption; and the first attempts at pushing land cases through the courts were largely smothered by a combination of bribery, bureaucratic delays and petty legalistic obstructions.

A growing sense of frustration and impatience forced the Indians to consider new tactics which might serve to accelerate the legal process. Foremost among these were the formation of a unified civil rights movement — an organ for publicizing their program and promoting inter-tribal solidarity — and the adoption of a more militant demeanour in the field, including land recuperation — the *de facto* occupation and cultivation of territory usurped from the *resguardos*. The first initiatives obviously came from those particular areas where the combative traditions were strongest: the civil rights movement, *Consejo Regional Indígena del Cauca* (CRIC), was formed on 24th February 1971 in Toribío, in the middle of the Army 'war zone'; and the initial occupations of land occurred in such places as the *finca* La Aurora, near Santander de Quilichao, and elsewhere in the *resguardos* of Tacueyó, San Francisco, and Jambaló, all of which were under considerable pressure from coffee farmers moving in from the main Cali-Popayán highway. In Jambaló, for example, an *escritura* (deed) of 1914 had recognized the Indians' right to a total area of 24,000 hectares. By the early 1970s, only 4,736 hectares were still administered as a *resguardo* — the balance being divided between a large expanse of high mountains which are of no agricultural use, and fully 7,845 hectares which had been illegally occupied by white landlords (see 'Unidad Indígena', no.6, July 1975).

In Tierradentro proper CRIC rapidly found allies in the traditionally radical communities of Huila, Tóez, San José, Mosoco and Vitoncó, and in the warmer climate reservations such as Tálaga, Belalcázar, Santa Rosa,

San Andrés and Yaquivá — all of which have lost substantial amounts of lower altitude land to white coffee farmers in this century. In San Andrés, for example, the original *área de población* from the 1920s — itself of questionable legality — was further extended into a valley known as La Rinconada, as well as being subject to the unfortunate expansion of 'tourist facilities' which have inevitably accompanied the creation of the *Parque Arqueológico de Tierradentro*. Elsewhere in the same reservation — such as the *veredas* of Coscuro and Pisimbalá — the land was declared *baldío* ('empty') by the local authorities and sold to white families from Inzá, who then proceeded to expel the native inhabitants and destroy all evidence of the original Indian occupation.

The more remote *resguardos*, on the other hand — Lame, Suín, Chinas and Calderas — are entirely surrounded by other Indian reservations, and therefore have little experience of the struggle against white colonization. They have been understandably slow to support CRIC, but there is evidence that this is changing rapidly, especially in the light of widespread dissatisfaction in Calderas with a recent, and quite unnecessary subdivision of the communical lands into private *parcelas* — a process which has spawned local Indian tyrants and blacklegs such as Justiniano Pinacué, who openly collaborate with the pressure groups of the white landowners. This change of attitude — led by Justiniano's brother, Victoriano Pinacué — is all the more significant since Calderas has strong traditions of independence from the other Paez resguardos, and in the past has usually voted Conservative as a means of distinguishing itself from its mainly Liberal neighbours. This is not, however, the only case of CRIC being able to overcome long standing ethnic frictions; it has also succeeded in breaching the gap between Paez and Guambianos, a remarkable feat, considering that these two groups have often in the past shown indifference or actual hostility towards one another. A Guambiano, Julio Tunubalá, was at one stage elected president of CRIC, and when — in July 1973 — the holding of the 3rd Congress of CRIC was prevented by the military occupation of the *resguardo* of Huila, it took place instead in Silvia, being attended by just as many Guambianos as Paez, and serving to underline the reconciliation of these two peoples.

Equally, the non-Paez *resguardos* of Puracé and Coconuco — among the most deprived of all Indian groups in Cauca, due to their close proximity with Popayán — have provided further indications that CRIC may no longer be thought of simply as a tribal institution, concerned solely with defending the interests of the Paez. On the contrary, the conflict in these two reservations illustrates perfectly the manner in which CRIC has succeeded in placing the Indian movement within the context of the universal struggle for national liberation. In Coconuco, for instance, the Indians occupied land which — illegally separated from their *resguardo* at the beginning of the century — had come to be 'owned' by the Bishop of Popayán, *monsenor* Arce Vivas — see Bonilla (1973) for the legal background to the case. Though subject to constant harassment and imprisonment by the police, they persevered in their occupation from mid-1972 to mid-1974, when the courts finally made a decision in their favour. Theirs was the first major victory for CRIC, and they had chosen their target well, for the bishop was — like *monsenor* Vallejo, the head of the Prefectura Apostólica in Belalcázar — a particularly loathsome example of the old school of patronizing, over-fed prelates who have consistently fed the reaction with their pious lies and shameless double-dealing.

The neighbouring Indians of Puracé had equally good cause for complaint: in the middle 60s Celanese de Colombia (a local holding company with 81% of its capital held by foreign multi-nationals) had begun to mine sulphur on the slopes of the volcano, immediately above the fields of the *resguardo*, polluting the atmosphere and the rivers with sulphureous waste and leading to a rapid decline in the fertility of the soil used by the Indians to grow potatoes, their main cash crop — see Patino (mss.) and 'Alternativa' no.17, 30th September 1974. The Indians' struggle to secure compensation from the mining company, and to promote a true ecological awareness in the region — as opposed to the tourist-oriented waffle emanating from the local national park of Puracé — held national headlines throughout the latter half of 1974, and showed to what extent the Indian cause could be employed to focus criticism on imperialist concerns like Celanese, and on inept government bureaucracies such as INDERENA, which administers the national park. It was also highly significant that the *resguardo* of Puracé was able to back up its demands by strike action from the largely non-Indian work force in the mine itself, thereby providing what is probably the very first example of the Indian land campaign being furthered by effective solidarity from other sectors of the working class.

Not surprisingly, however, the successes at Puracé and Coconuco — and the continuing efforts to recover usurped territory in other parts of the Cauca area — soon brought about a distinct hardening of attitudes among the landowning and administrative élite in Popayán. Again, it should be stressed that actual armed violence — including a number of cowardly murders, and countless mass arrests — was something initiated unilaterally by the propertied classes in the Cauca area, and in no way can be attributed to provocation on the part of the Indians. The fact is that CRIC always chose to fight its legal battles on grounds which would stand up to analysis within the terms of Ley 89 of 1890; the Indians were, in other words, morally and legally justified in reoccupying land which had been fraudulently separated from their *resguardos*. Faced by such a situation — in which the national institutions could no longer be warped in favour of

Calderas, Tierradentro.

San Andrés de Pisimbalá. The church burned down in early 1975.

naked class interests — the landowners had no other recourse but the time-honoured Colombian system of intimidation by the gun. It would be worth considering the latest developments in some detail; and while this most recent phase of the Indian struggle in the Cauca area has, it is true, occasionally provided sensational copy for a number of national and even international newspapers, by far the best accounts have been written by direct participants and close sympathizers, appearing especially in 'Unidad Indígena', an excellent monthly publication edited by CRIC and published in Bogotá, and in the weekly (formerly bi-monthly) magazine 'Alternativa', especially numbers 1, 3, 4, 6, 17, 19 (in 1974) 31, 40, 47, 48, 50, 53, 59 (in 1975) and 67, 70, 73, 96, 102 (in 1976).

Obviously it is difficult to do full justice to the theme in so short a space, but the more outstanding events of recent years seem almost to speak for themselves, and together add up to truly nauseating record of political violence on the part of the white landowners in Cauca, a record which cannot fail to suggest ominous parallels with the lead-up to the last major civil war in Colombia, in the late 1940s. The beginning of the new campaign of intimidation was dramatic, and intentionally so: on 2nd March, 1974, hired assassins killed Gustavo Mejía, a very well-known and widely respected white peasant organizer who had been one of the leading figures in the original foundation of CRIC. Insistent rumours maintained that the guilty party in this case was the mayor of Corinto, but — predictably — there was little hope of overcoming the indifference of the police in investigating the murder. A mere three days later Venancio Taquinaz, a Paez Indian and outspoken supporter of CRIC, suffered the same fate. By July of the same year the repression had escalated to gruesome multiple killings — such as that in Caloto, where Lisandro Tálaga, José Antonio Contono and Marco Tulio Tálaga were all killed in a single hit. At the same time, the Mosqueras — the same family who had once held the *encomienda* of Vitoncó — decided to take up the challenge which the Indian movement presented to their age-old position of privilege in the Cauca area. Aurelio Mosquera, a prominent *terrateniente* (landowner) in Silvia and a close collaborator with the locally active American anthropologists, proceeded to expel a number of Guambiano Indians from the *hacienda* El Chimán, a property which until recently had formed part of the *resguardo* of Guambía. A conflict ensued in which at least thirty Guambianos were arrested by the police, one of them a ninety-year old widow, and another a true destitute who died of hunger shortly after leaving gaol. Meanwhile Victor Mosquera Chaux, a senator and the leader of the Liberal party machine in the Cauca area — and, incidentally, one of the main movers behind the Army's assault on Rio Chiquito in 1965 — began to worry about the gradual erosion of the normally docile Indian vote by CRIC, which was actively supporting a dissident left-wing faction of the Liberals headed by Omar Henry Velasco. Despite innumerable attempts to revive the old system of patronage in Tierradentro, the returns in the mid-1974 elections showed that Mosquera had conclusively lost the support of the majority of the Indian population, and accordingly, he began to pepper his speeches with alarmist references to the menace of 'communism' and 'subversion', using the same style and language which had once justified the repressive operation in Rio Chiquito.

He was soon joined by his Conservative counterpart, senator Mario S. Vivas, in denouncing the threat which CRIC represented to property and the rule of law and order. Quickly overcoming the spurious 'liberalism' of President López's new régime, the landowners of Cauca succeeded in drastically escalating the level of social conflict in the area, subjecting such Indian areas as Caldono to a particularly heavy-handed military occupation and arresting, beating and intimidating the leaders of the local struggle to defend and recover *resguardo* lands. On 8th October 1974, Emiliano Ulcué, a member of an Indian *cabildo* in this region, was shot dead in cold blood; his assassination was followed on 18th October by that of two other Indian activists in Caldono, Joaquín Marino Yonda and Luis Enrique Ramos. Soon the 'security risk' posed by the activities of CRIC began to attract the attention not only of the local police and Army units, but also of the specialist intelligence outfits — our old friends the coke-dealing gangsters in DAS and F-2. An Indian from Tacueyó, Hector Cuchillo Tonguino, was taken to the F-2 offices in Cali and tortured for information on the activities of CRIC; a fate shared also by Guillermo Músicue, a local councillor and secretary of the *cabildo* of San Francisco. The *gobernador* of the same *cabildo*, Avelino Ul, was arrested by the Army and held for nine months in the gaol of Toribío, and two other Indians from Tacueyó, Lino and Antonio Mesa, were tortured by police on the *hacienda* of a local landlord, Juan Martínez.

Subsequent years have seen a gradual but inexorable intensifying of the land struggle in the Cauca area. The militarization of northern Cauca has included a permanent occupation of the offices of the *cabildos* of Toribío and San Francisco, where the soldiers are known to harass all comers and take great pleasure in making jokes about the Indians' language and pronunciation. Armed intimidation has continued apace, with the murder of Emiliano Mensa in Huila (February, 1975) and the wounding of José María Ulcué in Toribío on 23rd April, 1975. Though the latter was able to identify his assailants by name — they were farm managers for big landowners in the district — no action was taken by the authorities. In one particularly significant case, a leading Indian spokesman — Marco Aníbal Melenje, *gobernador* of the *cabildo* of Coconuco — was killed on 19th April 1975 by Luís Calambás, an Indian traitor who subsequently committed suicide. The gun used in the shooting — supposedly bearing the initials of a member of the landowning Valencia family — 'disappeared' shortly afterwards in a jeep of the Defensa Civil, a volunteer paramilitary organization which provides official, Army-sponsored 'cover' for local reactionary groups. Were this not enough, the murder was used as a cynical pretext to round up another 40 Indians, leading exponents of the land occupation program in Coconuco, and many of these languished for the rest of the year behind bars while the police carried out its 'investigations' into the crime.

Elsewhere the picture was monotonously similar — fifteen Indians imprisoned in Jambaló, ten in Santander de Quilichao — and, marking an extension of the struggle into hitherto 'quiet' areas, seventeen Indians from Santa Rosa and San Andrés were gaoled in Inzá for 'invading' *resguardo* land occupied by white coffee farmers, being also subsequently accused of collaborating with the guerillas of FARC. On attempting to investigate the case, an anthropologist from the *Facultad de Humanidades* in Popayán, Elias Sevilla Casas, was himself arrested in Inzá on 16th September by troops of the 3rd Brigade, under accusation of being a 'troublemaker'. Land recuperation continued to be practised in Santa Rosa, however, and in October 1975 a further 31 Indians were arrested and imprisoned in Inzá. The escalation of violence in this part of the Cauca area, and the active involvement of the police and Army in such violence, are both relatively novel developments — for San Andrés and Santa Rosa suffered little from the events of the Violencia, and until 1974 had not witnessed any major incursions by the uniformed authorities. On 27th January, 1976, the murder of Pablo Quinto in Santa Rosa provided the first clear indication that the local white landowners — themselves mainly composed of Liberal refugees from the Violencia — were beginning to go the way of similar groups elsewhere in the Cauca area. The tragic consequences of such action will undoubtably colour the future of all the *resguardos* on the previously peaceful southern borders of Tierradentro.

This prospect is far from being a cheering one for the Paez as a people. On the other side of the Central Cordillera, assassination has already become a very commonplace tactic, and should it continue to spread among the white landowners, the Paez may soon find themselves being subject to a greater threat than at any time since the Spanish first entered the area in the 1540s. In the single *resguardo* of San Francisco, for example, one year has seen the killing of at least six CRIC activists or sympathizers: Avelino Ramos and Manuel Dagua Taquinás in November, 1975; Ernesto Guejía and Isidoro Pilcué in August, 1976; and Alvaro Morales Ramírez and Ernesto Melo Avila in December, 1976. When the *gobernador* of the *cabildo* of neighbouring Tacueyó identified the killers in the second of these cases, he was arrested and taken away to F-2 headquarters in Cali in order to be tortured into changing his statement. In Coconuco, the reoccupation of *resguardo* lands produced on 29th September 1976, the first really important mass riot of recent years in any rural part of Cauca — with barricades being used to block the departure of police trucks full of arrested Indians, widespread hand-to-hand fighting, and a counter-attack by the police force with teargas and repeated salvos of gunfire just over the Indians' heads.

The same policy of deliberate intimidation continued elsewhere in the Cauca area with a long sequence of senseless murders: those of Isidoro Pilcué in Tacuyeyó (6th March 1976), of Benjamín Guetío in Siberia (November 1976), of Bernardino Ipia, Luciano Ramos and Antonio Yule in Jambaló (10th December 1976), of Pacho Fernández near Santander (2nd March 1977), and of Justiniano Lame in San Ignacio (2nd February 1977). The latter case occurred while Justiniano Lame was actually in the custody of the police; he had been shot in the leg when arrested, refused a torniquet, and told to walk several miles to the main road to Popayán. On arrival in this city, he was denied any medical attention, and locked up in a police cell, where he died a slow and sordid death from the loss of blood. On 7th February, CRIC called a mass meeting in Popayán to demand the return of his corpse — the city was 'militarized', the buses of Indian demonstrators turned away at roadblocks on the outskirts, the offices of CRIC occupied by troops and Marcos Avirama, the president of CRIC, arrested and taken away for interrogation at Army headquarters. Similar 'preventive measures' were taken during the general strike which paralyzed Colombia on 14th September 1977; with the town of Belalcázar placed under curfew and overrun by ten truckloads of soldiers, and ostensive military manoeuvres and multiple arrests in Caldono, Puracé, Inzá, Toribío and Tóez.

Events of this kind — with all their overtones of the *Violencia* — would perhaps be understandable, though hardly justifiable, if they appeared to result solely from the sort of rough justice that is part and parcel of the structure of corrupt local politics in the department of Cauca. They are, after all, no more than a reflection of the attitudes expressed by so many landowners — that it is necessary to *darles fuete* ('to whip them') or *echarles plomo* ('give them some hot lead') or, the favourite phrase of all, *bajar unos indios p'a que aprenden a respetar* ('kill a few Indians so that they learn some respect'). All the more damning, then, are the many indications that the policy of harassment of CRIC is not solely the result of excesses committed by purely local interests, but on the contrary, forms part of a nation-wide strategy of repression applied by successive governments and the military high command in Bogotá. Though in principle the legitimacy of the Indians' land claims in the northern *resguardos* of Pitayó, Jambaló, Tacueyó and Toribío had already been recognized in a document signed both by the Governor of Cauca, and by representatives of the Ministries of

Gobierno (Home Affairs) and Agriculture, no effective action to support these claims was ever taken by the government agencies concerned — see Corry (1976, p.26). Likewise, the promises made by the López administration in late 1974 — concerning the control of sulphur mining in Puracé, and the compensation to be paid by Celanese de Colombia to the neighbouring *resguardo* — had been completely put to one side by mid-1976. Not only had Celanese failed to come up with a single penny of the 5 million *pesos* (US $200,000) compensation — claiming that it would be used to buy arms and support 'insurgency' — but, even more alarming, the previous restrictions on open cast mining had actually been lifted, heralding the imminence by far more widespread ecological devastation than ever before.

Meanwhile, in an act of consummate cynicism, the government ecologists at INDERENA continued to judge that the real threat to the environmental balance of the area was being posed by a handful of destitute Indians collecting firewood in the National Park. Clearly, the ineffectual INDERENA considered it inopportune to take on the powerful multinationals backing Celanese: including, for the record, The Celluloid Corp., Pabin Corp., Ancell Co. Ins., Chancell Corp., Petrocel Corp., F.M.C. Corp., American Viscose, and the Celanese Overseas Corporation. There can be little doubt, therefore, as to where the sympathies of the Colombian government and its minions lie with respect to the land struggle of the Indians of Cauca. As if to underscore the overall repressive orientation of the police and military apparatus, Minister Cornelio Reyes (of the *Ministerio de Gobierno*) visited the Indian 'training' centre in Tóez on 7th September 1975 — a month after CRIC had held its fourth congress in the same place — and exhorted the Paez to abandon the 'subversive' CRIC, and support instead the newly formed pressure group of the large landowners, CRAC (*Consejo Regional Agropecuário del Cauca*), whose all-too-obvious whiplash sound caused the name to be changed later to the more conciliatory SAC (*Sociedad Agropecuário del Cauca*).

SAC? CRAC? ('I'll scratch your sack, if you . . . ') The Indians had no difficulty in identifying the fact that, in this case at least, the A stood quite simply for Authoritarian. Perhaps more troubling, however, was the growing realization that this kind of latent paternalism could not be considered a unique prerogative of the government and the uniformed authorities, but also extended to two other groups who — in theory, at least — had the Indians' own best interests at heart. The first of these was the group of American anthropologists working with the Guambianos — or, more specifically, Dr. Ronald Allan Schwarz and his students. Schwarz first came to Silvia as a Peace Corps volunteer fifteen years ago, and many local people have stated privately to me their suspicion that he is with the CIA. Such accusations are very common in South America — not surprisingly, for sure, since the CIA really does have a lot to answer for — but, lacking any concrete proof, I can only say that Schwarz's role in local affairs is rendered rather suspect by the fact that he long used Guambía as a 'field-laboratory' in which to train American graduate students, usually in groups of a dozen or so who infested the area for six months at a time (a 'semester' for which they got 'credits' back at their Stateside colleges).

When the Colombian Institute of Anthropology succeeded in putting an end to this practice, Schwarz started up a wooden toy factory in Silvia, using cheap local labour and selling the finished products exclusively on the North American market, a type of enterprise which is surely more characteristic of the small-time imperialist than the serious anthropologist. Furthermore, any outsider must stand or fall with the company he keeps; and the old millhouse which is used for the toy factory, as well as the house in which Schwarz was living in early 1975, both belong to Aurelio Mosquera, the notorious *terrateniente* and Indian persecuter. And, despite his frequent references to the American Anthropological Association's code of ethics, Schwarz sees no contradiction in using his considerable influence with the Guambianos to denigrate the CRIC organizers and deny the importance of the movement they have helped initiate. Indeed, rather than supporting the idea of pan-tribal Indian solidarity, he constantly plays on the traditional hostilitics bctwccn the Paez and the Guambianos, leading one to suspect that his motives include not only a desire to maintain Indian divisiveness, but also — repeating the sad experience of the Meo in South-East Asia — to actually use some of the Guambianos as a native intelligence force to spy on the activities of CRIC.

The other manifestation of this sort of disregard for the Indians' attempts at autonomous self-development comes at the opposite end of the political spectrum; for with CRIC growing from strength to strength, it was not long before the Indian movement began to attract the somewhat unwelcome attentions of a number of opportunist groups on the Colombian left, those whose rigid dogmatism and intellectualism have so consistently undermined the project of national liberation in this country, and in the continent as a whole. The middle-class posturing of such organizations — their 'vanguardism' and desire to exert a vertical hegemony over the entire revolutionary process — have been excellently analyzed by Debray (1974), and need not detain us in any great detail here. What is more important is to understand the manner in which the villains of this particular piece, the leadership of the Colombian peasants' union, the *Asociación Nacional de Usarios Campesinos* (ANUC), has managed to degenerate so rapidly from the position of national prominence in the struggle for land — which it held during the period 1971-1974 — adopting a position characterized by purely factional politics and a frankly counter-productive obsession with Power and Control, elements which have less to do with Revolution than with the

Colombian traditions of 'leadership' by the intellectuals in Bogotá.

Most elements of the confrontation between CRIC and ANUC were already apparent in 1974 — the dispute over the relevance of the coca habit, for example, discussed in Chapter VII — but they only surfaced in an explicit form in mid-1975, at the 4th Congress of CRIC held in Tóez at the beginning of August. Shortly before this congress, on 17th July, the executive committee of ANUC had attempted to disband the Indian secretariat (*Secretaría Indígena*) which worked within ANUC, replacing its pro-CRIC members with a number of figures such as Julio Tunubalá, himself an ex-president of CRIC who had been dismissed as the result of charges of embezzlement of funds. Frustrated in this attempt, the ANUC delegates arrived at Tóez literally spoiling for a fight, condemning in their speeches any separate *indigenismo*, any deviation from the common 'political orientation', and suggesting instead 'an Indian organization on a national scale which, within ANUC, may serve to orient the action of this specific sector . . . ' The issue was clearly one of ultimate control over the Indian movement and, understandably, the reaction of CRIC to such arrogance was suitably intense. 'Alternativa' no.48 (25th August 1975) provided an interesting first analysis of the confrontation; and the subsequent development of the debate can be followed in some detail in 'Unidad Indígena' nos.6, 8, 9, 16, 20, 25, 26 (July, October, November 1975; September 1976; March, October, November 1977) — which puts the CRIC point of view — and in 'Carta Campesina', the ANUC mouthpiece, especially nos.31, 35, 36 October 1975, November 1976, February 1977).

CRIC had always firmly asserted the Indians' right to an autonomous national union, one which would reflect the cultural traditions which distinguish the Indian from the white *campesino* — such as their languages, the *resguardo* organization, local government by *cabildo* and, above all, the principle of collective ownership of the land. To drive the point home to ANUC, the Indians at Tóez also made it clear that a militant *indigenismo* was just as important to them as the land struggle itself. In the general conclusions of the 4th Congress of CRIC (published in 'Unidad Indígena' no.7, August 1975) they made the following broad statements of policy with regard to culture and education:

1. To unite with the shamans in defending Indian traditions and in learning the botany of medicinal plants.

2. To recover the traditional myths and oral traditions which were beginning to disappear among the Paez.

3. To preserve Indian languages and ensure that they be used in missionary schools together with, or even instead of, Spanish. There was also a demand for the schools to teach local Indian history, and not the history of the European conquerors.

4. To recover all the old songs and musical forms and encourage the

A *minga* at Toez, in the upper valley of the river Paez.

proliferation of flute-and-drum bands in every Indian *resguardo*.

5. 'To conserve coca as part of Indian culture; for the purposes of shamanism and agricultural work, and as a medicine. It is necessary to stop trading coca with whites, because coca is a thing worthy of respect, and traders use it in a way which is not appropriate . . . ' (The defence of coca was also the subject of an excellent article written by Indians of the Amazonian lowlands, entitled *'Amazonas: el mensaje de la coca'* in 'Unidad Indígena' no.4, April 1975.)

All of this was too much for the leadership of ANUC to stomach. In October, 1975, they began to use words like 'irresponsible' and talked of 'Indianist opportunists infiltrated in the Indian movement' who 'aimed to anarchize (*sic*) the *Secretaría Indígena* of ANUC . . . ' ('Carta Campesina' no.31) CRIC counter-attacked in the November 1975 edition of 'Unidad Indígena', speaking of the 'progressive deterioration' of ANUC, of their bureaucratic ambitions and revolutionary adventurism, and especially of their desire to assume undisputed leadership and make the peasant movement *madurar biche* — that is, to turn ripe while still green. This earthy, direct metaphor was countered by the retreat of the Bogotá leadership of ANUC into ever more intellectualized insults — with copious references to themselves as the only true 'vanguard', and a proliferation of terms to describe the 'errors' of CRIC, such as 'revisionism', 'Trotskyism', 'populism', 'anarchosyndicalism', and above all, 'Indianism' or *indigenismo*. One assumes that they left out 'Maoism' only because this was the banner they subscribed to themselves, though it is hard to understand how they expected to perpetuate the late Chairman's breadth of vision with such unnecessary and small-minded bickering.

The divisive tactics of ANUC were further emphasized by their unilateral assertion that: ' . . . in general it can be said that the Indians proceed independently from the rest of the peasantry . . . ' (Carta Campesina no.36) Consistent with this disregard for any genuine grass-roots political initiatives, the organizers of the 4th Congress of ANUC at Tomala (February 1977) spared no efforts to fan the flames of contention with CRIC, providing their delegates with only the most inferior food and accommodation, and greeting their speeches with cat-calls of '*abajo los indios*' ('down with the Indians'). The leadership of ANUC gave further evidence of its patronizing attitudes in the carefully rigged launching of yet another 'vanguard' party, the *Organización Revolucionaria del Pueblo* (ORP), which effectively converted ANUC from a broadly-based union — a group responsible for reflecting the often divergent views of its many supporters — into a hierarchical organization whose only function was that of imposing acceptance of a 'correct' ideological line dictated from on high. Aware that it would ever be able to force its decisions on the leadership of CRIC, the next tactic of ORP/ANUC was to attempt to divide the Indian movement and win over the rank-and-file. Since it had never done any really serious canvassing in the Cauca area before, ORP/ANUC decided that the only way to achieve this objective would be to call mass meetings in Indian areas, bringing in large groups of outside supporters who could be used to focus criticism on the present orientation of CRIC. The first such attempt had occurred in Silvia in the middle of August 1976, and — though it had not been a great success — it was decided to repeat the experience in Corinto on 12th October, 1977. This time the repudiation of ORP/ANUC by the Indians was made perfectly explicit by the intervention of a speaker on behalf of CRIC, who succeeded in pointing out the crude manipulation being attempted by the rival group, and called on the assembled company to join him in a rival meeting organized by CRIC in the same town. All but a very small number of Indians did so, and ORP/ANUC was left talking to itself.

Sadly, this attitude towards CRIC is symptomatic of a failure widespread in Latin American leftist circles — the failure to consider social and cultural diversity as actually a *positive* factor in the class struggle, something conducive to new and imaginative forms of political and economic organization. CRIC has stated itself to be '...in open conflict with the dogmatism, sectarianism and vanguardism which have caused so many problems to the Colombian revolutionary process...' (Unidad Indígena, no.26, November 1977), proposing instead a return to the only kind of class unity which will resist the trials imposed by a savage repression — a unity based on the principle of mutual respect. This is something that the Indians of Cauca — for all their failure to grasp the niceties of the sacred texts — all share in abundance, a real understanding of the human scale of all non-coercive political endeavour, a fact which is perfectly evident in the spontaneity, humour and genuine warmth which they bring to direct personal encounters. For politics to them is not a task of simple quantitative organization, and much less of academic speculation. It is, rather, an encounter of the whole man with the total universe that surrounds him; and in this encounter the activities of the CRIC activist and his brother, the shaman, are but two aspects of a single, unifying vision, one which we — shrunken children of the industrial wasteland — would do well to consider in its own terms.

The cultural aspects of the CRIC platform have already been enumerated above, but to the list approved at the Tóez congress should also be added another very welcome clause on the control of archaeological sites within Indian territory — such as that at San Andrés de Pisimbalá — '...so that, being managed by the heirs of the culture of our ancestors, it should cease to function as a business enterprise in the interests of the tourists, and become a place where the people may understand and appreciate the culture of the indigenous inhabitants of Colombia.'

('Unidad Indígena' no.12, April 1976). Even more significantly, CRIC's very flexibility has allowed the organization to constantly invent new tactics to consolidate the position obtained in the initial spectacular land recuperation programs. In many newly recovered areas, there exists an increasing emphasis on the local institutions of collective labour — the *minga*, or large communal work-party, and the *mano prestada*, a system of reciprocal labour-sharing among a small number of neighbours — and as a result such customs are also beginning to find a renewed popularity in many of the *resguardos* where they had become relatively rare in the years since the *Violencia*. Furthermore, the proliferation of communal vegetable patches, the *huertas communales*, also indicates that the very land itself is once again being actively and effectively used as common property. This represents an important return to the ideals of the communitarian *resguardo*; in which, traditionally, each individual had the right to a life-time's usufruct of a determined piece of land, but in which he should also contribute to certain collective agricultural undertakings, the so-called *rozas de santo* ('saint's fields') which were appropriated by the Church during the colonial period.

Consonant with its support for the shamans, CRIC has also organized a number of short courses which aim at improving local health standards. Rather than imposing the sort of hygiene consciousness popular among the Western medical profession, these courses have aimed at four principal objectives: 1. self-medication and first-aid; 2. identification of all major diseases and complaints; 3. the dissemination of information regarding their effective cure and control; 4. the increase of cultivation of medicinal herbs; 5. the organization of small dispensaries and a collective for buying pharmaceutical products direct from the wholesalers. This latter feature is itself part of a much broader drive to set up cooperatives throughout the Indian reservations of the Cauca area, particularly for the sake of deriving the greatest possible benefit from market sales to white intermediaries (of coffee, potatoes, onions, grain), and of circumventing the retail distribution system for industrialized goods, until recently in the hands of the white shopowners in the towns. The *tiendas comunales* (communal shops) have become characteristic of many *resguardos*, and — despite a campaign from the local whites to destroy the buildings which house these shops — many of them still appear to be flourishing, and have managed to survive the occasional profiteering and dishonesty of a few of the original administrators. All this activity in developing an autonomous infrastructure has not, however, detracted from the land struggle itself, and CRIC has expanded its operations into many areas where the population is still predominantly Indian, but where the *resguardo* institution had been extinguished earlier in this century. It has reconstituted *cabildos* to press for the devolution of Indian lands in no fewer than eight localities in northern Cauca, two in the Western Cordillera, and one in Tierradentro — where the *cabildo* of Guanacas, near Inzá, took office again for the first time in almost forty years, on 15th February 1976.

At the same time, aware that this policy could lead to increasing confrontation with the poor white peasantry surrounding the Indian reservations, CRIC held a rally on 28th August 1977 in San Andrés de Pisimbalá, to stress the fact that its campaign was not racist in intent, but was aimed solely at the large landowners. One of these was the notorious Cenén Narváez, a white from Inzá who had fraudulently acquired a large expanse of land which belongs to the *resguardo* of Santa Rosa. The Indians who remained living on his estate had long been considered *terrajeros* — 'sharecroppers', but on land which is legally their own — and those who refuse to pay a share of their harvest to Narváez had suffered all kinds of violent intimidation, including the breaking down of their fences, the theft of their livestock, and the occasional beating of their womenfolk. Conscious of the fact that many of the small and medium-sized non-Indian peasants were themselves *terrajeros*, and often had to face very similar abuses CRIC pointed out the need for the white and Indian peasantry to overcome their ethnic and cultural differences, so that together they could fight more effectively against the excesses committed by the landowning élite. Clearly, such initiatives can only be applicable to a reasonably restricted area on the edge of Indian reservations. But even so, with the effective demise of ANUC, it may well be that CRIC will provide a spur for many non-Indian peasant groups to learn from its experience and reapply its programs in the rather different conditions of other parts of the Cauca area and of the country as a whole.

Such a prospect is by no means beyond the realms of possibility, for although CRIC is unlikely to assume any sort of 'leadership' — of the kind favoured by the cadres in ORP/ANUC — its example has already caused it to be recognized as the foremost exponent of a certain style of direct political action, a style which could usefully be used to accelerate the land reforms undertaken by INCORA — the Government's land reform agency — elsewhere in Colombia. Already CRIC has lent active support to the struggles of other Indian groups, particularly in the Sierra Nevada de Santa Marta and in the lowlands of Amazonia, and its reputation has grown to the point where it has received widespread international recognition. In England, for example, the early stages of its activities have already formed the basis of one study by the Projects Director at Survival International, Stephen Corry (1976), who also included a useful translation of the very first CRIC publication 'Our Struggles of Yesterday and Today' — (originally published in February 1973, as 'Nuestras Luchas de Ayer y de Hoy'.)

What CRIC needs, however
READER THIS IS DIRECTED AT YOU
is SUPPORT — moral, financial, or otherwise.

Please send any communications or contributions directly to:
Consejo Regional Indígena del Cauca,
Carrera 10-A No. 1N-17,
Popayán,
Colombia.

Or subscribe to Unidad Indígena,
Apartado Aéreo 32395,
Bogotá.

SOLIDARIDAD CON LAS LUCHAS DE LOS COMPANEROS INDIGENAS DEL CAUCA.

LIBERTAD PARA LOS INDIGENAS PRESOS.

LA TIERRA P'AL QUE LA TRABAJA.

Notes

Chapter 1. MAMA COCA

1 Mortimer (1901); and see also the new (1974) edition which contains the frontispieces from both the American (1901) and French (1904) editions.
2 *idem.*, p.66.
3 *idem.*, p.230.
4 See the discussion of Frazer in Uscátegui (1954, p.224).
5 Brundage (1963, pp.21 and 47).
6 *idem.*, pp.20 and 262.
7 *idem.*, p.199.
8 Chaves (1947).
9 Reichel-Dolmatoff (1951, pp.56 et seq.).
10 Reichel-Dolmatoff (1968).
11 Howard Reid, personal communication. (March, 1977).
12 In Patino (1967, p.222).
13 In Uscátegui (1954, p.224).
14 Christine Hugh-Jones, personal communication. (June, 1977).
15 Rostworowski (1973, pp.195 et seq.).
16 Mortimer (1901, p.232).
17 Donne (1972, p.335).

Chapter II. COCA AND THE WEST

1 Vespucio (1951, p.240). See also the excellent discussion of this letter in Vila (1972). The place described is the Guajira peninsula.
2 See Patino (1967, pp.201-223) for an introduction to the early chronicle sources on the use of coca.
3 Cieza de León (1962, p.249).
4 This usage is discussed extensively in Guerra (1971).
5 Cited in Hemming (1972, p.367, and footnote).
6 Begué (1971).
7 In Patino (1967, p.213).

8 Matienzo (1967, p.163).
9 See Begué (1971).
10 See Matienzo (1967, p.163).
11 In Patino (1967, p.213).
12 Aguado (1957, III, p.76). The full account of Francisco Martín's adventures is contained in Pedro de Aguado's 'Recopilación Historial' (1957, III, pp.59-65, 75-82). It is doubtful if the finished manuscript, submitted to the Council of the Indies in Spain in 1579, was all written by Aguado himself, who only arrived in South America in 1562. The more detailed descriptions — such as that concerning Martín — are probably derived from manuscripts collected by Antonio Medrano, who had made a number of transcriptions of oral accounts by eye-witnesses of the Spanish Conquest. In any case, Aguado's colourful description of Martín's life contrasts notably with the bland whitewashing which his story received in other official histories of the time, such as Castellanos (1944, pp.206, 210).
13 López de Gómara (1954, p.138).
14 Cobo (1964, I, p.216).
15 On Jussieu and Lamarck, see Mortimer (1901, p.166) and Freud (1884) in Byck (1974, p.55).
16 The diarist of the Expedición Botánica, Eloy Valenzuela, mentions coca three times (1952, pp.274, 350, 364). Gentner (1972, p.534) has identified Mutis' sample of coca as **E. novogranatense**.
17 See Bonnycastle (1818, p.275); Hamilton (1827); and the later account of Bollaert (1860).
18 See a letter, signed 'Academicus', in the Gentleman's Magazine (1814, II, p.217).
19 Miller (1828, II, p.198).
20 Markham (1862, p.152). Another enthusiastic report of this period, by a doctor with many years' experience of coca in Peru, was that of Mantegazza (1859).
21 The report of Fidalgo's expedition to Santa Marta (1793-1808) is referred to in Patino (1967, p.204).
22 The reader is referred to more exhaustive treatments of the early medical history of cocaine in Mortimer (1901), Byck (1974) and Ashley (1975).
23 Freud (1887) in Byck (1974, p.173).
24 Freud (1884) in Byck (1974).
25 *idem.*, p.53.
26 Rusby (1888) in Mortimer (1901, p.17).
27 Mortimer (1901, p.304).
28 *idem.*, p.171.
29 Poeppig (1836) in Gutiérrez Noriega and Zapata Ortiz (1947, p.27).
30 Lewin (1924) in Byck (1974, p.243).
31 *idem.*, pp.244-5.
32 Gutiérrez Noriega (1947) in Andrews and Solomon (1975, p.262).
33 Gutiérrez Noriega and Zapata Ortiz (1947, p.77).
34 See Ricketts (1952) and Bejerano (1953).
35 Gutiérrez Noriega and Zapata Ortiz (1947, Introduction).
36 See Monge (1953).

37 The papers describing the findings of the U.N. Commission, together with the later debate which followed with Dr. Monge's Peruvian Commission, are in 'Perú Indígena' vol. III, for December 1952, and are hereafter referred to as U.N. Commission (1952) and Monge (1952). América Indígena (vol. XII) contained two independent articles attacking Monge, one written by Gutiérrez Noriega (1952) and the other by Ricketts (1952). Volume XIII of América Indígena carried a report from Colombia by the man who, as Minister of Hygiene, had rendered the cultivation of coca illegal in Colombia — Bejerano (1953) — and a renewed defence from Dr. Monge (1953).

38 Gutiérrez Noriega (1952, p.118).

39 For an example of this, see Friede (1944, pp.16-19), and more recently, Galeano (1973, pp.71-72) who should know better than to condemn one of the most revolutionary sections of Latin American society — the Bolivian mining proletariat — for their coca habit, which he calls '...the sterile retaliation of the condemned'.

40 See González (mss., p.195).

41 See Begué (1971).

42 Buck *et al.* (1968).

43 *idem.*, p.174.

44 *idem.*, p.169.

45 *idem.*, p.173.

46 *idem.*, p.175.

47 See Grinspoon (1971), Rubin and Comitas (1975) and Rubin (ed.) (1975).

48 See Brecher *et al.* (1972).

49 See Martin (1970), Hanna (1974), Burchard (1975) and Bolton (1976).

50 Burchard (1975, p.475).

51 Bolton (1976, p.632).

52 Gutiérrez Noriega and Zapata Ortiz (1947, p.106).

53 Burchard (1975, p.464).

54 *idem.*, p.477.

55 Bolton (1976, p.630). A similarly anti-euphoria explanation of coca chewing, and a similar desperate obsession with the 'why' of the coca habit, was expressed in neo-Freudian terms by Stein (1961, p.169):
'...the oral ecstasies manifest in the eager devouring, vigorous chewing, and loud smacking of lips and tongue in connection with coca, leads me to the conclusion that the oral pleasure could be far more important to Hualcaínos than any narcotic (*sic*) values of the coca itself.'

56 Kaplan (1975, p.552).

57 See, for example, the opinion of a U.S. Senate committee on Rubin and Comitas' seminal study of *ganja* in Jamaica, describing it as '...an utterly worthless study, conducted under a National Institute of Mental Health grant, by a few Jamaican scientists of limited credentials.' quoted in the New York magazine 'High Times', September 1976 (p.55).

58 See Orcutt and Biggs (1975) for a comparison of marijuana and alcohol consumption on the campus of the University of Minnesota.

Chapter III. BOTANY, ARCHAEOLOGY, COLONIAL HISTORY, THE DEVELOPMENT OF THE COCA TRADE

1 Osborne (1968, p.89).
2 Plowman (1976a, 1976b) has recently clarified the confused botany of the genus **Erythroxylum**. Compare his studies with the mixed-up and often contradictory information to be found in Mortimer (1901), Gentner (1972) and Machado (1972).
3 Mortimer (1901, p.228).
4 Guerra and Olivera (1954, pp.105-109).
5 See the notes appended to samples of **E. orinocense** and **E. acutum** in the National Herbarium, Bogotá. Plowman (1976b) for the use of **E. hondense** in teas.
6 Holmstedt *et al.* (1976). In Plowman (1976b).
7 See Plowman (1976b) for a more detailed discussion of the negligible effects of domestication on **E. coca**. Native informants in the Cauca area have added — admittedly, with reference to the local **E. novogranatense** — that cultivation of coca under heavy shade tends to produce very unpalatable leaves. In that case, the removal of coca to an open environment may also have contributed to the emergence of a more chewable leaf.
8 See Plowman (1976b). The distinction between the 'bitter' Huánuco leaves (**E. coca**) and the 'sweet' Trujillo leaves (**E. novogranatense** var. **truxillense**) was repeatedly stressed by Mortimer (1901) and his informant Henry Rusby. See also Rostworowski (1973).
9 See Bushnell (1956, p.38) and Lanning (1967, p.77).
10 Fig.66 'Head of man chewing coca', in Lathrap (1975, p.48).
11 See Plowman (1976b).
12 Lanning (1967, p.89).
13 Lathrap (1975, p.48) supports the idea of coca coming to Valdivia from the eastern slopes of the Andes.
14 Cieza de León (1962, p.249).
15 For Tumaco, and Calima I, see Reichel-Dolmatoff (1966). For greater detail on Tierradentro, see the bibliography at the beginning of Appendix C.
16 Reichel-Dolmatoff (1972, p.139).
17 Warwick Bray (personal communication, July, 1976). See also Willey (1971, p.299, fig.5-46).
18 See Reichel-Dolmatoff (1972). Uscátegui summarizes various arguments on whether or not the cheek protuberances are indicative of coca chewing.
19 See Piedrahita (1881, p.14) and Patino (1967,m p.206).
20 Patino (1967, p.201) for the Sinú. Reichel-Dolmatoff (1953) describes Tairona coca-toasting pans almost identical to those used today in the Sierra Nevada.
21 Patino (1967, p.293) on tobacco. Rivet (1943) produced a synthesis of the Karib diffusion theories which were then popular in Colombia.
22 Uscátegui (1961).
23 Cieza de León (1962, p.249).
24 Uscátegui (1961, p.218).
25 Piedrahita (1881, p.14).

26 Uscátegui (1961, p.218).
27 See, for example, Brundage (1963, p.224), Hemming (1972, p.367), Ashley (1975, p.7), Andrews and Solomon (1975, p.7).
28 The discussion of these *Visitas* and the model of intra-ethnic trade are taken from Murra (1967) and especially (1972). The broad outlines of Andean prehistory are indebted to Lanning (1967).
29 See Rostworowski (1973).
30 See Murra (1972, p.458). For a very different interpretation of the same source, see Golte (1970).
31 On coca in the Chillón valley, see Rostworowski (1973).
32 See Begué (1971).
33 See Murra (1972, p.460).
34 See Cieza de León (1962, p.250).
35 See Matienzo (1967, p.163).
36 See Acosta (1940, p.286).
37 See Patino (1967, p.221).
38 Galeano (1973, p.71).
39 Espinoza (1973, p.24).
40 Murra (1972, p.440).
41 See Rostworowski (1973, p.214) on the decline of coca production in the coastal valleys of Peru.
42 A very detailed description of the labour arrangements in the coca plantations of the Spanish colony is contained in Matienzo (1967) who visited the area in the mid-sixteenth century. Bird (1967, p.367) has uncovered evidence of a small amount of migratory labour being practised in the Huánuco area before the Spanish Conquest.
43 See Hemming (1972, p.368) for a discussion of the contemporary sources.
44 Murra (1972, p.460).
45 Hanna (1974, p.291). Buechler and Buechler (1971, p.4, 105) also mention the importance of small-scale coca trading as a source of income for the Bolivian Aymara.
46 Cieza de León (1962, p.249). See Chapter II for the full quote.
47 Piedrahita (1973).
48 Matienzo (1967, p.163) on the use of coca by the black slaves taken to Peru by the Spanish. See also Patino (1967, p.210) for the Cali district.
49 Archivo Central del Cauca (Sig.8512).
50 Patino (1967, p.210).
51 Archivo Nacional, Quito, Ecuador (*Caja* 20, 1703, *fol.* 114 *et seq.*). I am indebted to David Earle for this and many other manuscript references.
52 See Arboleda (1948) and Archivo Central del Cauca (*Sigs.*8512 and 8462).
53 Archivo Central del Cauca (*Sig.* 8093). One *arroba* of coca was commonly sold for between 2 and 3 *patacones* in Guanacas (see footnote 25). One *patacón*, or piece of eight, was worth 272 *maravedís*, whereas a *peso*, also known as a *castellano*, varied between 450 and 490 *maravedís*.
54 Friede (1953, pp.161-174). Early chronicles on the use of coca in Timaná include Descobar (1938, p.161) and Vásquez de Espinosa (1948, *para.* 1044).
55 See Dollfus and Lavalle (1973) for a comparison of the ecological conditions in the Central and Northern Andes.

56 See Bray (1970) for an account of settlement patterns in the Buga district, just north of Cali. Cubillos (1959) has excavated the Morro de Tulcán, a ceremonial site in Popayán, but the existence of this large pyramidal structure does not necessarily imply any major nucleated settlement. Castellanos (1944) provides Conquest-period descriptions of a fort in Timbío and a large ceremonial hall in Popayán, but equally — although the existence of a dense population in the Popayán region cannot legitimately be disputed — there is still room to doubt whether this was ever organized in large nucleated villages. In my own surveys of habitation sites in the vicinity, I was rarely able to find clusters of more than two or three house platforms on a single site. And most of the larger sites — La Marquesa, Cerro de la Eme, Pubenza, etc. — were located on hill-tops, and the relative paucity of sherds and other refuse would tend to imply a funerary or ceremonial use, rather than a strictly habitational one. It is to be noted that these hill-top sites are often characterized by a large number of very deep (up to 20m.) shaft-and-side-chamber tombs, whereas the scattered house platforms and occasional intriguing hints of prehistoric drainage channels — notably in the *barrio* Los Sauces — are mainly located near the lower and flatter land, which was obviously more suitable for cultivation.

57 Patino (1967, p.208) cites a number of chronicle sources which describe this situation in the period immediately following the Spanish Conquest. It is not clear, however, whether these colonies were 'islands' in Murra's sense of the word, that is, whether they were separated from the main centres of population by any territorial discontinuity. Furthermore, the explicit mention of inter-tribal trading at the market in Tunja in 1550 — see Aguado (1956, I, p.406) — would indicate either that Spanish influence had already notably modified the indigenous economic practices, or that such exchanges between different groups had coexisted in the past with a more strictly intra-ethnic system of reciprocity.

58 Patino (1967, pp.211-213).

59 Ortiz (1973, p.237) has provided an acute analysis of the nature of reciprocal exchange obligations among the present-day Paez. That a similar situation existed in Popayán/Coconuco region prior to the Spanish Conquest could be inferred from the discovery of large, unstratified middens at the sites of El Mandur and Pozo Azul — on the *hacienda* Patugó, at 3000 metres, on the edge of the *páramo* of Paletará — whose pottery is unmistakeably similar in type to that published by Cubillos (1959) for the Morro de Tulcán, on the outskirts of Popayán (1760m).

60 Romoli (1962, p.283) refers to documentary evidence on the plantations and commerce of coca in Almaguer in the late sixteenth and early seventeenth centuries. Friede (1944, p.19) quotes various entries in the parish records of neighbouring San Sebastián, dated 21st April 1826, indicating that the local priest paid for Indian labour with coca leaves.

61 Friede (1953, p.110) provides evidence of the trading of the Timaná coca surplus towards Almaguer.

62 See especially Medina (1916, p.105) and Lunardi (1934, p.28). Pittier (1907) describes the classic pattern of localized exchange among the Paez at the turn of the century.

63 Guzmán (1929, p.7) writes of the Almaguer region: 'Commerce between members of the poorer classes is reduced to the exchange of food substances, with coca playing the principal part in their modest transactions... it is taken with profit to the markets of Popayán and Silvia...'

64 Friede (1944) provides a detailed description of the dismembering of many Indian reservations in southern Cauca. A similar synthesis is still lacking for Tierradentro, but Otero (1952) and González (mss.) both provide some good leads. See also Appendix C.

65 See Bernal (1954b) for a description of the Paez economy before it had been significantly affected by the *Violencia*. Though he tends to be a little vague in his discussion of the impact of coffee agriculture on the Paez, he provides an excellent account of the products of the higher altitudes, and of the trade that existed at that time between Mosoco and Silvia. This latter has since declined somewhat as the result of the *Violencia* and the construction of new roads.

66 Ortiz (1973, especially pp.237-9, and 271 *et seq.*). She has pointed out the difference of attitudes shares by the Paez in relation to coffee and other agricultural products. Her failure to recognize the importance of reciprocity when it is extended to more than one altitude zone (see p.215) — and with it her lack of emphasis on the coca crop — may be the result of the extremely narrow focus of her research, which was concentrated solely within the warm-climate valley of San Andrés de Pisimbalá. Schwarz (1973, p.143) has made the point that the situation in that valley cannot be made extensive to the Cauca area as a whole, as the higher altitude exports are primarily onions and potatoes, rather than coffee.

67 Begué (1971) gives an account of the Peruvian and Colombian legislation on the coca question. Lehmann (1949) wrote at the time: 'The prohibition of the sale of coca is a step forward in the Indian's dependence, it is a step towards his complete enslavement.' The last statistics on the Cauca coca crop were published before the prohibition by Bonilla (1945).

68 See Friede (1944, p.18) and Duque (1945).

Chapter IV. THE POLITICS OF COCAINE

1 'Hearings etc.' (1972, p.295) for the figures 1960-1972; 'The New York Times' (2nd January 1977) for 1976.

2 Rockefeller (1975, p.24).

3 For detailed descriptions of the process of refining cocaine, see Mortimer (1901, pp.309-319), Ashley (1975, pp.190-3), Trease and Evans (1972, p.469).

4 'El País', Cali, 7th July 1974.

5 'Papeles tocantes a la Nueva Granada'. Egerton collection, no.1807. Department of mss., British Museum. For the police chief in Barranquilla, see 'El Tiempo', Bogotá, 10th December 1974.

6 'Alternativa', Bogotá, 2nd August 1976.

7 'Alternativa', 22nd July 1974.

8 'Alternativa', 24th February 1975; 'Latin America Report', London, 28th May 1976.

9 'El Tiempo', 18th September 1974.
10 'El Tiempo', 6th December 1974.
11 Nicholas Gage in 'The New York Times', reprinted in 'O Estado de Sao Paulo', 27th April 1975.
12 'Alternativa', 24th November 1975.
13 'The Washington Post', 14th December 1976; 'Miami Herald', 15th December 1976; quote from 'High Times' for March, 1977.
14 'Alternativa', 29th September 1975.
15 'Latin America Political Report', 3rd October 1975, 30th January 1976.
16 'Alternativa', 24th February 1975.
17 'Latin America Political Report', 20th June 1975.
18 The drift to the right is charted in 'Latin America Political Report', 11th July 1975, 26th September 1975, 3rd October 1975, 16th July 1976, 10th December 1976, 18th March 1977.
19 'Alternativa', 2nd August 1976.
20 'Latin America Political Report', 16th July 1976, 10th December 1976, 18th March 1977. See also Postscript.
21 'Alternativa', 22nd July 1974, 11th November 1974, 24th February 1975; 'El Tiempo', 23rd September 1974.
22 'Alternativa', 1st September 1975.
23 Partridge (1975, p.156).
24 'Jornal da Tarde', Sao Paulo, 4th August 1975.
25 'El Espacio', Bogotá, 13th February 1974.
26 Mortimer (1901, p.317).
27 'El Tiempo', 12th December 1973.
28 'El Espectador', Bogotá, 29th October 1974.
29 'La Prensa', Lima, 19th December 1974.
30 See Weil (1976).
31 The 1926 figure is in Pérez de Barradas (1957, p.218); the 1950 figure in Begué (1971); and the 1974 figure in 'La Prensa', Lima, 19th December 1974.
32 See 'Bank of London and South America Review', vol.8, 1974.
33 *idem.*, see also the estimate of cocaine earnings in 'Latin America Political Report', 30th January 1976.
34 'Miami Herald', 24th January 1977.
35 'Latin America Political Report', 15th July 1977.
36 'The Guardian', Manchester, 4th June 1977.
37 UPI wire from Quito, 14th January 1976.
38 'El Tiempo', 28th September 1974.
39 'Latin America Political Report', 27th May 1977. See also Postscript.
40 On smuggling in Paraguay, see 'Latin America Political Report', 30th August 1974, 19th December 1975, 29th April 1977.
41 UPI wires from Washington D.C.: 5th July 1974 on the incrimination of the Chilean military, 8th July 1974 for the story on Allende.
42 'Latin America Political Report', 19th December 1975.
43 See Ashley (1975, pp.128 *et seq.*).
44 *idem.*, p.136.
45 *idem.*, p.137.

46 *idem*., p.139.
47 For an account of Santo Trafficante's operations, see McCoy (1972, p.55).
48 See Ashley (1975, p.137). See also footnote 13.
49 'El Tiempo', 23rd September 1974; 'Alternativa', 11th November 1974, and 24th February 1975.
50 An excellent exposé of the DEA's activities was published in Playboy magazine by Browning (1976).
51 Gage in 'The New York Times', reprinted in 'O Estado de Sao Paulo' 27th April 1975, contains a preliminary description of some of the abuses uncovered by the Jackson sub-committee.
52 Rockefeller (1975, p.54).
53 See 'The 31st Annual Almanac. 94th Congress, 1st Session, 1975.' (p.539).
54 See 'U.S. Narcotics enforcement assistance to Latin America. A new Counter-insurgency Training and Equipment Program?' Argentine Commission for Human Rights, Washington D.C. March 10th, 1977.
55 *idem*., see also 'counterSpy', Washington D.C., vol.3, issue 2, December 1976.
56 'The Guardian', 25th July 1977.
57 See the interview with the San Francisco attorney, Michael Stepanian, in 'High Times', September 1976.
58 'El Ticmpo', 30th July 1974.
59 'El Tiempo', 26th November 1974.

Chapter V. HOW TO CHEW COCA LEAVES

1 Andrew Weil (personal communication, March 1977).
2 Hanna (1974, p.284) has estimated a daily consumption of about six grams of *llipta* in the highlands of Peru. This is roughly a ratio of one gram of lime to every ten grams of coca.
3 See Hanna (1974).
4 See Brecher *et al*. (1972).
5 See Ritchie *et al*. (1965) and Julien (1975, p.90).
6 Mortimer (1901, p.420).
7 *idem*., p.355.
8 See Gutiérrez Noriega and Zapata Ortiz (1947, p.106), and Monge (1952, 1953).
9 See Julicn (1975, p.91).
10 See Nieschulz (1975) and Burchard (1975, p.477).
11 See Duke, Aulik and Plowman (1975).
12 See Monge (1952, 1953).
13 See Hanna (1974).
14 See Martin (1970) and Duke *et al*. (1975) for a complete list of coca alkaloids, and Nieschulz (1975) for the importance of cuscohygrine.
15 See Mortimer (1901) and Andrews and Solomon (1975, pp.14-15).
16 Rusby, in Andrews and Solomon (1975, p.14).
17 See Plowman (1976b).
18 Rusby, in Andrews and Solomon (1975, p.14).

19 See Hernández de Alba (1944, p.148) and Friede (1944, p.16).
20 See Buck *et al.* (1968, p.161).
21 Nieschulz (1975, p.273).
22 Burchard (1975, p.464).
23 Bolton (1976, p.630).
24 Nieschulz (1975, p.275).
25 *idem.*, p.273.
26 Montesinos (1965, p.16).
27 See Hanna (1974, p.284) who quotes Ciuffardi's estimates of the cocaine content in a quid of coca, which reach as high as 64 or even 112 mg.
28 Cooper's (1949) suggestion that coca is, in certain regions, used exclusively without an alkaline reagent does not appear to be supported by any conclusive evidence.
29 See Bolton (1976).
30 See Uscátegui (1954) and the discussion of the overlapping use of coca and tobacco in pre-Hispanic Colombia in the section (above) on the Pre-history of Coca. The use of tobacco probably coincided with that of coca in some of the Formative cultures of America, such as that of Valdivia, on the coast of Ecuador — see Lathrap (1975, p.48).
31 For a discussion of the very incompletely understood pharmacology of delta-9 tetrahydracannabinol, see Julien (1975), Rubin and Comitas (1975) and Rubin (ed.) (1975).
32 On the damage produced in the mouth by coca chewing, see Cuervo Márquez (1920, p.170), Lunardi (1934, p.29), La Barre (1948, p.44) and Wells (1964).

Chapter VI. ON GROWING YOUR OWN COCA

1 See Plowman (1976b).
2 See Mortimer (1901, p.238) and Weil (1976).
3 The situation in Cauca contrasts in this respect with that in the arid coastal valleys of Peru, where Rostworowski (1973, p.210) has suggested that the moderate shade cast by medium-sized fruit trees — such as *pacae* (**Inga recticulata**) *guamo* (**Inga feuillei**) and *guava* (**Psidium guajava** L.) — could actually stimulate the growth of coca, by protecting it from excessive heat and sunlight, and from abrupt changes in temperature.
4 See Rostworowski (1973, p.202) on the 18°C. isotherm; and Mortimer (1901, p.234) on the inferior alkaloid yield of lowland coca plants. Weil (1976, p.78) has also recently confirmed the effects of maximum frost-free altitude in producing the best quality *coca de altura* in the Valle de la Convención, near Cuzco, Peru.
5 See Mortimer (1901, p.237) and Plowman (1976b).
6 Irrigation is not usually considered necessary on the east-facing slopes of the Andes, such as those of Tierradentro, or of the *montana* of Peru and the *yungas* of Bolivia. Rostworowski (1973, p.203) has mentioned its application to the coastal valleys of Peru, and Patino (1967, p.203) cites evidence of irrigation among the Conquest period Indians who cultivated coca along the arid Caribbean coast of Venezuela.

7 Mortimer (1901, p.243) describes a number of pests that attack coca bushes in Peru.

8 Piedrahita (1881) described the toasting of coca leaves by this method in the vicinity of Bogotá in the sixteenth century. Uscátegui (1954) has summarized similar practices in the Sierra Nevada de Santa Marta, and in the tropical lowlands of the Vaupés and Putumayo drainages.

9 See Weil (1976) for a description of Peruvian drying techniques.

10 The need for this subsequent humidification was pointed out by Matienzo (1967) in his seminal work on coca agriculture in sixteenth century Peru; and also noted in eighteenth century Colombia by Santa Gertrudis (1970, IV, p.294).

11 A number of minor variants have been noted in the Amazon basin: see Schultes (1972, p.27) for the use of coca as snuff on the Miritíparaná river; and Schultes (1957a) for the scented coca of the Tanimuka Indians, which is made by the addition of the balsamic resin of **Protium Heptaphyllum** March.

12 The formula: $CaCO_3$ + heat → CaO + CO_2
CaO + H_20 → $Ca(OH)_2$ + heat. (thanks, Jonathan).

13 Cieza (1962, p.249).

14 Jorge Bejarano, cited by Rostworowski (1973, p.206). See also Pérez de Barradas (1957, p.217).

15 See Uscátegui (1954, p.272) for the Sierra Nevada, and (1961, p.226) for the Tunebo.

16 See Cooper (1949).

17 See Acosta (1940, p.286); La Barre (1948, p.69); Cooper (1949); Stein (1961, p.99); and Weil (1976).

18 See Patino (1964). It seems more likely, however, that the Kogi *popóro* should also be **Lagenaria siceraria**.

19 See Patino (1967).

Chapter VII. MAMA COCA REVISITED

1 Sigmund Freud (1884) in Byck (1974, p.73).

2 See Pérez de Barradas (1957, p.220); and the erotic section of the Larco Hoyle museum in Lima, Peru.

3 On coca chewing by Paez women, see Pittier (1907) '...the women do not use it...' Hernández de Alba (1944, p.199) who claims that coca was used '...very little by the women...' Douay (1890) describes the ceremonial chewing of coca by the neighbouring Guambiano women while they were engaged in singing a mournful chant. For other restrictions on the use of coca by women, see Uscátegui (1954, p.284) for the Witoto of the Putumayo drainage; Torres (1971, p.154) for the Barasana of the Vaupés; Reichel-Dolmatoff (1949-1950, pp.75-79) for the Kogi of the Sierra Nevada de Santa Marta; and Stein (1961) for the Quechua of Hualcán. The use of coca by post-menstrual women among the Barasana and Maku of the Vaupés has recently been confirmed by Christine Hugh-Jones and Howard Reid respectively (personal communications, June, 1977).

4 Reichel-Dolmatoff (1949-1950, pp.75-79). This excellent account of Kogi coca

chewing is often difficult to find in the original, but the relevant sections have been summarized in Uscátegui (1954, *passim.*) and reproduced almost verbatim in Pérez de Barradas (1957).

5 Bernal (1954a) is the classic account of Paez shamanism. Another useful short description is that of Nachtigall (1953). Hernández de Alba (1944) and (1946) is not entirely reliable. More recently, Schwarz (1973, pp.297-332) has provided a competent introduction to the largely similar ritual practices of the neighbouring Guambianos.

6 Jean-Paul Sartre 'Discours sur la méthode', quoted in Diamond *et al.* (1975, p.110). See also Jay's (1972) provocative discussion of the anthropologist's tendency to treat his informants as mere objects for study.

7 See Kroeber (1949) for a discussion of the Muiscas; and Reichel-Dolmatoff (1966) for the references to the Tairona and the Kogi.

8 See Bernal (1954a) for an attempt to define *senas* in an unacceptably rigid pattern. Jaulin (1973, p.438) has pointed out that divination must be '...intuitively compatible with what could happen, or what would be perceived as desirable to happen.'

9 See La Barre (1948, p.178).

10 See Cooper (1949), Stein (1961, p.318) and Rostworowski (1973).

11 The Muiscas used burning coca as an incense offering — Castellanos (1944) and Zamora (in Pérez de Barradas, 1957, p.221) — the Kogi offer crumbled coca leaves to the four cardinal points before proceeding with a human burial — Reichel-Dolmatoff (1967). For the various forms of offering customary in the Central Andes, see La Barre (1948), Rostworowski (1973) and especially Osborne (1968, p.89): 'The most perfect offering of all is to burn a block of llama fat with coca at midnight inside a ring of dried llama dung and to throw the ashes into a stream.'

12 See Hernández de Alba (1944) for Narino, and Schwarz (1973, p.328) for the Guambianos.

13 See González (mss., p.222).

14 Bernal (1955) on Paez kinship terminology; and Schwarz (1973) on that of the Guambianos, which is notably different.

15 Within the scheme outlined recently by Ioan Lewis (1971) it would appear that Paez shamanism fits into the category of a 'central possession religion', and more specifically, of that based on autonomous deities rather than on specific ancestor cults. (See Chapter Six of 'Ecstatic Religion'.)

16 Lewis (1971) (p.29 of 1975 ed.).

17 A very useful theoretical departure in this direction has been provided by Diamond (1974). The application of a militant anthropology to a specific social praxis has, however — especially in the state of diffuse, invisible war which characterizes Latin America today — tended to lag behind the welcome refinements in academic libertarianism. It goes without saying that the future of anthropology lies solely on the divising of means to perpetuate a concrete struggle *in* the field and *outside* the repressive apparatus of the State and its Universities.

Appendix A. DOPE AND MUSHROOMS

1 Emboden (1972, p.215); and Starks (1977, p.29).
2 Emboden (1972, p.232).
3 Patino (1969).
4 Araújo (1961, p.316). Wagley and Galvao (1947, p.144) also speak of the use of cannabis by the Tupi-Guarani-speaking Guajajara of Maranhao, who are neighbours of the Jê-speaking Canela Indians.
5 Rubin and Comitas (1975, p.15).
6 Partridge (1975, p.149).
7 Burroughs and Ginsberg (1963, p.41).
8 Patino (1969).
9 Guzmán (1968, p.262).
10 Partridge (1975) has described the situation in the *municipio* of Aracataca, located fifty miles south of Santa Marta. This town is supposed to have provided the inspiration for the Macondo of Gabriel Garcia Márquez's 'Cien Anos de Soledad'.
11 The classic study of **Stropharia cubensis** in Heim and Wasson (1958) remains the only major source of information on this mushroom. Furst (1976, pp. 172-173) cites the work of John Haines, a mycologist at the New York State Museum in Albany, for the clarification of the ecology of **Stropharia**, and points out the importance of the sixteenth century Mazatecs' regard for deer, the only animal which could have served as host to the spores of this mushroom before the arrival of European cattle. The report on the Lacandon use of **Stropharia** derives from a communication by Robertson in Dobkin (1974). The *derrumbe* mushroom was identified by Schultes (1972, p.10); and the British **Psilocybe** mushrooms described by the Red Shift Research Collective (1977).
12 On the use of **Banisteriopsis** in Colombia see Schultes (1957b); Uscátegui (1959); Burroughs and Ginsberg (1963); Reichel-Dolmatoff (1969); and Harner (1973). For the note on *pildé* see Uscátegui (1961, p.219).

Bibliography

MANUSCRIPT SOURCES

Archivo Central del Cauca, Popayán.
references to individual mss. by *Sig. (Signatura)* number — in the colonial period — or by *Paquete, legajo* and *comunicación* — in the Republican period.

Archivo Nacional, Quito, Ecuador.
references by *Caja*, date, and folio numbers.

González, Rev. P. David
'Los Paeces' mss. in collection of Prefectura Apostólica de Tierradentro, Belalcázar, Cauca. 260 pp. in typescript, written c. 1950.

'Papeles tocantes a la Nueva Granada'
in Egerton collection, Department of mss., British Museum, London.

Patino, Aníbal
'Impacto Ecológico y Socioeconómico de Industrias Puracé S.A.'
10 mimeographed pages dated 20th July 1974. Universidad del Valle, Cali.

Schwarz, Ronald Allan: 1973. 'Guambía: An Ethnography of Change and Stability. Ph.D. thesis submitted to Michigan State University.

'U.S. Narcotics enforcement assistance to Latin America. A new Counter-insurgency Training and Equipment Program?'
a memorandum prepared by the Washington DC Information Bureau and the Argentine Commission for Human Rights, 1912 'N' St. N.W., Washington DC 20036. (March 10th, 1977).

PRESS

'Alternativa', Apartado Aéreo 25496, Bogotá.

'Bank of London and South America Review', London.

'Carta Campesina', Asociación Nacional de Usuários Campesinos, Bogotá.

'counterSpy' Washington DC.20044 (P.O. Box 647 Ben Franklin Station).

'Documentos Políticos: Revista del Partido Comunista de Colombia.' Bogotá.

'La Prensa', Lima.

'El Espacio', Bogotá.

'El Espectador', Bogotá.

'El País', Cali.
'El Tiempo', Bogotá.
'High Times', Box 386 Cooper Station, New York, N.Y. 10003.
'Jornal da Tarde', Sao Paulo.
'Latin America Commodities Report', London.
'Latin America Political Report', London. (This has been the title used throughout in the footnotes, though prior to 1977 the correct name was 'Latin America: a weekly political report.')
'Miami Herald', Miami.
'O Estado de Sao Paulo', Sao Paulo.
'The Guardian', Manchester and London.
'The New York Times', New York.
'The Washington Post', Washington DC.
'Unidad Indígena', Apartado Aéreo 32395, Bogotá.

PUBLISHED SOURCES

Acosta, José de; 1940. 'Historia natural y moral de las Indias'. Fondo de Cultura Económica, Mexico. (1st ed. 1590).
Aguado, Fray Pedro; 1956 (vols. 1 and 2) and 1957 (vols. 3 and 4). 'Recopilación Historial'. Empresa Nacional de Publicaciones, Bogotá. (Written 1560s.)
Alape, Arturo; 1972. 'Las Muertes de Tirofijo'. Ediciones Abjón Mono, Bogotá.
Andagoya, Pascual de; 1938. 'Relación de los sucesos de Pedrarias Davila en las provincias de Tierra Firme o Castilla del Oro, y de lo ocurrido en el descubrimiento de la Mar del Sur y costas del Perú y Nicaragua.' in Jijón y Caamano (1938).
Andrews, George, and Solomon, David; 1975. 'The Coca Leaf and Cocaine Papers', Harcourt, Brace, Jovanovich; London and New York.
Aragón, Arcesio; 1939. 'Fastos Payaneses. 1536-1936.' Ministerio de Educación Nacional, Bogotá.
Araújo, Alceu Maynard; 1961. 'Medicina Rústica'. Companhia Editora Nacional, serie Brasiliana vol.300. Sao Paulo.
Arboleda, Gustavo; 1935. 'Historia Contemporanea de Colombia'. Vol.VI, 'La revuelta liberal hasta terminar el ana do 1860'. Cali.
1956. 'Historia de Cali'. (3 vols.) Biblioteca de la Universidad del Valle, Cali.
Arboleda Llorente, José Maria; 1948. 'El Indio en la Colonia'. Ministerio de Educación Nacional, Bogotá.
1952. 'Historia de Colombia. 'Publicaciones de la Editorial Universidad del Cauca, Popayán.
Arroyo, Jaime; 1955. 'Historia de la Gobernación de Popayán.' (2 vols.) Editorial Santafé, Bogotá. (Written 1862, 1st ed. 1907).
Ashley, Richard; 1975. 'Cocaine: Its History, Uses and Effects'. St. Martin's Press, New York.
Barclay, Arthur S.; 1959. 'New Considerations in an old genus: Datura.' in Botanical Museum Leaflets, Harvard University, vol.18, no.6. Cambridge, Mass.

Begué, Remedios de la Pena; 1971. 'El uso de la coca en America, según la legislación colonial y republicana.' in Revista Espanola de Antropología Americana, vol.6, Madrid.

Bejarano, Jorge; 1953. 'Nuevos capítulos sobre el cocaísmo en Colombia.' in America Indígena, vol. XIII, Mexico.

Bernal Villa, Segundo Eliécer; 1954a. 'Medicina y Magia entre los Paeces' in Revista Colombiana de Antropología, vol.2 no.2, pp.219-267. Bogotá.

1954b. 'Economía de los Páez' in Revista Colombiana de Antropologia, vol.3, pp.291-367. Bogotá.

1955. 'Bases para el Estudio de la Organización Social de los Páez.' in Revista Colombiana de Antropología, vol.4, pp.165-188.

Bird (1967) in Ortiz de Zúniga (1967).

Bollaert, William; 1860. 'Antiquarian, ethnological and other researches in New Granada, Ecuador, Peru and Chile'. London.

Bolton, Ralph; 1976. 'Andean Coca Chewing: A Metabolic Perspective' in American Anthropologist, vol.78, no.3.

Bonilla Iragorri, Gerardo; 1945. 'El Consumo de Hojas de Coca en el Departamento del Cauca.' in Revista de la Universidad Nacional de Colombia, vol.2. Bogotá.

Bonilla, Víctor Daniel; 1973. 'Coconucos: historia del despojo' in Lecturas Dominicales, 'El Tiempo', 27th May 1973. Bogotá.

Bonnycastle, R.H.; 1818. 'Spanish America'. London.

Bray, Warwick and Moseley, M. Edward; 1970. 'An archaeological sequence from the vicinity of Buga, Colombia' in Nawpa Pacha, vols.7-8. Berkeley, California.

Brecher, Edward M. *et al.*; 1972. 'Licit and Illicit Drugs: The Consumers Union Report on Narcotics, Stimulants, Depressants, Inhalants, Hallucinogens and Marijuana — Including Caffeine, Nicotine, and Alcohol'. Little, Brown and Co., New York.

Bristol, Melvin Lee; 1970. 'Tree datura drugs of the Colombian Sibundoy' in Botanical Museum Leaflets, Harvard University, vol.22. Cambridge, Mass.

Browning, Frank; 1976. 'An American Gestapo: the story of the Drug Enforcement Administration — perhaps the most ruthless and corrupt government agency ever' in Playboy magazine, February 1976, Chicago, Illinois.

Brundage, Burr Cartwright; 1963. 'Empire of the Inca'. University of Oklahoma Press, Norman, Oklahoma.

Buck, Sasaki, Hewitt and Macrae: 1968. 'Coca chewing and Health: An epidemiologic study among residents of a Peruvian village' in American Journal of Epidemiology, John Hopkins University, Baltimore, Md. vol.88, no.2.

Buechler, Hans C., and Buechler, Judith-Maria: 1971. 'The Bolivian Aymara', Holt, Rinehart and Winston, New York.

Burchard, Roderick E.: 1975. 'Coca Chewing: A New Perspective' in Rubin (ed) (1975), pp.463-484.

Burg, George: 1936. 'Informe sobre los estudios arqueológicos en la región de San Andrés en Tierradentro' in Revista Popayán, no.163. Popayán.

Burroughs, William, and Ginsberg, Allen: 1963. 'The Yage Letters'. City Lights Books, San Francisco, Calif.

Bushnell, G.H.S.: 1956. 'Peru'. Thames and Hudson, London.

Byck, Robert: 1974 (ed). 'The Cocaine Papers by Sigmund Freud'. New York.

Caro, Miguel Antonio: 1952. 'Noticia Biográfica de Julio Arboleda'. pp.7-80 in Julio Arboleda 'Poesias', Ministerio de Educación, Bogotá.

Castellanos, Juan de. 1944. 'Elegías de Varones Ilustres de Indias'. Biblioteca de Autores Espanoles, Madrid. (1st ed., 1589).

Castillo Cárdenas, Gonzalo: 1971. Introduction to Lame (1971, pp.xi-xiv).

Castillo I Orozco, Eugenio del: 1877. 'Vocabulario Páez-Castellano'. Paris.

Castrillón Arboleda, Diego: 1973. 'El Indio Quintín Lame'. Ediciones Tercer Mundo, Bogotá.

Chaves, Milciades: 1947. 'Mitología Kágaba' in Boletín de Arqueología, vol.II, nos.5-6, Bogotá.

Cieza de León, Pedro de: 1918. 'The War of Chupas' trans. C.R. Markham, Hakluyt Society, 2nd Series vol.42, London.

1962. 'Primera Parte de la Crónica del Perú'. Editorial Espasa-Calpe, Madrid. (1st ed. 1553). Also trans. C.R. Markham 'The Travels of Pedro Cieza de León'. Hakluyt Society, 1st series, vol.33, London, 1864.

Cobo, Bernabé: 1964. 'Historia del Nuevo Mundo', vol.I. Biblioteca de Autores Espanoles, Madrid. (1st ed. 1653).

Colmenares, Germán: 1973. 'Historia Económica y Social de Colombia 1537-1719'. Ed. Universidad del Valle, Cali.

Comité de Solidaridad con los Presos Políticos: 1974. 'Libro Negro de la Represión: Frente Nacional 1958-1974'. Ed. Gráficas Mundo Nuevo, Bogotá.

Cooper, John M.: 1949. 'Stimulants and Narcotics' in Handbook of South American Indians, vol.5. Bureau of American Ethnology, bulletin 143. US Government Printing Office, Washington DC.

Cooper, Richard: 1978. 'A Guide to British Psilocybin Mushrooms'. Hassle Free Press, London.

Corry, Stephen: 1976. 'Towards Indian Self-Determination in Colombia'. Survival International Document 11, London.

Cowley, Abraham: 1795. 'History of Plants' a poem in six books translated from the Latin by Nahum Tate, London. (1st ed. 1662).

Cuervo Márquez, Carlos: 1920. 'Prehistoria y Viajes. Estudios arqueológicos y etnográficos'. Madrid. (1st ed. 1893).

Cubillos, Julio César: 1959. 'El Morro de Tulcán' in Revista Colombiana de Antropología, vol.VIII, Bogotá.

Debray, Régis: 1974. 'La critique des armes'. Editions du Seuil, Paris.

Descobar, Fray Gerónimo: 1938. 'Relación de Fray Gerónimo Descobar, de la orden de San Agustín, sobre el caracter e costumbres de los indios de la provincia de Popayán'. In Jijón y Caamano (1938). (Written c. 1580.)

Diamond, Stanley: 1974. 'In Search of the Primitive. A Critique of Civilization'. Transaction Books, New Brunswick, N.J.

Diamond, Stanley, Bob Scholte, Eric R. Wolf. 1975. 'On Defining the Marxist Tradition in Anthropology: A Response to the "American Anthropologist".' In Critique of Anthropology, vols.4-5, London.

Dobkin de Rios, Marlene: 1974. 'The influence of psychotropic flora and fauna on Maya religion'. In Current Anthropology, vol.15 no.2, Chicago.
Dollfus, O., and Lavalle, D.: 1973. 'Ecología y ocupación del espacio en los Andes tropicales durante los últimos veinte milenios' in Bulletin de l'Institut Francais d'Etudes Andines, vol.II no.3, Lima.
Donne, John: 1972. 'Complete Poetry and Selected Prose'. The Nonesuch Press, London.
Douay, Léon: 1890. 'Contribution à l'Américanisme du Cauca'. Congrès des Américanistes: Sixième Séance ordinaire. Berlin. (pp.753-786 of 'Comp-terendu . . . ').
Duke, J.A., Aulik, D. and Plowman, T.: 1975. 'Nutritional value of coca' in Botanical Museum Leaflets, Harvard University, vol.24 no.6. Cambridge, Mass.
Dugue Gómez, Luís: 1945. 'Notas sobre el cocaísmo en Colombia' in Boletín de Arqueología, vol.1 no.5.
Emboden Jr., William A.: 1972. 'Ritual Use of **Cannabis Sativa** L.: A Historical-Ethnographic Survey' in Peter T. Furst (ed) 'Flesh of the Gods'. Praeger Publishers, New York.
Espinosa, José María: 1971. 'Memorias de un Abanderado'. Banco Popular, Bogotá.
Espinoza Soriano, Waldemar: 1973. 'La coca de los mitmas cayampis en el reino Ancara. Siglo XVI' in Anales Científicos de la Universidad del Centro del Perú, no.2. Huancayo.
Fals Borda, Orlando: 1956. 'Fray Pedro de Aguado. El cronista olvidado de Colombia y Venezuela'. Ed. Franciscana de Colombia, Cali.
Fluharty, Vernon Lee: 1957. 'Dance of the Millions. Military Rule and Social Revolution in Colombia 1930-1956'. University of Pittsburg Press.
Frampton, John: 1577. 'Joyfull newes out of the newe founde worlde, wherein is declared the rare and singular vertues of diverse and sundrie Hearbes, Trees, Oyles, Plantes, and Stones, with their applications, as well as Phisicke as Chirurgerie, etc.'. London.
Being a translation of Nicolas Monardes 'La Historia medicinal de las cosas que se traen de nuestras Indias Occidentales que sirven en medicina'. Seville, 1574.
Friede, Juan: 1943. 'Los Indios del Alto Magdalena (Vidas, Luchas y Exterminio) 1609-1931'. Ed. Instituto Indigenista de Colombia, Bogotá.
1944. 'El Indio en Lucha por la Tierra'. Editorial Espiral, Bogotá. (2nd ed., Editorial La Chispa, Bogotá, 1972).
1953. 'Los Andakí. 1538-1947. Historia de la aculturación de una tribu selvática'. Fondo de Cultura Económica, Medico.
1956. 'Introducción y Estudio Preliminar'. pp.5-104 in Aguado (1956, I).
1961. 'Vida y luchas de Don Juan del Valle, primer Obispo de Popayán y Protector de Indios'. Editorial Universidad del Cauca, Popayán.
Freud, Sigmund: 1884. 'Uber coca' in Byck (1974).
1887. 'Beitrage uber die Anwendung des Cocain' in Byck (1974).
Furst, Peter T.: 1976. 'Hallucinogens and Culture'. Chandler and Sharp, San Francisco.
Galeano, Eduardo: 1973. 'Las Venas Abiertas de America Latina'. Siglo XXI ed., Mexico and Buenos Aires.

Garcés, Jorge A.: 1935. (ed.) 'Colección de Cédulas Reales dirigidas a la Audiencia de Quito. 1538-1600'. Publicaciones del Archivo Municipal, Quito, Ecuador.
1936. 'Colección de Documentos Inéditos relativos al Adelantado Capitán Don Sebastián de Banlcázar. 1535-1565'. Publicaciones del Archivo Municipal, Quito.
Gentner, Walter A.: 1972. 'The Genus **Erythroxylum** in Colombia'. In Cespedesia, vol.I no.4, Cali.
Golte, Jurgen: 1970. 'Algunas consideraciones acerca de la Producción y Distribución de la Coca en el Estado Inca' in Proceedings of XXXVIII Congress of Americanists, Munich.
Gott, Richard: 1973. 'Rural Guerillas in Latin America'. Pelican Books, London.
Grinspoon, Lester: 1971. 'Marijuana Reconsidered'. Harvard University Press, Cambridge, Mass.
Guerra, Francisco: 1971. 'The Pre-Columbian Mind'. Academic Press, London.
Guerra, F. and Olivera, H.: 1954. 'Las plantas fantásticas de México'. Imprenta del Diario Espanol, Mexico.
Gutiérrez-Noriega, Carlos: 1947. 'Mental Alterations Produced by Coca' in Andrews and Solomon (1975).
1952. 'El Hábito de la coca en Sudamérica' in América Indígena, vol.XII no.2, Mexico.
Gutiérrez-Noriega, Carlos and Zapata Ortiz, Vicente: 1947. 'Estudios sobre la coca y la cocaína en el Perú'. Ministerio de Educación Pública, Lima.
Guzmán, Arcesio: 1929. 'Monografía del Distrito de Almaguer'. Bogotá.
Guzmán, Germán: 1968. 'La Violencia en Colombia'. Ediciones Progreso, Cali.
Hamilton, Col. J.P.: 1827. 'Travels through the interior provinces of Colombia'. London. Translated as 'Viajes por el interior de las provincias de Colombia'. Ed. Banco de la República, Bogotá.
Hanna, Joel M.: 1974. 'Coca Leaf Use in Southern Peru: Some Biosocial Aspects' in American Anthropologist, vol.76 no.2.
Harner, Michael J.: 1973. 'Hallucinogens and Shamanism'. Oxford University Press, London and New York.
Hearings Before the Subcommittee of the Committee on the Judiciary to Investigate the Administration of the Internal Security Act and Other Internal Security Laws, U.S. Senate, 92nd Congress, 2nd Session, September 18, 1972: 'World Drug Traffic and its Impact on U.S. Security'. U.S. Government Printing Office, Washington DC, 1972.
Heim, Roger and Wasson, R. Gordon: 1958. 'Les Champignons Hallucinogènes du Mexique'. Editons du Muséum National d'Histoire Naturelle. Paris.
Hemming, John: 1972. 'The Conquest of the Incas'. Abacus Books, London.
Hernández de Alba, Gregorio: 1938. 'Investigaciones Arquelógicas en Tierradentro' in Revista de Indias, vol.II no.10, Bogotá.
1944. 'Etnología de los ˆ ndes del Sur de Colombia' in Revista de la Universidad del Cauca, no.5. Popayán.
1946. 'The Highland Tribes of Southern Colombia' in Handbook of South American Indians, vol.2. Bureau of American Ethnology Bulletin 143, Washington DC.
1946b. 'The archaeology of San Agustín and Tierradentro' in *idem*.

Holmstedt, Bo, Eva Jäätmaa, Kurt Leander, and Timothy Plowman: 1977. 'Determination of cocaine in some South American species of **Erythroxylum** using mass fragmentography' in Phytochemistry, vol.16. Pergamon Press, England.

Iragorri, Luis Carlos: 1962. 'Apuntes para un estudio económico y fiscal del Cauca'. Editoriales del Departamento, Popayán.

Jaulin, Robert: 1973. 'Gens du soi, gens de l'autre'. Union Générale d'Editions. Paris.

Jay, Robert: 1972. 'Personal and Extrapersonal Vision in Anthropology' in Dell Hymes (ed) 'Reinventing Anthropology'. Random House, New York.

Jijón y Caamano, Jacinto: 1936 and 1938. 'Sebstián de Belalcázar' (2 vols.). Editorial Ecuatoriana, Quito.

Juan, Jorge and Ulloa, Antonio de: 1918. 'Noticias Secretas de América'. (2 vols.). Editorial América, Madrid. (Written 1740s, 1st ed. London 1826).

Julián, Antonio: 1787. 'La perla de la América, provincia de Santa Marta, etc.'. Published by Don Antonio de Sancha, Madrid.

Julien, Robert M.: 1975. 'A Primer of Drug Action'. W.H. Freeman and Co., San Francisco, Calif.

Kaplan, John: 1975. 'Intersections of Anthropology and Law in the Cannabis Area' in Rubin (ed) (1975).

Kroeber, Alfred L.: 1946. 'The Chibcha' in Handbook of South American Indians vol.2. Bureau of American Ethnology Bulletin 143. Washington DC.

La Barre, Weston: 1948. 'The Aymara Indians of the Lake Titicaca Plateau, Bolivia'. American Anthropological Association, Memoir no.68.

Lame, Manuel Quintín: 1971. 'En Defensa de Mi Raza'. Comité de Defensa del Indio, Bogotá. (mss. written in 1939 under the title 'Los Pensamientos del Indio que se Educó dentro de las Selvas Colombianas'.)
1973. 'Las Luchas del Indio que Bajó de la Montana al valle de la 'civilización'. Comité de Defensa del Indio, Bogotá.

Lanning, Edward: 1967. 'Peru Before the Incas'. Prentice-Hall, Englewood Cliffs NJ.

Las Casas, Bartolomé de: 1946. 'La Destrucción de las Indias'. Libreria Bouvet, Paris. (1st ed. Seville 1552).

Lathrap, Donald W.: 1975. 'Ancient Ecuador: Culture, Clay and Creativity. 3000-300 B.C.'. Field Museum of Natural History, Chicago.

Lehmann, Henri: 'Suppression of the sale of coca in Colombia'. Boletín Indigenista, vol.IX, pp.26-31. Mexico. 1949.

León Helguera, J.: 1969. 'The Problem of Liberalism versus Conservatism in Colombia: 1849-1885', in Frederick B. Pike, 'Latin American History: Select Problems'. Harcourt, Brace and World, New York.

Lewin, Louis: 1924. 'Phantastica: Narco and Stimulating Drugs, their Use and Abuse'. Berlin. A translation of the section on 'cocainism' can be found in Byck (1974).

Lewis, Ioan M.: 1971. 'Ecstatic Religion'. London. (Pelican ed., 1975).

Long, Stanley and Yánguez, Juan: 1971. 'Excavaciones en Tierradentro' in Revista Colombiana de Antropología, vol.XV, Bogotá.

López de Gómara, Francisco: 1954. 'Historia General de Las Indias'. Barcelona. (1st ed. 1551).

López de Velasco, Juan: 'Geografía y Descripción Universal de las Indias'. Publicado por Don Justo Zaragoza. Establecimiento Tipográfico de Fortanet, Madrid, 1894. (Written 1574.)

Lucena Salmoral, Manuel: 1962. 'Mitos, usos y costumbres de los indios pixaos' in Revista Colombiana de Antropología, vol.XI, pp.143-152. Bogotá.
1965. 'Datos antropológicos sobre los Pijao' in Revista Colombiana de Antropo logía, vol.XII, pp.357-387. Bogotá.

Lunardi, Mons. Federico: 1934. 'El Macizo Colombiano en la prehistoria de sur América'. Ed. Revista do Instituto Histórico e Geográphico Brasileiro. Imprensa Nacional, Rio de Janeiro.

Machado, Cazoma, E: 1972. 'El género **Erythroxylon** en el Perú'. Raymondiana vol.5, pp.5-101. Lima.

Mantegazza, Dr. Paolo: 'Sulie virtio igieniche e medicinale della Coca, a sugli Alimenti nervosi in generale'. Monograph. Milan. 1859.

Markham, Clements: 1862. 'Travels in Peru and India'. London, John Murray.

Martin, Richard T.: 1970. 'The Role of Coca in the History, Religion, and Medicine of South American Indians' in Economic Botany, vol.24. Cambridge, Mass.

Matienzo, Juan de: 1967. 'Gobierno del Perú'. Ed. Guillermo Lohmann Villena, Lima and Paris. (1st ed. 1567).

McCoy, Alfred W.: 1972. 'The Politics of Heroin in Southeast Asia'. Harper and Row, New York.

Medina, Leandro: 1916. 'Informe que el Secretario de Gobierno del Cauca rinde al senor Gobernador del Departamento'. Imprenta del Departamento, Popayán.

Miller, John: 1828. 'Memoirs of General Miller in the service of the Republic of Peru'. London (2 vols.).

Monge, Carlos; *et al.*: 1952. 'Documentos relacionados con la labor efectuada por la Comisión Peruana para el Estudio del Problema de la Coca' in Perú Indígena, vol.3 nos.7-8, pp.24-130. Lima.

Monge, Carlos M.: 1953. 'La Necesidad de Estudiar el Problema de la Masticación de las Hojas de Coca' in América Indígena, vol.XIII. Mexico.

Montesinos, F.: 1965. 'Cocaine metabolism' in Bulletin Narcotics, vol.17.

Mortimer, W. Golden: 1901. 'Peru: History of Coca'. J.H. Vail and Co., New York. New Edition under the title 'History of Coca: "The Divine Plant" of the Incas'. And/Or Press, San Francisco. 1974.

Murra, John V.: 1967. 'La Visita de los Chupaychu como fuente etnológica' in Ortiz de Zuniga (1967).
1972. 'El "control vertical" de un máximo de pisos ecológicos en la economía de las sociedades andinas' in Inigo Ortiz de Zuniga 'Visita de la Provincia de León de Huánuco (1562)' (vol2). Universidad Hermilio Valdizán, Huánuco.

Nachtigall, Horst: 1953. 'Shamanismo entre los indios paeces' in Revista Colombiana de Folklore, no.2. Bogotá.

Nieschulz, Otto: 1975. 'Cocaism and Cocainism', pp.269-276 in Andrews and Solomon (1975).

Olano, Antonio: 1910. 'Popayán en la Colonia'. Imprenta Oficial, Popayán.

Orcutt, J.D. and Biggs, D.A.: 1975. 'Recreational effects of Marihuana and Alcohol: Some descriptive dimensions' in The International Journal of Addictions, vol.10 no.2. New York.

Ortiz, Sutti Reissig de: 1973. 'Uncertainties in Peasant Farming: A Colombian Case'. University of London, The Athlone Press. London.
Ortiz de Zuniga, Inigo: 1967. 'Visita de la Provincia de León de Huánuco (1562)'. (vol.1) Universidad Hermilio Valdizán, Huánuco.
Osborne, Harold: 1968. 'South American Mythology'. London.
Otero, Jesús M.: 1952. 'Etnología Caucana'. Editorial Universidad del Cauca, Popayán.
Ots Capdequí, José María: 1957. 'El Indio en el Nuevo Reino de Granada durante la etapa histórica de la dominación espanola' in Revista de Indias, ano XVII no.67. Madrid.
Partridge, William L.: 1975. 'Cannabis and Cultural Groups in a Colombian Municipio'. pp.147-172 in Rubin (ed) (1975).
Patino, Víctor Manuel: 1964. 'Plantas Alimenticias'. Vol.II of 'Plantas Cultivadas y Animales Domésticos en América Equinoccial'. Imprenta Departmental, Cali.
1967. 'Fibras, Medicinas, Mescelaneas'. Vol.III of 'Plantas Cultivadas y Animales Domésticos en América Equinoccial'. Imprenta Departamental, Cali.
1969. 'Plantas Introducidas'. Vol.IV of 'Plantas Cultivadas y Animales Domésticos en América Equinoccial'. Imprenta Departamental, Cali.
Pérez de Barradas, José: 1937. 'Arqueología y Antropología precolombinas de Tierra Dentro'. Ministerio de Educación Nacional, Bogotá.
1957. 'Plantas Mágicas Americanas'. Consejo Superior de Investigaciones Científicas, Instituto 'Bernardino de Sahagún'. Madrid.
Piedrahita E., Presbítero Javier: 1973. 'Historia Eclesiástica de Antioquia 1545-1828'. Editorial Granamérica, Medellín.
Piedrahita, Lucas Fernández de: 1881. 'Historia General de las Conquistas del Nuevo Reino de Granada'. Bogotá.
Pittier de Fábrega, Henry: 1907. 'Ethnographic and Linguistic notes on the Paez Indians of Tierra Adentro' in Memoirs of the American Anthropological Association, Lancaster, Pa.
Plowman, Timothy: 1976a. 'Orthography of **Erythroxylum** (**Erythroxylaceae**)' in Taxon 25(1), pp.141-144.
1976b. 'Botanical Perspectives on Coca'. Paper delivered at the 75th Annual Meeting of the American Anthropological Association, Washington DC (November 20, 1976). 23pp.
Quintero Nieto, Ricardo: 1955. 'Tierritorio Ignoto (Tierradentro)'. Imprenta Márquez, Cali.
Red Shift Research Collective. 'A Guide to British Psilocybin mushrooms'. 240 Camden High St. London. 1977.
Reichel-Dolmatoff, Gerardo: 1949-1950. 'Los Kógi'. (vol.1) in Revista del Instituto Etnográfico Nacional, vol.IV, Entregas la y 2a. Bogotá.
1951. 'Los Kógi'. (vol.2) Editorial Iqueima, Bogotá.
1953. 'Contactos y Cambios Culturales en la Sierra Nevada de Santa Marta' in Revista Colombiana de Antropología, vol.I no.1, Bogotá.
1966. 'Colombia'. Thames and Hudson, London.
1967. 'Notas sobre el simbolismo religioso de los Indios de la Sierra Nevada de Santa Marta' in Razón y Fábula, no.1. Bogotá.
1968. 'Desana: Simbolismo de los Indios Tukano del Vaupés'. Universidad de los Andes, Bogotá.

1969. 'El Contexto Cultural de un Alucinógeno Aborigen: *Banisteriopsis Caapi*' in Revista de la Academia Colombiana de Ciencias Exactas, Físicas y Naturales, vol.XIII, no.51, pp.327-345. Bogotá.

1972. 'San Agustín: A Culture of Colombia'. Thames and Hudson, London.

Ricketts, C.A.: 1952. 'El Cocaísmo en el Perú' in América Indígena, vol.XII, Mexico.

Ritchie, Murdoch, Cohen and Dripps: 1965. 'Cocaine, procaine and other synthetic local anaesthetics' in 'The Pharmacological Basis of Therapeutics' (3rd ed.) edited by L.S. Goodman and A. Gilman, Macmillan, New York.

Rivet, Paul: 1943. 'La Influencia Karib en Colombia'. Revista del Instituto Etnológico Nacional, vol.I entrega la. Bogotá.

Rockefeller, Nelson *et al.*: 1975. 'White Paper on Drug Abuse: A Report to the President from The Domestic Council Drug Abuse Task Force'. U.S. Government Printing Office, Washington DC.

Romoli de Avery, Kathleen: 1962. 'El Suroeste del Cauca y sus Indios al tiempo de la Conquista espanola' in Revista Colombiana de Antropología, vol.XI, Bogotá.

1965. 'Apuntes sobre los pueblos autóctonos del litoral Colombiano del Pacífico en la época de la Conquista espanola' in Revista Colombiana de Antropología, vol.XII, Bogotá.

Rostworowski de Diez Canseco, María: 1973. 'Plantaciones prehispánicas de coca en la vertiente del Pacífico' in Revista del Museo Nacional, vol.XXXIX, Lima.

Rubin, Vera (ed.): 1975. 'Cannabis and Culture'. Mouton Publishers, The Hague and Paris.

Rubin, Vera and Comitas, Lambros: 1975. 'Ganja in Jamaica'. Mouton Publishers, The Hague and Paris.

Rusby, Henry H.: 1888. 'Coca at home and abroad'. Therapeutic Gazette, IV: 158-165 and 303-307, Detroit.

Santa Gertrudis, Fray Juan de: 1970. 'Maravillas de la Naturaleza'. (4 vols.) Ediciones del Banco Popular, Bogotá.

Sendoya, Mariano M.: 1964. 'La Nina María de Caloto' in Boletín de la Academia de Historia del Valle del Cauca, no.133, pp.248-257. Cali.

Schultes, Richard Evans: 1957a. 'A New method of coca preparation in the Colombian Amazon' in Botanical Museum Leaflets, Harvard University, vol.17, no.9, pp.241-246. Cambridge, Mass.

1957b. 'The identity of the Malpighiaceous narcotics of South America' in Botanical Museum Leaflets, Harvard University, vol.18, no.1, pp.1-56. Cambridge.

1972. 'An Overview of Hallucinogens in the Western Hemisphere' in Peter T. Furst (ed.) 'Flesh of the Gods'. Praeger, New York.

Schwarz, Ronald Allan: 1973. 'Guambía: An Ethnography of Change and Stability'. PhD. thesis submitted to Michigan State University.

Silva Celis, Eliécer: 1943-1944. 'La Arqueología de Tierradentro' in Revista del Instituto Etnográfico Nacional, vol.I entrega la., pp.117-130 (1943) and vol.I entrega 2a., pp.521-589 (1944). Bogotá.

Smith, T. Lynn: 1] 67. 'Colombia'. University of Florida Press, Gainesville.

Starks, Michael: 1977. 'Marijuana Potency'. And/Or Press, Berkeley, California.

Stein, William W.: 1961. 'Hualcán: Life in the Highlands of Peru'. Cornell University Press, Ithaca, N.Y.

'The 31st Annual Almanac. 94th Congress 1st Session 1975'. Published by Congressional Quarterly Inc. Washington DC 1976.

Torres, Laborde, A.: 1971. 'Mito y Cultura Entre los Barasana: Un grupo indígena del Vaupés. Ed. Universidad de los Andes, Bogotá.

Trease, G.E. and Evans, W.C.: 1972. 'Pharmacognosy'. Balliere Tindall, London.

Trimborn, Hermann: 1949. 'Senorío y Barbarie en el valle del Cauca'. Instituto Gonzalo Fernández de Oviedo, Madrid.

United Nations, Report of the Commission of Enquiry on the Coca Leaf of the ...
1950. Economic and Social Council, Special Supplement no.1, Lake Success, N.Y.
1952. (Abbreviated version in Spanish, together with the debate with Dr. Monge's Peruvian Commission) in Perú Indígena, vol.3 nos.7-8. Lima.

Uscátegui Mendoza, Néstor: 1954. 'Contribución al estudio de la masticación de las hojas de coca' in Revista Colombiana de Antropología, vol.III, pp.207-290.
1959. 'The Present Distribution of Narcotics and Stimulants Amongst the Indian Tribes of Colombia' in Botanical Museum Leaflets, Harvard University, vol.18 no.6, pp.273-304. Cambridge, Mass.
1961. 'Distribución Actual de las Plantas Narcóticas y Estimulantes Usadas por las Tribus Indígenas de Colombia' in Revista de la Academia Colombiana de Ciencias Exactas, Físicas y Naturales, vol.XI no.43, pp.215-228.

Valenzuela, Eloy: 1952. 'Primer Diario de la Expedición Botánica del Nuevo Reino de Granada. 29 Abril 1783-8 mayo 1784'. Ed. E.P. Arbelaez y Mario Acevedo Diaz, Bucaramanga, Santander.

Vásquez de Espinosa, Antonio: 1948. 'Compendio y Descripción de las Indias Occidentales' facsimile edition by Charles Upton Clark at the Smithsonian Institution, Washington DC (mss. completed 1629).

Vawell, Richard: 1974. 'Memoiras de un Oficial de la Legión Británica'. Biblioteca Banco Popular, Bogotá.

Vespucio, Américo: 1951. 'El Nuevo Mundo. Cartas Relativas a sus Viajes y Descubrimientos'. Estudio preliminar de Roberto Leviller. Buenos Aires.

Vila, Marco Aurelio: 1972. 'La Carta del 18 de julio de 1500 de Américo Vespucio' in Boletín Histórico, Editado por la Fundación John Boulton, Caracas. No.28.

Wagley, Charles and Galvao, Eduardo: 1947. 'The Tenetehara' in Handbook of South American Indians, vol.3. Bureau of American Ethnology, Bulletin 143, Washington DC.

Weil, Andrew: 1976. 'A Gourmet Coca Taster's Tour of Peru' in High Times Magazine, no.9, May 1976. New York.

Wells, Calvin: 1964. 'Bones, Bodies and Disease'. Thames and Hudson, London.

Willey, Gordon: 1971. 'An Introduction to American Archaeology. Vol.2; South America'. New York.